D1548598

**Microsoft**®

# Active Directory™

## Microsoft® Services for

# Windows® 2000

# Technical

# Reference

**The practical guide to planning and
deploying Active Directory services**

**David Iseminger**

PUBLISHED BY
Microsoft Press
A Division of Microsoft Corporation
One Microsoft Way
Redmond, Washington 98052-6399

Library of Congress Cataloging-in-Publication Data
Iseminger, David, 1969-
    Active Directory Services for Microsoft Windows 2000 : Technical Reference / David Iseminger.
        p.  cm.
    Includes index.
    ISBN  0-7356-0624-2
    1. Directory services (Computer network technology) 2. Microsoft Windows
(Computer file) I. Title.

TK5105.595 I84   1999
005.7'1369--dc21                                              99-046102

Printed and bound in the United States of America.

3  4  5  6  7  8  9     WCWC     5  4  3  2  1  0

Distributed in Canada by Penguin Books Canada Limited.

A CIP catalogue record for this book is available from the British Library.

Microsoft Press books are available through booksellers and distributors worldwide. For further information about international editions, contact your local Microsoft Corporation office or contact Microsoft Press International directly at fax (425) 936-7329. Visit our Web site at mspress.microsoft.com.

**Acquisitions Editor:** David Clark
**Project Editor:** Lynn Finnel
**Technical Editor:** Michael Hochberg

# Contents

## PART III  Appendixes

# Acknowledgments

Some projects fly smoothly from the start, others seem to hit turbulence as soon as they're off the ground. Generally, those who are committed simply must strap on their seatbelts and hold on for the ride. For most of this project the seat belt sign was illuminated—whether because of moving release dates, added or omitted features, or other reasons that don't lend themselves to short explanations. For some who were able to stay in their seats I'm grateful, including **Lynn Finnel** and especially **Mike Hochberg**.

Thanks are also in order for **David Clark** for acquiring the book, and for his occasional telephone call to see how things were going. Along those lines, thanks to **Anne Hamilton** for seeing this book idea from casual conversation to contract.

I've always been a fan of great graphics, and I believe you'll agree that the artwork in this book is excellent (noteworthy, even). For that, my special thanks are extended to **Joel Panchot,** who took my faxed scribbles and turned them into… well… artwork.

Thanks to **Ed Lance** for his contributions in Chapter 12, they were very useful. And as always, thanks go to **Margot Hutchison** for her ever-effective representation.

Despite challenges that seemed to dog this project from the beginning, everyone involved was able to focus on quality, readability, and value, and I hope the book's collaborative quality effort is reflected in the contents. (I think it is.) The reward for all of us will be readers who find its contents useful, educational, and maybe (hopefully) even a little enjoyable.

# Introduction

Welcome to *Active Directory Services for Microsoft Windows 2000 Technical Reference*, your complete source for the information you need to become an expert on Active Directory directory services. You probably already know that this technology is at the center of Microsoft Windows 2000, which makes getting familiar with it a must for IT professionals everywhere. Gathered here is the knowledge you need about directory services, the technical know-how about implementation of Active Directory technology in Windows 2000, and the step-by-step guidance to plan, implement, and manage Active Directory services in your organization. In short, this book is your one-stop reference for everything you need to make Active Directory services work for you.

## How This Book Is Structured

*Active Directory Services for Microsoft Windows 2000 Technical Reference* is structured to provide the best possible approach to explaining and detailing Active Directory technology. Since directory services haven't been around forever, this book starts with an explanation of directory services, why we need them, and how they make our computing lives manageable. Once directory services are explained, the particulars of Windows 2000's implementation of Active Directory services is explained in increasing detail.

Because there are two broad steps in getting Active Directory working for you and your organization—understanding the technology, and then implementing the technology—this book has been divided into two sections. As a result of this structure, you can quickly find a clear line of demarcation between gathering the knowledge you need to understand the technology and getting elbow-deep into its implementation. Again, the structure has been designed around your needs as an IT professional.

Part I, "Understanding Active Directory Services," explains directory services, Active Directory architecture, components, and features. Part I also explains how Active Directory is an improvement over the way directory structures were handled in other versions of Microsoft Windows, and how Windows 2000 domains differ from Windows NT domains and integrate with Active Directory services. Part I also explains how Windows 2000 base services—almost all of which are tightly tied to Active Directory services—are affected by the advent of Active Directory. The following list provides specifics on the chapters you'll find in Part I:

- **Chapter 1,** "Understanding Directory Services," explains what a directory service is and discusses the characteristics that directory services must have to be viable solutions in the distributed network environments that exist in today's organizations.

- **Chapter 2,** "Active Directory Services as a Directory Service Implementation," lists the features and technologies that enable Active Directory services to meet the requirements of an enterprise directory service. It also explains how features of its implementation can benefit an organization. Additionally, Chapter 2 compares the role of Active Directory directory service in Windows 2000 to the role of the directory in Windows NT.

- **Chapter 3,** "Windows 2000 Domains and Active Directory Services," explains how Windows 2000 domains and Active Directory services are tightly integrated and provides a foundation of Windows 2000 domain knowledge that facilitates understanding Active Directory technical concepts and deployment strategies.

- **Chapter 4,** "Active Directory Services Scalability Architecture," explains how Active Directory architecture enables Active Directory services to scale to the largest networks.

- **Chapter 5,** "More Active Directory Services Architecture," details the architectural components and approaches that enable Active Directory to fulfill the requirements of a directory service.

- **Chapter 6,** "Active Directory Services and DNS," introduces and explains the Windows 2000 base services that are integral to the enabling of Active Directory services. These base services are important to understanding how Active Directory delivers on Microsoft's promise of a centralized and administrator-friendly directory service.

Part II, "Deploying Active Directory Services," provides the technical information and the deployment recommendations that you need to get the most out of Active Directory services and to make Active Directory work for you. Part II includes exhaustive information on the technical issues that IT professionals, architects, and administrators will run into during the planning, securing, and managing of the varied services and offerings of Windows 2000 Active Directory. Part II provides explicit direction on planning an Active Directory services deployment, upgrading to Active Directory services from Windows NT, migrating to Active Directory technology from other directory services, and making organizational changes once Active Directory services is functioning. Part II consists of the following chapters:

- **Chapter 7,** "Planning an Active Directory Services Deployment," provides you with the information you need to ensure that your Active Directory deployment is well planned and that it will be able to handle the inevitable directory-related IT challenges, such as integration with Internet-related domain names. Understanding the concepts in this chapter is essential to ensuring that your directory service is ready for prime time.

- **Chapter 8,** "Active Directory Services and Security," examines in detail Active Directory security issues you'll face during the deployment and ongoing administration of Active Directory services and prepares you to deal with them.

- **Chapter 9,** "Managing Active Directory Services," describes in detail the Active Directory management interfaces and provides guidance for handling management issues such as delegation, backup, and remote management.

- **Chapter 10,** "Working with the Active Directory Services Schema," explains how Active Directory schema functions, details how it interacts with Active Directory services, and also provides schema extension guidance that enables you to further extend and tailor Active Directory services to your organization's needs.

- **Chapter 11,** "Upgrading to Active Directory Services," gives you the information you need to ensure that upgrading your Windows network—whether it's a single domain or a multiple master—goes as smoothly as possible. Make sure you read Chapter 7, "Planning an Active Directory Deployment," in conjunction with this chapter and before jumping into the upgrade process.

- **Chapter 12,** "Migrating to Active Directory Services," presents the information you need to migrate from another directory service to Active Directory services. Also included in this chapter is an exhaustive discussion of the issues involved in deploying Microsoft Exchange in conjunction with Active Directory services.

- **Chapter 13,** "Making Postdeployment Organizational Changes," addresses the challenges that IT professionals face once they deploy Active Directory services, such as domain changes or DNS changes, and provides the information they need to meet those challenges.

- **Chapter 14,** "Administratively Leveraging Active Directory Services," details the many features of Windows 2000 that are made possible with Active Directory services. Such features include IntelliMirror, distributed file system (Dfs), and others.

Despite the progressive structure of Part I, *Active Directory Services for Microsoft Windows 2000 Technical Reference* is a reference book in every sense of the word. Part II is less dependent on logical structuring; if you prefer to read about managing Active Directory (Chapter 9) before reading about securing it (Chapter 8), no problem. As with many reference books (such as dictionaries), you can dive right into any subject that interests you. This book is structured in such a way that individual subjects are as complete as possible. Perhaps the only exception to this philosophy is Chapter 7, "Planning an Active Directory Deployment"—you should read this chapter before one on upgrade or migration. Although Part II is geared toward real-life implementation, you should read Part I if you aren't familiar with Active Directory's architecture, its functions within Windows 2000, or its implementation capabilities.

If you want a comprehensive understanding of Active Directory services, start at the beginning and work your way through. The structure of the book reflects how most deployments are approached—first the technology must be understood; second the requisite planning, security, and management issues are addressed; and finally the actual implementation is set into motion.

## Conventions Used in This Book

Throughout the book, you will find special sections set aside from the main text. These sections, denoted by icons, draw your attention to topics of special interest and importance or to problems implementers invariably face during the course of a deployment. These features include the following:

**Note**   This is used to underscore the importance of a specific concept or to highlight a special case that might apply only to certain situations.

**More Info**   When additional material is available on a subject, whether in other sections in the book or from outside sources such as Web sites or white papers, I'll provide such information next to the More Info icon.

**Caution**   The *I told you so* of book features. When failure to take or avoid a certain action or situation could spell trouble for you, I point this out with the Caution feature. Don't say I didn't tell you.

**Tip**   This feature is reserved for directing your attention to advice on timesaving or strategic moves.

**Planning**   There are times when an ounce of prevention through planning is worth 20 hours of troubleshooting and downtime. Such times merit the Planning feature, which is also used for checklist-type planning that can ensure all your IT bases are covered.

**Best Practices**   Getting the most stable performance and the highest quality deployment often means knowing a few ins and outs. The Best Practices sections are where you'll find such pieces of knowledge.

### Real World

Many common problems that occur during deployment in the field can be solved easily, if you know how. The Real World sections provide workarounds and solutions to deployment problems without you having to learn the hard way.

When used judiciously, these features are especially helpful. I've included them only when I think they help you get more out of the book. Take notice of these features because ignoring them could come back to haunt you.

# Part I
# Understanding Active Directory Services

Active Directory services is the Microsoft Windows 2000 implementation of a directory service. What sets it apart from other directory services is its implementation design and comprehensive capabilities. A working knowledge of this new technology requires more than knowing what button to click and when; what's required is a fundamental understanding of directory services followed up with information specific to the operations and functionality of Active Directory services. In other words, to truly grasp the significance and power of this new directory technology and put it to work, it isn't enough to know *that* Active Directory services works; you must know *how* it works.

# Chapter 1
# Understanding Directory Services

In order to take your understanding of directory services one step forward, this chapter takes you one step back to the advent of directories. This slice of computer history makes clear today's need for a service such as Active Directory. Then, after defining what a directory service is and what one does, the chapter provides real-life examples of how directory services are used. Chapter 1 also lists attributes that directory services must have to serve the computing needs of organizations of all sizes. This list of necessary attributes is used in subsequent chapters to clearly detail how Active Directory services meets and even exceeds the requirements for an enterprise-class directory service.

## Network History and the Need for Directory Services

Our dependence on computers nearly equals our dependence on water and sunlight. We e-mail, we schedule, and we finish files and submit presentations that either get us promoted or land us in management. Imagine a day without e-mail, network capability, or even the ability to type a quick memo; such imagining wakes IT professionals at midnight in a cold sweat. Computers are part of the daily lives of both users and administrators; we depend on them and use them as extensions of ourselves and our productivity—quietly humming appendages that crunch numbers and meet deadlines.

But not long ago, computers came with green or amber screens, were booted with 5¼-inch floppies in five or more minutes, and were considered connected once the power outlet was located. There were mainframes and terminals, of course, but their user-friendliness ranked with that of IRS audits and root canals; few people other than tax advisers, dentists, and an occasional AS/400 programmer care much for any of those. With the advent of the mouse, the graphical user interface, and thousands of affordable applications that enabled all sorts of people to expand their productivity, computers began to flourish. Microsoft Windows platforms enabled IT professionals to use their knowledge of the Windows user interface and its navigational conventions to administer systems. Rather than having to endure some hybrid MS-DOS/UNIX command interface, administrators used Windows-based utilities and administration programs. The cost of administering networks came down; no longer were knowledgeable network administrators extremely rare, which meant their consulting fees were less astronomical. This enabled more companies to afford administrators, and therefore, to afford networks and increase efficiency and productivity.

Then computer prices started dropping and processors got more and more powerful. Soon users everywhere were connected to networks. That's when the real trouble began.

## The Growth of Networks

As computers became more powerful and less expensive, network operating systems (NOS's) such as Windows NT, Novell NetWare, and UNIX became viable solutions for the storage of mission-critical files and databases. Companies of all sizes and budgets could take advantage of networked computing, not just companies capable of shouldering the high cost of a "big iron" (mainframe) solution. As the computing paradigm shifted, an increasing number of applications were developed for the PC platform. The availability of applications contributed to a self-perpetuating circle of industry growth—more PCs meant a better potential return on applications developed for the PC platform, and the wider selection of applications was an inducement for companies to use PCs and server-class compatibles to run their back-office mission-critical applications. And with the growing number of reasons for companies to put computers on every employee's desktop came a growing need for companies to get those computers connected to networks.

But with more connected computers came more load on the server-class computer acting as mainframe pro tem, and soon the server couldn't handle the load. This was not such a big problem, though; computing hardware (server-class computers, in this case) was so affordable that the easy fix to an overloaded server was simply to add another server. The need for servers increased with user productivity and available applications, though, and servers began dotting the networking landscape.

What's more, the number of services available from these servers increased, each with its own interface and individual (read "completely different") way of accomplishing administrative tasks. Networks and the number of attached computers continued growing, spurred by Internet connectivity and benefits of the ubiquitous corporate local area networks (LANs). No longer was the availability of administrators a concern—the benefits of being networked far outweighed the costs associated with getting and keeping the network running. Instead, the concern was managing the sprawl of servers, all of which were interconnected, but like an uncharted archipelago, they were difficult to navigate and almost impossible to organize into a viable community. A better system was needed to enable administrators and users to view the network as a cohesive unit and not as the disjointed and scattered array of servers, services, and information it was becoming.

## The Expansion of the Enterprise Network

Not surprisingly, nowhere is the problem of the disjointed network more acute than in large corporate networks. Large corporations have compelling reasons to completely network their computer systems into a sort of digital information system: enhanced productivity, improved and extended communications, and increased employee access to resources that help them increase company profitability. Despite a shift in network computing that resulted in replacing mainframe computers with a few commoditized server-class computers, the paradigm of computing didn't shift when networks scaled beyond the capabilities of a few individual servers. Activities were still server-centric, so as the number of servers housing data increased, each server remained largely disconnected—at least in presentation and management—from the rest of the servers and the users themselves. Servers were distributed throughout a network in physical locations that suited their group's immediate needs, each server becoming little more than another name to add to the browser list or to be memorized by those who placed their files on its shares.

The distribution of such servers caused a certain dilemma: it increased the administrative burden and made finding useful information difficult for users. Rather than being spread out further, networks needed to be consolidated—networks needed to have a central point for network information that would provide more unified network resources for users and administrators. Rather than having to search the separate servers that dotted the LAN geography, users and administrators needed an interface to the network that enabled them to view the network as a unit and to utilize services that were a part of that unit. In other words, the network needed to be presented as a single entity, not a scattering of users, servers, and services. The difference is more than semantics; to be definable (that is, to be a thing) suggests an element either is or is not a part of the entity. A network with a scattering of users, servers, and services is a network without cohesion or definable bounds.

A tool was needed that could define the network—its users, servers, services, and other elements—as a bounded and isolated thing, not as a scattering of things. What was needed was a directory service that was comprehensive, extensible, and scalable. In addition, the directory service had to be easy to use and even easier to manage.

Windows 2000 Active Directory fills this tall order. Active Directory technology represents a shift in paradigm from traditional server-centric computing. Active Directory effectively embraces the network, creating a predictable, searchable, and unified system that represents the network as an individual unit. Active Directory is a centralized repository of information that unifies and organizes the many elements that make up the network, creating a logical, hierarchical, and scalable platform.

The implementation of a centralized repository of information is a powerful approach to network computing, and its advantages reach much farther than the large enterprise. Small-sized and midsize organizations might benefit most from the use of Active Directory services.

## Administration Needs in the Small Company

Small-sized and midsize companies must be lean, adaptive, and agile to survive in today's competitive business environment, and their dependence on computers is no less than that of large organizations. In fact, companies that aren't the behemoths of industry might rely more on their information systems since their ability to move quickly is essential to their success. Windows 2000 Active Directory services was designed to meet the needs of these growing, changing companies and to reduce the cost (and volatility) of maintaining a network and a company's digital information system. How can Active Directory do all this? By enabling administrators and users to do what they must do more easily, quickly, and intuitively.

Often in small organizations, the responsibilities placed on administrators are many and varied—at least as varied as the services and interfaces such administrators have to face. Administrators need an efficient means of taking advantage of their knowledge of a user interface as they administer network services. In Windows NT, administrators experienced with Microsoft Exchange Server who move to the Remote Access Service (RAS) Access Admin utility will find a vastly different way of performing administrative tasks, which results in a certain amount of ramp-up time. Small organizations normally have less time for such issues than large organizations; small organizations need the network and its services to be running soon and to be quickly administrable when problems arise. There is a need for a consistent user interface, one that is centralized and manageable and enables administrators to take advantage of their experience to put new and unfamiliar services into use as quickly as possible.

The result needs to be something centralized—some sort of lassoing of all the administrative interfaces into one consistent and isolated interface. Only a service such as Active Directory can deliver the degree of centralization required.

Administrators are often spread thin, leaving them little time to perform troubleshooting tasks that require them to travel to various locations on their networks. With the centralized and consolidated vision of the network that Active Directory services provides, navigation of the network becomes easier, which adds up to an easier approach for users who want to access resources on the network. The end result is increased productivity for administrators and users. As the network's uses are extended and connectivity grows, Active Directory services can help small-sized and midsize organizations more effectively use everything the network has to offer.

## The Laws of Computing

Some laws are difficult to break; others exist for no apparent reason. (The law of gravity and rural jaywalking laws, respectively, come to mind.) When it comes to computing, some laws have more influence and greater impact on the ongoing innovation of technology than others. While the laws of physics and chemistry certainly play roles in production lines, laws other than such hard-science laws arguably shape the industry and its cycle of innovation and evolution. These other laws—perhaps categorized as practical or demand-driven laws—are based on science but are driven by consumers. These practical laws of computing—Metcalfe's Law, Moore's Law, and Murphy's Law—have shaped information technology as we know it today and will probably shape the computing paradigm of tomorrow. Without question, these laws are important to the discussion of Active Directory services and contribute to the paradigm shift toward distributed computing.

## Metcalfe's Law

Metcalfe's Law, proposed by the same Robert Metcalfe who invented Ethernet and co-founded 3COM Corporation, is an observational law that attempts to quantify the effect of an interconnected system of machines (computers and telephones, for example). The technical definition of Metcalfe's Law is as follows: connect any number, $n$, of machines—computers, phones, or even cars—and you get $n$ squared potential value. In the postdigestion moments of reading that law, you realize that as computers become connected, each additional connected computer makes the value of all connected computers skyrocket. As the old adage goes, one telephone is useless (who are you going to call?); and a car in a driveway with no roads on which to travel to other places is similarly useless (where are you going to go?). Connect everyone in a neighborhood (by phone or by road) and then everyone in a city, and the increase in value becomes apparent. AT&T certainly knows this; their connections are valued at around $60 billion.

In terms of networking, Metcalfe's Law can be paraphrased like this: for each computer you add to a network, the value of the network grows exponentially. At first, there was a network, and then users (and the company) saw the advantages of the network and began connecting more computers to it. The trend continued until eventually all the computers on the network were interconnected in the corporate LAN. While this trend toward corporate LANs was taking hold, the land of the bulletin board system (BBS), where users connect to certain online locations for various reasons, began to give way to a network of interconnected users (the Internet). As more users (networks) became interconnected to the Internet, tremendous value was created, which compelled larger networks (such as corporate LANs) to also connect. This trend was the embodiment of Metcalfe's Law, and we've only begun to see its impact.

Metcalfe's Law is an accurate reflection of the effect of connecting more computers to a network, and those continued interconnections have resulted in distributed networks of mammoth value, but also mammoth administrative burden. The value was first seen in the LAN (and continues to be seen there—the ongoing addition of connected computers still increases the value of every LAN) and extends to the Internet. The trend of interconnecting computers, however, brought with it administrative growing pains that Active Directory is designed to assuage.

## Moore's Law

Many people are familiar with Moore's Law, which is attributed to former Intel executive Gordon Moore based on an observation he made during preparation for a speech in 1965. Moore's Law states: the processing power of computers doubles every 18 months.

There has been some variation to this timeline—it has sometimes been as long as two years and as short as one year—but over the years, 18 months has been proven to be most accurate. This pace of increased processing power explains the ever-slippery grasp one has on possessing a cutting-edge powerhouse desktop computer, which requires endless upgrades or replacements along a similar timeline. But for the sake of our discussion, Moore's Law has much broader implications. This constant increase in processing power brought about a fundamental change in the way networks needed to function; in the beginning, processing power needed to be in the network (rather than in the clients), as the following paragraph explains.

Not too terribly long ago, a wide area network (WAN) technology called X.25 was the WAN of choice because at every hop over the WAN, network switching devices checked packets for integrity and passed them to the next network-switching device, which would do the same. This process enabled computers on either end of a connection to rest assured (literally) that the data they sent over the X.25 network would reach its targeted device intact. Such built-in network intelligence was necessary because the computers at either end had limited processing power and were unable to check packets for integrity (and handle problems that arose with corrupted packets). In other words, these computers didn't have the processing power to handle the communications overhead. Today, the X.25 network is not very popular. The overhead associated with all that packet-checking introduces latency, and because computers have continued to double their processing power every 18 months, they are now easily able to handle the communications overhead associated with checking packet integrity.

The same shift is happening with networks. Mainframes are no longer needed to perform the processing for desktop computers because desktop computers have sufficient processing power. But with this distribution of computing power across a network—or more simply put, with the advent of distributed computing—resources that users need have also become distributed. Administration has been decentralized with the distribution of networks, and as a result, the workload and scope of responsibility for administrators have grown. Thus, Moore's Law has created a dilemma: increased processing power enables users to do more, process more, and use empowering new technology, but increased processing power also scatters users and the resources they need across the networked landscape, spreading information—and the administrators who must ensure information is available—across that same ever-broadening network landscape.

Resource distribution leads to difficulty in finding and organizing useful information. When users are unable to find information or administrators have to manage numerous, dispersed services, a network becomes less useful and more difficult to own. Therefore, the growth and distribution of the network becomes its own nemesis. Any solution, then, must enable users and administrators to shift back toward a more centralized view of the network, while also accounting for (and encouraging) continued growth of the network. This centralizing of ideas, attributes, and capabilities must be accomplished without undermining the broadened physical reach of the distributed network. In short, there must be distributed computing and networks with centralized presentation and administration.

Moore's Law has shaped computing by encouraging the creation of a distributed environment where desktop computers currently have the processing power that mainframes had less than 10 years ago. Increased processing power has been a boon to networking and computing, but with it has come a scattering of resources and ideas. The solution is a centralization of those resources and ideas, and that is exactly what Active Directory services does.

## Murphy's Law

Most of us have firsthand experience with Murphy's Law, which is less a law of computing (administrators, I hear your objection to that statement) than a general law aligned with a cynical view of life. Murphy's Law states that "anything that can go wrong will go wrong." Anyone who's installed a garage door opener can attest to its validity.

Hardware fails. Network connections get unconnected, wires work loose, domain controllers go off line, users move to different offices, and hard disk space inevitably runs low. These are facts of computing life and, in general, users and administrators are required to consider them when going about their daily routines.

When this trio of computing laws—Metcalfe's Law, Moore's Law, and Murphy's Law—is considered together, it provides a perspective of the current computing environment that makes the benefits of Active Directory services nearly irrefutable. With increasing processing power spreading networks over numerous computers and varied geographies, much can go wrong. Users can become inundated with details or lost in highly connected networks; resources get scattered and placed on servers that process requests with lightning speed but whose usefulness is limited by the necessity to commit their murky names and services to memory. What could go wrong has gone wrong—users are lost in distributed information overload, and the administrative difficulties have created a bottleneck.

Fortunately, a well-designed, enterprise-ready directory service can provide a real solution to these modern-day computing dilemmas; it can centralize the view and administration of a network, while enabling and even fostering growth of the network and computing power. Keeping Metcalfe's Law of spiraling network value, Moore's Law of doubling processor power, and Murphy's Law of inevitable bumps in the deployment road in balance necessitates the advent of a well-designed directory service. Otherwise, we will become mired in a distributed network that we can't administer, can't really use, and can't control.

## The Directory Defined

As an IT professional who eats, breathes, and sleeps networks, you undoubtedly know you need a tool that will enable you and your network users to view the network as a cohesive unit and not as a scattered collection of servers, services, and information. The need has existed for a while, and Microsoft isn't the only company trying to address it. (Novell Directory Services [NDS], the directory service offering from Novell, has been out for some time now.) But what is a directory service, really? That question needs to be answered before a firm grip on the sometimes slippery term can be had.

So let's back up a bit and examine the particulars. Specifically, let's explain in detail what a directory is, how it differs from a directory service, and what the difference is between a simple directory (single-purpose) and a complex directory (multipurpose).

## What Is a Directory?

You probably know the meaning of the word *inhibitor,* and if you can tell me what a covalence inhibitor is, you certainly know what *covalence* means. But if you're not clear on the meaning of either of the words, you'll never understand the term. Similarly, you probably know what a *service* is, but if you want to know what a directory service is, you must first be certain that you know the meaning of *directory.*

A *directory* is a catalog of information (such as names, phone numbers, or restaurants) that is listed and grouped in a particular way; often, the listing or grouping of such information is geared toward making the information as easily accessible to its users as possible. For a couple of quick examples, the white pages and yellow pages are directories that are organized differently, one alphabetically and one categorically, that give people convenient access to essential information.

What makes a directory powerful is its ability to accept all sorts of information and then use that information in ways that empower the users or expand the richness of services. But for such services and uses of the directory to be a reality, the information in the directory must be accessible.

## What Is a Directory Service?

A directory service is a computer service that enables users to store and access information stored in a computerized directory. A directory service often defines, or is based on, an interface protocol or protocols for interacting with the directory. An example of a directory service is the Domain Name Service (DNS), which you use every time you connect to the Internet. Another commonly used directory service is Windows Internet Naming Service (WINS). The effectiveness and scalability of a directory service are not guaranteed. Some directory services are expertly conceived such that they can scale to the entire Internet without outgrowing their usefulness. (DNS is a good example.) Other directory services are limited by their design and structure to a ceiling of scalability suitable only to moderately sized organizations. (WINS comes to mind.)

The point is that directory services aren't all created equal; some are created only to provide the names of employees within an organization—perhaps with their extensions, office numbers, employee numbers, and departments—and serve their intended purpose perfectly well. Others have the much more complex task of centralizing all networking, security, user, and resource information into one extendable and scalable directory service solution—absorbing other directory services and abstracting system management activity to familiar snap-in user interfaces. Some directory services have proprietary interfaces that make interacting with the information in the directory possible for only certain users (such as other operating system components); others have an open, standardized interface that enables any standards-compliant user to access its directory information.

Each of these kinds of directories has its place—that is, unless the more complex directory service makes the simple directory service unnecessary or absorbs its information altogether. Examining a simple directory service in detail is in order. After that, we'll look at a complex directory service.

## The Simple Directory Service

To keep things simple, you must limit the tasks being performed; this is true for directory services as much as it is for building a birdhouse.

DNS is a good example of a simple directory service. DNS has one goal: to translate host names to IP addresses, such as translating *http://www.microsoft.com* to 207.46.130.14.

When we take a closer look at DNS and how it qualifies as a directory service, we see that it has the following directory and directory service traits:

- Lists and groups a catalog of information in a particular way. DNS organizes its information based on specific categories, such as .com or .org, and is hierarchical in nature, so you can have valid hosts with names such as microsoft.com and microsoft.org.
- Defines a computer service that enables its users to access its information; DNS has a particular format and particular commands that must be followed to interface with its directory of information.

We can define the bounds of what DNS can do and what it's intended for, and can essentially define its uses in their entirety. If we add one or two more easily definable capabilities, we can still understand the service. But computing environments require more services than simple host-to-IP mappings these days and more than the capability to provide only a couple of services. As these bounds increase and as the lines that define what a directory service can do become fuzzy, understanding can wane unless we're prepared for the fact that a directory service's capabilities are meant to be fuzzy—or in more technical terms, more extensible.

## The Complex Directory Service

For many computing environments, the reasons for using directories are varied and numerous, resulting in the proliferation of separate directory services, some of which are single-purpose and some of which are multipurpose. The previous section describing the single-purpose DNS directory service provides a great example of a useful directory service, but we would have limited computing functionality if that were the only directory service available.

Imagine for a moment what would happen if we were to increase the capabilities of DNS so that it could provide more information than just the IP address of a given host. What if it could, for example, provide us with a list of the host's computer resources, the host's user accounts, and security settings placed on those accounts? If it could do those things, it would be a multipurpose and more complex directory service. Figure 1-1 illustrates a simple single-purpose directory service that has been turned into a complex multipurpose directory service.

**Single-Purpose Directory**      **Multipurpose Directory**

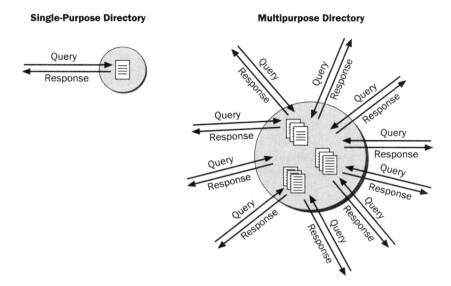

**Figure 1-1.** *A simple directory service, and opposite it, the same directory service as a complex directory service.*

With the complex directory service, an economy of scale is achieved because one directory can service requests for multiple types of information. The basic idea of the directory, and its corresponding service, has not changed. It is still a catalog of information and is still accessed by some defined interface protocol—only the protocol might be more complicated than it was before and the catalog of information more extensive.

Because a complex directory service can do the work of multiple simple directory services, complex directory services are essential parts of today's complex distributed computing environments—such as the computing environment found in enterprise networks.

## The Enterprise Directory Service Shopping List

Enterprise computing environments, as well as small computer networks that make significant use of computer technology, use many network services. These services, such as WINS servers, Dynamic Host Configuration Protocol (DHCP) servers, and security subsystems, have individualized catalogs of information that they must use to carry out their network-based operations. The result has been a scattering of these services across the network and across administrative bounds.

Administrators have had to manage these network services separately and ensure that proper security is enforced on the catalogs of information, and users have had to deal with an increasing number of directories and directory services to do their work. As a result, the complexity of the network has been increasing for both administrators and users, making it more difficult for both to do their respective jobs and curtailing the effectiveness and usefulness of the network.

Clearly, organizations that use numerous network services need a way to consolidate these services' catalogs of information into some centralized, inclusive catalog that takes advantage of a security, administrative, and user infrastructure by being completely integrated with the operating system. An enterprise-class directory service is the solution to the problem of dispersed catalogs of information. In the following section, I will explain the requirements that such a directory service must meet.

## Enterprise Directory Service Requirements

A directory service that can serve the needs of organizations of all sizes, including organizations with enterprise networks, must meet a number of general and specific requirements. In general, a directory service must:

- Help users and administrators work better
- Be tightly integrated with security
- Be able to absorb other directories

The following is a shopping list of specific network requirements for a directory service:

- **Centralization**   Also known as consolidation, centralization involves reducing the number of directories an organization must contend with. Centralization also reduces administrative burden, and administration is one of the most expensive aspects of a computer network. However, just as important to centralization is the capability for all such centralized catalogs to share information among one another. For example, one catalog might have information about which machines and shares are associated with user JamieW, and another might have information about what her security access restrictions are on Printer7; these catalogs must communicate to create effective centralization. An enterprise-ready directory service must be able to absorb other directories, consolidating network information in a central location.

- **Scalability**   Simply put, any enterprise directory service must be able to grow gracefully with an organization. Better yet, a directory service should be able to grow as large as it must by somehow partitioning the information it stores. For example, DNS has been created so that a DNS server is required to know only a certain number of host-to-IP addresses at any given time. A DNS server has built-in mechanisms that enable it to pass a request to other DNS servers if it doesn't know the information a user is looking for. This combination (partitioned responsibility and hierarchical architecture) enables multiple DNS servers to communicate so that they appear to act as a whole. Since no single DNS server is responsible for all DNS queries, and because growth can be handled simply by adding partitions to the network and creating new DNS servers responsible for handling those partitions, scalability is not only achieved, it's ensured.

- **Ease of Administration**  Regardless of how centralized or scalable a solution is, if the solution is difficult to administer or to navigate, it isn't viable. Network administrators have more to do than ever before, and their jobs are getting more complex. If increased scalability, centralization, and consolidation of network directories make network administration even more complex, the battle is lost. Centralization and scalability must be implemented so as to make administration easier, not more complex.

- **Integration with Security**  There must be inherent mechanisms to secure the data that is placed into a directory, and the more information placed into a directory, the more important such security measures become. Without strong security integration, the usefulness of a directory service is diluted because much of the information in a network has some degree of security requirements associated with it. The challenge is in managing that security. Of course, you could put passwords on every resource or subset of information stored in a directory, but that debilitates the directory service's capability to help users and administrators work better. Security in a directory service must be integrated with the operating system's security subsystem to be effective.

- **Integration with Applications**  For a directory service to be embraced by its users and application developers, its central repository of information must be available to more than just the operating system. The directory service must have a built-in capability that allows applications to utilize the information in the directory service.

- **Standardization and Openness**  Access to a directory service must be available to application developers and users through standardized, open access mechanisms. As I mentioned earlier in this chapter, a directory service defines the means by which its users interact with its information. Often the interaction mechanisms are defined by protocols. A defined interaction mechanism must be standardized and open for the directory service to be viable for any organization, but especially in the enterprise.

## How Active Directory Services Meets Enterprise Directory Service Requirements

Active Directory services meets the requirements of an enterprise directory service in the following ways:

### Active Directory Is Centralized

Through its centralized repository of information, Active Directory services provides one-stop shopping for fulfilling your network information storage and retrieval needs—whether you're a user, an administrator, or an application developer.

### Active Directory Is Scalable

The Windows 2000 domain model is a hierarchical domain model (which is significantly different from the domain model used in prior versions of Windows NT). As a result, Active Directory services can be partitioned across the entire multidomain enterprise yet behave like a cohesive unit. (Does this sound familiar? Remember DNS?) More discussion about the structure of Active Directory and about the new Windows 2000 domain model can be found in the next chapter.

### Active Directory Makes Windows Networks Easier to Administer

Windows 2000 includes the Microsoft Management Console (MMC), which provides a centralized and common-interface approach to system administration. Many services in Windows 2000 are now performed through MMC using "snap-in" tools, which are required to share a common administrative look and feel. With Active Directory service's capability to store information for all sorts of objects—including network hardware devices—it's much simpler for an administrator to use a variety of tools with a common Windows 2000 interface than to use specialized tools and to possess specialized knowledge that used to be required. For example, configuring a router used to require telneting information from a hybrid MS-DOS/UNIX character-based command line utility to a router, and then typing arcane commands to implement relatively simple changes. With Active Directory services, such commands and administrative tasks can be performed with an MMC snap-in from any computer that has access to Active Directory services' catalog of information.

### Active Directory Is Built on Windows 2000 Security

As part of the Windows 2000 operating system, Active Directory services is completely integrated with Windows 2000 security. Any time a user (or a service or application) queries a directory for information it holds in its catalog, Active Directory checks whether that user has proper permission. Because Active Directory is so tightly integrated with Windows 2000, and because Windows 2000 security information is actually stored in the Active Directory repository, Active Directory services can implement pervasive security by simply comparing Windows 2000 security information against access control information for any given object being queried. Also, because Active Directory can store all sorts of information, administrators can create extended security services—such as those based on digital certificates, the Kerberos protocol, or even smart cards.

### Active Directory Is Application-Rich

To attract developers to use the powerful features of Active Directory technology, Microsoft has made Active Directory accessible through multiple protocols such as Lightweight Directory Access Protocol (LDAP) and Active Directory Services Interface (ADSI). Application developers can use the host of existing application programming languages, such as C, C++, and Microsoft Visual Basic, to write directory-enabled applications. Application developers can use the LDAP application programming interface (API) to store and modify information in an Active Directory directory. The recommended API for use with Active Directory is ADSI; ADSI provides a single interface to ADSI-compliant directory services and shields application developers from the details of LDAP programming, enabling developers to concentrate on their application rather than on how to communicate with Active Directory.

### Active Directory Implements Industry Standards

As mentioned in the previous section, Active Directory services is accessible programmatically through LDAP. LDAP is an Internet standard overseen by the Internet Engineering Task Force (IETF) and is defined in Request for Comments (RFC) 2251. Thus, programmers and users can be assured that programs built to adhere to the LDAP standard will work with Active Directory. To get a sense of how important adhering to such standards is and how open the standards are, consider that DNS is also a standard overseen by the IETF and because it is open and standardized, it can be implemented and accessed around the world and all across the Internet.

### Active Directory Is Open (Extensible)

As you might have gathered, developers or administrators who use this central repository of information might have a need to store (and later retrieve) information specific to their applications or networks. Fortunately, Active Directory services is extensible. By providing extension capabilities, Active Directory services can be tailored to an organization's specific needs.

### Active Directory Is Ready to Use

All of these attributes are nice, but if Active Directory services started as an empty shell waiting for information, most networks and their administrators would be at a loss as to how to make it work for them. Fortunately, Active Directory services is automatically populated with interesting and useful information upon installation for an immediate, broad foundation of network computing objects. These objects include user information, group information, security information, and all sorts of other Windows 2000 network operating system objects that can be accessed by the operating system and by network administrators and users.

And what about the general directory service requirements outlined previously? If Active Directory is to be truly ready to use in an enterprise environment or a small organization's environment, those requirements must be met. Let's see how Active Directory's functionality fulfills them:

- **It must help users and administrators work better** By providing a central repository of information that is available to both users and administrators, Active Directory services enables users and administrators to work more efficiently.

- **It must be tightly integrated with security**   No problem here. Active Directory services is hooked to the Windows 2000 security subsystem like Velcro.

- **It must be able to absorb other directories**   Because Active Directory services is extensible (and because certain directories have already been designed to run as part of Active Directory services), other directories—such as e-mail server applications—can and will be absorbed by Active Directory so that their services are simply another aspect of the capabilities of Active Directory services.

# Real-Life Directory Examples

Now that you've read all sorts of facts about directories (the catalog of information) and directory services (the network protocols used to interface with the catalog of information), it's time to move on to some real-life, everyday examples. Let's start simple and get more complex.

## The Simple Directory Example

Imagine you walk into a large building that houses mainly doctors' offices. Rather than jumping in the elevator and searching each floor for the doctor (or type of doctor) you're looking for, you walk over to a large, felt-backed, glass-covered display that presents information about the building and its tenants—the directory.

When you approach the building directory board, you see that the information is arranged by floor; at the top of the directory board, set to the left, is a title that states "Floor 10" and to its right are suite numbers (starting with 1001), the name of the health-care organization that rents each suite, and then the doctors who are associated with each organization. This is consistent for each of the other nine floors. This particular approach is fine if you are interested in finding out who is on each floor (the search criteria being floor number), but it isn't particularly efficient if you're interested in finding the location of the doctor you're coming to visit. You'd have to read through each floor's listing until you happened to come across your doctor's name. Now imagine that there are three of these felt-backed, glass-covered displays placed in a row along a large wall near the entrance of the 10-story building. The first directory is arranged as previously described—by floor—but the second directory is listed alphabetically by the doctor's last name, with his or her floor number, suite number, and organization listed to the right. Aha! Since the directory is arranged, or published, alphabetically by the last name of the doctor (your search criterion, as previously mentioned, is the name of your doctor), you simply go to the second felt-backed directory, read down the list until you come across your doctor's name, gather the floor, suite, and organization information associated with the doctor, and hop on the elevator.

But what if you don't have a specific doctor and instead have come because you've broken your leg (OK, so you're hobbling). You need an osteopath, but when you hobble to the first directory and see that it's organized by floor, you get no help finding your osteopath.

And then you wince and move to the second directory, where information is published based on the doctor's last name. This still doesn't help you because your search criterion is not the doctor's last name. You limp to the third felt-backed directory board and find that it is organized alphabetically by specialty. You finger down the list until you find *osteopath* and then follow the entry to the right where it lists the doctor's name, his or her suite number (which implies the floor on which the doctor can be found—10*xx* for the 10th floor, 9*xx* for the ninth floor, and so on), and the organization with which the doctor is associated. You quickly locate the information you need from the third directory and then get on the elevator (no stair climbing in your state) and hurry up to the doctor's office.

These types of static directories—ones that cannot be rearranged based on real-time input from users—are useful in places such as buildings and telephone books, but their usefulness and accuracy are also dependent on the volatility of their information. If, in the example of the building directories, people in the medical building rarely change suites (which is probably the case) and if the person in charge of the directory boards on the big wall quickly makes changes whenever a tenant moves, the building's directory actually remains quite useful. However, if no one bothers to update the directory for months or years, the usefulness of that directory diminishes increasingly as time goes by.

So a directory must not only contain interesting or useful information, it must also be kept current. Generally, the best way to keep information current is to store it on some sort of computer system. When you computerize a directory and add retrieval capabilities, you have a directory service.

## The Advanced Directory Service Example

As information gets more abstract, vague, or perhaps dispersed, the need for a directory service that can organize such information intensifies.

You could compare the approach a directory service takes in organizing information to the way that online booksellers organize the information on their Web sites. There are a number of online booksellers, including Amazon.com, BarnesAndNoble.com, Borders.com, and Fatbrain.com, and most of them have organized their Web sites to enable users to search for interesting or useful items in a centralized, cogent way—much the same way that directory services enable users to locate information. In the spirit of alphabetical listings, we'll use Amazon.com as representative of booksellers for the rest of this discussion.

Online booksellers are clearinghouses of information. They generally have every type of book a person could want, in all sorts of categories, with all sorts of information for any particular book. Categories of books are often specifically defined (such as fiction vs. nonfiction, thrillers vs. horror, etc.), and at many online booksellers, even larger divisions of hierarchies are provided when products other than books (such as movies and CDs) are offered—though the information for those products is generally published in a similar way to the information about books. At *http://www.amazon.com*, users can search for items of interest with the search capability that is built into the *http://www.amazon.com* interface, or they can narrow a search by choosing a particular category (Mystery & Thrillers, or Computers & Internet, for a couple of examples). From there, users can hone their search criteria by choosing subcategories from within that category, or they can perform a text-based search with keywords. In other words, users can search for items of interest by starting with broad categories and moving toward more specific categories. When *http://www.amazon.com* visitors finally get to a handful of entries that meet their criteria, they can view specific book entries that enable them to choose the book that most appropriately fits their need. Relevant, too, is that information for each book conforms to a certain set of criteria—such as title, author, publisher, and page count—that are common attributes of any book. What has happened throughout the course of the user's search of the sea of *http://www.amazon.com* information? Diverse, distributed, and otherwise segmented pieces of information have been gathered into one central site, where users interested in certain information can search based on a known attribute (topic, title, or author) and find all relevant information.

Each object of a search (a book) has a set of discrete attributes, and the body of information from which users can search is finite. There is an organizational hierarchy, in which categories contain other categories—the Computers & Internet category contains groups such as Certification and Programming—until they reach the final object that cannot contain other objects: the book itself. When initiating the search, users can narrow it to a particular section, such as Literature & Fiction, or they can search the entire site. Note, however, that some pieces of information about particular books are not exposed to the *http://www.amazon.com* search engine—for example, you cannot do a search based on the page count of a book. Why not? There might be a number of reasons, but the important one is that page count is not included as a searchable piece of information in the *http://www.amazon.com* search engine because it is not an attribute of a book that is likely to be useful as a basis for performing a search.

Now imagine that Amazon.com wants to publish a piece of information that previously did not exist about one of its books—perhaps the book's sales ranking. First the body of information that it publishes about its books—called a *schema*—must be expanded to incorporate the new piece of information, or *attribute*. If the designers of *http://www.amazon.com* choose, they can require each book to have a value for the attribute, or they can make the attribute an optional piece of information. Either way, its inclusion as an attribute for each book object in their site equates to an extension of their schema, and that extension to their schema enables the designers of *http://www.amazon.com* to tailor their site to contain information that they believe is important or relevant.

In many ways, the online bookseller's approach to information organization is similar to the Active Directory approach. But how does it really compare? How does the online bookseller's directory stand up to the criteria for a computer network directory service?

First let's look at the general requirements for a directory service and see whether the online bookseller's directory meets the following requirements.

- **It must help users and administrators work better.** It's hard to say whether it helps their administrators work any better, but it certainly helps users find the books they're looking for. We'll give a passing grade, then, for this item.

- **It must be tightly integrated with security.** Most online booksellers want you to find all the information you're interested in on any of the books you look for, so this doesn't apply as directly as it could. However, when placing an order with one of these booksellers for the first time, you generally set up an account with a username and password that's transmitted through a secure line of communication. Also, credit card information is secured. So as far as security is concerned, I think the online bookseller meets the criteria.

- **It must be able to absorb other directories.** Many booksellers these days are also selling movies and music—some even sell electronics, toys, and gifts and host auctions—all through the original (or primary) interface. So the online bookseller example gets another passing grade for meeting the directory service requirements.

Next, let's look at the specific directory service requirements.

- **Centralization**   Yes, online booksellers are centralized on a particular Internet Web site.

- **Scalability**   Well, the book offerings seem to continually expand, so as far as the bookseller is concerned, this solution is probably as scalable as it needs to be.

- **Ease of administration**   This one is an unknown.

- **Integration with security**   Yes, online booksellers provide adequate integration with security, by providing Secure Sockets Layer (SSL) or Transport Layer Security (TLS) for placing orders.

- **Integration with applications**   Since you could consider the order placement and tracking as an application, it seems as though these online bookseller directory services do a fair job of integrating with the kind of applications they need.

- **Standardization and openness**   These online booksellers' directories are absolutely standardized and open because they use an industry-standard, open protocol and language (Hypertext Transfer Protocol [HTTP] and Hypertext Markup Language [HTML], respectively) to enable users to interact with the directories they maintain.

---

**More Info**   The last point is worth commenting on further; because online booksellers have implemented open, standardized interfaces, they have experienced tremendous success and acceptance and have been able to expose their services to millions of users. That is the idea behind using an industry standard and an open standard. Active Directory services uses the same approach with its use of LDAP as its protocol of choice for interaction with its catalog of information.

We still have one question left to answer: how is all the information in a directory stored, organized, and updated? The answer is: by using a database. But a directory service is more than just a database, as you'll learn in the following discussion.

## Directory Service vs. Relational Database

There are important distinctions to be made between a directory service and a relational database. A directory service is a specialized kind of database—one that is built and tuned around being queried and is queried much more than it is written to. To further distinguish a directory service from a database, a directory service's distinctive qualities are not how it stores its information, but rather how it publishes and uses that information.

So a directory service is a specialized database. This specialization means that information appropriate for a directory service can be different than information appropriate for storing in a relational database. For example, a relational database might contain fields or entries that store volatile data or large pieces of data, whereas Active Directory services' core functionality—such as its storage, search, and retrieval capabilities—has been tuned so that Active Directory is a great place for user names and group memberships but not for volatile or large pieces of data. This is much like how an enterprise e-mail application works; the attributes of its objects (e-mail address, office location, and distribution list membership) are read much more often than they are written to. In fact, the core engine of Active Directory services is built upon the tried-and-true Exchange Server directory engine, which means Active Directory services had real-world deployment experience behind it before it was even rolled out.

The details of which objects are appropriate to store in Active Directory services and which objects are not are the subject of a more detailed discussion—which appears in Chapter 14, "Leveraging Active Directory Services." For now, though, the important fact to know about Active Directory services and databases is that Active Directory services stores its information in a specialized kind of database—one that has complete operating system integration, security integration, and specialized interfaces for the operating system as well as standardized interfaces so that other users of its services (applications, administrators, and users) can make use of it through Windows user interfaces and programmatically.

## Conclusion

As the PC-based distributed network began to gain momentum and replaced the centralized mainframe-based network, the varied services required to maintain interoperability across a distributed network increased and dispersed. Windows NT networks were no exception to the dilemma of ever-growing, more distributed networks, and the users, administrators, and developers of Windows-based applications and services found it increasingly difficult to work. Networks had become disjointed, spread out, and difficult to navigate.

A solution was needed that centralized resource information yet encouraged and enabled growth and scalability. Moore's Law and Metcalfe's Law showed no indications of being disproved, and to circumvent Murphy's Law, a solution to the difficulties and challenges of an ever more dispersed network had to be created, provided, and implemented.

The solution that was needed was a directory service that was enterprise-ready, scalable, secured, and standardized—a directory service that could centralize the varied network information pertinent to a Windows network.

This enterprise-ready directory service solution needed to be built into the base operating system, around which all other operating system activities are based and in which all pertinent network-computing information is stored, retrieved, manipulated, and extended. That's easy to say, but a directory service of such ambitious proportion cannot simply be added to an operating system; rather, the operating system must be built around the directory service. That is precisely what has happened with Active Directory services, and the major changes in Windows architecture implemented in Windows 2000 are a direct result of the central role of Active Directory services.

# Chapter 2
# Active Directory Services as a Directory Service Implementation

Microsoft Windows 2000 has incorporated its directory service, Microsoft Active Directory services, into the heart of the operating system's functionality. As a result, computing in the Windows 2000 network environment is significantly different from computing in the Microsoft Windows NT environment, and Active Directory services is at the center of it all.

You can think of Active Directory services as the information hub of a Windows network—the virtual brain of the digital nervous system. In Active Directory, information is stored and retrieved, added and removed, and extended or pruned, providing the entire network with a centralized repository that is *the* definitive source for information on the network.

Because Active Directory is such an all-encompassing service and such a vital part of Windows 2000, it's easy to be intimidated by its importance and complexity. Don't be. The Active Directory architecture isn't intimidating if you keep one thing in mind: Active Directory services is just an information store. That's all it is—a specialized database. Its features and benefits are varied and complex, but when all is said and done, the architectural details of these features are simply derivatives of how information is stored or presented. Once that's understood, it's easy to turn feelings of intimidation about Active Directory services into eagerness or even excitement.

This chapter provides a list of technical details that Active Directory services implements and introduces the deployment features that Windows 2000 makes available—each of which is made possible by the presence of the centralized Windows 2000 directory service. This chapter also explains where Active Directory technology is physically implemented in the Windows 2000 operating system, and then explores how Active Directory functions as the centralized information repository on a Windows 2000 network.

# Active Directory Technical Specifications

In Chapter 1, "Understanding Directory Services," the requirements for an enterprise directory service were outlined. For convenience, here they are again:

- Centralization
- Scalability
- Ease of administration
- Integration with security
- Integration with applications (interoperability)
- Standardization and openness

The technical specifications of Active Directory services map to this list of requirements. Of course, there is some overlap—for example, centralization and ease of administration go hand-in-hand—so some features or technologies apply to more than one item and therefore might be listed more than once.

## Centralization and Scalability

For a directory service to provide a centralized information store accessible through the use of any given access protocol, a certain set of directory service features must be implemented. Additional features are necessary to ensure that the directory service can be scaled to large, enterprise networks. Some features are basic and necessary; others establish the difference between the best directory service available and all others.

The following is a list of the features, specifications, and technologies that enable Active Directory services to provide a centralized information store and that allow Active Directory to scale with growing networks:

- All directory interfaces are exposed to Lightweight Directory Access Protocol (LDAP)
- Base-level operating system integration
- Catalog services (the Active Directory Global Catalog)
- Domain Name Service (DNS) support
- DNS/Directory namespace integration
- Enhanced (real-time static) inheritance model
- Extensive search capabilities, based on LDAP search conventions
- Flexible single-master operation for collision-averse domain services
- Hierarchical directory
- Integrated development model
- LDAP support features use the same directory security model as the operating system

- Migration tool for migration from other directory services
- Multimaster replication
- Native LDAP integration
- Optimized replication based on network topology
- Partitioning support
- Pervasive security for catalog service and directory information
- Real-time catalog/directory access
- Schema extensibility
- Single network logon
- Synchronization and consolidation platform (absorption of other directories)
- Transitive domain trust relationships (vs. explicit trust relationships)

## Ease of Administration

Ease of administration—or manageability, as it's sometimes called—is at the heart of any directory service. In fact, directory services were created because a tool was needed to centralize distributed networks so that they would be easier to manage. Active Directory services includes features and technologies that consolidate administrative activities and that enable administrators to use a somewhat standardized and familiar interface (based on the existing Windows 2000 interface) to perform administrative tasks. As a result, a networked administrative infrastructure is created that allows your organization's network to be managed (or administered) more efficiently and, perhaps, more accurately.

The following is a list of the Active Directory features, specifications, and technologies that make network administration easier than ever before:

- Advertised applications
- Application deployment services
- Application installation services
- Assigned applications
- Centralized and standardized management interface (Microsoft Management Console [MMC])
- Command-line administration
- Delegated administration
- Desktop application management
- Extensible management tools (MMC snap-ins)
- Extensible scripting engine
- Group policy services
- Integrated management tools (MMC)

- Java scripting support
- JavaScript scripting support
- JScript scripting support
- Lockdown of user desktop settings
- Management scripting
- Predefined desktop settings for users (Group Policy)
- Published applications
- Quality of Service (QoS) profile management (users and network devices)
- Remote operating system installation
- Roaming user support
- Security-based and non-security-based groups for increased group usage flexibility
- Simple Network Management Protocol (SNMP) support
- Synchronization of user data between client and server
- Use of organizational units (OUs) for fine-grained administrative control and delegation
- User data management services
- User settings management
- VBScript scripting support
- Web Based Enterprise Management (WBEM) support
- Windows (graphical) administration
- Windows Scripting Host (WSH) integration

## Security

When security capabilities are built into a directory service, the operating system and any service that is a client of the directory service's store are able to authenticate any action based on the centralized repository of security information. This pervasive and highly available security information enables applications and services to offload security-related functions to the directory service, which allows these applications or services to focus on providing their intended functionality rather than a security infrastructure. Also, robust and centralized security capabilities provide a secure environment for sensitive documents, communications, and even commerce.

The following is a list of the features, specifications, and technologies that enable Active Directory to provide robust, centralized security:

- 40-bit Secure Sockets Layer (SSL) support
- 128-bit SSL support
- Centralized security management

- Certificate server/directory service integration
- File system encryption
- Kerberos authentication
- Smart Card support
- Transport Layer Security (TLS) authentication
- X.509 certificate server integration

## Interoperability and Standardization

When standards support is implemented in a directory service such as Active Directory (and thereby, openness is achieved), all the capabilities of the directory service become available to anyone who cares to develop to the interface standard. Standards support not only enables quick deployment and porting of programs to Active Directory services, but also ensures that applications, services, administrative tools, or even other directories that are compliant with the standards can interoperate with Active Directory or make use of its features and capabilities. Without standards support, directories proliferate, creating an environment where administrative tasks are not centralized and increasing the administrative burden (and thereby, the cost of ongoing management) of the network and its services. Fortunately, Active Directory services includes extensive support for Internet and other industry standards.

When interoperability is implemented in a directory service, the directory service becomes capable of synchronizing services with other directories. Interoperability provides the Synchronization necessary to make all services in Active Directory (such as security) available to other directories and vice versa.

The following is a list of the standards that Active Directory services implements, with the associated Internet Engineering Task Force (IETF) Requests for Comments (RFCs) in parentheses beside ratified standards. Note that support in Active Directory for these standards ensures that Active Directory will interoperate with any directory service that also complies with the standards. For example, because Active Directory services supports LDAP standards, it can interoperate with any LDAP-compliant directory service.

- Directory Synchronization (DirSync) support (Internet Draft)
- Dynamic DNS (RFCs 2052 and 2136)
- Dynamic Host Configuration Protocol (DHCP) (RFC 2131)
- LDAP (RFCs 1777 and 2247)
- LDAP C application programming interface (API) (RFC 1823)
- LDAP Data Interchange Format (LDIF) (Internet Draft)
- LDAP version 3 (RFCs 2251, 2252, and 2256)
- LDAP version 3 C API (Internet Draft)
- MIT version 5 Kerberos (RFC 1510)

- Simple Network Time Protocol (SNTP)(RFC 1769)
- Transmission Control Protocol/Internet Protocol (TCP/IP) (RFCs 791 and 793)
- X.509 version 3 public key security (International Organization for Standardization [ISO] standard)

Interoperability requires that access to Active Directory and its services be made available to applications or services outside the operating system itself. Active Directory services achieves such interoperability through its support of the following interfaces, protocols, and languages:

- Active Directory Service Interfaces (ADSI)
- C
- C++
- Java
- LDAP
- Messaging API (MAPI)
- Microsoft Visual Basic

# Active Directory Features

The features discussed in this section are creations made possible by the building blocks available through the specification details outlined in the previous section. These implementation features are available with any Windows 2000 deployment and are provided as part of the base Active Directory capabilities provided by Microsoft.

As you read about these implementation features, you'll see that many of them enable Active Directory services to meet the requirements for an enterprise directory service. For example, the administration delegation feature reflects the effort made to ensure that ease of administration is achieved.

## Administration Delegation

Active Directory services allows network administrators to delegate administrative duties while maintaining network security. The security scheme applied to Active Directory services makes fine-grained security available to all objects in Active Directory. Among those many and varied objects are domains, sites, and OUs. In addition to enabling administrators to assign administrative control and administrative capabilities for such objects and containers, Active Directory lets administrators apply permission settings to all objects in a given container (inheritance).

Administration delegation capabilities of this sort are greatly needed because in previous versions of Windows, the only way to provide enough permission rights to subsets of administrators for a given domain was to grant the administrators sweeping permissions across the entire domain, which posed potential security risks and resulted in a less-than-ideal blanketing of permissions. With the Windows 2000 administration delegation feature, administrative rights can be fine-tuned, and the scope of administrative rights can be more narrowly defined than it could previously. (For example, administrative permissions can be provided to administrators for an OU within a domain, rather than for the entire domain. In Windows NT, providing such administrative rights meant giving sweeping domain-wide administrative rights to administrators who only needed administrative access to a portion of that domain.)

## Automated Software Distribution

Active Directory services enables administrators to automatically distribute software to users based on their roles in the organization. For example, an organization that has licensed Microsoft Word 2000 could automatically distribute that software (and maybe their licensed copies of id Software's Quake III Arena) to the computers of all writers in the organization.

## Backup Services

Windows 2000 comes with a backup utility, supplied by VERITAS Software Corporation, that can back up the entire Active Directory database. (You must configure the backup to include the Active Directory database by selecting to either back up everything on the computer or back up the System State data. The configuration is geared toward backing up the Active Directory database as part of the basic backup routine.)

## Backward Compatibility

In any Windows 2000 environment, full backward compatibility with downlevel clients, such as Windows NT, Windows 95, and Windows 98, is provided by default. In fact, backward compatibility was one of the primary design requirements of Active Directory services.

When Windows 2000 servers and Windows NT servers exist in a given network deployment, that deployment is considered to be a mixed environment. In a mixed environment, Windows 2000 domain controllers appear to downlevel clients as Windows NT 4 domain controllers.

## DEA Platform

Windows 2000 provides a platform for Directory-Enabled Applications (DEAs), which allows these applications to take advantage of the centralized, distributed features of Active Directory to automate various aspects of their functionality. Some of the functionality that can be automated includes the installation, distribution, and maintenance of these DEAs.

## DEN Platform

Windows 2000 has more integration with the network than did previous versions of Windows. Not only is site information used to produce replication scenarios that reduce Active Directory services' use of network and wide area network (WAN) bandwidth, but also network devices use the Active Directory database to store and retrieve configuration and policy information.

This interaction between Active Directory services and the network is called Directory-Enabled Networking (DEN). This platform has hardware and software support from major vendors such as Cisco Systems. Administrators can assign resources such as network bandwidth allocation and QoS settings for users (or applications) based on their role in the organization.

## IntelliMirror

One of the most important network management features of Active Directory services is IntelliMirror. With IntelliMirror, administrators can automatically distribute software, provide for automated software maintenance, centrally manage desktop configuration, and install operating systems remotely. The benefit for the administrator is clear: less administrative, management, and maintenance headaches.

IntelliMirror provides three primary functions: user data management, software installation and maintenance, and user settings management.

With its user data management functionality, IntelliMirror provides users with independence from their personal workstations, enabling users to roam to any Windows 2000 Professional computer and retain their data, applications, and system settings preferences. This independence is possible because Active Directory stores user information, so IntelliMirror can make that information available to the user anywhere on the network and on any Windows 2000 computer.

IntelliMirror also allows users to work with network data when the network is down or they're disconnected. We'll examine how this is accomplished in Chapter 14, "Leveraging Active Directory Services."

With its software installation and maintenance functionality, IntelliMirror allows administrators to specify an application or a set of applications to always be available to a user or a group of users. Whenever an application is not available to a user or a group when that user or any member of the group logs on to a particular workstation and the group profile specifies that the user or group should have the application available, the unavailable application is installed and configured. Conversely, the removal of applications is also supported, as is automated repair of disabled applications.

With its user settings management, IntelliMirror enables administrators to centrally manage and control desktops across the enterprise. For example, administrators can lock desktop configurations to certain specifications and settings. The user settings management facilities of IntelliMirror also enable administrators to associate network settings with users or groups of users.

## Printer Search Capabilities

Active Directory services contains information about all shared printer resources in a Windows 2000 network environment. It organizes printers by business purpose rather than by network location. This type of organization enables users to search for a printer based on its features rather than having to know the name of the server share and the name of the printer. Also, by maintaining information about printer resources in Active Directory, administrators can easily change permissions or other settings on one or all printers from an easily accessed central point of administration.

## Required Authentication Mechanism

Active Directory services allows administrators to require a certain type of logon authentication, including Kerberos authentication, X.509 certificate authentication, or NT LAN Manager (NTLM) authentication.

# Where Is Active Directory Services?

Although we've discussed the technical specifications and the features of Active Directory services, we still have a void in our understanding of how Active Directory is implemented in Windows 2000. That void is expressible in the form of a question: where is Active Directory? The need to know the answer to this question comes from a need to understand *how* Active Directory services works, not just *that* it works. Understanding how Active Directory works starts with knowing where it resides. Does the Active Directory database sit on one computer? If it's entirely new to Windows and so mission-critical and central to Windows deployments, how did previous versions of Windows function without it? Is it a service that runs on every Windows 2000 server, or is it something else?

The answers to these questions are best provided by comparing Active Directory services to the directory service capabilities in Windows NT. Windows NT 4 and Windows NT 3.51 used Windows NT domains, and within each of those Windows NT domains, certain Windows NT servers acted as domain controllers. There was one Primary Domain Controller (PDC) and generally multiple Backup Domain Controllers (BDCs). On each of these domain controllers, certain information about the Windows NT domain was housed so that the domain controller could perform domain-centric activities, such as logging on users or authenticating access to restricted resources. For example, if JohnDoe wanted to read a restricted file housed on a computer running Windows NT Server, the read request would be sent to the nearest domain controller to query whether JohnDoe had proper access permission to read the file. The domain controller, which housed all security information for the domain (among other domain-specific information), would authenticate whether JohnDoe had proper permission to read the file. It would then return the information to the server on which the file was housed, enabling that server to admit or reject JohnDoe's read request.

All BDCs in Windows NT 4 domains maintained copies of the domain-specific information store housed on the PDC. Loosely speaking, they maintained copies of the PDC's *directory store,* which of course was specific to the Windows NT 4 domain. This enabled organizations to make network information available across potentially large and geographically diverse domains. But the copies that the BDCs housed were read-only; information could be written to only the information repository on the PDC.

Active Directory replaces this directory store, this information repository that was kept at the PDC and copied to BDCs in Windows NT domains, but its approach to doing so is very different, and its architecture and capabilities enable it to do much, much more than Windows NT's domain-specific information store ever considered doing.

In Windows 2000 domains, there is no PDC and there are no BDCs. Instead, all servers in a given domain are peers, called *domain controllers,* and each domain controller has a read/write copy of the Active Directory database (the much enhanced and reengineered information repository for domain-specific information). Therefore, Active Directory is essentially a completely new, vastly enhanced incarnation of the information repository that used to be housed by Windows NT domain controllers. Active Directory services has not only absorbed the functionality of the old Windows NT directory stores, it has greatly extended these stores, providing a centralized repository for all network information. In other words, the Windows NT directory stores have been absorbed by the full-fledged directory service that is Active Directory. Thus, in Windows 2000, the entire concept of domain management has been redesigned from the ground up, based on the centralization and scalability needs of ever-expanding networks.

**Real World**

In physical terms, the Active Directory information repository is encompassed by a file called ntds.dit, which is stored in the %systemroot%\ntds folder, such that a Windows 2000 installation placed in the C:\Win2000 folder would implement the Active Directory information store in C:\Win2000\NTDS\ntds.dit. For convenience, Active Directory services also keeps a basic pre-deployment version of an Active Directory information store (database) as the file ntds.dit in the %systemroot%\system32 folder; this file enables a Windows 2000 Server computer to be promoted to a domain controller without the Windows 2000 Server CD. Once promoted (and the ntds.dit file written to the %systemroot%\ntds folder), the newly promoted domain controller synchronizes with other domain controllers to bring its information up to date.

## Departure from the Windows NT 4 Approach

In Windows NT 4 (and earlier), the domain-based information repository was largely closed. Sure, you could add users to the domain and create local or global groups, but the type of information that went into the information store was dictated by Windows NT. While the information repository was used by the Windows NT operating system to keep its predefined information centrally and highly available and enabled a somewhat centralized point of administration and security, it couldn't be used or extended by other applications or by administrators. Nor was it available to application services that were largely part of the domain-based network system itself, such as corporate e-mail. Figure 2-1 illustrates how Windows NT 4 kept its directory store under the hood, so to speak.

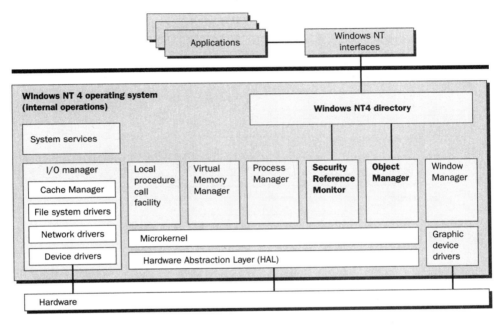

**Figure 2-1.** *The Windows NT 4 directory store.*

In Windows 2000, the directory plays a very different, very central, and highly extensible role, and has taken an evolutionary step forward in networked computing. In Windows 2000, almost everything that has to do with the operating system stores its information centrally, in Active Directory. This Windows 2000 directory information store model enables applications, administrators, services, network devices, users, and the operating system to make use of the directory, in effect making Active Directory itself a service provider on a grand, distributed scale. Figure 2-2 illustrates how this approach enables all sorts of software and administrative components to use Active Directory technology.

It's worthwhile to discuss how these two different approaches to the domain-based information store—keeping it isolated to the operating system or making it available to the entire network—affect the network environment. In Windows NT 4, the result of keeping the repository of domain-based information closed was that other services and applications (such as e-mail, databases, or application servers) were distributed across the network landscape. This created an ever-broadening scope of management responsibility and an ever-diluting sense of "the network," as Figure 2-3 illustrates.

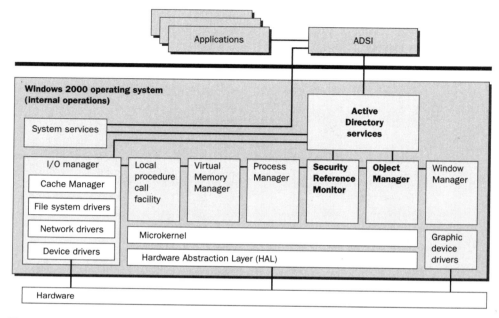

**Figure 2-2.** *The Windows 2000 directory store.*

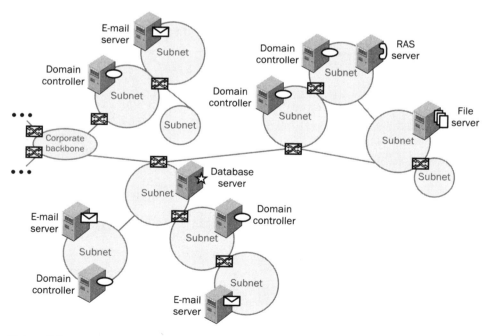

**Figure 2-3.** *A Windows NT 4 domain with directories scattered across the network.*

When the domain-based information store is opened to use by other services, applications, or network administrators who need to manage the corporate network, the separate components of the network become united. Information pertinent to applications or servers can be placed in Active Directory and easily retrieved (remember, the Active Directory database is propagated to each domain controller in the domain), providing cohesiveness for the network that can be maintained regardless of how big the network gets. Figure 2-4 illustrates how a large network can appear as a cohesive unit; contrast this to the network illustrated in Figure 2-3.

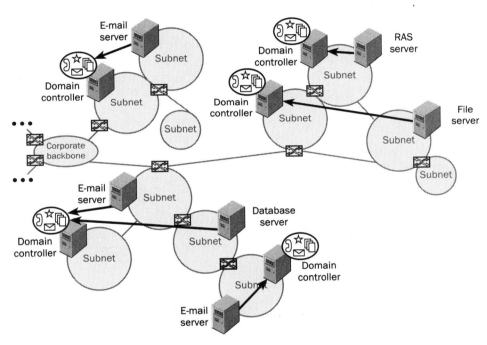

**Figure 2-4** *A Windows 2000 domain with directory information centralized on domain controllers.*

Note that an increase in the number of servers or services won't cause a segmentation of the network. Regardless of where additional servers are deployed, policies or application information is still published in the Active Directory database, which, due to its propagation and publication throughout the domain in domain controllers, is always available and "nearby."

As you can see from Figure 2-4, the Windows 2000 approach is a significant improvement over the Windows NT approach. Active Directory services not only effectively takes over the responsibilities and services formerly performed by the PDC and its BDCs, but also its introduction in Windows 2000 fundamentally changes the way the operating system does its work.

While it's easy to report that Active Directory services has brought a centralized and open directory service to Windows 2000 and the change will turn a distributed network problem into a centralized computing environment, the truth of those statements is difficult to emphasize enough. In fact, this change in the way directory-based information is stored, retrieved, and published fundamentally affects the way the entire network functions. It's not just a new way of implementing PDCs and BDCs; it's a new computing approach. I'd say this 20 times in a row to underscore the importance of these facts, but my editors won't let me. Once (OK, a few times throughout the book), with a little italicizing to spice it up, will have to suffice: Active Directory changes *everything*.

One of the main reasons that Active Directory services is capable of achieving centralization is that its schema is extensible. If it were not extensible, application developers would not be able to use Active Directory to centrally store information objects particular to their programs. The result would be that applications would have to create and then maintain their own information stores (or directories), as is the case with applications that were written to function under Windows NT 4 and earlier. Without the extensibility of the Active Directory schema, the availability of programmatic interfaces to manipulate and interact with Active Directory, and the standardization on LDAP, Active Directory services would fall short of achieving centralization. But Active Directory does deliver on those requirements and capabilities and on all the other requirements of an enterprise-class directory service. As a result, Active Directory is a centralized solution that can bring a distributed, growing network together under the auspices of one integrated, open, extensible, and scalable directory service solution.

# Conclusion

When all is said and done, Active Directory services is really a simple thing: it is an information repository. This information repository comprises the set of requirements for an enterprise-class directory service and all features related to such a complex animal. Don't confuse what it *is* with what it is *capable* of doing. Remember that Active Directory is simply a directory service, or information repository, and that all of its fancy, robust features are what make it such a complex animal.

The notion of a directory service in Windows NT has actually been around for the past few versions, but until Windows 2000 and Active Directory the information repository was a private tool, available primarily to the operating system and closed to the rest of the network. With Windows 2000 and Active Directory services, the basic design of the directory store has completely changed, creating a solution that can unify enterprise networks.

# Chapter 3
# Windows 2000 Domains and Active Directory Services

The Microsoft Windows 2000 domain structure and its associated objects have changed significantly from their Windows NT 4 incarnations, reflecting Active Directory services' central role in Windows 2000 and the design requirements that make it a scalable, enterprise-ready directory service. Some of these changes are obvious, such as the movement to a transitive trust relationship model, while others are subtler, such as the introduction of organizational units. Whether the issues are obvious or subtle, explaining them is central to understanding the interaction and dependencies between Windows 2000 domains and Active Directory services.

Active Directory services emulates the Windows 2000 domain model—or vice versa, if you'd like to look at it that way. Either way, Windows 2000 domains and Active Directory services are dependent on one another and even defined by each other's characteristics. The close and indivisible relationship between Windows 2000 domains and Active Directory services requires an explanation of the Windows 2000 domain model and how it interacts with Active Directory services. Therefore, this chapter begins with an explanation of the Windows 2000 domain model and examines why that model is so different from the Windows NT domain model.

## Windows 2000 Domains

Windows NT 4 domain models didn't scale well. There are other ways of stating this fact that would sugarcoat the truth, but the simple fact of the matter is that the Windows NT 4 domain model—with its one-way nontransitive trusts—required lots of administrative overhead in large-enterprise implementations. This is no longer the case with Windows 2000 and its domain model, largely because of the new approach to trusts, but also because the entire domain concept has been revamped to align with industry standards such as Lightweight Directory Access Protocol (LDAP) and Domain Name Service (DNS).

## The Domain Hierarchy

In Windows 2000 networks, domains are organized in a hierarchy. With this new hierarchical approach to domains, the concepts of forests and trees were created. These new concepts, along with the existing concept of domains, help organizations more effectively manage the Windows 2000 network structure.

### Domains

The atomic unit of the Windows 2000 domain model hasn't changed; it is still the domain. A domain is an administrative boundary, and in Windows 2000, a domain represents a namespace (which is discussed in Chapter 4) that corresponds to a DNS domain. See Chapter 6, "Active Directory Services and DNS," for more information about how Active Directory services and DNS interact.

The first domain created in a Windows 2000 deployment is called the *root domain,* and as its name suggests, it is the root of all other domains that are created in the domain tree. (Domain trees are explained in the next section.) Since Windows 2000 domain structures are married to DNS domain hierarchies, the structure of Windows 2000 domains is similar to the familiar structure of DNS domain hierarchies. Root domains are domains such as *microsoft.com* or *iseminger.com*; they are the roots of their DNS hierarchies and the roots of the Windows 2000 domain structure.

Domains subsequently created in a given Windows 2000 domain hierarchy become *child domains* of the root domain. For example, if *msdn* is a child domain of *microsoft.com,* the *msdn* domain becomes *msdn.microsoft.com.*

As you can see, Windows 2000 requires that domains be either a root domain or a child domain in a domain hierarchy. Windows 2000 also requires that domain names be unique within a given parent domain; for example, you cannot have two domains called *msdn* that are direct child domains of the root domain *microsoft.com.* However, you can have two domains called *msdn* in the overall domain hierarchy. For example, you could have *msdn.microsoft.com* as well as *msdn.devprods.microsoft.com*; the *microsoft.com* namespace has only one child domain called *msdn,* and the *devprods.microsoft.com* namespace also has only one child domain called *msdn.*

The idea behind domains is one of logical partitioning. Most organizations large enough to require more than one Windows 2000 domain have a logical structure that divides responsibilities or work focus. By dividing an organization into multiple units (sometimes called divisions in corporate America), the management of the organization is made easier. In effect, the organization is being partitioned to provide a more logical structure and perhaps to divide work among different sections of the organization. To look at this another way, when logical business units (divisions) are gathered collectively under the umbrella of one larger entity (perhaps a corporation), these logically different divisions create a larger entity. Although work within the different divisions might be separate and very different, the divisions collectively form a larger but logically complete entity. This concept also applies to the collection of Windows 2000 domains into one larger, contiguous namespace entity known as a tree.

## Trees

*Trees*—sometimes called *domain trees*—are collections of Windows 2000 domains that form a contiguous namespace. A domain tree is formed as soon as a child domain is created and associated with a given root domain. For a technical definition, a tree is a contiguous DNS naming hierarchy; for a conceptual figure, a domain tree looks like an inverted tree (with the root domain at the top), with the branches (child domains) sprouting out below.

The creation of a domain tree enables organizations to create a logical structure of domains within their organization and to have that structure comply with and mirror the DNS namespace. For example, David Iseminger and Company could have a DNS domain called *micromingers.iseminger.com* and could have various logical divisions within the company, such as sales, accounting, manufacturing, and so on. In such a situation, the domain tree might look like the domain tree in Figure 3-1.

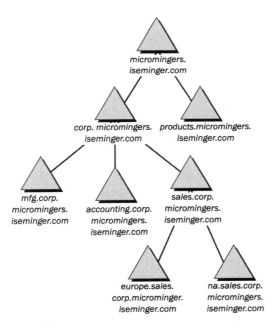

**Figure 3-1.** *The domain tree for micromingers.iseminger.com.*

**Note**  By now you've noticed that *iseminger.com* is being used all over the place. This isn't vanity on the author's part; it's a legal consideration the publisher insists upon. "No domains that are potentially contentious please," they said. "Only author-owned domains or really, really dull ones." The author has an in at *www.iseminger.com*, so that domain name has to be used everywhere in this book. I had more inventive names, but alas, we must please the lawyers.

This organization of logical divisions within the company works great for companies that have one DNS domain, but the issue of companies that might have more than one "company" in their larger enterprise must be addressed. That issue is addressed through the use of Windows 2000 forests.

## Forests

Some organizations might have multiple root domains, such as *iseminger.com* and *microsoft.com*, yet the organization itself is a single entity (such as the fictional David Iseminger and Company in this example). In such cases, these multiple domain trees can form a noncontiguous namespace called a *forest*. A forest is one or more contiguous domain tree hierarchies that form a given enterprise. Logically, this also means that an organization that has only a single domain in its domain tree is also considered a forest. This distinction becomes more important later in this chapter when we discuss the way that Active Directory interacts with Windows 2000 domains and forests.

The forest model enables organizations that don't form a contiguous namespace to maintain organization-wide continuity in their aggregated domain structure. For example, if David Iseminger and Company—iseminger.com—were able to scrape together enough pennies to purchase another company called Microsoft that had its own directory structure, the domain structures of the two entities could be combined into a forest. There are three main advantages of having a single forest. First, trust relationships are more easily managed (enabling users in one domain tree to gain access to resources in the other tree). Second, the Global Catalog incorporates object information for the entire forest, which makes searches of the entire enterprise possible. Third, the Active Directory schema applies to the entire forest. (See Chapter 10 for technical information about the schema.) Figure 3-2 illustrates the combining of the iseminger.com and Microsoft domain structures, with a line between their root domains indicating the Kerberos trust that exists between them and establishes the forest. (The Kerberos protocol is explained in detail in Chapter 8.)

Although a forest can comprise multiple domain trees, it represents one enterprise. The creation of the forest enables all member domains to share information (through the availability of the Global Catalog). You might be wondering how domain trees within a forest establish relationships that enable the entire enterprise (represented by the forest) to function as a unit. Good question; the answer is best provided by an explanation of trust relationships.

## Trust Relationships

Perhaps the most important difference between Windows NT 4 domains and Windows 2000 domains is the application and configuration of trust relationships between domains in the same organization. Rather than establishing a mesh of one-way trusts (as in Windows NT 4), Windows 2000 implements transitive trusts that flow up and down the (new) domain tree structure. This model simplifies Windows network administration, as I will demonstrate by providing a numerical example. The following two equations (bear with me—the equations are more for illustration than pain-inducing memorization)

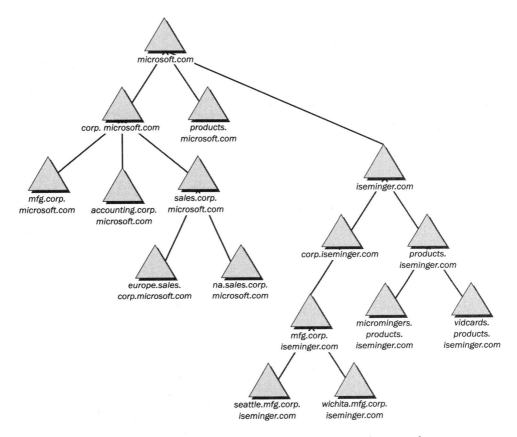

**Figure 3-2.** *The combining of domain trees for iseminger.com and Microsoft.*

exemplify the management overhead introduced with each approach; the equations represent the number of trust relationships required by each domain trust approach, where *n* represents the number of domains:

Windows NT 4 domains—$(n * (n-1))$

Windows 2000 domains—$(n-1)$

Just for illustration purposes, let's consider a network that has a handful of domains and see how the approaches to domain models compare. (Assuming that five domains fit in a given hand, $n = 5$ in the following formulas.)

Windows NT 4 domains: $(5 * (5-1)) = 20$ trust relationships

Windows 2000 domains: $(5-1) = 4$ trust relationships

That's a significant difference in the number of trust relationships that must be managed, but that reduction is not even the most compelling strength of the new approach to domains. With Windows 2000 domains, the trusts are created and implemented by default. If the administrator does nothing but install the domain controllers, trusts are already in place. This automatic creation of trust relationships is tied to the fact that Windows 2000 domains (unlike Windows NT 4 domains) are hierarchically created; that is, there is a root domain and child domains within a given domain tree, and nothing else. That enables Windows 2000 to automatically know which domains are included in a given domain tree, and when trust relationships are established between root domains, to automatically know which domain trees are included in the forest.

In contrast, administrators had to create (and subsequently manage) trust relationships between Windows NT domains, and they had to remember which way the trust relationships flowed (and how that affected user rights in either domain). The difference is significant, the management overhead is sliced to a fraction, and the implementation of such trusts is more intuitive—all due to the new trust model and the hierarchical approach to domains and domain trees.

In Windows 2000, there are three types of trust relationships, each of which fills a certain need within the domain structure. The trust relationships available to Windows 2000 domains are the following:

- Transitive trusts
- One-way trusts
- Cross-link trusts

### Transitive Trusts

Transitive trusts establish a trust relationship between two domains that is able to flow through to other domains such that if domain A trusts domain B, and domain B trusts domain C, domain A inherently trusts domain C and vice versa, as Figure 3-3 illustrates.

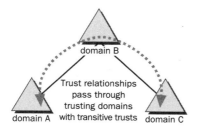

**Figure 3-3.** *Transitive trust among three domains.*

Transitive trusts greatly reduce the administrative overhead associated with the maintenance of trust relationships between domains because there is no longer a mesh of one-way nontransitive trusts to manage. In Windows 2000, transitive trust relationships between parent and child domains are automatically established whenever new domains are created in the domain tree. Transitive trusts are limited to Windows 2000 domains and to domains within the same domain tree or forest; you cannot create a transitive trust relationship with downlevel (Windows NT 4 and earlier) domains, and you cannot create a transitive trust between two Windows 2000 domains that reside in different forests.

### One-Way Trusts

One-way trusts are not transitive, so they define a trust relationship between *only* the involved domains, and they are not bidirectional. You can, however, create two separate one-way trust relationships (one in either direction) to create a two-way trust relationship, just as you would in a purely Windows NT 4 environment. Note, however, that even such reciprocating one-way trusts do not equate to a transitive trust; the trust relationship in one-way trusts is valid between only the two domains involved. One-way trusts in Windows 2000 are just the same as one-way trusts in Windows NT 4 and are used in a handful of situations. A couple of the most common situations are described below.

First, one-way trusts are often used when new trust relationships must be established with downlevel domains, such as Windows NT 4 domains. Since downlevel domains cannot participate in Windows 2000 transitive trust environments (such as trees and forests), one-way trusts must be established to enable trust relationships to occur between a Windows 2000 domain and a downlevel Windows NT domain.

> **Note**  This one-way trust situation doesn't apply to the migration process (such as an upgrade of an existing Windows NT 4 domain model to the Windows 2000 domain/tree/forest model). Throughout the course of a migration from Windows NT 4 to Windows 2000, trust relationships that you have established are honored as the migration process moves toward completion, until the time when all domains are Windows 2000 and the transitive trust environment is established. There's a whole lot more detail devoted to the migration process in Chapter 12, "Migrating to Active Directory Services."

Second, one-way trusts can be used if a trust relationship must be established between domains that are not in the same Windows 2000 forest. You can use one-way trust relationships between domains in different Windows 2000 forests to isolate the trust relationship to the domain with which the relationship is created and maintained, rather than creating a trust relationship that affects the entire forest. Let me clarify with an example.

Imagine your organization has a manufacturing division and a sales division. The manufacturing division wants to share some of its process information (stored on servers that reside in its Windows 2000 domain) with a standards body. The sales division, however, wants to keep the sensitive sales and marketing information that it stores on servers in its domain private from the standards body. (Perhaps its sales are so good that the standards body wants to thwart them by crying, "Monopoly!") Using a one-way trust keeps the sales information safe. To provide the necessary access to the standards body, you establish a one-way trust between the manufacturing domain and the standards body's domain, and since one-way trusts aren't transitive, the trust relationship is established only between the two participating domains. Also, since the trusting domain is the manufacturing domain, none of the resources in the standards body's domain would be available to users in the manufacturing domain.

Of course, in either of the one-way trust scenarios outlined here, you could create a two-way trust out of two separate one-way trust relationships.

### Cross-Link Trusts

Cross-link trusts are used to increase performance. With cross-link trusts, a virtual trust-verification bridge is created within the tree or forest hierarchy, enabling faster trust relationship confirmations (or denials) to be achieved. That's good for a short version of the explanation, but to really understand how and why cross-link trusts are used, you first need to understand how interdomain authentications are handled in Windows 2000.

When a Windows 2000 domain needs to authenticate a user (or to otherwise verify an authentication request) to a resource that does not reside in its own domain, it does so in a similar fashion to DNS queries. Windows 2000 first determines whether the resource is located in the domain in which the request is being made. If the resource is not located in the local domain, the domain controller (specifically, the Key Distribution Center [KDC] on the domain controller) passes the client a *referral* to a domain controller in the next domain in the hierarchy (up or down, as appropriate). The next domain controller continues with this "local resource" check until the domain in which the resource resides is reached. (This referral process is explained in detail in Chapter 8.)

While this "walking of the domain tree" functions just fine, that virtual walking up through the domain hierarchy takes time, and taking time impacts query response performance. To put this into terms that are perhaps more readily understandable, consider the following crisis:

You're at an airport whose two terminal wings form a V. Terminal A inhabits the left side of the V, and Terminal B inhabits the right. The gates are numbered sequentially, such that both Terminal A's and Terminal B's Gate 1s are near the base of the V (where the two terminals are connected) and both Gate 15s are at the far end of the V. All gates connect to the inside of the V. You've hurried to catch your flight and arrive at Terminal A Gate 15 (at the far end of the V) only to realize that your flight is actually leaving from Terminal B. You look out the window and can see your airplane at Terminal B Gate 15, but in order for you to get to that gate you must walk (OK, run) all the way back up Terminal A to the base of the V and then jog (by now, you're tired) all the way down Terminal B to get to its Gate 15—just in time to watch your flight leave without you. As you sit in the waiting area, biding your time for the two hours until the next flight becomes available and staring across the V to Terminal A, from which you thought your flight was departing, you come up with a great idea: build a skybridge between the ends of the terminals so that passengers such as yourself can quickly get from Terminal A Gate 15 to Terminal B Gate 15. Does this make sense? It makes sense only if there's lots of traffic going between each terminal's Gate 15.

Similarly, cross-link trusts can serve as an authentication bridge between domains that are logically distant from each other in a forest or tree hierarchy and have a significant amount of authentication traffic. What amounts to lots of authentication traffic? Consider two branches of a Windows 2000 domain tree. The first branch is made up of domains A, B, C, and D. A is the parent of B, B is the parent of C, and C is the parent of D. The second branch is made up of domains A, M, N, and P. A is the parent of M, M is the parent of N, and N is the parent of P. That's a bit convoluted, so check out Figure 3-4 for an illustrated representation of this structure.

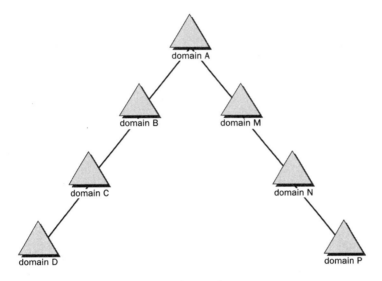

**Figure 3-4.** *A sample domain hierarchy.*

Now imagine that you have users in domain D who regularly use resources that, for whatever reason, reside in domain P. When a user in domain D wants to use resources in domain P, Windows 2000 resolves the request by walking a referral path that climbs back to the root of the tree (domain A in this case) and then walks back down the appropriate branch of the domain tree until it reaches domain P. If these authentications are ongoing, this approach creates a significant amount of traffic. A better approach is to create a cross-link trust between domains D and P, which enables authentications between the domains to occur without having to walk the domain tree back to the root (or the base domain at which the tree branches split). The result is better performance in terms of authentication.

## Administrative Boundaries

The reduction of the number of trust relationships that must be managed is a great improvement in Windows 2000. However, another improvement was greatly needed in Windows 2000, and that had to do with administrative boundaries. In Windows NT 4 and earlier, administrators who needed the capability to administer subsets of users or groups within a given Windows NT domain had to be given sweeping, domain-wide administrative permissions. Even if their administrative rights shouldn't have spanned the entire domain, the rights they needed required that such sweeping rights be granted. In Windows 2000, that has changed with the advent of organizational units (OUs).

## Domains

The Windows 2000 domain is an administrative boundary. Administrative rights do not flow across domain boundaries, nor do they flow down through a Windows 2000 domain tree. For example, if you have a domain tree with domains A, B, and C, where A is the parent domain of B and B is the parent domain of C, then users with administrative rights in domain A do not have administrative rights in B, nor do users with administrative rights in domain B have administrative rights in domain C. To obtain administrative rights in a given domain, a higher authority must grant them. This does not mean, however, that an administrator cannot have administrative rights in multiple domains; it simply means that all rights must be explicitly defined.

## Organizational Units

Organizational units enable administrators to create administrative boundaries within a domain. With OUs, administrators can delegate administrative tasks to subordinate administrators without granting them sweeping administrative privileges throughout the domain. Let's clarify with an example of why OUs are so useful. Say the sales force within your organization has its own network administrators and resources, such as printers and servers, and funds all these network resources with its own budget. The network administrators from the sales force want control over the sales force resources, policies, and other administrative elements within the sales force group. However, the sales force is part of the corporate domain. If this were a Windows NT 4 network, the administrators of the sales force unit would have to be added to the Domain Administrators group to get the administrative privileges they need to administer the sales force unit. Such membership in the Domain Administrators group gives the sales force administrators administrative control over the entire corporate domain (not just the sales force unit). Such sweeping administrative control isn't appropriate, but it's the only way to provide the sales force administrators with administrative control over the sales force's resources and policies. With Windows 2000 and the advent of OUs, that's changed. In a Windows 2000 network, the supervising network administrators can create OUs, including a sales force OU, within the domain structure and thereby establish new and more limited administrative boundaries. The solution could go something like this: Create an OU for the sales force unit, and give the sales force administrators full administrative privileges only for the sales force OU and not for any other area of the corporate domain. With the creation of OUs, membership in the Domain Administrators group (which grants administrative privilege for the entire domain, including its OUs) can be restricted to only those administrators who have administrative responsibilities that cover the entire domain. This results in a more secure and better-run network.

What if your organization needs to have OUs within OUs? Can you nest OUs? The answer to that question is yes, but performance becomes an issue after you go deeper than about 15 OUs. There are other issues you should consider when deciding whether to nest OUs (and whether to use OUs at all), and I'll discuss them in detail in Chapter 7, "Planning an Active Directory Services Deployment."

# Active Directory Services Interaction

Where does Active Directory services fit into all of this? Why is it absolutely necessary to fully understand domains and domain structure in order to understand the planning requirements of Active Directory services? Because Active Directory is inextricably tied to the domain structure of your Windows 2000 deployment.

## Emulating the Domain Hierarchy

As we already know, Windows 2000 domains form a domain hierarchy and one or more domain hierarchies can form a forest. The directory, as a complete unit, is simply the collection of all objects in the forest. To ensure that Active Directory services would scale to millions of objects in a single directory, however, there had to be a strategy for "breaking up" the directory into parts because, simply put, one mammoth unpartitioned directory would not scale well. The solution was to partition the directory.

The Active Directory partitioning schema emulates the Windows 2000 domain hierarchy. The unit of partition for Active Directory services, then, is the domain.

This emulation of the domain hierarchy achieves a number of goals.

- Scalability is ensured.
- Performance is maximized.
- Replication overhead is minimized.

The following section explains in detail how the Active Directory partitioning schema emulates the domain hierarchy, why scalability is ensured and performance is maximized, and how this emulation of the domain structure minimizes replication overhead.

## Cataloging the Domain (the Directory Partition)

The primary goal of Active Directory services is to create a catalog of objects that reside in the forest. Of course, the catalog wouldn't be too terribly useful if it were so big that it became slow and clumsy. For example, imagine all the friends you could take on a skiing trip if only you had a school bus—but try parallel parking that bus, climbing a mountain pass with that bus, or parking it in your garage. A better approach would be to have a convoy of cars, each of which could carry skiers who lived near each other. You would then avoid the painfully slow climb up the pass, and you could find parking places scattered about the parking lot. Best of all, each car could service the getting-home requirements of a few skiers, thereby getting everyone home faster than if they were loaded in the single bus.

To take the bus comparison a bit further, imagine the problem you'd run into if you made more ski-frenzied friends. If there were too many, not all of them would fit on the bus. In such a situation, you would have to get an entirely new, bigger bus, which would be even more cumbersome. And as more skiers are invited, the time it takes to get every-one home after the skiing trip gets longer and longer. In comparison, when cars are used, you simply have to add more cars to the convoy as you invite more friends; the result is essentially no additional inconvenience for any existing skiers, nor any additional tran-sit time when getting skiers home. Of course, you must have a road that can accommo-date more cars.

Active Directory services helps you avoid getting on the overloaded bus. Instead, the directory is broken into pieces—just like the convoy of cars—and the benefits of such an approach are similar to the benefits of using a convoy, but much farther reaching.

### Partitioning the Directory

To help you picture how Active Directory services gets partitioned within the forest, I'll provide an example of a simple forest. Figure 3-5 illustrates the sample forest and its single domain tree.

The forest consists of all of the domains illustrated in Figure 3-5. The entire directory consists of all the objects contained in all the domains in the forest. However, to increase scalability and performance, you must break the directory into multiple pieces, the aggregation of which creates the complete directory.

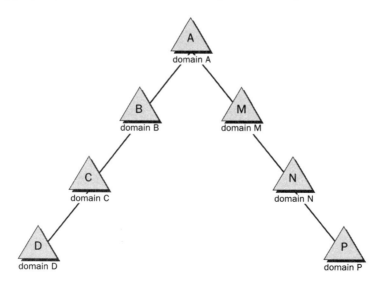

**Figure 3-5.** *The A, B, C, D, M, N, and P domain hierarchy.*

Remember that in Windows 2000 the unit of partitioning is the domain. So, when we take another look at our domain hierarchy example, we can compare the logical domain hierarchy to the way that the directory is partitioned. Figure 3-6 compares the domain hierarchy to the directory catalog. As you can see, the directory is simply the aggregation of each domain's partition.

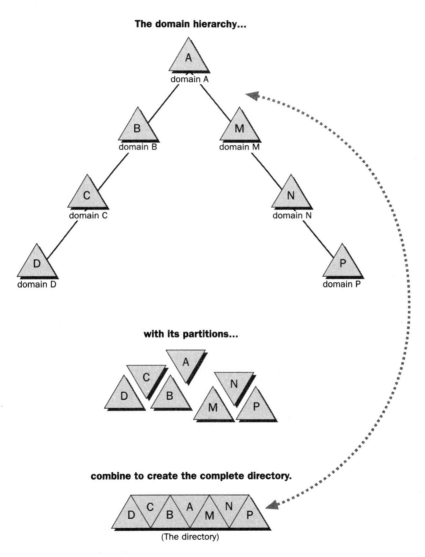

**Figure 3-6.** *The domain hierarchy/directory partition schema relationship.*

Remember that noncontiguous trees in the same forest still form one directory. Don't confuse trees with forests, and don't confuse the boundary of the enterprise (the forest) with the contiguous nature of a given domain tree within the forest (the tree). Most organizations, hopefully, will be able to plan and deploy a single tree—equating to a single namespace—that constitutes their entire forest. That's the easiest deployment to envision, manage, and maintain. But deployments aren't always that neat, and acquisitions happen, so you need to remember the following logical equation:

one forest = one schema = one directory catalog

Also realize that a single domain still constitutes a forest. If you're fortunate enough to be able to sensibly design your Windows 2000 domain structure as a single domain, realize that your single domain constitutes the forest. What does that mean? It means that the entire directory catalog will be in one unpartitioned unit. (The domain is the unit of partitioning—one domain = one partition.)

Perhaps one of the most important advantages of partitioning the directory catalog has to do with the catalog's scalability, specifically in terms of the effect of adding a domain to the domain tree or even adding another entire domain tree to the forest. Adding a domain or a domain tree does not add administrative or replication burden to the existing domain hierarchy and administrative structure. Because of the partitioning of the directory, and because each domain controller in any given domain contains only directory catalog information particular to its domain, when a domain or even a domain tree is added to the forest, network performance and scalability are not affected. When combined with the new transitive trust relationships established among domains in the same forest, this partitioning of directory catalog information makes scaling to very large enterprise deployments with Windows 2000 and Active Directory services possible.

### Getting Information About Objects in Another Domain

With all this talk about partitioning the directory catalog, you might be wondering how information from one domain partition gets accessed by users in another domain. After all, if the domain controllers in one domain contain information about objects only in their domain, what happens when users need to get information about objects that reside in another domain? Good question, and fortunately the answer is straightforward: Active Directory services uses DNS lookups and queries to resolve queries, just like the Internet.

Although Active Directory services and Windows 2000 use DNS for their lookup service, they both use a special service (SRV) resource record (RR) entry that designates a given DNS entry as a domain controller. Domain controllers, in turn, determine whether they are able to resolve a query, such as would be the case if the query were about an object in their local domain. If they cannot, the request is referred to a domain controller that either can resolve the request itself or can point the domain controller to the next logical server to which the request should be made. Eventually, the domain controller that can resolve the query is found (or is definitely not found), at which time the client is referred to that server to continue with the query process.

DNS queries are explained in more depth in Chapter 6, "Active Directory Services and DNS."

## Distributing the Directory

The next points to make clear are how the partitioned directory is distributed and how it interacts with the Windows 2000 domain model. In Windows 2000, each domain controller in a given domain contains a copy of the directory partition for its domain, enabling each domain controller to locally resolve queries for information about objects in the domain to which it belongs.

This approach makes sense because in many cases users (or other entities that make use of Active Directory services) make more use of domain-local network resources than they make of resources located in a remote domain. By distributing a copy of the domain partition to each domain controller in the domain—and by making each of those copies readable and writable—the following enhancements and improvements are realized:

- Performance is increased because any domain controller can perform local searches for objects found in its domain.
- Scalability is increased because each domain controller contains a readable and writable master copy of the directory catalog partition.
- Scalability is also increased because no single machine is burdened with performing all the updates for the directory.

This approach is especially useful when remote sites or branch offices are part of the network topology. By putting a domain controller (which, by definition, contains a copy of the directory catalog partition) at a remote site, user queries can be resolved locally. This means that the use of perhaps expensive or limited wide area network (WAN) resources can be minimized. The benefit of placing a domain controller at a remote site or branch campus isn't confined to WAN resource savings because, of course, the performance of queries will also be improved by having the domain controller (and its directory catalog partition) available on the remote site's local area network (LAN).

## Replicating the Directory

Since each domain controller contains a writable master copy of the Active Directory partition for its domain, changes can be made to a domain's partition on any available domain controller. When changes are made on one domain controller, there must be a way to get change updates replicated to other domain controllers. This process of distributing updated information to appropriate domain controllers is called *replication*.

In Windows 2000, the unit of replication is the domain partition. However, only changes at the attribute level of a given object are replicated to other domain controllers, rather than entire objects. The result is a significant savings in replication traffic, and any time operationally required network traffic can be reduced, the better the solution.

Update priority is determined through the use of Update Sequence Numbers (USNs). Rather than comparing the values for object attributes, Active Directory services uses a running number—the USN—to determine whether replication is needed, and if so, which object attribute values need to be transmitted. For more information on USNs, see the "Replication" section in Chapter 4, "Active Directory Services Scalability Architecture." This implementation of USNs is another advantage of having the domain as the unit of partitioning; it limits replication traffic (which is already limited to attribute changes) to the confines of the domain in which the changes were made.

## Cataloging the Enterprise (the Global Catalog)

Finally, there must be some way for Active Directory services to quickly respond to user queries. Although many user queries pertain to the domain in which the users belong, many others are not domain specific, but rather, are made throughout the enterprise. For example, e-mail name queries. A truly enterprise-ready and performance-minded directory service must service such frequent and global queries without generating undue network traffic and without having to jump through multiple query referrals. The answer is a directory catalog that contains a subset of attributes for every object in the enterprise. In effect, it must be a catalog of object attributes that are globally interesting. For Active Directory services, that answer is the Global Catalog. The Global Catalog consists of selected attributes from every object in the enterprise, which means that selected attributes from every object in the forest are available for domain-local querying. Just as Microsoft has created a default set of objects in the schema, default attributes from each schema object are tagged for inclusion in the Global Catalog. (You might never need to modify these—but you can.) Most objects have approximately 15 attributes, and approximately seven of those attributes are tagged for inclusion in the Global Catalog.

The Global Catalog sits on selected domain controllers within each domain and services queries that are specific to global searches. When a user submits a global query based on an object's attribute and that object's attribute is tagged for inclusion in the Global Catalog, the query can be resolved by a domain controller in the local domain that is configured to keep a copy of the Global Catalog. Because there is at least one domain controller housing the Global Catalog in each domain, queries directed at global searches can be performed and resolved quickly. Attributes included in the Global Catalog by default were chosen because they don't change very often, and that's the way it should be. Using static information in the Global Catalog minimizes replication traffic; after all, when an object's attribute that's tagged for inclusion in the Global Catalog changes, that change must be replicated to all Global Catalog domain controllers across the entire enterprise. Apart from the minimizing of replication traffic, static information in general is more appropriate for global searches.

## Conclusions

Windows 2000 domains and Active Directory services are two sides of the same coin; domains are administrative boundaries, as well as partition and replication boundaries for Active Directory services. Just as the Windows 2000 forest is the all-inclusive organizational structure for Windows 2000 domains, the Windows 2000 forest is the all-object-inclusive structure for Active Directory services, as well as the framework within which all objects are defined by a single schema. In short, the domain structure *is* the

Active Directory services structure. If you don't understand Windows 2000 domains, you can't understand how Active Directory services operates—which is why domains have received as much attention in this chapter and this part of the book as they have.

Scalability is achieved in Windows 2000 because domains no longer require exhaustive two-way trust relationships; now trusts are implicitly created and then augmented when a Windows 2000 domain must interact with downlevel domains or when trusts must be established with forest-external domains. Scalability is also achieved because the domain-level partitioning schema of Active Directory services minimizes the impact of adding domains—so much so that Active Directory services can scale to networks as large as the Internet.

Despite the partitioning of Active Directory services and the Windows 2000 domain model, the cohesiveness of a Windows 2000 networking environment is ensured by virtue of the Global Catalog. By keeping selected object attributes in a catalog that spans the entire enterprise, often-searched object attributes can be readily accessible, regardless of where the query originates or where the target object resides in the organization.

Of course, keeping all the Windows 2000 domain terminology straight can be difficult, as can getting a clear understanding of why such organizational and hierarchical containers—such as forests, domains, and OUs—were created in the first place. It might help if you consider the following loose associations between Windows 2000 domain terms and how a large organization might apply the structure to its environment:

- Enterprise boundaries—forests
- Corporate boundaries—trees
- Division boundaries—domains
- Departmental boundaries—organizational units

But what if your organization doesn't look like this? What if you aren't an enterprise or a corporation, or you don't have departmental boundaries? If any of those responses reflect your thoughts, don't worry—these loose associations are only guidelines to give you an idea of how forests, trees, domains, and OUs can meet the requirements and requests of large and small organizations alike. Maybe you don't need OUs, or maybe you need only one domain (which you determine after reading Chapter 7, "Planning an Active Directory Services Deployment," right?). Regardless, you should keep one thing in mind throughout the planning, deployment, and management processes.

Keep it simple.

Domains, directories, and networking are complex enough on their own without the burden of an overly complex deployment plan. Can your network work with one domain? Can your network work with only a few OUs? If so, great—then use only one domain and a few OUs. You'll hear this call for simplicity throughout Part II of this book because simplicity works: keep things simple, and they'll be easier to manage, easier to administer, and easier for your users to use. And after all, that's the goal, isn't it?

# Chapter 4
# Active Directory Services Scalability Architecture

Scalability is one of the primary goals of Microsoft Windows 2000, and at the center of that goal is ensuring that the information repository for Windows 2000—Active Directory services—can scale to meet today's enterprise computing requirements. To understand the architecture of Active Directory services and how its central role in the operating system requires that it scale gracefully with the operating system is to understand the operational framework of Windows 2000.

## The Importance of Scalability

As discussed in Chapter 2, Active Directory services must meet specific directory service requirements in order to be a viable enterprise-ready directory service. These requirements are

- Centralization
- Scalability
- Ease of administration
- Security
- Integration with applications
- Standardization and openness

The explanation of how Active Directory services meets these requirements is split into two chapters: this chapter and the next. In this chapter, we will examine in detail the architectural elements of Active Directory services that enable it to meet what is arguably the most complex requirement for an enterprise-ready directory service: scalability. Since achieving scalability sets the foundation for meeting many of the other requirements, scalability is explained first (and individually) in this chapter, and the achievement of the remaining requirements is explained in the following chapter.

Active Directory services is capable of scaling from small implementations, such as single-server or single-domain deployments, to enterprise-sized implementations as large as the

Internet. The reason Active Directory scales so well to both small and very large deployments is rooted in a handful of architectural design elements. These elements are

- Partitioning approach
- Catalog service implementation
- Replication scheme

## Partitioning Approach

Active Directory services scales well because its approach to partitioning is designed to enable it to hold millions of objects. Active Directory bases its partitions on Windows 2000 domains so that any given Windows 2000 domain equates to one Active Directory partition. If an organization consists of three Windows 2000 domains, the organization also has three Active Directory partitions. Since more Windows 2000 domains can be added as the organization grows (and since each domain's Active Directory partition can hold up to 1 million objects), Active Directory services can scale in step with the growth needs of the organization.

But why is partitioning important? Why is it that partitioning in this way helps Active Directory achieve such scalability? To answer these questions, we must take a step back, look at the overall information needs of a given network system, and explain how Active Directory service's partitioning approach meets those needs.

Let's use an example with some easy numbers. Let's say that the fictional midsized Iseminger Corporation has a network environment that consists of 10 DNS domains, and it's using some random and fictional operating system that has a directory service that isn't partitioned at all. The primary domain is called *iseminger.com*, and the rest of the domains are child domains of that domain, all of which are in the same tree. In this example, the full body of information that Iseminger Corporation uses is the information contained in all 10 domains. However, most of the information that individual users and administrators use within the *iseminger* domain resides in their own domain. For example, users in the *midtower.cases.iseminger.com* domain do most of their searches on information that resides in the *midtower.cases.iseminger.com* domain. They also store most of their files in that domain, and most of the printers they access are in that domain.

The total amount of information in all 10 of *iseminger*'s domains is vast and scattered throughout the organization, and it somehow needs to be available in a coherent manner. With the company's fictional operating system and its mammoth directory, no one can get information very quickly, and adding even a single domain increases the size of every directory-hosting server's load by 10 percent. However, by partitioning the information, an intelligent approach can be taken to managing *iseminger*'s vast amount of information, and as a result, the amount of information that can be handled efficiently is greatly increased. If *iseminger* moved to Windows 2000 and Active Directory services, its 10 domains could immediately be partitioned according to its Windows 2000 domains. Figure 4-1 depicts a domain controller search both with and without partitioning.

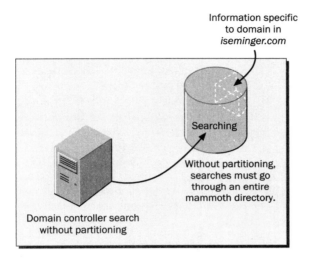

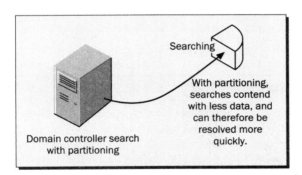

**Figure 4-1.** *Domain controller searches with and without partitioning.*

Since Active Directory services' unit of partitioning (or slicing) is the Windows 2000 domain, scalability is achieved on a couple of levels. These efficiencies have a lot to do with why Windows 2000 partitions Active Directory based on domains.

First, any given Active Directory partition must contain only part of a network's body of information—in the case of *iseminger.com*, only one-tenth of the network's full body of information. Limiting the number of objects that can exist in one partition or domain (if you call 1 million objects limiting) ensures superior performance, and enabling multiple domains to exist in a given organization ensures Active Directory can scale to the largest of organizations. Partitioning in this way makes Active Directory services more efficient and better performing, especially since most users' Active Directory queries are searches for information in their own domain.

Second, when growth occurs and a domain must be added to an organization's network, the new domain's Active Directory partition will not have a large effect on Active Directory partitions in other domains. By contrast, consider what would happen if a domain were added to a network with an unpartitioned directory service—let's use the Iseminger network as an example again. The result of adding a domain to that network would be a 10 percent increase (10 domains' information plus 1) in an already vast amount of information that would have to be held on each directory-hosting server—that's not a good, scalable approach. Using the Active Directory approach to partitioning, the effect of adding new domains to the overall enterprise deployment is minimized.

> **Note**  While each Windows 2000 domain equates to one Active Directory partition, all domain controllers in a given domain contain a readable and writable copy of the domain's Active Directory partition.

After this discussion of the Active Directory partitioning approach, you might be wondering how users and administrators find objects (such as information about printers, files, or people) stored in partitions other than their own. Clearly, some mechanism must be in place that enables users to access information from Active Directory partitions located throughout the enterprise. Such access is provided by the Active Directory catalog service, the Global Catalog.

## Catalog Services (the Global Catalog)

To provide scalability, a directory service must not only be able to partition the information it stores, but it must also provide a mechanism that enables all the partitions to act as a single entity. Although these two requirements—enterprise-wide information availability and information partitioning—might seem mutually exclusive, they can both be met if a directory service provides a catalog service. The catalog service provided by Active Directory services is called the Global Catalog.

Briefly, a catalog service is an information store that contains selective information about every object in the entire directory and services queries specifically targeted for an "entire enterprise" search. To understand how the Global Catalog functions, you must first understand how information is stored in the Active Directory information store (including the Global Catalog). What follows are explanations (or definitions, if you care to consider them as such) of four terms—namespace, object, naming context, and schema—that you must be familiar with to understand how information is stored in the Active Directory database.

## Namespace

The concept of a namespace is central to any directory service, including Active Directory services. Despite the sometimes vague and foggy impressions that get conjured when discussing the definition of a namespace, the definition is actually quite straightforward. A *namespace* is simply a defined space in which a given name can be resolved (matched) to some object. By *defined space,* I mean some definable, bounded area such as a corporation, a Windows 2000 domain hierarchy, or the city of Seattle. To use a simple but effective analogy, compare a namespace to an extended family: You generally have a couple of parents, some kids, a few pets, some grandparents and cousins, and perhaps some houseplants. In the extended family namespace of Olson, for example, the name Pokey (of the fourth-generation Olsons) can be resolved to the family's domesticated cheetah. The name, then, can be uniquely resolved to a certain object. Similarly, in the Windows 2000 domain namespace of *iseminger.com*, the name *printer1.corp.iseminger.com* can be resolved to the printer on floor 776 of the Iseminger corporate campus. That name, then, can be uniquely resolved to a certain object in the *corp.iseminger.com* domain hierarchy (that is, the *iseminger.com* namespace).

Since a domain hierarchy equates to a namespace, many Active Directory implementations will also equate to a namespace. However, recognize that forests can consist of more than one namespace. That is, forests can consist of more than one hierarchical Domain Name System (DNS) domain tree, as would be the case if *microsoft.com* and *msn.com* were part of the same forest.

## Object

An *object* is some item that can be defined by a set of attributes. Each object type (a class of object) has particular attributes that differentiate that object type from other object types in a given namespace. For example, you can have a feline object (an instance of the feline class) that has certain attributes, such as a name (Pokey), color (spotted), and species (cheetah). A special kind of Active Directory object, a *container,* is similar to an object in that it has attributes, but it doesn't refer to an item; rather, a container contains objects and other containers. Containers are somewhat difficult to compare to real life because they don't represent a concrete item (like a cheetah). Rather, a container is generally characterized (if not defined) by its contents; you might call your home a container because it generally contains your family, your pets, some houseplants, and perhaps a mortgage. The home container is defined not by its own attributes (like its architectural style or its square footage), but rather by its contents. A Windows 2000 domain is another example of a container.

Objects are identified by a name. In Windows 2000, there are two different kinds of names: the distinguished name and the relative distinguished name.

### Distinguished Name

The *distinguished name* identifies the object's path through the directory service's entire hierarchy. The following is an example of a distinguished name for a user object found in *midtower.cases.iseminger.com*:

```
O=Internet/DC=COM/DC=iseminger/DC=cases/DC=midtower
/CN=Operators/CN=Line11/CN=CynthiaRandall
```

Don't worry about memorizing the way this particular naming scheme is structured or about what the various symbols and conventions represent. This naming scheme is just to provide you with an example of a distinguished name and to illustrate how distinguished names find their way through the directory service hierarchy. For those with inquiring minds, though, here's a short legend to the conventions used in this particular example.

*O = Organization*
*DC = Domain Component*
*CN = Common Name*

### Relative Distinguished Name

The *relative distinguished name* is the part of the distinguished name that is actually an attribute of the object. In the *midtower.cases.iseminger.com* example, the relative distinguished name is the following:

```
CN=CynthiaRandall
```

The object in question is a user, and the name attribute of this particular user object in the Iseminger organization is CynthiaRandall; since CynthiaRandall is an attribute of the actual object, this attribute becomes the relative distinguished name part of the larger distinguished name.

To stretch the application of distinguished names and relative distinguished names to our cheetah example, you might contrive some sort of organizational hierarchy for a family of which the cheetah named Pokey is a part by designating the following as the pet's distinguished name. (Remember, the distinguished name resolves the name through the entire hierarchy.)

```
O=Olson/DC=Generation1/DC=Generation2/DC=Generation3/CN=Pets
/CN=Pokey
```

And of course, the relative distinguished name would simply be:

```
CN=Pokey
```

Remember that only certain object types can be placed in certain containers. In this example, you can't place a member of the feline class (such as a cheetah) in the Children container; it breaks all sorts of rules, including genetics. Similarly, you can't have a member of a Houseplant object in the Children container either.

## Naming Context

One or more *naming contexts* can exist within the scope of a namespace. It's easy to confuse a naming context with a namespace, so let's clarify the two right off the bat. A namespace generally equates to a naming hierarchy; *microsoft.com* is a namespace, and it might have a bunch of child domains in its domain tree. All of this would be part of the *microsoft.com* namespace. In contrast, each given domain within the *microsoft.com* namespace is a distinct naming context—for example, *corp.microsoft.com* is a naming context, as is *example.microsoft.com*.

The important distinction between a namespace and a naming context has to do with naming objects within a given naming context. In the *corp.microsoft.com* naming context, there can be only one printer named Printer30 because the context in which Printer30 has been named requires that the name Printer30 resolve to a unique object. It's somewhat akin (no pun intended) to the dilemma of having two brothers with the same first name: "This is my brother Darryl, and that's my other brother Darryl." You'll see this analogy and another explanation of the naming context in Chapter 6, "Active Directory Services and DNS." Rather than interrupting this explanation by sending you there right now, I am providing an explanation in this chapter as well.

Back to the *corp.microsoft.com* and *example.microsoft.com* printer example: we have a printer called Printer30 in the *corp.microsoft.com* naming context, and because of that, we can't have another printer named Printer30 in *corp.microsoft.com*. However, we can have a printer called Printer30 in *example.microsoft.com*. Why? Because it's a different naming context—just like it's OK to have two different-family cousins named Darryl, but not OK to have two same-family brothers named Darryl.

In Active Directory, each partition is a naming context. Since Active Directory partitions equate to Windows 2000 domains, each Windows 2000 domain is a naming context.

## Schema

Active Directory services has a specific set of objects that can exist in a given namespace (or namespaces, in the case of a multi-namespace forest). To ensure that the universe of objects that exists in Active Directory fits within this specific set of objects, Active Directory maintains something called a schema. The *schema* is essentially an extensive object model from which any object within Active Directory must be derived. The schema also dictates the attributes of any given object; it specifies which attributes a given object must have and which attributes a given object can have. Essentially, the schema is a skeleton of objects that can exist in an Active Directory deployment.

Active Directory services comes with an extensive schema, but the provided schema might not include all the objects a given organization wants to include in its directory service. For example, an organization within *iseminger* might need to create a new object with attributes that include color, size, weight, cost, and type, which its sales force, product managers, or customer service technicians can search for in the Global Catalog. For that reason, the Active Directory schema can be extended (by administrators with appropriate permissions) to meet the needs of users. In a word, the schema is extensible.

The schema, then, is the scaffolding of your directory information tree. What you do once that scaffolding is erected (or expanded) determines the usefulness of this structure.

## How the Global Catalog Operates

Now that we're familiar with the terms we need to know to understand how Active Directory services stores information, we can return to the subject we started to explain in this section: how does the Global Catalog provide access to information about the entire organization? It does this by being the information service provider that covers all namespaces in the forest. While the namespaces can be divided into two or more naming contexts (Windows 2000 domains) for the purposes of the Active Directory partitioning scheme, the Global Catalog is not bound by individual Windows 2000 domains or individual domain trees. Instead, the Global Catalog is a collection of selected object attributes from every domain (that is, every naming context in the namespace). Notice I specify the term *selected*.

All objects in Active Directory services are based on objects available in the schema; there are no objects in Active Directory that are not defined in the schema. Therefore, you can take a representative view of the objects in Active Directory by viewing the objects available in the schema. The creation of the Global Catalog is based on this logic.

The attributes that any Windows 2000 Active Directory deployment includes in (replicates to) the Global Catalog consist of a base set of default attributes, which means that if an administrator does nothing to modify those attribute settings, a representative (default) set of attributes preselected by Microsoft will automatically be included in the Global Catalog. By providing these default items, Windows 2000 allows administrators to focus on selecting additional attributes that they believe are necessary to meet the global search needs of their organizations. Figure 4-2 depicts selected attributes of an object being stored in the Global Catalog and distributed to various servers.

The Global Catalog is not housed on every domain controller. Administrators determine which domain controllers should house a copy of the Global Catalog, generally considering such issues as site location and bandwidth. Administrators can use Active Directory Schema Manager to designate appropriate domain controllers as Global Catalog holders.

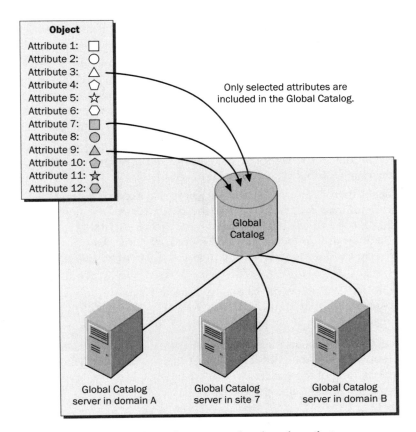

**Figure 4-2.** *The Global Catalog stores only selected attributes.*

Global Catalog searches occur in the following circumstances:

- When searches are directed at the root of a domain tree (the "." that is the technical parent of the root domain). This is what happens when Windows 2000 user interface searches are used by clients and such searches specify a global search.

- By a direct reference to the Global Catalog port at a Global Catalog replica.

- By explicit reference (as in GC://) to the Global Catalog Active Directory Service Interfaces (ADSI) provider.

When one of these Global Catalog searches is initiated, the following occurs:

1.  The client queries its designated DNS server for a (Windows 2000) domain controller housing the Global Catalog. Domain controllers that house a copy of the Global Catalog register a special DNS resource record (RR) (a special kind of service [SRV] record, to be exact) with DNS servers when they boot up, enabling those DNS servers to search their zone files (the DNS information store) for records that designate the servers as Global Catalog servers.

2.  The DNS server searches its zone file and returns the results of its query to the client. Of course, the response includes an Internet Protocol (IP) address for any matching Global Catalog domain controllers.

3.  The client then makes a Lightweight Directory Access Protocol (LDAP) query to the IP address returned by DNS (the IP address of the domain controller housing a copy of the Global Catalog). The Global Catalog query is sent to port 3268 on the domain controller. (Standard Active Directory queries, which are directed to the domain-local partition, are submitted to port 389, which is the standard LDAP port.)

4.  The Global Catalog server listens for Global Catalog queries on that port, processes each query, and then provides the client with an appropriate response.

In Windows 2000 deployments that use only one domain, each domain controller actually contains the equivalent of the Global Catalog (if there's only one Windows 2000 domain, there is no partitioning of the Active Directory database), and therefore each domain controller responds to Global Catalog requests.

# Replication

*Replication* is the process of copying (replicating) parts of an information repository to other locations. Replication enables distributed information stores like Active Directory services to remain synchronized, an important factor in an information repository's capability to scale. In a Windows 2000 network, replication ensures that changes made to one copy of an Active Directory partition are copied to all other replicas of the Active Directory partition. (You might remember from Chapter 2 that each Windows 2000 domain controller contains a copy of the Active Directory partition for the domain it belongs to.)

Windows 2000 takes what is called a *multimaster approach* to replication. In a multimaster approach, changes can be made to any copy of a part of an information store, and those changes are propagated to all other copies. In Windows 2000, this is possible because each copy of an Active Directory partition is writable—changes to the directory store can be written to any Active Directory partition on any domain controller, and those changes are propagated to all other domain controllers in the domain.

Contrast this to the replication approach in previous versions of Windows NT, in which domain controllers were either the Primary Domain Controller (PDC) or one of many Backup Domain Controllers (BDCs). In that approach, only the PDC was writable; the BDCs were read-only. This *single-master* architecture meant that any changes to a domain's information store had to be made on the PDC, and copies would then be propagated to the read-only BDCs. This approach, in which only the PDC has a writable copy of directory information, scales poorly.

With Active Directory services and its multimaster approach to replication of changes or updates to directory information, each domain controller is capable of handling changes to the Active Directory information store, which effectively distributes the load associated with updating directory information. A superior replication scheme must do more than ensure that the load associated with replication is distributed, though. It must also ensure that the replication process is automatic and transparent to users and administrators and is performed as efficiently as possible.

The method that Active Directory services uses for its replication of information has been developed to favor volatility over time, to avoid the use of (often unreliable) timestamps for validity, and to dampen network traffic associated with updates. The following sections take a closer look at how Active Directory replication occurs.

## Replication Process Overview

Windows 2000 uses a 64-bit number called the *Update Sequence Number* (USN) on each domain controller to maintain a value that identifies changes to its Active Directory services store. When a change is made to any object in Active Directory, the domain controller advances the USN and stores it with the changed object (or attribute). Now the change must be distributed to other domain controllers. To accomplish this distribution without being wasteful, each domain controller maintains a table of USNs that are associated with all its replication partners (other domain controllers with which replication information is exchanged). In that table, the highest USN received by each replication partner is stored. When one of the domain controller's replication partners initiates the replication process, the domain controller consults its table of USNs for that replication partner and requests only the changes associated with USNs that are greater than the value stored in its table for that replication partner. This approach limits the amount of data passing between replication partners, effectively limiting the transmitted data to the data that changed since the last successful replication update. Note that the USN stored in the domain controller's table for a given replication partner is not changed (to the new USN) until all changes associated with the most recent replication exchange are completed successfully.

## Failure Recovery

The use of USNs also makes failure of a given domain controller easy to recover from. A domain controller that has failed for any given length of time can, once it is brought back on line, consult its list of replication partner USNs and request updates for all changes above the USN number stored in its USN table for a given controller.

## Resolving Collisions

Because most Windows 2000 domains contain multiple writable partition replicas, the same attribute of a given object could be modified at or near the same time on different domain controllers. When an attribute is modified on a domain controller before a change to that attribute that was made on another domain controller is completely propagated, a *collision* occurs. Domain controllers detect collisions by comparing the property version numbers in the changes they receive during replication with locally stored property version numbers. *Property version numbers* differ from USNs (which are specific to each domain controller) because they are specific to a given object's attribute and are initialized upon creation of the attribute. Property version numbers are advanced only when an attribute is changed (not when the attribute is updated through the normal process of replication). These changes are called *originating writes,* to differentiate them from changes applied to a given attribute through the replication process. A collision is detected by comparing property version numbers for a given attribute.

When a collision occurs, Active Directory services evaluates the following properties of each modification request, in the order presented, to resolve the collision:

1. The property version number
2. The timestamp
3. The IP address

The change with the higher value is the change that is replicated. If the values are identical in one instance, Active Directory moves to the next item to resolve the collision. If a domain controller receives an update that has a property version number that is lower than the locally stored number, the update (with the lower property version number) is discarded. Such favoritism toward more recent versions, and the fact that timestamps are used *only* to resolve collisions, results in Active Directory favoring volatility over time.

## Reducing Network Traffic

To reduce the use of network bandwidth for the propagation of replication information, Active Directory services employs several strategies. The premise behind such bandwidth usage dampening is obvious: there's never enough bandwidth, let alone too much, and its use by system-specific activities should be kept at a minimum. There are other reasons as well, as the following paragraphs explain.

The first approach that Active Directory uses reduces the amount of data transmitted by compressing it before sending it over wide area network (WAN) links.

Secondly Active Directory services uses information about network topology, specifically about Windows 2000 sites, to send replication information more efficiently over high-cost network links. Sites (which are described in more detail in Chapters 5 and 7) are essentially one or more IP subnets that are linked by high-bandwidth connections (10 Mbps or faster). From the information about sites that Active Directory stores, the replication mechanism within Active Directory is able to create a sense of site topology and interconnections and uses that information to create replication partners in an intelligent way.

For instance, when replication information is sent from a server across a high-cost link to a server in another site, replication to other servers in that distant site is done within the site rather than from the server across the high-cost link again. The following example will help you visualize how this process works.

Say that the Windows 2000 domain *midtower.cases.iseminger.com* consists of two sites, one in Amsterdam and one in Miami. Changes are made to the Active Directory services partition that resides on a domain controller in Amsterdam, and those changes must be propagated to the domain controllers in Miami holding Active Directory partition replicas for the *midtower.cases.isemingers.com* domain. The appropriate replication partner would compress the changed information and then send it to its replication partner in the Miami site. The server at the Miami site would receive and decompress the updated information and then apply the changes to its Active Directory store. Next all other domain controllers in the Miami site would get that replication information (which originated in Amsterdam) from the domain controller in Miami, avoiding more usage of the high-cost link between Amsterdam and Miami. This approach not only conserves bandwidth on high-cost links, but it also makes use of the high-bandwidth connections that interconnect domain controllers in the same Windows 2000 site. Figure 4-3 illustrates this method.

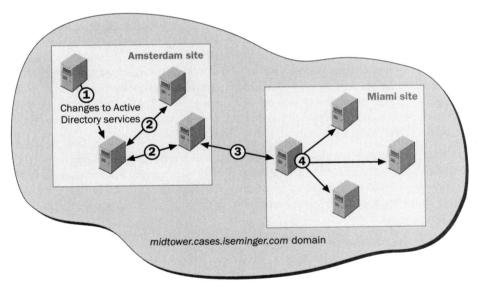

1. Changes to Active Directory information occurs on a domain controller in the Amsterdam site.

2. Replication of the changes propagates throughout the site.

3. The domain controller, configured to be a replication partner with a corresponding domain controller in the Miami site, compresses the change information and sends it to its replication partner at the Miami site.

4. Within the Miami site, the changed information gets replicated (without compression) to the domain controllers in Miami.

**Figure 4-3.** *Using compression to replicate data across a high-cost link.*

The third mechanism that Active Directory services employs to reduce the amount of bandwidth used to propagate replication information is called *propagation dampening*. Propagation dampening keeps replication information from endlessly looping through the network. This is necessary because Active Directory allows loops (multiple replication paths) in the Active Directory replication topology to provide fault tolerance and increase performance. Without propagation dampening, replication updates would be endlessly propagated through the loops, consuming large amounts of bandwidth.

Windows 2000 achieves propagation dampening by keeping up-to-date vectors comprised of domain controller/USN (DC/USN) pairs. In any Windows 2000 site, each domain controller contains an up-to-date vector for every other domain controller in the site; when replication begins, the requesting domain controller sends its up-to-date vector to the sending domain controller. If the DC/USN pair indicates that the requesting domain controller has an up-to-date version of the Active Directory partition (that is, if its USN matches the USN that the sending server has in its DC/USN table), then no update information is transmitted.

# FSMO Roles

A multimaster operation such as the one that Windows 2000 implements with its new approach to domain controllers is superior to its predecessor (single-master operations). While there are many benefits to multimaster operations, certain network operations that are necessary components of a Windows 2000 network environment don't adapt well to the multimaster paradigm. For the most part, these are operations that must have a unique master copy (or authority or version) through which all requests for service must go. In other words, these network operations require that one server contain the master copy and be the master servicer of the operation.

To enable these single-master operations to take place in a multimaster environment, Windows 2000 implements the idea of a *flexible single-master operation* (FSMO) (pronounced FIZZ-mo). When a given server holds the "right" to be the FSMO server for one of these multimaster-averse network operations, it becomes the "single master" for that particular service.

The main reason why some of these special network operations don't function well in a multimaster environment is that they deal with collisions poorly. While Active Directory services has mechanisms that can resolve replication-related collisions should they occur (as we saw in the previous section), the sensitive network operations that require FSMO operations do a better job avoiding collisions altogether. In the Windows 2000 environment, there are five situations in which it is better to prevent collisions than resolve them, and the domain controllers that provide FSMO services in these five situations are called FSMO role holders.

In FSMO, a single-master role holder provides the necessary master role services for the Active Directory functionality it provides. However, these roles can change and can be offloaded to other domain controllers in the case of shutdown or failure. Since there is the capability for a given FSMO role holder to hand its role to another domain controller, the approach is considered flexible, hence the term flexible single-master operation.

The five roles that FSMO role-holding domain controllers can have are the following:

- Domain Naming Master
- Infrastructure Master
- PDC Emulator
- Relative ID (RID) Master
- Schema Master

Each of these five FSMO roles is explained in detail in Chapter 7, "Planning an Active Directory Deployment." However, a fundamental understanding of their operation is important to understanding how Active Directory services achieves its scalability, so concise explanations of each are provided here.

The *Domain Naming Master* is the only domain controller from which administrators can perform a number of domain creation or deletion operations. New domains can be added to the namespace or namespaces (the organization's forest) only from the Domain Naming Master. Likewise, only from the Domain Naming Master can existing domains be deleted or cross-references to external directories be removed or both.

The *Infrastructure Master* is the domain controller that is responsible for keeping track of objects that reside in another directory but are referenced in the current directory. Any record in Active Directory services that references such extra domain objects contains the object's globally unique identifier (GUID) to ensure that the object is referenced properly (even if it moves from one location or domain to another) and its security identifier (SID) to ensure that security for the object is maintained. The Infrastructure Master is responsible for updating the SIDs and distinguished names in cross-domain object references in the domain in which it resides.

The *PDC Emulator* provides support for downlevel clients, such as Windows NT 4, Windows 95, and Windows 98 clients without the appropriate directory-enabling service packs applied. Simply put, the PDC Emulator appears as the PDC for downlevel clients attempting to reach the equivalent of the PDC in a Windows 2000 domain and provides functions such as directory writes, downlevel BDC replication service, and domain master browser for downlevel clients and servers. Obviously, only one server can act as a PDC for a given domain; therefore, only one Windows 2000 domain controller can manage emulation of that single PDC. Once all downlevel clients and servers are upgraded, however, the PDC Emulator still retains some functionality, including being the preferential password replication domain controller for other Windows 2000 domain controllers, processing account lockouts, and authentication failure (on other domain controller) retries.

The *RID Master* is responsible for maintaining RIDs for a given domain. RIDs are used as part of the creation of SIDs to enable the uniqueness of SIDs over time. The RID Master is also responsible for being the gatekeeper for objects in its domain so that objects cannot be moved from its domain to another domain. When an object is moved from one domain to another, its SID (which is comprised partially of its RID) changes. By ensuring that only the RID Master can move objects from its domain to another domain, Windows 2000 ensures that two objects will never have the same SID, even across domains. This, in turn, ensures that no two objects will have the same GUID, as could happen if an object were moved to two places from two different domain controllers (rather than one—the RID Master) at approximately the same time.

The *Schema Master* is the only domain controller on which schema changes can be performed.

Each of these FSMO roles can be held by any domain controller in a given Windows 2000 domain; however, there are certain constraints and requirements that apply to them. First there is one Domain Naming Master and one Schema Master for each namespace. (A namespace is the collection of all domains in a given enterprise domain tree hierarchy, as you might remember.) This makes sense: the addition or deletion of domains is an enterprise-wide activity, and the schema applies to the entire namespace.

Second there is one Infrastructure Master, one PDC Emulator, and one RID Master for each Windows 2000 domain. This also makes sense: The Infrastructure Master tracks references to objects that are external to its particular domain and therefore is a per-domain operation. The PDC Emulator and the RID Master also function on a per-domain basis.

## Conclusion

Scalability is one of the primary features of Active Directory services. It has to be; otherwise, Active Directory could not meet the needs of enterprise networks.

When you add scalability to a directory service, you enable large organizations to create a comprehensive and cohesive computing environment and to make that computing environment function without the need for complex, labor-intensive management. The next step is ensuring that such scalability doesn't distribute administration or services such that they get lost in the extended tangle of the network. In other words, scalability must come with centralization. The next chapter continues the explanation of how Active Directory achieves its requirements and in doing so achieves the distinction of being an enterprise-ready directory service.

# Chapter 5
# More Active Directory Services Architecture

This chapter continues the explanation begun in Chapter 4 of how Active Directory services meets the requirements of an enterprise-class directory service.

The requirements we will discuss in this chapter include the following:

- Ease of administration
- Security
- Integration with applications
- Standardization and openness
- Centralization

## Achieving Ease of Administration

Active Directory services is administered with relative ease because it takes advantage of centralization and standards compliance, and it makes use of building blocks. For instance, when network information is consolidated in a centralized repository (that is, when the centralization requirement is met), network administration immediately becomes easier. Active Directory provides a centralized repository for information about all network resources, which means that multiple separate directories of information, such as RAS account information or e-mail distribution lists, are obviated.

In addition, when a directory service is open and complies with industry standards (that is, when the standardization requirement is met), network administration can be simplified because widely available (or widely used) tools can be used for what might otherwise have required a proprietary, unfamiliar interface.

## Easing Administration with Centralization

With centralization achieved, administration immediately becomes easier. Rather than administrators having all sorts of directories to manage, such as RAS accounts, database permissions, and SNA Server policies, all directories can be subsumed by Active Directory services and therefore be centrally located. The centralization of administration information in Active Directory, coupled with the standardization of the administration interface provided by the Microsoft Management Console, goes a long way in promoting easier administration.

## Easing Administration with Standards Compliance

Other contributing factors to the ease of administration attributed to Active Directory services are its standards compliance and openness. Such standardization results in administrative tools, whether provided by Microsoft or developed by outside vendors with similar interfaces. Chapter 2, "Active Directory Services as a Directory Service Implementation," goes into detail about the various standards to which Active Directory services is compliant. It also provides insight into just how many different standards there are for administrative interfaces or administrative programs.

One large contributor to achieving ease of administration with Active Directory services is its complete, ground-up integration with Internet standards. One of the most important of these standards is Hypertext Transfer Protocol (HTTP). The result of complying with this particular standard is that Active Directory can be managed by any Web browser on any machine (providing the user has appropriate permissions) from anywhere in the organization or, with the proper connections, from anywhere on the Internet.

## Administration Building Blocks

Perhaps the most important, pervasive, and potentially powerful tools that Active Directory provides to help ease the burden of administration are administration-empowering building blocks. The architecture of Active Directory, with its centralization, scalability, and vast repository of information, provides building blocks that can be used to make administration of Microsoft Windows 2000 domains, and the clients who aren't necessarily directly making use of Active Directory services, potentially much easier. For example, with the publication of available applications in the Active Directory database, as well as pointers to necessary application files, it becomes possible to create an application that senses when crucial files are missing from a given user's desktop installation of the program. The application can then direct the operating system to check Active Directory for the location of such files on the network and to copy those files to the local "broken" installation of the program—in short, to fix the broken program. This "self-healing" approach is an administrator's best friend; what would otherwise entail a service log, a service call, administrator time, downtime for the users, and all associated costs becomes an automated update made possible by a centralized repository of information (for both published applications and their files' locations on the network). And remember that this example is but a small taste of what can be done administratively with a centralized information store such as Active Directory. It will likely be some time before we tap the full extent of its capabilities.

# Achieving Security

The advent of the Internet and open networks is a great thing, but with it comes unavoidable security baggage. Security, especially in a directory service that intends to make objects selectively available in its information repository, must be both pervasive and industrial-strength. Active Directory services meets the requirement for security by completely integrating with Windows 2000 security. All the information stored in the Active Directory information repository—all the way down to the attributes of a given object—is protected from unauthorized access. This protection is made possible by securing every object, and every object attribute, with Windows 2000 Discretionary Access Control Lists (DACLs). The application and protection of DACLs for each object, and each object attribute, in Active Directory means that the permissions most administrators are familiar with applying to familiar securable objects, such as a file in an NTFS volume, can also be applied to Active Directory objects. If a user attempts to access an object but does not have the proper permission settings, the Active Directory security implementation will not reveal the presence of the object, let alone allow manipulation of its attributes.

In addition to the capability to apply security properties to objects and attributes, administrators can direct Active Directory services to propagate security settings down the hierarchical object path (that is, to child objects and containers) of any given Active Directory object. In other words, child objects and containers can inherit permission settings applied to parent objects or containers. This capability is aptly called *inheritance,* and it enables administrators to efficiently apply security settings to entire trees or branches of the Active Directory information repository.

With Active Directory services' capability to assign certain permission rights to objects and to enable children of such objects to inherit those security settings, an administrative phenomenon called *delegation* can be achieved. With delegation, Active Directory enables the administration of entire sections (such as a Windows 2000 site) of a given Active Directory tree to be assigned to a different administrator. In Windows NT, such delegation wasn't as accessible, and the result was that administrators were often given unnecessarily broad administrative rights over an entire Windows NT domain in order to provide the necessary rights to administer even parts of the domain. With Active Directory's flexible object permission assignments (DACLs), which can easily be propagated to children objects and containers (inheritance), you can provide administrators with only the administrative rights they need—and only over the objects for which such permissions should be granted—to do their job. This more fine-tuned approach to assigning rights and permissions to objects, and its consequential reduction in the required set and scope of administrative rights that a given administrator or group must be assigned, effectively tightens the security of the Windows 2000 domain (and Active Directory) overall. Why? Because the number of administrators with sweeping administrative rights can be reduced, and the number of administrators who can be provided with the subset of required permissions to do their (more focused and more site-specific or organization-specific) jobs is increased.

# Achieving Application Integration

Active Directory services enables application integration by providing an extensible schema and multiple application interfaces to its information store.

The power of a directory service becomes more evident when applications and services are able to take advantage of its centralized structure. Though a slew of new and empowering capabilities are built into Active Directory services, the true power of this distributed and scalable directory service can be seen when applications integrate with and leverage Active Directory. Microsoft has taken steps to ensure application integration is available, one of the most important of which is including the capability to extend the Active Directory schema.

## Schema Extensibility

The schema, as defined in Chapter 4, is the universe of objects that can be instantiated in the Active Directory information store. Microsoft provides mechanisms to extend the schema, enabling applications to create objects in the schema that can then be used in Active Directory to provide extended or formerly unavailable application services. This enables Active Directory to be more than a central repository of information—these mechanisms allow Active Directory to become an active information store that can be used by applications or users throughout the enterprise.

## Application Interfaces

For Active Directory services to integrate with applications, its information store must be accessible through application interfaces. Active Directory provides many application programming interfaces (APIs), including Active Directory Service Interfaces (ADSI), Lightweight Directory Access Protocol (LDAP), and Messaging Application Programming Interface (MAPI). ADSI is the Microsoft-provided interface to Active Directory. It is the most commonly used (and the most versatile, powerful, and full-featured) interface available for programmers to integrate their applications with Active Directory services. ADSI is an object-oriented interface. Perhaps its most attractive feature is that it hides the details of LDAP-based communications from its users. ADSI can be accessed from every programming language that Windows 2000 supports, including Microsoft Visual Basic, C, C++, Java, and others.

The LDAP API is a C programming language API that has been standardized in Request for Comments (RFC) 1823. The LDAP API is a low-level interface that exposes many of the LDAP-based communication interfaces that ADSI hides.

> **More Info**    For more information about LDAP, see the complete text of RFC 1823 at *http://www.ietf.org*.

MAPI is supported in Active Directory strictly for backward compatibility. Application developers building applications that will interface with Active Directory should use ADSI instead of MAPI.

## Achieving Standardization and Openness

Active Directory services meets the requirement for standardization and openness by embracing Internet standards and using LDAP as the directory-wire protocol.

Active Directory services was designed from the ground up to adhere to Internet standards and to be a native LDAP server. For example, the entire structure of the Windows 2000 directory scheme and Active Directory's locator service are based on the Internet-standard locator service Domain Name Service (DNS). Windows 2000 clients and Active Directory services no longer use NetBIOS name resolution; rather, the more hierarchical and scalable solution, DNS, is used natively by Windows 2000 to provide all locator service activity. NetBIOS name resolution (such as that provided when WINS is implemented) is provided in Windows 2000 only for backward compatibility; once all clients are Windows 2000 capable or outfitted with the appropriate directory services updates, you can take your WINS servers out of service. We already use DNS every day; DNS translates familiar names into IP addresses, such as translating *www.microsoft.com* into 207.46.131.13.

> **Note**    Well, Active Directory services was not entirely built from the ground up. It is based on the Microsoft Exchange directory service engine, but its capabilities have been greatly extended. From an operating system perspective, it's been completely rebuilt and its design has been tailored to meet the requirements of an enterprise-class directory service.

In addition, the information store (database) that previously managed domain-based information in earlier versions of Windows NT has been revamped and extended to embrace the openness and flexibility of the LDAP standard, and it now (in the form of Active Directory services) is an LDAP-native directory service information store. Being such, Active Directory natively implements LDAP commands, which means that it accepts standardized LDAP protocol messages and responds to such commands without having to translate them into another command. Such native support for LDAP, the language of directory services, enables Active Directory to easily interoperate with and even subsume other directory services; it also enables Active Directory to interoperate with any application written to the LDAP standard.

Although Active Directory is standards compliant and is a directory service in every sense of the word, it does not implement the X.500 standard and its associated directory access protocols. X.500 is a directory standard that was created in the late 1980s and revised in the early 1990s, but the X.500 specification and its directory access protocols (DAP, DSP, DISP, and DOP) were too complex and introduced too much overhead to be commercially viable or attractive, and therefore did not garner much acceptance or support. To complicate things further, two X.500 "standards" were released, and there were no assurances that different X.500-compliant implementations would be interoperable. In response to this dilemma, people at the University of Michigan (and other places) decided that a lightweight client-server access protocol that interacted with X.500 might spur the acceptance and deployment of X.500. The result proved their theory to be somewhat true; LDAP is now the protocol of choice for accessing directory services, and X.500 is largely unused and unsupported.

The fact that Active Directory services does not support X.500 is not a limiting factor, nor is it a drawback to standardization or openness. LDAP is sufficient for directory services and especially attractive due to its lightweight design, and there really isn't much interest in the industry for support of X.500 anyway (for reasons of overhead and ambiguity as previously explained).

When Active Directory services' support of DNS, LDAP, TCP/IP, and other Internet standards is combined with its programmatic interfaces such as ADSI, LDAP C, and MAPI, its openness and standardization become evident.

**More Info** In addition to these standards and open architecture, Active Directory services supports many other Internet and open standards, a detailed listing of which is provided in Chapter 2, "Active Directory Services as a Directory Service Implementation."

# Achieving Centralization

Active Directory services meets the centralization requirement by consolidating network information in the Active Directory information store, by providing a centralized administrative interface (with MMC), by allowing a single logon to control all network access permissions, by creating Active Directory Connectors, and by having an extensible schema. The following sections discuss these centralization features in detail.

## Centralized Administrative Interface

Since Active Directory is at the heart of Windows 2000 and of all information associated with a networked Windows 2000 environment, and since Active Directory services' logical presentation is that of a single entity (rather than, say, this domain controller or that domain controller), centralization is achieved. The requirement that domain controllers be placed throughout the network is a purely physical one. When user interfaces (such as searches) or management interfaces (such as MMC snap-ins) are utilized, Active Directory responds as a centralized entity regardless of which particular domain controller physically responds to the inquiry or request. And since all domain controllers contain replicas of domain-based Active Directory partitions, which domain controller actually responds to a request is of no consequence. Active Directory appears to users and administrators as a centralized entity, not as a group of domain controllers.

> **More Info**    For more information on Active Directory management interfaces, check out Chapter 9, "Managing Active Directory Services."

## Single Sign-on

Another way Active Directory services achieves centralization, which works in tandem with a pervasive security system, is by allowing users to access all network resources with a single sign-on (logon) rather than by requiring users to sign-on to multiple systems. All access control information is based on Windows 2000 security identifiers (SIDs) and individual object (and attribute) DACLs, all of which are stored in Active Directory. With the implementation of a single sign-on, when a user logs on to a Windows 2000 network, the logon credentials initially provided (and the associated permissions for resource access throughout the directory service offerings) carry through to all user activities in that logon session, as shown in Figure 5-1.

> **More Info**    For more information on the logon process and how security credentials follow a user throughout a logon session, check out Chapter 8, "Active Directory Services and Security."

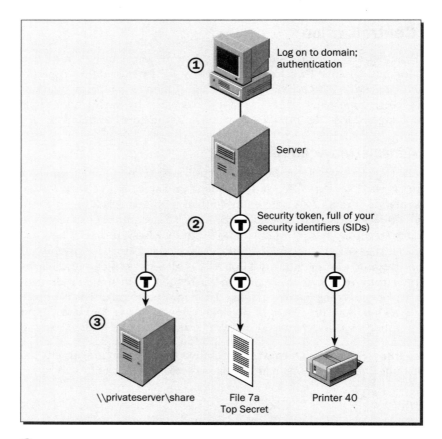

Log on to domain; authentication

Server

Security token, full of your security identifiers (SIDs)

\\privateserver\share

File 7a
Top Secret

Printer 40

**(1)** You log on to your domain/machine, and are authenticated.

**(2)** An access token (commonly called a security access token) is associated with your logon session.

**(3)** All attempts to access resources throughout your logon session, from printing documents to running applications on remote computers, base your request on your security access token, which is transparently transmitted whenever you make a request.

**Figure 5-1.** *Windows 2000 single sign-on.*

## Active Directory Connectors

Active Directory services also provides centralization by enabling users to access other directories directly through Active Directory itself. The access mechanism it provides, called *Active Directory Connectors,* enables users to transparently access any LDAP-compliant directory. Active Directory stores information about the LDAP-compliant directories that its Active Directory Connector exposes, including DNS information, and determines from that information where the foreign directory should appear within the Active Directory information repository.

> **More Info**   For more information on Active Directory Connectors, check out Chapter 12, "Migrating to Active Directory Services."

## Extensible Schema

One of the most important ways that Active Directory achieves centralization is by providing an extensible schema. If application developers could not extend the schema, they would not be able to use Active Directory services to centrally store information objects unique to their programs. The result would be that applications would have to create and then maintain their own information stores (or directories), as is the case with applications that were written to function under Windows NT 4 and earlier.

> **More Info**   For more information on the Active Directory schema, check out Chapter 14, "Administratively Leveraging Active Directory Services."

# Chapter 6
# Active Directory Services and DNS

Active Directory services is the hub of most operations that occur in Microsoft Windows 2000, so it's no surprise that there is a lot of interaction between many Windows 2000 base services—both network-related and others—and Active Directory. Of particular interest are the interactions between Active Directory services and the Domain Name Service (DNS), and the new capability for dynamic DNS updates, both of which are integral to Windows 2000 and Active Directory services.

To understand many of the locator and client/server interactions that occur in a Windows 2000 Active Directory environment, you need to understand DNS. The de facto standard for providing name resolution in previous versions of Windows—the Windows Internet Naming Service (WINS)—hasn't been completely supplanted, but it is inferior to DNS and is included in Windows 2000 only to provide compatibility with Windows clients that aren't configured to use DNS. You can be sure that DNS is the locator service of the future, and once you deploy Windows 2000 and Active Directory services, DNS automatically becomes your default locator service.

DNS is the primary locator service for Active Directory, and many other components in a Windows 2000 network also rely on DNS for locator services. DNS can therefore be considered a base service for both Windows 2000 and Active Directory services. This chapter provides an extensive treatment of DNS. The topics covered are:

- Understanding how DNS operates
- Getting familiar with DNS, including its concepts and components
- Learning about DNS functional operations, including query resolution
- Learning about how Active Directory services uses DNS as its locator service

As you read this chapter, you'll notice similarities between the way DNS functions and the way Active Directory services functions. This is no coincidence—the way DNS scales and operates is a model many computer systems would do well to emulate. After all, DNS scales to the entire Internet.

# Understanding DNS

As you probably know, DNS is an industry-standard protocol (and service) used to locate computers on an Internet Protocol (IP)–based network. IP networks, such as the Internet and Windows 2000 networks, rely on number-based addresses to ferry information throughout the network. Network users, however, are better at remembering word-based and letter-based names, such as *www.microsoft.com,* than they are at remembering number-based addresses, such as 207.46.131.137. Therefore, it is necessary to translate user-friendly names (*www.microsoft.com*) into the number-based addresses that the network can recognize (207.46.131.137). DNS is the service of choice in Windows 2000 to locate resources and translate resource names into their corresponding IP addresses.

Accordingly, you need to thoroughly understand DNS to understand Windows 2000 and Active Directory services. This section provides the information you need to understand DNS. It examines how DNS works, including discussions about DNS's resource records (RRs) and hierarchical namespace, and then examines in detail how Active Directory services, Windows 2000 domain controllers, and clients interact with DNS to get the locator services they require.

**Note** DNS can also translate an IP address into a user-friendly name using in-addr.arpa. To see this type of translation in action, try pinging an IP address with the –a parameter on, such as in the following command prompt command:

ping –a 207.46.131.137

DNS uses a specialized database of RRs to respond to client name-resolution queries. Before DNS, name resolution on the Internet was achieved with *hosts files,* which were manually created files that associated host names with IP addresses. Whenever a new client was added to the network, an administrator had to manually update the hosts file and then copy (replicate) that file to all other computers on the network so that the new host could be reached by all the other computers. As the Internet grew, this form of name resolution was clearly insufficient; it was too management intensive, and it didn't scale. The file just got bigger, and because it used a flat namespace, it could not be partitioned and had to be distributed in its entirety. The solution was DNS.

DNS replaced a hosts file's flat namespace with a hierarchical namespace. With a hierarchical namespace, information about host names and IP addresses can be partitioned and distributed; thus, scalability is achieved. In the *widgets.products.microsoft.com* domain, for example, responsibility for name resolution can be partitioned so that various servers can handle name resolution for different parts of the namespace. One server can be responsible for resolving the first part (*microsoft.com*), and that server can forward the name-resolution request to the DNS server deeper in the *microsoft.com* DNS hierarchy that is responsible for resolving the next part of the namespace (the *products* part of *products.microsoft.com*). Finally the request can be forwarded to yet a different server that is responsible for resolving the last part of the name (the *widgets* part of *widgets.products.microsoft.com*). DNS servers in each part of the hierarchical namespace need to maintain a database of resource records for hosts in only their part of the hierarchy. Thus the servers in the *products* part of *widgets.products.microsoft.com* maintain resource records for only the *products* part of the hierarchical namespace, and not for the *microsoft.com* part or the *widgets* part of the namespace.

As you've probably noticed, this approach to partitioning a potentially large database is essentially identical to the way Active Directory partitions its directory of information into Windows 2000 domains.

## Computer Names, Host Names, FQDNs, and Relative Distinguished Names

The first step in understanding DNS is understanding the differences among the handful of terms associated with a given computer's name. Since Microsoft Windows NT went through an evolutionary process that pushed it toward DNS as its locator service (and away from the poorly scaling WINS approach), Windows NT users and administrators have had to become familiar with several name-resolution schemes and their associated naming conventions. Now Windows 2000 users and administrators must learn about DNS and its naming conventions. The following is a list of the naming conventions that have been used to identify computers in the various Windows name-resolution methods, including the Windows 2000 method. (IT professionals who have already transitioned to DNS should consider this discussion a refresher and think about how fortunate they are to be ahead of the curve.)

- Computer name
- Host name
- Fully qualified domain name
- Relative distinguished name

These naming conventions share a common goal: to unambiguously resolve a name to a network address, generally an IP address. The difference between naming conventions lies in each convention's distinct approach to resolving names.

In the flat NetBIOS namespace, a single name unambiguously resolved a computer name to a network address. This is the name that early Windows versions stored in browser and master browser lists, enabling peer Windows networks to browse resources on networked Windows computers. In this scenario, the term associated with the computer was the *computer name*, and registration of the computer name depended on network broadcasts (and a master browser, determined by elections, by later Windows version numbers or Windows NT operating system usage, or by a combination of both). This was fine for small, peer-based Windows networks, but networks soon grew beyond what the use of broadcasts and simple flat-file master browser lists could service.

Next came WINS, which enabled a dynamic and centralized repository of NetBIOS-based computer names stored on WINS servers. These repositories could service a larger network. This was a step in the right direction because name-resolution queries could be directed to a WINS server (rather than being broadcast—which is a method with a slew of drawbacks) and conflicts could be centrally arbitrated. With WINS, the term *computer name* was retained, but the term *host name* also appeared (perhaps it was borrowed from DNS, which was being widely used in the firmly established non-Windows network world) and was used interchangeably with computer name. At the time, WINS was the default name resolver for Windows platforms, but DNS was gaining popularity in step with the popularity and proliferation of increasingly larger networks.

Networks grew, and WINS became less and less capable of handling the sheer volume of names. The decreasing capability of WINS to handle the name-resolution load was not due to the processing power required for resolution, but instead, was due to the fact that generating unique names in an organization with lots of computers became an ever-increasing management burden. DNS was (and is) a better solution. As a result of DNS's hierarchical namespace, the need for unique computer names was isolated to a given domain, enabling a computer name such as server1 to exist in different domain locations in the same hierarchy. With DNS the necessity came (to the Windows world) for a name that properly addressed the DNS hierarchy. The name had to include not only the computer, or host, name, but also a name that could unambiguously identify, or fully qualify, that computer within the entire DNS hierarchy. That name is the *fully qualified domain name* (FQDN)—for example, *server1.widgets.microsoft.com*.

But in certain situations, the domain-hierarchy part of the FQDN is cumbersome and a "local" name for a given computer (or any other DNS host) that is relative to the DNS domain in which the host resides is needed. That name is the *relative distinguished name*. The relative distinguished name is simply the single host name to the left of the leftmost dot in the FQDN—for example, an FQDN of *server1.widgets.microsoft.com* has *server1* as its relative distinguished name.

But what about all those NetBIOS names that users have become accustomed to throughout the evolution of Windows toward its enterprise-ready Windows 2000 incarnation? Conveniently enough, rather than imposing new names or new naming conventions on those poor users, DNS simply uses the computer name (or host name) as the relative distinguished name and appends the DNS domain hierarchy to that name to create the FQDN.

To clarify these concepts, Figure 6-1 illustrates how to identify the computer name (or host name, or relative distinguished name) part of the FQDN.

Remember these computer name (or host name) conventions, as well as how the conventions fit into the creation of the FQDN; the concepts will reappear throughout this chapter.

## DNS Concepts

There are a handful of basic concepts on which the functional structure of DNS operates. These basic concepts range from namespace definitions to demarcation of name-resolution responsibility boundaries. Understanding these concepts goes a long way in getting a solid working knowledge of DNS. And since Active Directory functions in much

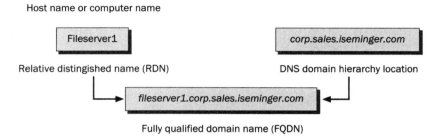

**Figure 6-1.** *The relationship between the FQDN, the relative distinguished name, and the DNS domain hierarchy location.*

the same way as DNS, understanding these concepts also goes a long way toward understanding how Active Directory provides its information repository services. The following is a list of the DNS concepts that are defined and explained in this section:

- Namespace
- DNS domains
- DNS zones
- Root
- Name resolution

### Dealing with Fugitive DNS Characters

As you probably know, certain characters, some of which were widely used in computer names during the NetBIOS name-resolution years of Windows, are illegal in computer names in DNS. Since Windows has moved from NetBIOS to DNS, a dilemma arises when administrators convert computer names or host names into DNS relative distinguished names or FQDNs. What happens to computers that have consistently used DNS-illegal characters such as underscores (_) as part of their computer names?

The answer is that Windows 2000 DNS has been designed to provide backward compatibility—or rather, to provide an upgrade/evolution path—for computers making the transition from NetBIOS naming conventions to DNS. Specifically, Microsoft DNS Server (and only Microsoft DNS Server) allows you to continue to use a number of characters that are illegal in standard DNS. The characters that are illegal with other DNS software, but are legal as long as Microsoft DNS is the DNS software being used, are the following:

- Underscore (_) for service (SRV) RRs
- Asterisk (∗) for mail exchange (MX) RRs

Windows 2000 DNS also has support for Unicode characters.

This support for otherwise illegal characters is quite useful for IT administrators who don't want to rename their potentially numerous computers that have illegal DNS characters.

## Namespace

A *namespace* is a context within which the names of all objects must be unambiguously resolvable. For example, the Internet is a single DNS namespace—within which all network devices with a DNS name can be resolved to a particular address, such as *www.microsoft.com* to 207.46.131.13.

Namespaces can be flat or hierarchical. Flat namespaces do not scale well because they can grow only so large before all available names are used up, and once a name is used more than once in a namespace, the namespace violates the "unambiguously resolvable" requirement. For an everyday example of a flat namespace, an immediate family can be compared to a flat namespace. You wouldn't have two brothers named Darryl in the same family. If the last name was, say, Smith, determining which Darryl Smith was being addressed would be too difficult. However, you might have a cousin from the Jones family named Darryl. That would present no difficulties because that's a different namespace—you'd have Darryl Smith and Darryl Jones.

A hierarchical namespace is divided into different areas, which might be easier to understand if you think of these hierarchically organized areas as *subnamespaces*. Each area is its own subnamespace within the overall namespace. Therefore, each object must have a unique name only within its subnamespace in order to have an unambiguously resolvable name within the namespace hierarchy. Hierarchical namespaces, then, can scale to extremely large networks—as you add more objects to the overall namespace, you have to find unique names for them within only the subnamespace to which they belong.

All DNS namespaces are hierarchical. The subnamespaces in the DNS hierarchical namespace are called *domains*. As you may remember, the unique name of a computer within a domain is called a relative distinguished name. Computers with the same relative distinguished name can exist in different subnamespaces (domains) of the namespace hierarchy because they can be fully resolved to a unique object within the entire DNS hierarchy, using an FQDN. For example, you can have a server called server1 in the *widgets.microsoft.com* domain (the *widgets.microsoft.com* namespace), and you can have server1 in the *gadgets.widgets.microsoft.com* namespace. Because they are in different subnamespaces in the hierarchical namespace, they can be resolved to different FQDNs— *server1.widgets.microsoft.com* and *server1.gadgets.widgets.microsoft.com*.

Compare this hierarchical namespace to a family with Darryl Smith the father and Darryl Smith the son. In computer terms, their relative distinguished names are both Darryl Smith, but their FQDNs are Darryl Smith Sr. and Darryl Smith Jr. (More information about relative distinguished names and FQDNs is provided earlier in this chapter, in the "Computer Names, Host Names, FQDNs, and Relative Distinguished Names" section.)

## DNS Domains

Domains in DNS are familiar to most computer professionals who've used the Internet; *domains* are nodes in the DNS hierarchical namespace, and domains can be further divided into *subdomains*. Domains in the *gadgets.widgets.microsoft.com* hierarchy, for example, include the *gadgets*, *widgets*, *microsoft*, and *com* domains.

### DNS Zones

A *DNS zone* is a set of files or records (more precisely, a database of resource record entries) that corresponds to part of the DNS hierarchical namespace. DNS zones are used to delineate which DNS servers are responsible (authoritative) for resolving name-resolution queries for a given section of the DNS hierarchy. DNS zones differ from the domain structure in the following fashion: Zones can be composed of one or more DNS domains. One zone in the *gadgets.widgets.microsoft.com* domain tree might be authoritative for the *gadgets* and *widgets* domains. In other words, there is not a requirement for DNS zones to have a 1:1 relationship with DNS domains.

### Root

The uppermost domain in a hierarchical namespace such as the DNS namespace is called the *root*. The root, which is defined as " " (nothing) or, more accurately, "." (a dot), is the base at which any entire-domain-tree search must be initiated.

### Name Resolution

The purpose of DNS is to provide name resolution. *Name resolution* in DNS is the process of comparing a host name (such as a computer name) to a list of RRs and identifying the corresponding IP address. *Reverse name resolution* is the process of comparing an IP address to a list of RRs and identifying the corresponding host name. These resolution processes are initiated when a DNS server receives a query.

## DNS Components

With the basic concepts of DNS explained and defined, the basic components of DNS that are used by Windows 2000 and other clients of DNS can now be presented. The following components implement the DNS-facilitated name-resolution process. Each of these components merits its own section and a thorough explanation.

- DNS servers
- DNS resolvers
- Resource records
- Zone files

### DNS Servers

A *DNS server* is a computer that completes the process of name resolution in DNS. DNS servers contain files, called *zone files*, that enable them to resolve names to IP addresses (or vice versa). When queried, a DNS server will respond in one of three ways:

- The server returns the requested name-resolution or IP-resolution information.

- The server returns a pointer to another DNS server that can service the request.
- The server indicates that it doesn't have the requested information.

DNS servers might, during the course of preparing to return the requested resolution information, query other DNS servers. (For more information, see the "DNS Name-Resolution Operations" section later in this chapter.) But beyond that, DNS servers do not perform any operations other than those mentioned in the preceding list.

There are two main kinds of DNS servers—primary servers and secondary servers.

The *primary server* is the authoritative server for the zone. All administrative tasks associated with the zone (such as creating subdomains within the zone or other similar administrative tasks) must be performed on the primary server. In addition, any changes associated with the zone or any modifications or additions to RRs in the zone's zone files must be made on the primary server. For any given zone, there is one primary server (except when you integrate Active Directory services and Microsoft DNS Server, as I explain later in this chapter).

*Secondary servers* are backup DNS servers. Secondary servers receive all of their zone files from the primary server's zone files in a zone transfer. You can have multiple secondary servers for any given zone—as many as necessary to provide load balancing, fault tolerance, and traffic reduction. Additionally, any given DNS server can be a secondary server for more than one zone. Let me provide an example.

Imagine you have DNS zones named zone1 and zone2 in your organization. For simplicity's sake, let's say they cover domain A and domain B, respectively. In this configuration, you could have a DNS server in zone1 that is a secondary server for both zone1 and zone2. Figure 6-2 illustrates how this might be configured.

In addition to primary and secondary DNS servers, there are three additional DNS server roles you can use when you deem such servers are appropriate for your DNS infrastructure. These additional servers are caching servers, forwarders, and slaves.

*Caching servers* (also known as caching-only servers) perform as their name suggests; they provide only cached-query service for DNS responses. Rather than maintaining zone files like other secondary servers do, caching DNS servers perform queries, cache the answers, and return the results to the querying client. The advantage to using caching servers is that network traffic associated with the replication of zone transfers is completely avoided. The disadvantage, however, is that whenever a caching server is bounced (rebooted), the cache is flushed and must be regenerated through the process of performing queries and caching the answers. The primary difference between caching servers and other secondary servers, then, is that other secondary servers maintain zone files (and do zone transfers when appropriate, thereby generating whatever network traffic is associated with the transfer).

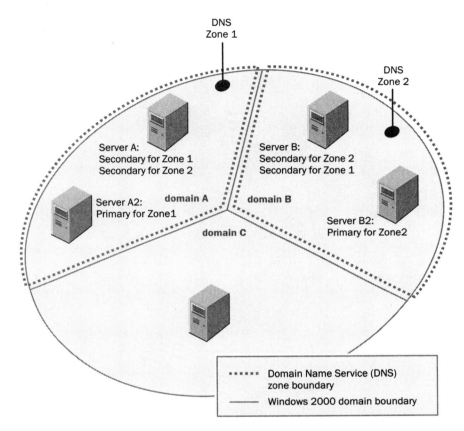

**Figure 6-2.** *Using a single DNS server as a secondary server for more than one zone.*

**Note** All DNS servers, not just caching servers, cache results. DNS servers cache information for a period of seconds known as *Time to Live (TTL)*. TTL is configured on the primary server, and it applies to all DNS servers in the domain. When determining the TTL value, balance the need for quick query responses with the need for consistent cache information across your organization's DNS servers. If you use low TTL values, your cache information will remain consistent, but your DNS servers will not keep quickly accessible cached information as long. DNS servers can also cache negative responses, decreasing the response time for queries about domains or nodes that don't exist or are unavailable.

*Forwarders* are DNS servers that have been designated to handle communication with off-site DNS servers. The idea behind forwarders is that it's better to have one DNS server communicating with outside DNS servers instead of all DNS servers doing so. (Caching, network traffic, and other considerations might drive your decision to use a DNS forwarder in your deployment.) Figure 6-3 illustrates how forwarders work.

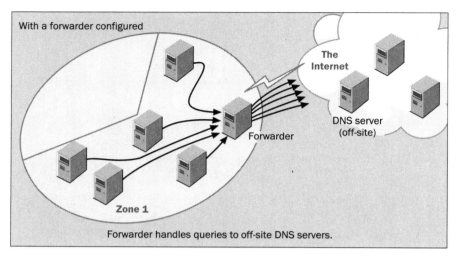

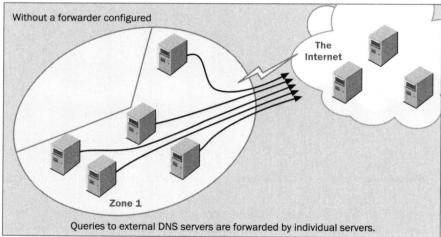

**Figure 6-3.** *Using forwarders to minimize the number of DNS servers communicating with the outside world.*

DNS servers that make use of a forwarder (that is, the forwarder's "clients") can use the forwarder in one of two modes: *exclusive* or *nonexclusive mode.*

A DNS server configured to use a forwarder in nonexclusive mode submits the query to its forwarder or forwarders and receives the result of the query to pass back to the originator of the query. If the forwarder can't resolve the query or doesn't receive a response, the DNS server using the forwarder attempts to resolve the query using its own zone files.

DNS servers that are configured to use their forwarder in exclusive mode depend entirely on the forwarder to resolve queries; these DNS servers are called *slaves*. Slaves behave the same as DNS servers configured to use a forwarder in nonexclusive mode with one exception: if the forwarder cannot resolve a forwarded query, the slave DNS server does not attempt to resolve the query on its own and simply returns a query failure to the DNS client that initiated the query.

## DNS Resolvers

The *resolver* is a software component bundled in the Windows 2000 Transmission Control Protocol/Internet Protocol (TCP/IP) stack (and is also available in any DNS-capable non-Microsoft client) that communicates with DNS servers to create and resolve name-resolution queries. Resolvers exist on DNS clients and DNS servers.

## Resource Records

A *resource record* (RR), is the unit of information entry in DNS zone files; RRs are the basic building blocks of host-name and IP information and are used to resolve all DNS queries. While there are only a handful of commonly used resource record types, resource records actually come in a fairly wide variety of flavors in order to provide extended name-resolution services.

Different flavors of resource records have different formats, as they contain different data. In general, however, many resource records share a common format, as the following address resource record (a type of resource record) example illustrates. Following the example are explanations of all of its fields.

```
iseminger.com. 600 IN A 150.150.150.1
```

- The first field (iseminger.com) denotes the owner.
- The second field (600) is the TTL parameter, in seconds.
- The third field (IN) is the class field that represents the protocol family, which is almost always IN, for Internet class.
- The fourth field (A) is the type of resource the resource record is representing. I'll describe the commonly used types of resources in a moment.
- The fifth field (150.150.150.1) is the resource data, or RDATA. This field is a variable type that provides information appropriate for the type of resource; in this case, it's a 32-bit IP address.

The following resource record types are commonly used in DNS:

- Start of authority (SOA)
- Name server (NS)
- Pointer record (PTR)
- Address (A)
- Mail exchange (MX)
- Canonical name (CNAME)
- Windows Internet Naming Service (WINS)

- WINS-reverse (WINS-R)
- Service (SRV)
- Load-sharing

Each of these resource record types merits further explanation. In the explanations, I provide examples of these RR types taken from a private test deployment of *www.iseminger.com* (the site over which I had the most control) after the first domain controller was brought on line. The sample resource records are provided to help you get familiar with how they look when you pull up Notepad and start looking at the DNS files. Note that in these examples I use parentheses to identify the sample values of certain fields; remember that these values are the sample values and won't or shouldn't necessarily be the values in your DNS deployment's resource records.

**SOA resource records:** The start of authority (SOA) record is the required first entry in all forward and reverse (in-addr.arpa) zone files, and it defines the zone for which the DNS server is authoritative, as well as the specific server that is authoritative for the domain. The following is an example of an SOA record:

```
@  IN  SOA    server4.iseminger.com.  dnsadmin.iseminger.com. (
                          1            ; serial number
                          3600         ; refresh   [1h]
                          600          ; retry     [10m]
                          86400        ; expire    [1d]
                          3600 )       ; min TTL   [1h]
```

The SOA RR has the following fields:

- Owner (@) specifies the owner of the record (the DNS server on which the zone file resides). The use of a freestanding @ specifies that the owner (generally the machine being used, or the server on which the file resides) is the current origin.
- Class (IN) specifies the protocol family—in this case (and in most cases), the Internet protocol family.
- Type (SOA) indicates that this is an SOA RR.
- Authoritative server (server4.iseminger.com) specifies the DNS server that is authoritative for the zone.
- Responsible person (dnsadmin.iseminger.com) specifies the mailbox address of the person—presumably an administrator—who is responsible for the zone. Note that this field uses a period instead of an @, as in *dnsadmin.iseminger.com* instead of *dnsadmin@iseminger.com*.
- Serial number (1) specifies the number of times the zone has been updated. When secondary servers contact the primary server to determine whether a zone transfer is necessary, the secondary servers compare their individual serial numbers with the primary server's serial number. If the primary server's serial number is higher, a zone transfer is necessary.

- Refresh number (3600) specifies the interval, in seconds, that secondary servers should wait between checks with the primary server for zone changes. The bracketed notation to its right denotes the time in common terms, such as [1h], which stands for one hour (which equates to 3,600 seconds).

- Retry number (600) specifies the delay time, in seconds, between retries (implying a previously unsuccessful attempt) that secondary servers should use when contacting the primary server.

- Expire number (86400) specifies the time, in seconds, that secondary servers should wait for a response from the primary server before discarding their copies of the zone file as invalid.

- Minimum TTL (3600) is the default TTL value applied to resource records in the zone that do not specify their own TTL.

**NS resource records:** Name server (NS) records describe which servers are secondary servers for the zone specified in the SOA record and indicate which servers are primary servers for any delegated zones. The following are examples of NS RRs:

```
@       IN  NS      server4.iseminger.com.
@       IN  NS      dnsserver1.iseminger.com.
```

- Owner (@) specifies the owner of the record. As mentioned previously, the use of a freestanding @ specifies that the owner is the current origin.

- Class (IN) specifies the protocol family—in this case (and in most cases), the Internet protocol family.

- Type (NS) indicates that this is an NS RR.

- Authoritative server (server4.iseminger.com in the first record, dnsserver1.iseminger.com in the second) specifies the name of the server that houses information about the zone.

**PTR resource records:** The pointer (PTR) record provides reverse address resolution (called reverse lookups); PTR RRs map an IP address to a host name, as the following example illustrates:

```
17.152.151.150.in-addr.arpa.   IN  PTR   filesrv1.iseminger.com.
```

Notice that the order of the IP address octets is reversed in this example.

- Class (IN) specifies the protocol family—in this case (and in most cases), the Internet protocol family.

- Type (PTR) indicates that this is a PTR RR.

The last field indicates the owner (host) of the record.

**A resource records:** The address (A) record is the most common; it simply maps a host name to an IP address, as the following example displays:

```
filesrv1     IN  A    150.151.152.17
```

The first field is the owner (host) of the record. Next comes the class, record type, and authoritative server—the standard structure explained earlier in this section.

**MX resource records:** The mail exchange (MX) record specifies where mail is to be routed for users in the given DNS domain. In addition to standard fields, the MX RR contains a field that enables administrators to weight multiple MX RRs based on whatever criteria seem appropriate. This field is called the *preference field*. Consider the following examples:

```
iseminger.com      IN  MX    4  mailsrv1.iseminger.com.
iseminger.com      IN  MX    9  mailsrv3.iseminger.com.
```

In these examples, the assignment of values in the preference fields (4 and 9) has the following effect: A mail server that needs to send mail to the *iseminger.com* domain would contact a DNS server for *iseminger.com* and retrieve all of the MX records for the domain. This mail server would then attempt to contact the mail server with the lowest preference-field value (mailsrv1.iseminger.com according to these sample MX entries). If contact with the host associated with the lowest preference value was not possible, the mail server would attempt to reach the MX-designated host that had the next lowest value for its preference field (mailsrv3.iseminger.com in this example).

**CNAME resource records:** The canonical name (CNAME) record provides a mechanism by which you can assign an alias to a given host. CNAME RRs are useful for keeping the naming conventions of your network infrastructure hidden from the outside world (or the inside world, for that matter). When DNS resolves a CNAME RR, it uses the owner field (filesrv1.iseminger.com. in the following example) to subsequently find an A RR to resolve the name. The following is an example of a CNAME RR:

```
drawings      IN  CNAME     filesrv1.iseminger.com.
```

**WINS resource records:** The WINS record is implemented only by Microsoft DNS Server and is used when dynamically created host names registered with WINS are unavailable in a static DNS zone file. In essence, this resource record enables Microsoft DNS Server to make a request to a WINS server when DNS is unable to resolve a given host name. If the host name exists in the WINS database, WINS returns the query to DNS and DNS resolves the query. The following example illustrates a WINS RR:

```
@       IN  WINS     150.150.150.19
```

As you remember from the explanation of the SOA RR, an @ specifies that the owner is the current origin. This is followed by the class, record type, and authoritative server fields. Class (IN) specifies the protocol family, type (CNAME) indicates that this is a CNAME RR, and the last field indicates the owner (host) of the record.

> **Tip** NS records must not point to a host that resolves to a CNAME RR; that is, an NS record can't point to an alias. Also, NS records must have an A record in the same zone file as the NS record so that the name can be locally resolved.

> **Caution**   The WINS and WINS-R RRs are specific to Microsoft DNS Server and won't work if you attempt to use them with other DNS server software.

**WINS-R resource records:** The WINS-reverse (WINS-R) record provides administrators the capability to perform reverse lookups through WINS. Consider the following WINS-R RR example:

```
17.152.151.150.in-addr.arpa.    0   IN   WINS-R       filesrv1 iseminger.com.
```

As you probably noticed, the WINS-R RR has a structure that is similar to that of the PTR RR, with the WINS-R RR containing some additional information.

- The first field is the reverse-lookup in-addr.arpa address.
- The TTL is specified in the second field (0). This is usually set to 0 to keep WINS-R records, which are often volatile, from being cached by DNS.
- Class (IN) specifies the protocol family, which is the Internet protocol family.
- Type (WINS-R) indicates that this is a WINS-R RR.
- The next field indicates the WINS NetBIOS name of the owner of the record.
- The domain name that should be appended to the host name for creation of the FQDN is specified in the final field (iseminger.com.).

**SRV resource records**: The service (SRV) record enables administrators to specify what service a server provides, what protocol it uses, and what domain it services. SRV RRs have their own special syntax, as the following example illustrates:

```
http.tcp.iseminger.com. 600 IN SRV 0 100 80 web1.iseminger.com.
```

- The first field (http.tcp.iseminger.com.) follows a specific dot-delimited formatting convention, which can be defined as:
  [service].[protocol].[name].
- In this example, the service (http), protocol (tcp), and name (iseminger.com) are dot-delimited and contain a trailing dot.
- The second field (600) specifies the TTL.
- The third and fourth fields (IN and SRV) specify class and type, respectively.
- The fifth field (0) specifies host priority. As with the MX RR preference field, clients give preference to hosts with the lowest values in their SRV RR priority fields.
- The sixth field (100) specifies weight and can be used for load balancing when SRV RRs have the same values in their SRV RR priority fields. Clients should give preference to hosts with higher weight-field values.
- The seventh field (80) specifies the port number on which the server is listening for requests pertaining to the specified service.
- The last field (web1.iseminger.com.) is the FQDN for the host associated with the SRV RR.

**Load-sharing resource records:** This is less a resource record type and more a means of incorporating load-sharing mechanisms into your DNS deployment. DNS can perform load sharing in a round-robin fashion. When multiple A RRs for a given host name exist in the zone file, DNS servers that are Request for Comments (RFC) 1794–compliant distribute the load across those entries' hosts by rotating which entry is returned when queries for the given host name are serviced. Take the following example:

```
www.iseminger.com.      IN  A     150.150.150.31
www.iseminger.com.      IN  A     150.150.150.32
www.iseminger.com.      IN  A     150.150.150.33
```

If *www.iseminger.com* were an internal site that was receiving lots of hits, I could mirror the site onto three (or more) servers, enter the sample RRs into DNS, and voilá! I get round-robin load balancing across all three servers. Windows 2000 DNS servers and versions of BIND 4.9.3 and later implement this kind of round-robin load balancing.

## Zone Files

A *zone file*—sometimes referred to as a db file or, simply, the database—is the complete collection of resource records for a given DNS zone. In all DNS server implementations (other than an Active Directory–integrated DNS server implementation), the zone file contains all the information (resource records) necessary to resolve queries for the zone in which the DNS server is authoritative.

> **Note** When Microsoft DNS Server is integrated with Active Directory, the zone file is obviated because all DNS resource records are placed into the Active Directory services information repository.

The primary server in any given DNS zone is the only server on which zone file updates can be made. The primary server is the master source for the zone file; when secondary servers need to update their zone files (that is, when conditions occur that compel them to check whether they need to update their zone files), they do so through a *zone transfer*. There are three types of zone transfers:

- Full zone transfers
- Incremental zone transfers
- Transfers using DNS Notify

In a *full zone transfer*, the primary server transmits the complete contents of the zone file to the zone's secondary server or servers. The following is a list of actions taken by the primary server and the secondary servers before a full zone transfer is performed:

1. Secondary servers poll the primary server at the interval specified by the refresh value in the SOA RR.

2. The primary server responds by transmitting its SOA RR, which includes its serial number. (See the SOA RR explanation in the previous section for details.)

3. If a secondary server determines that the primary server's serial number has a higher value than the serial number in its copy of the SOA RR, the secondary server makes an AXFR request (a full zone transfer request). After the primary server receives the request, it responds by sending the full zone file to the secondary server.

Figure 6-4 illustrates the process of a full zone transfer.

The drawback to full zone transfers is obvious. Full zone transfers consume a considerable amount of network bandwidth because the entire zone file must be transferred every time an update needs to be made, and even minor changes to the zone file can trigger an update.

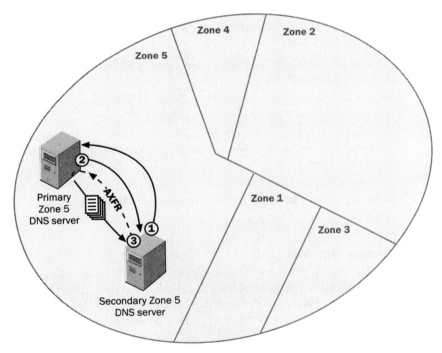

① Secondary servers poll the primary DNS server at the Start of Authority (SOA) resource records specified interval.

② Primary server responds with its SOA RR.

③ Secondary server evaluates the SOA RR and, if appropriate, requests a full zone using an AXFR request. Primary server sends entire zone file.

*Note that the secondary server could reside, physically, in another zone.

**Figure 6-4.** *The process involved with a full zone transfer.*

DNS servers that support RFC 1995 can perform *incremental zone transfers*. A primary server that supports this type of zone transfer maintains a recent-version history of the zone file (a record of recent changes) and can identify which records have changed since the most recent update. When secondary servers that support incremental zone transfers determine that changes to the zone file have occurred (which they do in the same way that other secondary servers do), they submit an IXFR request (incremental zone transfer request). The primary server then transmits only the changed files. During incremental zone transfers, the primary server transmits the oldest records first. To maintain compatibility with DNS servers that do not support incremental zone transfers, primary servers do not have to perform incremental zone transfers in response to IXFR requests; they can perform a full zone transfer instead.

When *DNS Notify* is used in a zone transfer, the initiator of the process is the primary server rather than the secondary server. DNS servers using DNS Notify take the following steps when a zone file is updated:

1. A change in the zone file triggers the primary DNS server to increment the serial number in the SOA RR.

2. The primary server sends a notify message to secondary servers that have been placed (by an administrator) in its notify set.

3. Secondary servers in the notify set send back SOA-type queries, enabling them to determine whether the primary server's zone file is more recent than their copies of it.

4. If any secondary server in the notify set determines that its zone file needs updating, it submits an AXFR or IXFR request to the primary server.

Figure 6-5 illustrates how incremental zone transfers occur.

### Getting dynamic with DNS

A relative newcomer to the DNS scene is Dynamic DNS. DNS was originally designed to require manual updates of resource records on primary servers. With Dynamic DNS (defined in RFC 2136), a means of dynamically updating zone files on primary servers has come into being. Secondary servers receive these updates as they would manual updates—through zone transfers.

Dynamic DNS also enables administrators to configure primary servers to allow updates to originate from other servers, such as secondary servers, that support the dynamic update feature of Dynamic DNS. This is especially useful in an environment in which Dynamic Host Configuration Protocol (DHCP) is used; with dynamic update, the DNS servers can be automatically updated when computers come on line and are leased IP addresses and the like from DHCP.

Dynamic updates are driven by UPDATE messages, which can specify the creation or deletion of RRs or RR sets. Administrators can specify the conditions that must occur before an RR is updated, thereby protecting the zone files from unwanted updates.

Using DNS Notify helps keep the zone files of secondary servers consistent; rather than waiting for each secondary server's refresh interval to expire, primary servers can push zone file changes to secondary servers. Using DNS Notify also makes zone transfers more secure; because notifications are sent only to secondary servers in the primary server's administratively specified notify set, nefarious or rogue DNS servers that might initiate zone transfers by making pull requests can be ignored. Microsoft DNS Server in Windows 2000 implements the notify set as part of its security strategy and sends zone file updates exclusively to members of its notify set. Figure 6-6 illustrates the process involved with DNS Notify.

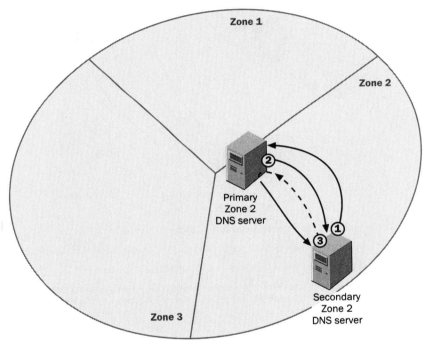

1. Secondary servers poll the primary DNS server at the Start of Authority (SOA) resource records specified interval.

2. Primary server responds with its SOA RR.

3. Secondary server evaluates the SOA RR and, if appropriate, requests an incremental zone transfer using an IXFR request. Primary DNS server sends <u>only</u> the changed files.

**Figure 6-5.**  *The process involved with an incremental zone transfer.*

# DNS Name-Resolution Operations

With all of its concepts, components, resource records, and zone file nuances, DNS has a single purpose: to resolve names to IP addresses (or vice versa). Name-to-IP-address resolutions are called forward lookups, while IP-address-to-name resolutions are called reverse lookups.

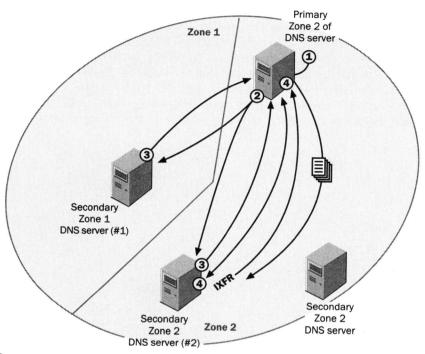

1. The primary DNS server increments its SOA RR serial number.

2. The primary DNS server sends a notify message to secondary servers in its notify set.

3. Notified secondary servers return an Start Of Authority (SOA) query.

4. Secondary servers in the notify set that determine their zone file is outdated submit an AXFR or IXFR request. In this example, secondary server #2 submits an IXFR request initiating an incremental zone transfer.

**Figure 6-6.** *Using DNS Notify for zone file updates.*

The process of resolving names (in both forward and reverse lookups) is carried out through the submission and handling of queries. DNS handles two types of queries: recursive queries and iterative queries.

## Recursive Queries

In a *recursive query,* the requesting client demands that the DNS server reply with either the resolved name or an error message that states the requested data or name doesn't exist. Recursive queries don't allow the DNS server to return a referral to another DNS server to the client, so if the DNS server can't locally resolve the query, it has to query other DNS servers in the hierarchy until it either resolves the name or IP address or determines that the requested data or name doesn't exist. Figure 6-7 illustrates the steps that occur during a recursive query.

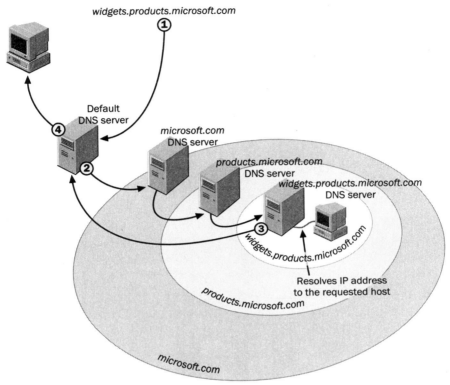

**(1)** Client "asks" its DNS server how to reach *server1.widgets.products.microsoft.com*—technically, the client is asking for server 1's IP address.

**(2)** Client's DNS server doesn't know the mapping isn't in the zone file, but it does know the address of the *microsoft.com* DNS server and submits a query on the client's behalf. The *microsoft.com* DNS server submits a similar request to the next DNS domain server in the hierarchy and so on, until the IP address associated with *server1.widgets.products.microsoft.com* is found.

**(3)** The resolved IP address is sent back to the client's DNS server.

**(4)** The DNS server responds to the client with *server1.widgets.products.microsoft.com*'s IP address (or an error, if no address can be found).

**Figure 6-7.** *What happens during a recursive query.*

DNS clients often use recursive queries, but recursive queries are not generally used when DNS servers query other DNS servers.

## Iterative Queries

In an *iterative query,* the requesting client allows the DNS server to return the best answer it can provide based on its local zone file or cached data. If the queried DNS server can't resolve the name, the reply might be in the form of a referral to another DNS server that the client should try. In an iterative query, the client continues this process until it gets a pointer to a DNS server that can answer the query using its local zone file or cached data (which is most likely a DNS server that is authoritative for the domain in which the target host in question resides). Figure 6-8 illustrates the process involved in an iterative query.

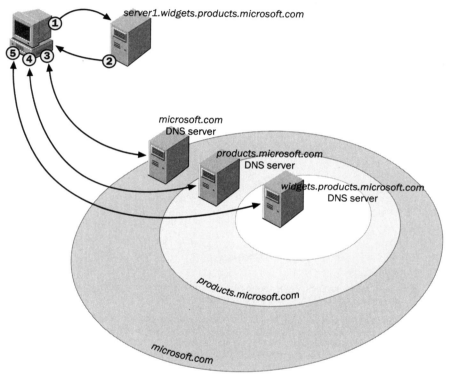

① Client "asks" its DNS server for the IP address of *server1.widgets.products.microsoft.com*.

② Client's DNS server doesn't know the address and refers client to the *microsoft.com* DNS server. At this point, the work of the client's defaut DNS server is complete, and after this, it is no longer active in the client's query process.

③ Client queries the *microsoft.com* DNS server; it refers the client to the next DNS server in the hierarchy—*products.microsoft.com*.

④ Client queries the *products.microsoft.com* DNS server and gets referred to the *widgets.products.microsoft.com* DNS server.

⑤ Client queries the *widgets.products.microsoft.com* DNS server, which replies with the server's IP address (which it has in its zone file).

**Figure 6-8.** *The process involved in an iterative query.*

Iterative queries are generally performed by DNS servers acting on behalf of DNS clients that have presented the DNS servers with recursive queries. In other words, when a client sends a recursive query to its local DNS server that the server cannot resolve locally, the server, in an effort to find the host and return a definitive answer to the DNS client, sends a series of iterative queries to other DNS servers until it contacts the server that can respond to its iterative query with locally housed zone-file information.

# How Active Directory Services Uses DNS

DNS is a crucial base-service provider to Windows 2000 and Active Directory because Active Directory makes its services available by publishing them in DNS. Because Active Directory services information is published in DNS, Active Directory services can be located by simple queries to the nearest DNS server. This process is known as *domain controller registration*. During the course of domain controller registration, each domain controller uses dynamic updates to register multiple SRV resource records with the DNS database (the DNS database is equal to the DNS zone file). Once domain controller registration is complete with the domain controller's SRV resource records dynamically updating the DNS database, clients are able to locate a domain controller and make use of the services that Active Directory offers.

Clearly, then, these three steps—registration of the domain controllers, dynamic updates of SRV resource records, and location of domain controllers by using DNS—are the building blocks by which the services provided by Active Directory are made available to every client on the network. Clients must be able to use DNS (all modern clients can) to be able to get information about, and thereby make use of, Active Directory services. As an IT professional, you need to understand the process associated with each of these three steps.

**Caution**   Even if your organization chooses not to be part of the Internet's DNS hierarchy, you'll still need to implement DNS in your private network infrastructure. Windows 2000 clients use DNS to locate resources, other Windows 2000 clients, and, most importantly, Windows 2000 domain controllers (and, therefore, Active Directory services).

## Domain Controller Registration

Upon startup, Windows 2000 domain controllers register their host name with DNS. Domain controllers use dynamic updates—which are defined in RFC 2136—when registering.

In addition, domain controllers register their NetBIOS name with WINS, either using a broadcast or directing a NetBIOS registration request to a WINS server (or, if appropriate, to another NetBIOS name server). Registration with WINS enables clients that are not DNS capable to use NetBIOS name resolution to find domain controllers. NetBIOS name registrations are performed using 1C registration, enabling the registered NetBIOS name to be recognized as a domain controller.

## SRV Resource Record Registration

In addition to registering host names, domain controllers register a number of SRV RRs upon bootup. Specifically, the Netlogon service registers the SRV RRs, again using dynamic updates.

> **Note** In addition to registering the SRV RRs, domain controllers register a single A RR (a simple host record). This enables clients that are unable to recognize SRV records to use a standard DNS lookup to locate the domain controller.

As already explained, SRV resource records indicate the services servers provide, the protocols they use, and the domains they service. Since domain controllers are really Lightweight Directory Access Protocol (LDAP) servers that use Transmission Control Protocol (TCP), and since, consequently, LDAP and TCP are services and protocols available for registration with DNS through SRV resource records, clients can locate domain controllers by simply querying DNS for LDAP servers that use TCP. (For more information about how clients locate domain controllers, see "Locating a Domain Controller" later in this chapter.)

### Conventions

Windows 2000 and Active Directory services use certain conventions regarding the registration of SRV RRs in DNS. I discuss these conventions in the following paragraphs.

First service and protocol strings use an underscore prefix to prevent potential collisions with existing names in the namespace. Thus, the TCP protocol is registered as _tcp and the LDAP service is registered as _ldap.

Second Microsoft implements a subdomain called _msdcs to enable clients to locate domain controllers that are specifically Windows 2000 domain controllers. This new subdomain is necessary for a number of reasons—chief among them is that some mechanism of distinguishing Windows 2000 domain controllers from other LDAP servers potentially residing on the network is necessary.

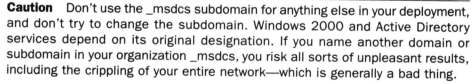

> **Caution** Don't use the _msdcs subdomain for anything else in your deployment, and don't try to change the subdomain. Windows 2000 and Active Directory services depend on its original designation. If you name another domain or subdomain in your organization _msdcs, you risk all sorts of unpleasant results, including the crippling of your entire network—which is generally a bad thing.

Third note that multiple domain controllers can offer the same services in a given DNS zone. That's fine with DNS; it simply creates multiple resource records. When a DNS server can respond to a client query with multiple resource records, it does so—that is, it responds to the client by providing information about all matching or applicable servers—and lets the client decide which server it should use.

## Server Types

Netlogon specifies a handful of well-known server type designations when it registers SRV resource records with DNS. These designations enable clients that perform DNS queries for these well-known server types to find the server type they need. These server types are inserted right before the _msdcs designation. These acronyms and their corresponding server types are the following:

- dc = domain controller
- gc = Global Catalog server
- pdc = Primary Domain Controller
- domains = globally unique identifier (GUID)

Inclusion of the domains server type enables servers to be located by GUID, which is useful in the event of name changes. (GUIDs, which are 128-bit numbers that are automatically generated for referencing objects in Active Directory services, never change, regardless of object name changes.)

## Examples of Resource Records

The following is a sample listing of SRV resource records that are registered with DNS upon startup. This sample was taken from a private domain controller (*iseminger.com*); to find the file containing this information on your own domain controller, open Netlogon.dns—located in %SystemRoot%\System32\Config—with your favorite text editor.

```
iseminger.com. 600 IN A 150.150.150.1
_ldap._tcp.Iseminger.com. 600 IN SRV 0 100 389 DCSERVER1.Iseminger.com.
_ldap._tcp.pdc._msdcs.Iseminger.com. 600 IN SRV 0 100 389 DCSERVER1.Iseminger.com.
_ldap._tcp.a681e15a-0eff-11d3-b4e5-00a0c90d0656.domains._msdcs.Iseminger.com.
    600 IN SRV 0 100 389 DCSERVER1.Iseminger.com.
    a681e159-0eff-11d3-b4e5-00a0c90d0656._msdcs.Iseminger.com.
    600 IN CNAME DCSERVER1.Iseminger.com.
_kerberos._tcp.dc._msdcs.Iseminger.com. 600 IN SRV 0 100 88 DCSERVER1.Iseminger.com.
_ldap._tcp.dc._msdcs.Iseminger.com. 600 IN SRV 0 100 389 DCSERVER1.Iseminger.com.
_kerberos._tcp.Iseminger.com. 600 IN SRV 0 100 88 DCSERVER1.Iseminger.com.
_kerberos._udp.Iseminger.com. 600 IN SRV 0 100 88 DCSERVER1.Iseminger.com.
_kpasswd._tcp.Iseminger.com. 600 IN SRV 0 100 464 DCSERVER1.Iseminger.com.
_kpasswd._udp.Iseminger.com. 600 IN SRV 0 100 464 DCSERVER1.Iseminger.com.
_ldap._tcp.seattle._sites.Iseminger.com. 600 IN SRV 0 100 389 DCSERVER1.Iseminger.com.
_kerberos._tcp.seattle._sites.dc._msdcs.Iseminger.com. 600 IN SRV 0 100 88 DCSERVER1.Iseminger.com.
_ldap._tcp.seattle._sites.dc._msdcs.Iseminger.com. 600 IN SRV 0 100 389 DCSERVER1.Iseminger.com.
_kerberos._tcp.seattle._sites.Iseminger.com. 600 IN SRV 0 100 88 DCSERVER1.Iseminger.com.
```

All domain controllers register the following SRV RRs:

- _ldap._tcp.[domain].
- _ldap._tcp.[site]._sites.[domain].

- _ldap._tcp.dc._msdcs.[domain].
- _ldap._tcp.[site]._sites.dc._msdcs.[domain].
- _ldap._tcp.[domain GUID].domains._msdcs.[forest root domain name].

All domain controllers that are running the Kerberos V5 Key Distribution Center (KDC) service register the following RRs:

- _kerberos._tcp.[domain].
- _kerberos._udp.[domain].
- _kerberos._tcp.[site]._sites.[domain].
- _kpasswd._tcp.[domain].
- _kpasswd._udp.[domain].

All domain controllers that are running Microsoft's extended version of the Kerberos KDC service, which implements a public key extension to the Kerberos protocol's initial Authentication Service Exchange subprotocol, register the following resource records:

- _kerberos._tcp.dc._msdcs.[domain].
- _kerberos._tcp.[site]._sites.dc._msdcs.[domain].

All domain controllers that are running the Kerberos Password Change service register the following RRs:

- _kpasswd._tcp.[domain].
- _kpasswd._udp.[domain].

**More Info**   See the Internet Engineering Task Force (IETF) document "draft-ietf-cat-kerb-chg-password-02.txt," found at *http://www.ietf.org*, for more information about the Kerberos Password Change service.

For the benefit of clients that cannot understand SRV RRs, domain controllers also register the following A records. (Note that Windows 2000 clients do not use these records.)

- [domain].
- gc._msdcs.[forest root domain name].

While I'm sure these lists are interesting, they don't explain what functions these SRV resource record types serve. The sample file from *iseminger.com* on page 105 also provides an example but no definitions. Thus, some definitions of the SRV resource records that can be registered with DNS are needed. Here they are:

**_ldap._tcp.[domain].**
Example: _ldap._tcp.iseminger.com.

This record enables clients to locate an LDAP server based on domain name. Note that not all resource records of this type in the DNS zone file necessarily point to a domain controller; the RR could point to any LDAP server registered with DNS.

### _ldap._tcp.[site]._sites.[domain].

Example: _ldap._tcp.seattle._sites.Iseminger.com.

This record enables clients to locate a server that is running LDAP in the domain named in [domain] in a particular site. Again, note that the server is not necessarily a domain controller.

### _ldap._tcp.dc._msdcs.[domain].

Example: _ldap._tcp.dc._msdcs.Iseminger.com.

This record enables a client to locate a domain controller in the [domain] domain.

### _ldap._tcp.[site]._sites.dc._msdcs.[domain].

Example: _ldap._tcp.seattle._sites.dc._msdcs.Iseminger.com.

This record enables clients to locate a domain controller in the [site] site and in the [domain] domain.

### _ldap._tcp.pdc._msdcs.[domain].

Example: _ldap._tcp.pdc._msdcs.Iseminger.com.

This record enables clients to locate the server acting as the Primary Domain Controller (PDC) in the mixed-mode [domain] domain. Only the domain controller holding the PDC Emulator flexible single-master operation (FSMO) role registers this resource record.

### _ldap._tcp.gc._msdcs.[forest root domain name].

Example: _ldap._tcp.gc._msdcs.Iseminger.com.

This record enables clients to locate a Global Catalog server for this forest. Only domain controllers functioning as Global Catalog servers for the [forest root domain name] forest register this resource record.

### _ldap._tcp.[site]._sites.gc._msdcs.[forest root domain name].

Example: _ldap._tcp.seattle._sites.gc._msdcs.Iseminger.com.

This record enables clients to locate a Global Catalog server for the [forest root domain name] forest in the [site] site. Only domain controllers functioning as Global Catalog servers for the [forest root domain name] forest register this resource record.

### _gc._tcp.[forest root domain name].

Example: _gc._tcp.Iseminger.com.

This record enables clients to locate a Global Catalog server for the [forest root domain name] domain. Note that not all records of this type in a DNS zone file necessarily point to a domain controller. Only a server running LDAP and functioning as a Global Catalog server for the [forest root domain name] forest registers this resource record.

### _gc._tcp.[site]._sites.[forest root domain name].

Example: _gc._tcp.seattle._sites.Iseminger.com.

This record enables clients to locate a Global Catalog server for the [forest root domain name] forest in the [site] site. Note that not all records of this type in a DNS zone file necessarily point to a domain controller. Only a server running LDAP and functioning as a Global Catalog server for the [forest root domain name] forest registers this resource record.

### _ldap._tcp.[domain GUID].domains._msdcs.[forest root domain name].

```
Example: _ldap._tcp.a681e15a-0eff-11d3-b4e5-
            00a0c90d0656.domains._msdcs.Iseminger.com.
```

This record enables clients to locate a domain controller in a domain on the basis of the domain's GUID. This record is used only if the domain name has changed, the forest name is known, and the forest has not also been renamed. All domain controllers register this SRV record.

### _kerberos._tcp.[domain].

Example: _kerberos._tcp.Iseminger.com.

This record enables clients to locate a server that is running the Kerberos KDC for the [domain] domain that is accessible using TCP. Note that not all records of this type in a DNS zone file necessarily point to a domain controller.

### _kerberos._udp.[domain].

Example: _kerberos._udp.Iseminger.com.

This record enables clients to locate a server that is running the Kerberos KDC for the [domain] domain that is accessible using User Datagram Protocol (UDP). Note that not all records of this type in a DNS zone file necessarily point to a domain controller.

### _kerberos._tcp.[site]._sites.[domain].

Example: _kerberos._tcp.seattle._sites.Iseminger.com.

This record enables clients to locate a server running the Kerberos KDC service for the [domain] domain that is located in the [site] site. Note that not all records of this type in a DNS zone file necessarily point to a domain controller.

### _kerberos._tcp.dc._msdcs.[domain].

Example: _kerberos._tcp.dc._msdcs.Iseminger.com.

This record enables clients to locate a domain controller running Microsoft's extended Kerberos V5 KDC service in the [domain] domain.

**_kerberos._tcp.[site]._sites.dc._msdcs.[domain].**
Example: _kerberos._tcp.seattle._sites.dc._msdcs.Iseminger.com.

This record enables clients to locate a domain controller that is running Microsoft's extended Kerberos V5 KDC service for the [domain] domain in the [site] site.

**_kpasswd._tcp.[domain].**
Example: _kpasswd._tcp.Iseminger.com.

This record enables clients to locate a Kerberos Password Change server for the [domain] domain that is accessible using TCP. Note that not all records of this type in a DNS zone file necessarily point to a domain controller.

**_kpasswd._udp.[domain].**
Example: _kpasswd._udp.Iseminger.com.

This record enables clients to locate a Kerberos Password Change server for the [domain] domain that is accessible using UDP. Note that not all records of this type in a DNS zone file necessarily point to a domain controller.

**[domain].**
Example: Iseminger.com.

This record enables a client that cannot recognize SRV resource records to locate a domain controller by using a standard A RR lookup.

**gc._msdcs.[forest root domain name].**
Example: gc._msdcs.Iseminger.com.

This record enables clients to locate a Global Catalog server by using a standard A RR lookup.

## Locating a Domain Controller

Once domain controllers register their SRV and A resource records with DNS servers, Active Directory services is ready to provide services to clients. Before any of these services can be provided, however, clients must go through the process of locating a domain controller.

Clients locate domain controllers through an algorithm, running in the context of Netlogon, called the *domain controller locator*, or *locator* for short. A locator can find a domain controller in either of the following ways:

- Using a DNS name
- Using a NetBIOS name

The process that a client (using its locator) goes through in locating a domain controller varies depending on whether the client is attempting to locate the domain controller by using a DNS name or by using a NetBIOS name.

## Locating Domain Controllers Based on DNS Name

DNS is the primary mechanism by which Windows 2000 clients attempt to locate domain controllers. However, a client will not use DNS if any of the following conditions exist:

- A NetBIOS domain name is supplied to the **DsGetDcName()** function. (The role of **DsGetDcName()** is explained shortly.)
- Internetwork Packet Exchange (IPX) or NetBEUI is the only available transport.
- A Windows NT 3.51 or Windows NT 4.0 domain controller is being located.
- The locating client is a Windows 3.1, Windows for Workgroups 3.1, Windows for Workgroups 3.11, Windows NT 3.51, Windows NT 4.0, Windows 95, or Windows 98 client.

When a client does use DNS to find a domain controller, the client (through its locator) implements calls to the **DsGetDcName()** function with particular flags indicated in the function call. The **DsGetDcName()** function essentially enables the locator to specify, in its query to a DNS server, what kind of service or resource it's looking for. Rather than go into detail about the **DsGetDcName()** function, I've listed the steps a client takes to locate a domain controller and included in them the **DsGetDcName()** function flags without explanation because the names of the flags indicate what services are being requested.

**More Info** Check out *http://msdn.microsoft.com* for specifics on the **DsGetDcName()** function as well as its flags.

Even if you don't know much about programming, you will better understand the process that a client goes through to locate a domain controller after you read the following steps:

1. The client's locator queries DNS and specifies a service-specific DNS host name. DNS is queried based on the following parameters of the **DsGetDcName()** function:

    - If the DS_PDC_REQUIRED flag is specified, the client requests a lookup for _ldap._tcp.pdc._msdcs.[domain name]. The client requests that the DNS server return any success or failure to the function caller.
    - If the DS_GC_SERVER_REQUIRED flag and the *SiteName* parameter are specified, the client requests a lookup for _ldap._tcp.[site]._sites.gc._msdcs.[forest root domain name]. If a domain controller isn't found, the client goes to the next step. Otherwise, the client requests that the DNS server return any success or failure to the function caller.

- If the DS_GC_SERVER_REQUIRED flag is specified, the client requests a lookup for _ldap._tcp.gc._msdcs.[forest root domain name]. The client requests that the DNS server return any success or failure to the function caller.

- If the DS_KDC_REQUIRED flag is specified and the *SiteName* parameter is specified, the client requests a lookup for the following domain: _kdc._tcp.[site]._sites.dc._msdcs.[forest root domain name]. If no domain controller can be found, the client goes to the next step. Otherwise, the client requests that the DNS server return any success or failure to the function caller.

- If the DS_KDC_REQUIRED flag is specified, the client requests a lookup for _kdc._tcp.dc._msdcs.[forest root domain name]. The client requests that the DNS server return any success or failure to the function caller.

- If the DS_ONLY_LDAP_NEEDED flag is specified and the *SiteName* parameter is specified, the client requests a lookup for _ldap._tcp.[site]._sites.[domain]. If no LDAP server is found, the client goes to the next step. Otherwise, the client requests that the DNS server return any success or failure to the function caller.

- If the DS_ONLY_LDAP_NEEDED flag is specified, the client requests a lookup for _ldap._tcp.[domain]. The client requests that the DNS server return any success or failure to the function caller.

- If the *SiteName* parameter is specified, the client requests a lookup for _ldap._tcp.[site]._sites.dc._msdcs.[domain]. If no domain controller is found, the client goes to the next step. Otherwise, the client requests that the DNS server return any success or failure to the function caller.

- The client requests a lookup for _ldap._tcp.dc._msdcs.[domain]. If no domain controller has that name (not the same as "if no domain controllers can be found"), the client goes to the next step. Otherwise, the client requests that the DNS server return any success or failure to the function caller.

- If the *DomainGuid* parameter is specified, the client requests a lookup for _ldap._tcp.[domain GUID].domains._msdcs.[forest root domain name]. The client requests that the DNS server return any success or failure to the function caller.

2. If IP is not supported or if DNS is not supported (indicated by a specific error returned from the locator), the client uses the NetBIOS locator.

3. If the specified name cannot be resolved, the client uses the NetBIOS locator.

4. DNS returns a list of matching IP addresses, which are sorted by priority and weight, and the client pings each IP address in the order returned. The ping that the client performs is a UDP LDAP query to port 389. The client waits 1/10th of a second after each ping for a response and then pings the next domain controller.

5. The pinging continues until the client receives a viable response or until it has tried all returned IP addresses.

6. When a domain controller responds to the ping, the client compares the information supplied in the response to the information specified in the **DsGetDcName**() function call. If the information does not match, the client ignores the response.

7. The first domain controller to respond to a ping is returned to the caller.

8. If the client does not have site information or if none of the pinged domain controllers respond, the client submits a DNS query for a non-site-specific DNS name.

### Locating Domain Controllers Based on NetBIOS Name

If a client cannot use DNS to locate domain controllers, or if any of the conditions outlined in the previous section exists, the client attempts to locate a domain controller using NetBIOS name resolution. To do this, the client sends a NETLOGON_SAM_ LOGON_REQUEST message to the \mailslot\net\ntlogon mailslot on the server in [domain] that resolves to the [domain][1C] NetBIOS name record. The client uses the first domain controller that responds to the message.

Regardless of whether DNS or NetBIOS is used to locate a domain controller, once a domain controller has been found, the client caches the information so that subsequent logon sessions don't require additional queries.

# Integrating DNS with Active Directory Services

Microsoft DNS Server runs on every Windows 2000 domain controller by default and is optimized for use with Active Directory. That means that if you have deployed a Windows 2000 network infrastructure and you have implemented Active Directory services, Microsoft DNS Server is running on your domain controllers—and providing many features necessary for Windows 2000 and Active Directory to function—without any additional installation steps being necessary on your part.

Microsoft DNS Server has a number of advantages for Active Directory implementations:

- It supports dynamic update, which is necessary for domain controllers to dynamically register their SRV RRs upon startup. Dynamic update is also very administrator-friendly, in that administrators deploying networks that use DHCP can configure DHCP and DNS services to communicate so that hosts can be dynamically added to the DNS database.

- When Microsoft DNS Server is integrated with Active Directory, DNS zone files and a DNS-specific zone update strategy or mechanism are not necessary. DNS resource records become part of the Active Directory information repository and are replicated to every domain controller (each of which is running DNS by default, as you remember) through the standard replication mechanisms included in Active Directory.

- Since DNS coverage requirements are often similar (in terms of their placement throughout the network topology) to Active Directory partition and domain controller coverage requirements, you can simplify server deployment and the decision-making processes associated with determining where to place DNS servers throughout your network.

- In an Active Directory–integrated DNS environment, all domain controllers that are also DNS servers act as DNS primary servers. The advantage to this approach is that changes can be made on any Active Directory/DNS domain controller (rather than on the single primary server for a given DNS zone, as is required in other implementations of DNS server software), enabling administrators to modify DNS resource records on any domain controller and enabling clients to dynamically update resource records on the nearest available DNS server.

You can have additional DNS servers in your deployment that are not Windows 2000 domain controllers; however, those non-domain controller DNS servers cannot load Active Directory–integrated zone information. This makes sense; unless the server is a domain controller, it doesn't have an Active Directory information repository and therefore cannot house DNS database information that has been absorbed by Active Directory.

Note that you do not have to use Active Directory–integrated DNS in your Windows 2000 deployment. You must, however, use DNS server software that supports dynamic update. It's important to remember that Active Directory and DNS, while sharing a domain naming system, are separate. While there are certain benefits to using the Active Directory database as your DNS database (zone file) and while Microsoft DNS Server has been designed to make use of the replication, availability, and security features of Active Directory, DNS is still a discrete service.

# Part II
# Deploying Active Directory Services

Part II provides the technical information and the deployment recommendations that you need to get the most out of Active Directory services and to make Active Directory work for you. It also includes exhaustive information on the technical issues that IT professionals, architects, and administrators will run into during the planning, securing, and managing of the varied services and offerings of Microsoft Windows 2000 Active Directory. Part II provides explicit direction on planning an Active Directory services deployment, upgrading to Active Directory services from Microsoft Windows NT, managing Active Directory services once it's deployed, and making organizational changes once Active Directory services is functioning.

# Chapter 7
# Planning an Active Directory Services Deployment

Before you start upgrading any domain controllers, rolling out any directory service deployments, or implementing any of the nifty new features of Microsoft Windows 2000, you need a plan. You need to think about issues surrounding the deployment of Active Directory services, such as the creation of your forest and its domains and organizational units (OUs), and then you need to recheck that plan to make sure it makes sense. And of course, you need to have information so that you can evaluate how to best develop your plan and prepare for issues you're likely to run into during the plan's development. That's where this chapter comes in.

In the grand scheme of a Windows 2000 deployment, the most important set of tasks you will complete is to think about, create, test, and then re-create your Active Directory services deployment plan. Active Directory is a fundamental and crucial part of any enterprise-based Windows 2000 deployment, and as the saying goes, "An ounce of prevention is worth a pound of the cure." A good plan can keep your Active Directory deployment from coming down with a terminal case of the unscalables (a little-known network disease that prevents a deployment from scaling with network growth, requiring a complete redesign down the road that is painful and costly).

To prepare you for issues you'll face as you work your way through this chapter, the first section introduces some of the considerations, choices, and trade-offs you'll have to make during your Active Directory services planning phase. I've found that learning about some of these issues from an overview level first can help round out your understanding of how many of the decisions and implementation guideline details are interdependent and affect each other. Following the overview section are sections that explain the details you'll need to consider when creating your Active Directory deployment plan. All these planning issues are then discussed together at the end of the chapter to provide the full perspective you'll need for a successful deployment.

Keep in mind that you'll probably have to revise your plan several times before it's complete and suits the needs of everyone involved. The planning process is like buying a car as a married couple; what's great for you and what's the perfect vehicle in your mind gets shaped, remolded (often with extra seats and a sliding side door), and revamped once the needs and requirements of other members of the group are considered. In the end, you get something that everyone can live with, that provides the functionality necessary for the ongoing operations of the organization, and that enables scalability for future growth.

# Overview of Planning Decisions

It's very important to realize that planning your Active Directory services deployment equates to determining the effectiveness of many Windows 2000 enterprise features and that such planning is closely aligned with the physical topology of your network. You need to have knowledge of your physical network topology to complete your Active Directory plan. You also must realize that choices you make in your Active Directory deployment plan will greatly affect the capability of your deployment to fully take advantage of the scalability, availability, and security features of Windows 2000. In the final section of this chapter, these scalability, availability, and security features are addressed and the elements of your plan that affect such important deployment requirements are explained.

Keep in mind when creating your Active Directory services plan that there are significant costs associated with maintaining any network; the steps you take and the decisions you make during the planning of your Active Directory deployment can help you significantly reduce the costs of maintaining your network. One overriding philosophy you should remember as you make these decisions is this: keep it simple. Simpler is better. The simpler your Active Directory deployment is, the easier it will be to manage and the easier it will be to manage change. The simpler it is, the easier it will be for users to make use of it. The simpler it is, the easier your life will be. Realize that creating a simpler deployment plan is often more difficult than creating a complex plan. Sometimes you will have to deal with complex issues when you develop your plan, such as the issue of an existing Windows NT deployment that has to be upgraded to Windows 2000 (covered in Chapter 11), but you should still strive for simplicity. If you can create a plan for a simple, one-domain and single-forest environment (perhaps with many nested OUs scattered across a handful of sites and a comprehensive security-group strategy) that works for your organization and if that plan remains simple after you rethink it and bounce it off the appropriate groups and people, you should get a bonus or a hefty pat on the back because your entire organization will benefit from your efforts.

## Components of Your Active Directory Services Plan

The task of planning the structure of an Active Directory services deployment can be divided into four distinct smaller tasks: creating a forest plan, creating a domain plan, creating an OU plan, and creating a site plan. As mentioned above, your prevailing philosophy when you create each of these plans should be simplicity, and generally, simpler is better. If you have to manage complexity that is simply inherent in your organization, it's best to push such complexity farther down in the logical trio of forest, domain, and OU—meaning that it's better to have a complex OU plan than it is to create complexity at the forest level. Having said that, I'll allow that there are circumstances under which simple plans are not ideal for a given organization; I'll point out such cases as we come across them. First, however, let's get a general sense of what's involved in each of the four Active Directory planning tasks.

## Forest Plan

The forest is the largest unit of organization in a Windows 2000 deployment, and it generally encompasses the entire organization. A forest can be one domain, or it can comprise multiple domains that share a single schema and a single Configuration container. Within any given forest, trust relationships between domains are simple: all domains trust all other domains with transitive trusts.

The primary activity associated with creating your forest plan is the creation of a plan for the overall domain tree hierarchy; in other words, you'll need to determine how your Windows 2000 domains are related to each other in the Domain Name Service (DNS)–like domain hierarchy that constitutes your forest.

## Domain Plans

Creating a domain plan consists of determining the number of domains your forest requires, the name of each of those domains, and the hierarchical relationships that the domains have with one another. Each domain will need a DNS name associated with it, part of which is determined by the domain's position within the domain tree hierarchy; such domain name planning, and each domain's associated position within the domain hierarchy, are also part of domain planning.

In general, it's best to structure domains based on something that's not volatile and that can endure even significant change within your organization. This generally means organizing your domains based on geopolitical boundaries (cities, states, or regions). What about distinguishing the business-based structure from the activity-based structure within your organization? Simple: use groups to create that distinction, not domains or OUs. That way, your domains will be stable even when significant organizational changes occur, and only your groups will need to change. Domains are not easy to modify once created—groups are much simpler to form, move, and modify.

## Organizational Unit Plans

When you create your OU plan, you map the organization of your IT department to the Windows 2000 OU structure. In other words, you determine which segments or departments of the overall organization are associated with which administrative teams and create OUs based on that determination. This task has nothing to do with your organization's business management structure, the chain of command, or any other structure within the organization; it has to do with the IT administrative structure, and when we go into more detail about OU structures, you'll understand why.

## Site Plan

When you create your site plan, you create a map of your physical network topology, break that topology into well-connected sites (sites that have local area network (LAN)–speed connections or better), associate each well-connected site with the IP subnets that compose it, and define the physical topology of your network based on your findings.

You'll also identify site links, which are sub-LAN-speed connections (or oversubscribed connections) between well-connected sites. Active Directory services takes the information about your IP subnets (which are defined by you as well-connected sites) and builds a virtual map of your organization's network topology. This virtual map enables Active Directory to direct client requests, replication traffic, and other administrative transmissions along the most appropriate route in terms of network traffic and bandwidth availability.

## Understanding Windows 2000 Groups

The next stop on the overview tour is an explanation of Windows 2000 groups. Windows 2000 has doubled the available group offerings, taking advantage of Windows 2000 trust capabilities and Active Directory services' availability to create a more comprehensive set of groups.

When you are working on certain parts of your plan, you'll be required to understand the proper use of each of these groups, how the groups differ, and where each group type's membership and assignment scopes can be applied. When used properly, groups can greatly simplify the life of the administrator; understanding how to properly use them is a must. This being so, you need a good, complete explanation of them before we get too far into this chapter.

You'll likely see references to *security groups* and *non–security groups* during the course of preparing or administering your Windows 2000 groups and users. Simply put, security groups are groups to which resource permissions can be assigned, and all four of the groups discussed in this book are security groups. The reason for the distinction between security groups and non–security groups in Windows 2000 is that Active Directory services enables the integration of e-mail-based distribution lists (such as the distribution lists you send e-mail to within your organization's e-mail environment) with Active Directory services. With the integration of e-mail services and Active Directory services, the line between e-mail distribution lists (which appear as groups) and Windows 2000 security groups (such as the four group types explained here) has blurred. Don't let these two group categories (security and non–security) confuse you; we're going to discuss only security groups in this book.

There are four security group types:

- Local groups
- Global groups
- Domain local groups
- Universal groups

Windows 2000 groups are named for the scope in which they can be used. Creating and using groups are integral to creating a working, effective, and manageable Windows 2000 administrative and security structure. Differentiating among group types and trying to figure out how they work are often causes for confusion, so this section explains groups clearly and concisely, wrapping up the discussion of groups with a matrix of the groups and the scopes in which they can be used.

Don't be surprised if you find that the number of groups you create ends up creeping toward the number of users in your corporate network, and don't be surprised if one user becomes a member of 10 different groups. If that's how the structure of your well-planned domain strategy pans out, so be it. Keep in mind, though, that the maximum recommended number of members of any group is 5,000. But since a user or a group equates to one member, you can get around this maximum by nesting groups—that is, by creating groups with fewer than 5,000 members and then collecting those groups into other groups. For example, you could create two groups with 2,500 members each (maybe called engineers and testers), then create a third group (maybe called WashingtonHQ) and get around that maximum by including the engineers and testers group in the WashingtonHQ group. At this point, the WashingtonHQ group would have two members, not 5,000.

## Local Groups

*Local groups* are named for the scope in which they can be used—that is, the local computer. Local groups can contain user accounts and global groups from the forest in which they are created (including downlevel domains) and from any trusted forests. Local groups cannot contain other local groups. Local groups let you combine global groups and user accounts from the entire forest and any trusted forest to share local computer resources. Local groups have not changed from their implementation in Windows NT.

Local groups are generally used only for allowing users (or groups) from across the enterprise to use resources on the local computer.

## Global Groups

*Global groups* are named for the scope in which they can be used—throughout the forest and in any trusted forest or domain. Global groups can contain only users or global groups from the domain in which they are created. Global groups in Windows 2000 have not changed from their implementation in Windows NT, but they are used slightly differently because of the addition of universal groups. Here is a one-sentence definition of global groups: global groups are collections of user accounts that can be used throughout your enterprise.

Global groups are good for gathering users (or groups) from a local domain for the purpose of specifying permissions to use resources located across the enterprise and are effective for managing the traffic associated with replicating the Global Catalog across site links (wide area network [WAN] links).

## Domain Local Groups

*Domain local groups* are new to Windows 2000, but this type of group existed as local groups on Primary Domain Controllers (PDCs) in Windows NT. The most important aspect of domain local groups is that they are available only when Windows 2000 is running in *native mode*. Native mode is explained in detail in Chapter 11, "Upgrading to Active Directory Services," but a short definition is in order: native mode is when all domain controllers are running Windows 2000 and the native-mode software switch has been set by an administrator. If you have begun installing Windows 2000 in your environment and your domain is not in native mode, your domain is in *mixed mode*. There are a handful of advantages to operating in native mode (including the availability of domain local groups), all of which are detailed in Chapter 11. When a domain is switched to native mode, local groups on a given domain controller become domain local groups.

Domain local groups can include users, global groups, and universal groups from anywhere in the forest or from any trusted forest or domain (including downlevel domains) and can contain other domain local groups from their own domain. Domain local groups are similar to local groups, only domain local groups can be used to control access to any computer in the local domain. Again, the name reflects the scope in which the group can be used—the local domain. Domain local groups are great for gathering users (or groups) from across the enterprise for the purpose of specifying permissions to use the local domain's resources and are effective for managing the traffic associated with replicating the Global Catalog across site links (WAN links)—but remember, they can be used only when native mode is enabled.

### Universal Groups

Universal groups are completely new to Windows, and they are named for the scope in which they can be used—they can contain users, computers, universal groups, and global groups from anywhere in the forest and can be granted permissions to access resources anywhere in the forest and in other forests with which the forest has an established trust relationship. Universal groups are available only when Windows 2000 is running in native mode. When working with universal groups, you need to remember that their membership is published in the Global Catalog.

All global, domain local, and universal groups are published in the Global Catalog; however, universal groups' members are also published in the Global Catalog. This fact has significant implications for Global Catalog replication traffic—whenever membership in a universal group changes, replication traffic is required. Note that membership changes in global or domain local groups will not generate Global Catalog replication traffic. If your entire network is connected by LAN-speed connections or better (meaning that you don't have slow WAN links over which Global Catalog replication traffic must travel), you don't need to worry too much about this replication and can probably use universal groups for all your groups—and do away with worrying about the management of global and domain local groups.

Universal group membership is added to a local user's security token during startup. The Local Security Authority (LSA) queries the Global Catalog for the user's universal group membership when the user logs on—and only at that time—and incorporates universal group membership information into the user's security token. If the Global Catalog cannot be queried (as is the case in a mixed-mode domain), membership in universal groups can't be added to the token and as a result, the user cannot be granted access to resources in the enterprise that have access restrictions based on universal group membership.

Here are some universal group guidelines:

- Add only other groups to universal groups; don't add individual users.
- Groups that don't change often and are widely used make good universal groups.
- Universal groups can be used to reflect organization-wide teams, to which resource access can be granted or denied.

Table 7-1 puts all of these groups into perspective by providing a chart that will let you quickly compare these groups and determine which group type is most appropriate for a given situation.

**Table 7-1. The Windows 2000 group matrix.**

| Group Type | Membership Scope | Usage Scope | Availability |
| --- | --- | --- | --- |
| Local | Users and groups from its own forest. | Local computer | Mixed mode, native mode |
| Global | Users and global groups from its own domain | Entire forest, any trusted domain | Mixed mode, native mode |
| Domain local | Users, global groups, universal groups anywhere in the forest, domain local groups from its own domain | Its own domain only | Native mode only |
| Universal | Users, computers, global groups, universal groups anywhere in the forest | Entire forest, any trusted forest | Native mode only |

Remember you can use groups to determine or create the user-based or enterprise-based organizational structure that your Windows 2000 deployment needs to be navigable and workable for its users. The rest of the structure of your Windows 2000 deployment, including your Active Directory services hierarchy and its corresponding DNS hierarchy, should be created to provide the most manageable, simple design as possible, which in turn makes the administration of this structure easier and more straightforward. Users generally won't navigate the domain hierarchy, the OU hierarchy, or the site hierarchy, so you should design them to fit administrative requirements, not user (or business-related organizational structure) standards. The only semiexception to this navigation rule is the forest, and it's more of a reinforcement of the impact of design decisions than an exception to the rule: if you have multiple forests, users will be required to know which forest they should navigate or search when looking for resources. I'll leave the explanation of that for the following section.

## Noteworthy Built-In Windows 2000 Groups

Windows 2000 has a number of built-in groups, but two of them are of particular interest to administrators who are developing an enterprise-wide Active Directory services deployment plan. Windows 2000 includes two administrator groups—Enterprise Administrators and Schema Administrators—whose members have significant control over the entire organization and forest.

Members of the Enterprise Administrators group have administrative authority in every domain in the forest and therefore have sweeping administrative power in your organization. This group is necessary because as you'll learn, domains are distinct administrative units regardless of their position in the domain tree hierarchy, which means that administrators in a parent domain do not have administrative authority in any child domain by default. The Enterprise Administrators group's members have authority that extends throughout the hierarchy, so you should consider the group's membership carefully.

Members of the Schema Administrators group are the only administrators who have the capability to make any modifications to the Active Directory schema. As such, they have complete control over the objects in Active Directory. Thus, the membership of the Schema Administrators group should also be considered carefully.

# Active Directory Services Planning Recommendations

You've heard this before, but I'll mention it again (and again, later on): the best thing you can do for your Windows 2000 deployment is to simplify your Active Directory services structure—by doing so, you will streamline your administrative process, increase the effectiveness of your IT staff, and simplify your life.

The following sections provide explanations and recommendations that will help you generate your Active Directory services plan and provide reasons for and exceptions to the simplicity maxim.

## Planning the Forest

We already know that a forest is a collection of one or more Windows 2000 domains in an Active Directory services environment. We also know that all domains in a forest share a single schema and a single Configuration container. (The Configuration container is a naming context that creates a virtual map of a network's physical topology, enabling directory-aware applications to take advantage of such information.) Recall from previous chapters that each domain controller maintains three naming contexts: the directory partition (the Active Directory information store for a domain controller's domain), the schema, and the Configuration container. Some domain controllers also maintain a copy of the Global Catalog when configured by an administrator to do so.

When you are developing your forest plan, you'll take the following steps:

1. Determine whether your organization needs more than one forest.
2. Show the plan to appropriate IT groups in your organization.
3. Rework the plan, based on the feedback you receive.

The first step from this list is discussed in detail in the following section.

## Making Logon Easy for Users

We know that whatever we can do to make it easier for users to get their work done is a good thing, and we also know that making the administrator's life easier is a good thing.

One capability of Active Directory services and its Global Catalog implementation has to do with user principal names (UPNs) and user logons. As a result of the availability of the Global Catalog, users can log on using a UPN, without needing to specify (or remember) the domain in which they have their user account. For example, imagine that a user named Paul has his user account in the *sales.corp.iseminger.com* domain, such that his UPN is paul@sales.corp.iseminger.com. You could abstract that domain name's hierarchical location in the domain tree and make it easier on Paul so that he would have to type only paul@iseminger.com during logon to get logged on. If Paul were moved to another domain (for whatever reason), he could still log on using his paul@iseminger.com address—making it easier on him, further abstracting the domain and forest structures, and making everyone happy.

## Determining the Number of Forests

Ideally, you should need only one forest for your organization. There are circumstances under which you might need more than one forest, but realize that having more than one forest in your organization will affect how users view the directory, will force users to take extra steps when using the directory, and will require that users understand the (supposedly transparent) implementation structure you've created. The result is that users will need to be trained how to work in a multiforest environment.

A multiple-forest environment creates additional work for users primarily because it makes the process of searching for a resource more involved. When users attempt to find a resource, they can specify the scope of their search—and the broadest search they will generally perform will be based on the Global Catalog. To users, the Global Catalog is represented simply as **Entire Directory** during searches. When they search for something located somewhere in the organization, it makes sense that they search the entire directory. (This will be more sensible as computing life with a directory becomes more commonplace.) As we know, each forest has exactly one Global Catalog associated with it. Having more than one forest means having more than one Global Catalog, and therefore, users in a multiforest environment must know that they need to specify which forest to search when looking for resources. That might sound simple to administrators or techno-savvy power users, but the vast majority of users out there aren't power users. Even when trained to search multiple directories (or Global Catalogs, or forests), users will search one forest, and if they don't find what they're looking for, they will either give up or decide that the resource they need doesn't exist. Worse yet, they'll get a partial list of resources and believe that the list is complete. (The list is partial because it will reflect resources in only one of the forests.) Not a good administrative situation by anyone's standards.

OK, so now that I've bemoaned the evils of multiple forests, I'll concede there might be specific reasons that force you to have more than one forest. Reasons that, presumably, preclude workarounds or concessions that might remedy the multiforest situation.

Let's enumerate the reasons why you might need to have more than one forest:

- Network administration is broken into multiple autonomous groups.
- The multiple autonomous groups don't trust each other.
- Each autonomous group wants individual control over the schema.
- You need to limit trust relationships between domains or domain trees.

Even if it appears you need multiple forests based on the reasons in this list, you should start your plan with one forest and then add another forest only if all other administrative mechanisms are exhausted.

If you need more than one forest, you need to know the various consequences of having multiple forests, which extend beyond the issues I outlined in the previous paragraph. Let's enumerate the consequences of having multiple forests:

- You will have multiple schemas. Maintaining consistency between them will create overhead and be difficult.
- You will have multiple Configuration containers. Network topology changes will have to be replicated to each affected forest, and maintaining consistency will create additional overhead.
- Explicit trusts between individual domains will need to be established and maintained. There are no transitive trusts between forests, so multiple domains requiring interforest trust relationships will require a mesh of one-way explicit trusts.
- Users will need to make explicit queries for resources outside their forest (as explained previously in this section).
- Any replication of information between forests will be manual and will require an administrative process for keeping such information up-to-date.
- Users logging on to computers in forests outside their own must use the default (full domain path) UPN when logging on. (For more information on UPNs, check out the sidebar entitled "Making Logon Easy for Users" earlier in this chapter.) To reuse my previous example, Paul would have to use his default UPN (paul@sales.corp.iseminger.com) when logging on to a computer outside his own forest since his abstracted address wouldn't reside in the computer's local-forest Global Catalog. Smart card logons would also require default UPNs, thus disabling the use of an abstracted UPN for smart card users.
- You cannot easily move accounts between forests. Any account moves between forests require that the user account be cloned.

There's no way of synchronizing information automatically between forests, so whenever you create more than one forest in a given organization, you are unavoidably creating additional administrative and coordination overhead. This is not a trivial amount of administrative overhead, either. If at all possible, use a single forest in your organization and find other ways (such as administrative delegation through the use of domains or OUs) to create a segregated administrative environment.

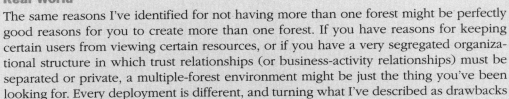

**Real World**

The same reasons I've identified for not having more than one forest might be perfectly good reasons for you to create more than one forest. If you have reasons for keeping certain users from viewing certain resources, or if you have a very segregated organizational structure in which trust relationships (or business-activity relationships) must be separated or private, a multiple-forest environment might be just the thing you've been looking for. Every deployment is different, and turning what I've described as drawbacks into great tools for privacy and security can be as simple as changing your perspective (your security-minded perspective, that is).

## Planning Domains

The next task in your Active Directory services planning list is the creation of a domain plan, which includes determining the hierarchical relationships between domains—that is, determining the parent/child domain hierarchy.

A domain is simply an administrative boundary that equates to one partition of the Active Directory information store. If a forest has three domains, that forest contains three partitions of its Active Directory information store, each corresponding to one of the forest's domains. The domain is also the boundary of Group Policy objects, which means that Group Policy can be applied to a given domain but that Group Policy does not get enforced outside the domain. (You can, however, explicitly set Group Policy to function in more than one domain.)

When you create a domain plan, you will complete the following steps:

1. Determine how many domains you will need.
2. Choose the root domain for each forest.
3. Determine DNS names for each domain.
4. Optimize authentication with cross-link trusts.

### Things to Consider When Planning Your Domains

Throughout the domain-planning process, there are some issues that you should keep in mind to provide the best domain plan possible. Some of these issues are not necessarily intuitive and require that you step outside the management pecking-order perception associated with any hierarchical system. Being aware of the following issues should help you keep such perspective:

- Domain hierarchies do not reflect administrative pecking orders. Hierarchical domains are based on administrative efficiencies, not organizational or management hierarchies. Administrators from child domains can be managerial peers or even superiors of administrators from parent domains.

- A single Windows 2000 domain can handle more than a million objects. The previous Windows NT limitation on the number of objects a given domain could maintain no longer applies. (Forty thousand user or computer accounts was the rule.) As a result, resource domains and domains divided based on the number of serviced accounts should be things of the past.

- Domains no longer depend on the availability of one computer. In Windows NT, only the PDC could save changes to domain-based information, and dependence on any one computer often was avoided by creating multiple domains. Windows 2000 uses a multimaster model, providing automatic fault tolerance and thereby removing the need for smaller domains based on this consideration.

- Domains are no longer the smallest units of administrative delegation. With Windows 2000, you can use OUs to create and delegate fine-grained control. In Windows NT, additional domains were sometimes created to reduce the scope of resources over which certain administrators had control. Limiting administrative control no longer requires creating subdomains (nor will administrators need to be granted more control than they really need to do their jobs): OUs can be created and their administration delegated as needed, all within a larger domain structure.

Before you start developing your domain plan, you will need certain information, and this information doesn't fit nicely into the discussions of the individual steps in the domain-planning process. I've provided the information here in the bulleted items in the preceding paragraphs and in the rest of this section rather than waiting until you get through the first few steps so that you can apply it to each of the steps as you go through them. Hopefully, this will save you from having to reread all this information once you've made it through this section, at which time you'd have to reapply it to earlier explanations. (I am looking out for you—simplicity, remember?) Of course, you'll be revamping your original, ideal plan after you've solicited feedback from various appropriate groups (meaning you'll need to revisit your plan—if not reread these steps and this information), right?

Remember when creating your domain plan that domains are named based on a DNS naming hierarchy, and that hierarchy provides parent/child relationships in which the name of a child domain differs from the name of the parent domain by *only* one label. For example, the *sales.corp.iseminger.com* domain is a child of the *corp.iseminger.com* domain and its name differs from the name of its parent domain by only one label—the *sales* label that is placed in front of *corp.iseminger.com*. Despite its apparent top-down structure, realize that the DNS domain hierarchy does not have to mirror an organization's administrative hierarchy. Administrators in a child domain can be, but aren't necessarily, subordinate to administrators in a parent domain. Administrators in the parent domain can have administrative privileges in the child domain, but they don't have privileges just because they are in the parent domain. Since that's a lot of words to choke down, let me provide an example.

Imagine an organization that has a handful of departments—sales, marketing, and manufacturing, among others—and also imagine that the administrative structure of the organization is such that all users within a given domain tree need the same applications to be available on their workstations and the same computer-setting restrictions applied to their accounts. The domain tree is shown in Figure 7-1.

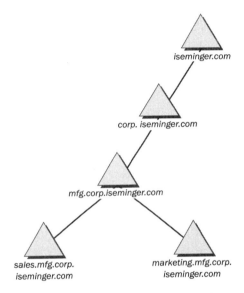

**Figure 7-1.** *An organization with a domain tree that's based on user application needs and Group Policy settings.*

Let's go through this example, point out some facts, and then conclude with the points that you can take away from the example and apply to your own deployment plan. In this example, certain password-restriction requirements in the sales, marketing, and manufacturing domains required that the IT department create multiple domains. The administrators for the sales, marketing, and manufacturing domains are all peers—none of those administrative departments is subordinate to any other, and the director of each administrative department sits on the IT executive board for Iseminger.com. Each administrator group has administrative control over its domain, though all domain administrator accounts are housed in the *corp.iseminger.com* domain. (More on why this was done is provided in the section titled "Delegating Administrative Responsibility" later in this chapter.)

The reason these domains were put into this domain tree structure was so that Group Policy could be set in the *mfg.corp.iseminger.com* domain and propagated to all domains in the tree. Also, certain Group Policy settings were specific to the three domains—though the sales and marketing domains required modifications to those policies—and since sales and marketing are in separate domains, each can subjectively filter or reject certain inheritance traits of Group Policy objects as appropriate for the users (or computers) in its domain. Administrators from the manufacturing domain do not have administrative control or any administrative rights in either the sales or marketing domain. Only the Enterprise Administrators have administrative rights throughout the organization and the capability to take ownership control of any object in the forest.

The important facts to take away from this example are the following:

- Although there are parent/child relationships between domains, administrators in parent domains do not automatically have administrative rights in child domains.

- Domain tree hierarchies do not need to mirror an organization's business hierarchy—peer groups can have parent/child relationships without affecting administrative control.

- Group Policy can flow down a domain tree, and such inheritance can make the application of administratively controlled Group Policy objects easier to control.

- The Enterprise Administrators group is the only group with default interdomain administrative rights.

One of the final pieces of information you should keep in mind when going through the steps of creating your domain plan is your organization's physical network topology and its ability to handle replication traffic. Windows 2000 domain controllers that belong to the same domain replicate information on a fairly consistent basis, due largely to the multimaster characteristics of Windows 2000. Because of this, if your domain spans more than one site, the WAN connection between sites will endure intradomain replication traffic. You also will need to consider whether remote sites are remote branches (with little administrative autonomy) or campuses (with on-site administrators and site-local server needs). Creating your domain plan, then, as well as your OU plan and certainly (primarily) your site plan, will depend in part on the physical topology of your network. No use putting such issues or discussions off: get out two big pieces of paper, some pencils, an eraser or two, some tape, and additional pieces of paper, and get ready to create a map of your physical network.

Let's define a few things before we start drawing: your *primary campus* is a LAN-speed-or-better-connected collection of users or offices; *secondary sites* are also LAN-speed-or-better-connected collections of sites or campuses that are smaller than the primary campus, but still significant in size. You could have any number of these. *Additional sites* are everything else; an additional site is any presence your organization has that isn't a primary campus or secondary site but that consists of LAN-speed-or-better-connected collections of users or computers. Now, on with the drawing.

First take out one of the big pieces of paper and draw your primary campus (or head-quarters or whatever else you might call it). Draw this as a square that's big enough to write a few lines in, and put it near the top of your piece of paper. If your organization is so evenly distributed that you don't have a central site, start with the location where your primary or senior IT staff resides, presuming they haven't for some reason been shoved into a remote corner. Your map should look something like Figure 7-2.

Next draw the secondary sites (or campuses or branches) as squares and distribute them evenly throughout the rest of the page. If you run out of room, tape a piece of paper to your main piece and continue until all your secondary sites are drawn. Connect these sites to one another with dotted lines that represent the actual physical connections between these sites (such as WAN links). Then draw a small square beside each link and put a number in each square (which needs to be only big enough to fit the number) that corresponds to the physical link associated with the square. On a separate piece of paper, draw these same small number-filled squares, and then jot down the characteristics of the links they represent, including whether any of these sites are connected to each other only through Simple Mail Transfer Protocol (SMTP) (e-mail transmission) connectivity. These links will be the *site links* that will get more attention in the section describing creation of your sites. Your map should now look something like Figure 7-3.

Finally draw your additional sites and then draw in their connections (site links) to the secondary sites and the main campus. By this time, your map is probably a mess, with more eraser marks than actual drawings. Ponder it for a moment, and then take out your second large piece of paper and redraw it, this time with the appropriate spacing and dotted lines (representing site links) so that the map is actually readable. Once you're done with that, make two more copies of it—you'll use copies of this map during domain planning (including domain controller placement) and site planning, and to determine whether any holes exist in your deployment plan (which is explained the last section in this chapter). Your map should look something like Figure 7-4.

Now that you have the map, gather information about usage of the site links—usage information that covers all hours of the day when the site links are available. Work with your other network engineering groups to gather this information; you'll use it to determine whether you can create domains that cross site boundaries. If a given site link can bear the burden of intradomain replication in addition to its normal usage, you can create a domain that crosses the link. If it can't (because it's already near capacity, its bandwidth is so expensive that your organization cannot afford the costs associated with the additional traffic replication would introduce, or it's too unreliable to depend on for important data such as replication traffic), you'll likely need to create domains on either side of that site link. Defining what *near capacity, too expensive,* or *too unreliable* is, is something you have to do on your own, based on your network group's past experiences with the link and your organization's assessment of costs and reliability.

**Figure 7-2.** *Drawing your primary campus onto your soon-to-be network topology map.*

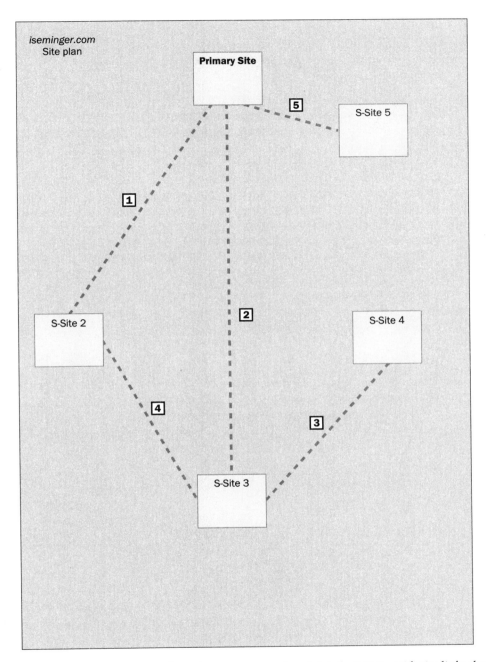

**Figure 7-3.** *Drawing secondary sites onto your network topology map, with site links drawn as dotted lines and site-link information placed on a separate sheet.*

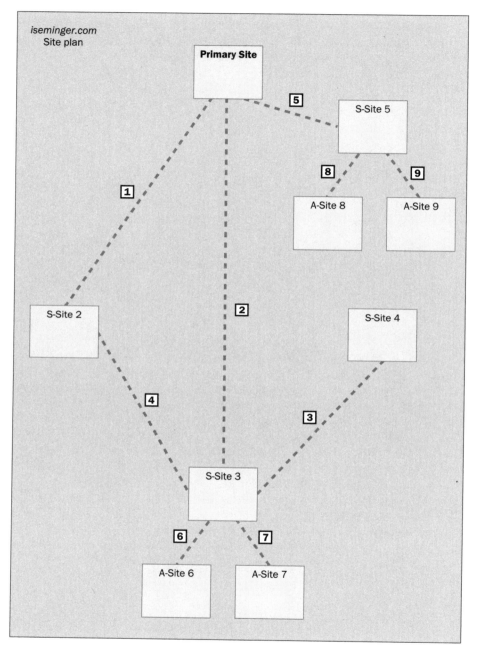

**Figure 7-4.** *Drawing additional sites on your network topology map.*

Now for the easy part: stare at your map for a while, concentrate, ponder it a bit, and then consider this map of yours and its links as you read through the following sections. With your map in hand and your assessment of its site links either written down or in the back of your mind, consider as you move through the following sections how many domains your organization's Active Directory deployment will need. Remember that you should be going through a few iterations of your domain-planning task; though the map might get messier as more iterations are done, your plan will become more solid, and the feedback you get from other groups in your organization will help you make better-informed decisions about your domain and site plans.

### Determining How Many Domains You Need

The simpler your domain plan is, the better off you're going to be in the long run: you've heard this before, but repetition is the stuff of memorization. A good policy is to start with one domain and add domains only as each additional domain can be technically justified. Additional domains are guilty until proven innocent: they add administrative overhead, and there should be substantial, technical explanations for using them. Adding a new domain "just because one domain would be too big" is not a valid reason. Windows 2000 and Active Directory services have done away with the need to do such object-limit juggling.

That said, I'll not deny that there are circumstances under which creating more than one domain for your organization will be a good, sound, and technically defensible approach. The following list provides compelling reasons for doing so:

- **Unique security requirements** dictate creating another domain.
- **Administrative requirements** dictate creating another domain.
- **Replication traffic** dictates creating another domain.
- **Existing Windows NT domains** need to be kept.

### Unique security requirements

Certain security settings are domain-wide, and these settings cannot be modified within a domain (such as at the OU level). If your organization or plan has unique security requirements, it makes sense to create a domain. The security settings that can be set at only the domain level are the following:

- Password policy, such as password length and expiration period.
- Account lockout policy, which aids in intruder detection and sets policy for account deactivation.
- Kerberos ticket policy, which determines the life of a Kerberos ticket granting ticket (TGT). Although tickets are automatically and transparently requested when the TGT expires, certain user bases might require shorter TGT lifetime cycles.

**More Info** For more information on the Kerberos protocol and TGTs, including the process involved when a client attempts to obtain a TGT from an Active Directory domain controller, check out Chapter 8, "Active Directory Services and Security."

### Administrative requirements

During your domain planning, you might discover that you need to create extra domains because of special administrative requirements. For example, you might have a certain user and computer base that requires administration from a particular group of administrators (such as an assigned IT department). You might have a certain part of the organization that requires administrative autonomy, as is the case when a set of administrators does not want any outside administrators to have access to certain resources within the domain (such as Human Resource files associated with pay scales, reviews, or other sensitive information). There might, in fact, be legal requirements for such segregation and guaranteed autonomy, which is certainly reason enough for the creation of an individual domain. Administrative requirements can be considered together with other factors, such as replication considerations or the application of Group Policy, when establishing justification for adding a domain.

### Replication traffic

If your organization has multiple sites, you might need more than one domain to avoid the replication traffic associated with having one domain span multiple sites. To determine whether you need multiple domains, you need to figure out whether your site links can handle the extra traffic associated with intradomain replication traffic. There's no way for me to quantifiably specify the usage level, per-usage cost, or reliability rating your site links need to meet to be viable for intersite replication associated with having one domain span multiple sites. When determining the coverage of your domains and where domains are placed in terms of physical network topology, you must take the establishment of Active Directory services sites into consideration. Whether a given site link can handle the traffic associated with intradomain replication is something you must determine in your plan because intradomain replication can have a significant impact on the responsiveness and overall consistency of your Active Directory deployment.

**Note** If you have a site that is connected to another site through only an SMTP link, that site should have its own domain. An SMTP link can be used only to transmit interdomain replication information, not intradomain replication information; therefore, the site isolated by the SMTP link (that is, connected through only an SMTP link) needs to have its own self-contained domain.

One important fact to keep in mind regarding intersite replication (whether that replication is of intradomain or interdomain information) is that all replication traffic between sites is compressed prior to being sent over the link. What does that mean for your calculations? It means you need to add an extremely difficult formula to them to accurately determine how much replication traffic your Active Directory services environment will need to support. For more information about replication and site considerations, see the "Planning Sites: Getting Tight with the Network" section later in this chapter.

### Existing Windows NT domains

You might have important reasons for keeping your existing Windows NT domain structure and thus for having multiple domains. Issues surrounding upgrading an existing Windows NT domain structure to Windows 2000 are covered in depth in Chapter 11, "Upgrading to Active Directory Services."

## Planning and Naming Your Domains

Once you go through the process of determining how many domains your organization needs, you'll need to determine the structure of your Active Directory services deployment's domain hierarchy, which includes determining the DNS names of each domain in each tree in your forest. Each domain tree begins with the forest's root domain, which is the first domain you create in Active Directory. For example, in the Active Directory deployment of Iseminger.com, the *iseminger* domain was created first and therefore is the root of the *iseminger.com* hierarchy.

Ideally, you should have a single domain tree in your forest. One tree is better than multiple trees because one tree introduces less administrative overhead and fewer domains than multiple trees. (Two trees require at least two domains; one tree requires only one domain.) When creating your domain tree plan, you should first create your ideal plan, and then solicit feedback from appropriate groups, and then reevaluate your plan to incorporate their feedback (as appropriate). Although a one-tree forest is ideal, you might have good reasons for ending up with more than one domain tree in your Active Directory services plan.

One important reason for having more than one domain tree is as follows:

- Your organization has more than one registered DNS name.

Having more than one registered DNS name is the primary reason for creating more than one tree in your forest, but there are actually a number of issues to consider when it comes to naming your domains and creating the DNS domain hierarchy in which all such domains must be placed. The following paragraphs outline guidelines to bear in mind when creating your domain plan. Some of the guidelines are straightforward and some are not, but all of them can help make the task of administering your Windows 2000/Active Directory deployment anywhere from slightly easier to monumentally less headache-inducing.

**Base domains on geography, not business structure.** I've mentioned this before, but it's worth restating here. Business structure, project lifecycles, and all other such organizational mechanisms found within many organizations are prone to change. In fact, they're guaranteed to change, and your Windows 2000 domain structure is not nearly as adaptable to change as businesses are. In fact, once you create a domain within a given DNS hierarchy, that domain cannot be easily moved. There is significant administrative effort associated with moving any domain—and the root domain (such as *iseminger.com* or *microsoft.com* in those domain tree hierarchies) cannot be moved or renamed *at all*. If you base your domains primarily on geography, you have a better chance of being able to gracefully adapt to inevitable changes within your organization. There is one exception to this rule, and that is the root domain, as explained in the following paragraph.

**Use a dedicated root domain.** The root domain can be either an existing domain, such as one that exists in a Windows NT deployment, or a domain that you create, but it should be a domain that does not house user accounts or many computer accounts; it should be dedicated to the operations associated with enterprisewide management. Using a dedicated root domain has a few advantages:

- Domain administrators in the root domain can manipulate the membership of the Enterprise Administrators and Schema Administrators groups. By having a dedicated root domain and limiting the membership of its Domain Administrators group to administrators who should be granted such enterprisewide administrative authority, you avoid a situation in which "regular" administrators in the root domain also have the capability to manipulate the membership of powerful, enterprise-wide, built-in groups.

- Replication across the enterprise protects the root. Since the dedicated root domain will likely be quite small (compared to regularly populated domains), you can place domain controllers in various geographical sites and provide extended fault tolerance against catastrophes. The importance of this strategy for a root domain is this: if all domain controllers in the root domain are lost and cannot be restored, the Enterprise Administrators and Schema Administrators groups will be lost as well, and there's no way to reinstall the root domain.

- Obsolescence is avoided. With a dedicated root whose name is presumably based on an Internet-based DNS name—which often is a reflection of the overall organization rather than a geographic location—you can avoid the domain's (unchangeable) name from becoming obsolete. For example, I might use the *iseminger.com* Windows 2000 domain (or even maybe the *corp.iseminger.com* domain) as the root domain, under which all other domains will be created. In using that rather than, say, the *seattle.iseminger.com* Windows 2000 domain, I avoid the possibility that moving headquarters from Seattle would relegate the unchangeable *seattle.iseminger.com* domain to irrelevance.

**Use a registered Internet DNS name as a base for your root.** Even if you don't use the root of your Internet-registered DNS hierarchy as your Active Directory services domain hierarchy root, you should base your root on the registered Internet DNS name to avoid confusion and maintain consistency. For example, using *corp.iseminger.com* as the root, based on the Internet-registered DNS root *iseminger.com,* maintains consistency in the internal structure and makes it easier for users who are less technically inclined than your IT staff to understand the navigational structure. Your next question might be: if I use the same DNS name internally as I do for the Internet, how will users (both internal and on the Internet) be able to navigate between them—both in instances where I want them to navigate both (for example, when internal employees are connected to both the intranet and the Internet) and in instances where I do not want them to (for example, when external users shouldn't be viewing intranet sites)? That's where the next point comes in.

**Use DNS structure to differentiate between the Internet and your intranet.** If you want to use your organization's intranet for internal Web information yet still expose your Internet-based Web information with the same domain name base, you can do so through a combination of DNS structure and proxy settings. Let me give you an example: Iseminger.com has an Internet presence that uses domains such as *novels.iseminger.com* and *winprs.iseminger.com* to direct Internet-based traffic to appropriate Web pages. (Don't get confused here—DNS uses the term *domain* to mean a naming context, as does Windows 2000, but a DNS domain does not have to be a Windows 2000 domain.) Internally, Iseminger.com uses its root structure—which has *corp.iseminger.com* as its Active Directory services root—to differentiate between internal sites, such as *sales.corp.iseminger.com,* which directs users internally to the sales team's internal Web site. Since employees have access to the Internet as well as the company intranet, the proxy server at Iseminger.com is configured such that any DNS addresses that have *corp.iseminger.com* as a suffix are directed to the intranet (with other queries passing through to the Internet). Since the firewall software is in place, external users can't see any of the *corp.iseminger.com* sites. (The Internet-based DNS server that's authoritative for *iseminger.com* returns errors for any queries based on *corp.iseminger.com.*) By taking this approach with your DNS hierarchy and by ensuring that proper security measures are in place and reviewed to ensure that your intranet is protected from outside viewing, you can use your DNS structure to create seamless and unified, yet secure, intranet and Internet access (and exposure) for your Windows 2000/Active Directory deployment.

**Don't use the same domain name twice.** It doesn't matter that you *can* do this as long as the two domains are on different networks that are not connected to each other. What matters is that using the same domain name twice is an effective way to create confusion among users and administrators alike and can cause unpredictable behavior (such as ranting and expletives from users and administrators). You could also cause ambiguity with DNS search results, in which case you could cause all sorts of additional grief. For example, imagine that I deploy an internal forest that has absolutely no connection to the Internet and use *iseminger.com* as its root. I can do this because I will never connect this private, internal deployment to the Internet. Then, in my daily routine, I sit at my unconnected *iseminger.com* workstation, and because I need to see the latest technology news, I connect to the Internet and bring up my favorite news site. Then I decide to open another browser and connect to an internal *iseminger.com* site to check some important internal document that contains all sorts of time-sensitive, crucial information. To which site will I be connected? The internal site or the Internet site? Answer: whichever DNS server happens to answer first. If the Internet-based DNS server answers first (and there's a good chance of that happening), I will see an external site and fly into a panic because my time-sensitive, crucial internal information is no longer available. Maybe

I mistyped, so I try again—and because the address is now cached in my browser, I will get the same site and go into a panic again.

Avoid such panic attacks. Don't use the same domain name twice.

**Use Windows 2000 DNS in your Active Directory services deployment.** This isn't a product pitch, just a sound recommendation. Using Windows 2000 DNS enables your deployment to take advantage of the fault tolerance and multimaster replication capabilities inherited by using the Active Directory information store to house DNS information. In addition, using Windows 2000 DNS enables previously deployed Windows NT domains—which didn't have to adhere to the same strict legal-character naming standards applied to DNS—to function in Windows 2000 environments without the need to rename them. For example, I've seen a fair amount of domain names containing the underscore ( _ ) character. The underscore is illegal in DNS, but if you deploy Windows 2000 DNS, you get to continue using the domain name and still get all the advantages of using DNS in your Active Directory environment. (In addition, you meet the infrastructure requirements of a DNS locator service.)

> **Caution** Even though Windows 2000 DNS can work with the nonstandard characters, don't name new domains with nonstandard DNS characters. It's kind of like using the electricity created by a battery charger to dry out your waterlogged clothes—sure, you can do it, but there are better, safer approaches that will get the job done without the associated risks.

**Use cross-link trusts to optimize authentication performance.** Once you've created your DNS domain hierarchy and determined which domains will be placed in which domain tree (hopefully, you have only one tree), you should analyze usage of resources in other domains and, if necessary, create cross-link trusts (sometimes referred to as shortcut trusts) to optimize and speed up the authentication process.

> **More Info** For more information about how cross-link trusts function, check out the "Trust Relationships" section in Chapter 3, "Windows 2000 Domains and Active Directory Services."

## Planning Organizational Units

OUs are organizational structures that you use to organize objects such as users, computers, or other resources within any given domain into logical administrative subgroups. OUs must be contained within the domain in which they are created, which means that only objects that reside in one domain can belong to any given OU.

There are a handful of important OU facts that you should keep in mind throughout your OU-planning process:

- **OUs are not security principals.** You can't base access control on OUs; that's a job for Windows 2000 security groups such as global groups, domain local groups, or universal groups.

- **Users will not navigate the OU hierarchy.** Don't create an OU plan with users in mind; create the plan with administration of the Windows 2000/Active Directory deployment in mind.
- **OUs have less effect on performance than Group Policy.** OUs are the best way to create administrative organization in your Active Directory deployment. Unless you're doing a whole lot of nesting (such as more than 15 levels deep, at which point you should reconsider your organizational approach), the impact of OUs on performance is not significant. If you're finding that performance isn't what it should be, scrutinize the number of Group Policy objects you have applied to various groups—that's a more likely culprit than your OU structure.

The best approach that you can take with OUs is to create them based on your IT administrative structure and not on your organization's management structure (or any other structure, for that matter). As mentioned previously, OUs are not navigated by users, and they are available in Windows 2000 and Active Directory services to provide IT administrators with the tool they need to better delegate administration and to do so based on administrative boundaries.

There are some other reasons why you might want to create OUs, such as to use them as Group Policy boundaries. In fact, since OUs can be nested into many levels, there are a number of reasons why you might create additional (nested) OUs to make your administration of Windows 2000 and Active Directory easier, such as to provide administrative delegation and control in hierarchical fashion.

**Real World**

While the theoretical limit on how many OUs can be nested is somewhat fuzzy, the practical and performance-based limitation has been fairly well defined. In its performance testing and in other testing, Microsoft has found that going any deeper than 15 levels of nested OUs begins to impact performance. This doesn't mean that you have to go 15 levels deep (that's a lot of OU nesting), but it means that if necessary, you can go that deep. Such nesting capabilities can go far in enabling simpler forest and domain designs, essentially placing the responsibility of implementing organizational hierarchy onto OUs—which is where it should be, since OUs are so easy to move, create, delete, and modify.

The previous sections that outlined your forest and domain plans went on and on about simplicity; I'll begin this one in a similar, if less stringent, tone: start with one OU, and then technically justify any additional OUs you must create. Chances are, though, that you'll have plenty of technically justifiable reasons in your OU plan for creating and even nesting OUs. If you do have plenty of reasons (and you probably will), you should first create an OU structure based on the IT administrative structure and then make modifications or additions based on other considerations.

The following is a list of reasons why you might need more than one OU:

- You need to delegate administrative responsibility.
- You want to delegate specific administrative tasks to certain groups.
- You want to apply Group Policy to particular subsets of users or computers within a given domain.

### Delegating Administrative Responsibility

With OUs, you can effectively delegate administrative responsibility of the contents of the OU container (that is, over all user, computer, or resource objects associated with a given OU). Creating OUs to delegate administration is synonymous with creating OUs based on an IT administrative structure. There are two options for how administrators are assigned to a given OU, and the option you choose determines the freedom an administrator has to create objects in the administrator's OU.

- **Full control:** Create a security group, and place OU administrators for whom you want to provide full control into the group. On the OU over which the OU administrators need administrative privileges, assign full control.
- **Discretionary control:** Create a security group, and place OU administrators for whom you want to provide discretionary OU control into the group. Assign control over objects such as user accounts, computer accounts, Group objects, or OU objects, as necessary.

There are a couple of issues you should keep in mind regarding whether you provide full control or discretionary control to a given group of administrators. Full control enables administrators in that OU to create objects in that OU, and since Active Directory services grants full control to the creator of objects, such administrators have full control over any objects they create. A better approach is often to enable discretionary control over commonly created objects.

While granting full control might sound like you're providing a key to the OU city, you can rest a little easier by realizing that domain administrators can take full ownership of any object in their domain—including OUs—regardless of the access control restrictions placed on the objects. That means that a renegade administrator of an OU cannot lock domain administrators out of the OU. However, much damage can be done by a renegade administrator during such a period (requiring significant administrative work to undo) if you aren't careful about whom you choose to provide OU-based administrative control to.

### Delegating Specific Administrative Tasks

You can get more granular with certain permissions within any given OU. Delegating specific tasks differs from delegating administrative responsibility in that implied in delegating specific administrative tasks is an absence of any autonomy. For example, if your help desk is responsible for managing the resetting of passwords for certain groups in a given domain, you could enable the reset password permission for the security group that encompasses the help desk, and thereby delegate that specific administrative task. And since the OU structure is based on administrative structure, chances are good that the help desk group is aligned with OU administrative boundaries as well. Another example: you could allow the accounting group to create Salary objects in the OUs over which they have responsibility and automatically populate them with pertinent information—perhaps through a macro with a simple user interface that enables them to fill out a few lines and then click a button to create or modify the attributes of the object they created. You can do all sorts of things with the marriage of fine-grained administrative capabilities and Group Policy.

The easiest way to delegate administration in this way is to use the Delegation Of Control wizard, available through the Active Directory Users And Groups snap-in. Another way to achieve this is to modify the access control rights on the object by selecting the object from Active Directory and modifying its security properties.

### Applying Group Policy to OUs

Group Policy can be applied at the forest level, the domain level, and the OU level. By enabling Group Policy to be applied to OUs, Windows 2000 enables administrators to have fine-grained control over policies and user and workstation management within a given domain, providing compelling reasons for creating fewer, larger domains with multiple OUs—which is an easier structure to administer than a structure with many domains.

## Planning Sites: Getting Tight with the Network

Much of the information pertaining to sites that we will cover in this chapter has already been either alluded to or explained, but in this section, that information is brought together, clarified, and tucked into one nice, neat little section.

Active Directory services stores site information in its Configuration container—a naming context that resides on every domain controller in every Windows 2000 domain—and uses site information to provide appropriate connections and domain controller selection during client/domain controller and domain controller/domain controller communications. The logical premise of creating sites and managing communication from client to domain controller and domain controller to domain controller is based on a combination of network bandwidth considerations and response times. Essentially, clients are directed to domain controllers that reside within their site whenever possible, and domain controllers base whether or not they compress replication traffic on whether the domain controller with which they communicate is within their own site (compression off) or in another site (compression on).

Because an organization's site structure is based on the structure of the organization's physical network, you do not have as much discretion when planning sites as you do when planning forests, domains, or OUs. Does that mean site plans are easier to develop than the other plans you need to create when planning your Active Directory deployment? Not really, because once you have selected your sites, you have to decide where to place domain controllers and other infrastructure-based controllers. Such planning is integral to more than just a well-conceived site plan; proper domain controller placement can be the difference between Active Directory deployments that are smoothly run and responsive and those that are not.

Let's quickly revisit definitions of sites and site links:

- A site is a collection of well-connected (LAN-speed or higher) IP subnets.
- A site link is a slow (sub-LAN-speed) or unreliable connection between sites.

Site links correspond only to physical (or logical) connections between sites; you do not need to create virtual connections if site links between three or more sites are implied. For example, imagine the site called Primary is connected with a 256-kbps frame relay connection to the site called Secondary, and the secondary site is connected to yet another site called Additional through a 384-kbps asymmetric digital subscriber line (ADSL). You would create only two site links in this situation—one for the frame relay connection between Primary and Secondary, and one for the ADSL connection between Secondary and Additional. You would not create a virtual site link that connected Primary to Additional (through Secondary). Additionally, if you have a WAN backbone that connects many sites—such as a frame relay cloud that has multiple DLCIs that interconnect four individual sites—you can create one site link that connects multiple sites (rather than the alternative method, which would be creating a mesh of site links similar to the mesh of trust relationships necessary in a Windows NT domain environment).

Remember the map of your network's physical topology that you created earlier in the "Things to Consider When Planning Your Domains" section? That's essentially your site plan—the squares that you drew for your primary and secondary sites represent easily identifiable sites. The additional sites are a little more difficult, and recommendations on how to handle them are given throughout the rest of this section. But before we go too much further, some clarifications about the nature of sites and how they interact with domains need to be made:

- One site can house multiple domains. There's no rule that states any relationship—one-to-one or otherwise—between sites and domains.
- One domain can span multiple sites. This sounds like the issue mentioned in the previous bullet, but there's a significant difference that has to do with the replication of domain-based information between sites. Replication traffic must be considered when determining whether a domain can or should span more than one site. There are also fault-tolerance and logon-performance considerations that are associated with one domain spanning multiple sites. All these issues are explained and clarified throughout the rest of this chapter.

**Caution** Site names are registered and replicated throughout the DNS hierarchy; therefore, site names must be valid DNS names.

## Managing Active Directory Replication

For you to properly consider the coverage of sites and how sites and their respective site links can affect Active Directory services performance, you need to understand how Active Directory handles replication traffic. Table 7-2 provides a matrix that shows how Active Directory implements replication.

**Table 7-2 How Active Directory implements and transmits its replication traffic.**

| | Intrasite replication (within a site) | Intersite replication (between sites) |
|---|---|---|
| **Compression** | No compression is done in order to preserve CPU time. (Compression is CPU intensive.) | Compression is used to preserve WAN bandwidth. |
| **Notification** | Replication partners within a site notify each other when changes need to be replicated (reduces replication latency). | Replication partners in different sites do not notify each other of changes (preserves bandwidth). |
| **Polling** | Replication partners poll each other for changes on a periodic basis. | Replication partners poll only at specific intervals and only during scheduled periods. |
| **Transport mechanism** | Replication partners within a site use remote procedure call (RPC). | Replication partners in different sites use TCP/IP or SMTP. |
| **Replication connections** | Replication connections can be created between any two domain controllers. | Replication connections between sites are made between bridgehead servers only. |

When planning your domains and determining whether a domain should span a given site link, you should review and consider the matrix in Table 7-2 as part of the process of ensuring that the site link can handle the increase in replication traffic. You should also consult your site-link usage information (which you gathered earlier and included as part of your physical network topology map) to determine whether special consideration should be given to the time of day during which replication should occur. Can you replicate only at night? Can you schedule the replication interval to correspond to times of low site-link usage—such as during lunch times or at night—and still maintain the level of domain controller synchronization that your organization requires? Is the cost for transmission of any additional data (such as the frequent intradomain replication) too high? For sites that don't have their own domain controller and therefore depend on the site link for connectivity to domain controllers, is the site link reliable enough to depend upon for authentication? These are all questions you should be asking as you plan your domain and the placement of your domain controllers. There are no hard-and-fast answers; the answers to these questions depend on your network topology, the cost of transmission on your site links, the reliability of those links, and your organization's tolerance for stale domain information.

Site links should be subjected to special scrutiny and will have significant influence on your creation and placement of domains, primarily due to the cost of intradomain replication. When any domain spans more than one site, replication traffic crosses that link. You must determine whether that site link's characteristics (including cost, bandwidth availability for more important data such as mission-critical applications, and reliability) allow you to span that site link or prevent you from spanning it. Your options: allow the domain to span the site link or divide the domain that spans the site into two domains— one on either side of the site link.

Once your sites and site links have been planned and your domain controllers have been scattered across your physical network in appropriate places, any issues associated with managing the replication topology itself must be addressed. (Since sites largely define how replication traffic occurs, most of this is automated, though you can manually specify any replication characteristics you deem necessary.) The process of specifying and configuring replication management is covered in detail in Chapter 9, "Managing Active Directory Services."

**Note**   What if a client's IP address doesn't place the client into one of Active Directory services' administratively defined sites? In such cases, communication with domain controllers is performed on a random basis.

## Placing Domain Controllers

The placement of domain controllers can greatly influence the responsiveness of Active Directory services. Issues that generally affect the number of domain controllers you need to deploy for a given site or a given domain are discussed in the following sections.

### Fault tolerance

You should never have only one domain controller for any domain. Doing so completely undermines the fault-tolerance and multimaster features of Windows 2000 and in general is a bad practice. Two domain controllers is the bare minimum, but there are certainly reasons to have more than two domain controllers, such as for capacity planning. Remember, too, that any given domain controller services exactly one domain. If you have multiple domains in any given site or if one of your domains spans more than one site, keep in mind that one domain controller is associated with exactly one site. You can't double-up the duties of domain controllers by having them service more than one domain.

### User account location

User accounts need to reside on domain controllers located in the same site as the user. There's too much traffic generated by user activity to push such traffic onto a site link.

### Capacity planning

This is a difficult issue to quantify or pin down, but in simplistic terms it means having enough domain controller processing power (or bandwidth or availability) to service the needs of the domain. As part of your ongoing administrative effort, you should monitor the usage of your domain controllers through tools such as the System Monitor snap-in and the Performance Logs And Alerts snap-in (formerly known as Performance Monitor) and review their performance (especially % CPU Utilization) to ensure that they have sufficient processing power and bandwidth to service requests. Telltale signs that your capacity is insufficient—and that your deployment is taking a performance hit as a result—are slow logon times, slow authentication when attempting to use resources, and other domain controller–related activities. Get a baseline (such as timing logons or authentications in your test environment, where presumably the DCs are not overburdened), and then take performance measurements in your production environment over a pertinent time period (such as throughout the work day on varying days of the week), find the trend, and compare that to your baseline. If you find that performance is significantly and noticeably lagging (from the user's perspective), you need to consider deploying additional domain controllers. Note that this is the extremely quick and concise version of capacity planning; there's much more to capacity planning than these simple steps, but these steps can get you pointed in the right direction.

Remember that domain controllers service logons and authentications, as well as replication traffic and servicing queries. Any site that has a significant number of domain users should have its own domain controller. So, if you have a site that houses three domains and a significant number of users (or resources such as file servers) in that site belong to each of the three domains, you should have at least three domain controllers—a minimum of one for each domain—in that site.

### Site-link reliability

When clients attempt to access domain controllers, Active Directory services first attempts to connect clients to domain controllers in their own site, and if no domain controllers are available, connection to a domain controller requires crossing a site link. You need to determine how reliable a given site link is in order to determine the placement of domain controllers in its site. For example, if you deploy one domain controller in a site that houses one domain and that domain controller goes down, do you trust the reliability of that site link for user logons? Remember that users cannot log on to their computers in a native-mode Windows 2000/Active Directory environment if the client cannot contact a Global Catalog server (which is a domain controller that houses the Global Catalog). If your site link is not reliable and you have not deployed a second (fault tolerant) domain controller on the site, users on that site will not be able to log on to their computers—which generally is detrimental to their productivity and their perception of the network's effectiveness.

### Global Catalog server availability

As mentioned a couple of times already, Global Catalog servers must be available when a user logs on to a native-mode Windows 2000 domain; without access to a Global Catalog server, the LSA on the user's computer cannot include the user's universal groups in his or her security token. Since such groups might be used to deny access to certain resources, the absence of such groups in a security token equates to a security breach. As such, Windows 2000 will refuse a logon request in a native-mode Windows 2000 domain if a Global Catalog server cannot be reached. That means you also must scrutinize the assignment of Global Catalog domain controllers to provide the same kind of availability and fault tolerance that standard domain controllers must have. Take a close look at your site links as well, and determine whether having a Global Catalog server available only on the other side of a site link is reasonable in case the site-link goes down. (It almost certainly is not reasonable.) Global Catalog servers replicate more data than standard domain controllers, so you should factor that into your planning process when determining whether your existing site links have the capacity necessary to handle replication traffic.

## Conclusions

The creation of an Active Directory services deployment plan is probably the most important task associated with a Windows 2000 deployment. Part of the challenge associated with creating a plan is dealing with the associated information overload; you must consider the forest plan, the domain plan, the OU plan, and the site plan all at once, make sure they're all in agreement and that their intermingled issues work out, and then somehow make sense of all their requisite interdependencies. This is not an easy task, but you can handle it like you handle many other challenges—you simply must start somewhere and work your way through.

This chapter was designed to guide you through the challenge. You started with some information that you needed to have before reading through the rest of the explanation of the planning process, and then you created a forest plan, a domain plan, and an OU plan. Then you had to revisit nearly all of those plans (especially the domain plan) when you went through the site plan. Fortunately, going through a handful of Active Directory plan iterations—complete with getting feedback from groups who likely have insights that you don't have—should result in a stronger, more appropriate plan that everyone involved can live with.

# Chapter 8
# Active Directory Services and Security

An important part of your Active Directory deployment is ensuring that proper security measures are in place throughout your network and your organization. Active Directory services is the central repository of information, including security information, for Microsoft Windows 2000. It maintains security information and provides a centralized foundation for extended security services. From this it follows that any thorough treatment of Active Directory technology must include a thorough treatment of Active Directory and Windows 2000 security. Windows 2000 and Active Directory were built with security in mind and depend on each other to create a robust and secure distributed networking environment.

## Windows 2000 Security

Security in the Windows environment has changed quite a bit with the advent of Windows 2000. While security primitives such as security identifiers (SIDs), access control entries (ACEs), and access control lists (ACLs) remain central to Windows security, the means by which their authorization information is accessed has changed dramatically. Also, with the integration of Internet-based communication into the fundamental operations of Windows 2000, another type of security has been implemented; or, rather, the infrastructure for another type of security has been implemented, which is the public key infrastructure (PKI).

### Windows 2000 Security Primitives

Windows 2000 uses a handful of primary information units to establish and implement pervasive security throughout any given Windows 2000 and Active Directory deployment. Through these primitive objects, Windows 2000 can build security information and enforce specified access control.

#### ACEs, DACLs, and SIDs

Windows 2000 security works on the basis of objects. Everything you can see or work with in Windows 2000 is an object; users, domains, organizational units (OUs), files, folders...everything. Most of these objects are represented in Active Directory, and each object has security information associated with it. (Files are securable objects, but are not represented in Active Directory.) An object's security information is collectively represented in the object's security descriptor. Windows 2000 uses the security descriptor information on each object in Active Directory (and for objects outside of Active Directory, such as a file on an NTFS partition) to enforce access and control rights to the object on a user-basis and group-basis. Access rights are often also called *permissions*. A security descriptor for any object contains the following information:

- The *security identifier* of the object's owner. SIDs are explained in more detail in a few paragraphs.
- The SID of the object's primary group.
- The *discretionary access control list* (DACL), which is an ACL that maintains data indicating which users have access to the object and the access permissions those users have.
- The *system access control list* (SACL), which is an ACL used by the system to track events for auditing purposes.

The entries in an object's ACLs are called *access control entries*. ACEs specify permission settings for users and groups. For example, if the users of an organization's marketing group have read and write access to a given object in Active Directory services, a corresponding ACE for that group is included in the DACL of the security descriptor object. If users of another group also have a set of permissions for that object, another ACE is added to the DACL of the security descriptor. Windows 2000 has a special mechanism for identifying users and security groups—sometimes referred to as *security principals*. Windows 2000 uses this special identification mechanism, called a security identifier, to apply user and group permissions to all objects in Windows 2000. Rather than identify users and security groups based on names, Windows 2000 identifies all users and groups through SIDs. A SID is simply a guaranteed unique identification that is associated with one, and only one, user or group in any given deployment. SIDs are guaranteed to be unique for all time; if you have any given user, delete that user, and then later create a new user with exactly the same name and exactly the same attributes, the SID will still be different from the original (and previously deleted) user.

SIDs follow a logical alphanumeric structure; they begin with a section that identifies the domain to which the user or security group belongs, and that is followed by a unique alphanumeric sequence that unambiguously identifies the user or group within the domain. This structure enables Windows 2000 to quickly identify domain membership for a given user or group. All authorization to use objects in Windows 2000, implemented in the security descriptor of each object with ACEs (collectively termed the DACL) is based on SIDs.

## Security Tokens

Users generally belong to a number of groups. As such, their access permissions are cumulative; if a user belongs to one group that has read access to a particular object and to another group that has read and write access to the object, the user has read and write permissions to the object.

When a user attempts to access a given object, all of the user's permissions must be checked against the object's security descriptor to fully evaluate whether the user has permission (and what kind of permission) to access the object. To reflect the need to collect all permissions a user has, Windows 2000 packages all SIDs associated with a user or group when attempting to access a given object. This collection of SIDs is called a *security token*.

### SIDs Outside Active Directory Services

SIDs, security descriptors, and DACLs aren't used solely by Active Directory services. You're probably already familiar with SIDs and ACEs because they've been used for a long time in Microsoft Windows NT to secure all sorts of network resources. The approach hasn't changed in Windows 2000; files and other network resources outside the Active Directory information repository still use security primitives to secure their resources.

For example, NTFS partitions use SIDs and security descriptors to determine which users can perform various tasks (such as read, write, or delete) on a given file. Although files that reside on an NTFS partition are not objects in Active Directory, they can share in the Windows 2000 security infrastructure because security is built into the Windows 2000 operating system and is pervasive in a Windows 2000 deployment.

## Security Implementation vs. Security Protocols

Regardless of *how* a server or Active Directory services obtains security information, access rights are determined based on a user's access token (which includes any group membership SIDs). It's important to distinguish this security information from the security protocol an operating system uses to ferry the security information from one location (the user's computer or the Active Directory repository) to another. That ferrying mechanism (such as the Kerberos protocol, or NTLM) is separate from the security primitives found in Windows 2000.

This distinction is important because the security information and the security protocol are each very different technologies. The system by which objects in Active Directory and other Windows 2000 network resources are secured can be compared to a system of padlock devices and their combinations. Security descriptors and their associated DACLs can be viewed as the padlocks, and the security tokens can be considered the combinations to the padlocks. The protocols that transport these combinations throughout the network can be viewed simply as delivery people carrying important envelopes (the contents of which are the combinations to the padlocks). Notice that the delivery people aren't part of the padlock-combination pair, even if they *are* an important part of the overall solution. Delivery people can deliver all sorts of things for all sorts of different organizations, and some delivery people are better suited for the job than others.

In the case of Windows 2000, the security implementation is the DACL and security token working relationship (the padlock/combination pair), and the security protocols are

Kerberos and, to a lesser extent in Windows 2000, NTLM (the delivery people). Remembering this distinction can help your understanding of Windows 2000 security overall, and will help when the Kerberos protocol and NTLM are discussed in more detail later in this chapter.

## Active Directory Security

Active Directory services introduces some new concepts and requirements to the security mechanisms in a Windows environment, namely the securing of Active Directory objects and their attributes. This addition to the security requirements of Windows results in a change in the way Windows 2000 handles security (when compared to the way Windows NT 4 handled security), and is a direct result of the availability of Active Directory services' centralized, distributed information repository.

Windows 2000 security and Active Directory are completely integrated. Since Active Directory is capable of scaling to millions of objects, the constraints on the number of users or groups that a given Windows NT 4 domain was capable of servicing (approximately 40,000) are no longer an issue. With the advent of Active Directory, domain controllers no longer require the Security Account Manager (SAM). Also, since the Active Directory repository performs better than the registry approach used in Windows NT, overall performance in Windows 2000 is improved when compared to Windows NT. Plus, since Active Directory is distributed and replicated as multimaster, enabling any domain controller to write changes to the information repository, performance and availability are even further enhanced.

As a result of these performance and security improvements, the number of domains that have to be created for an organization and the complexity of their deployments can be greatly reduced. The integration of Windows 2000, Windows security, and Active Directory can make your job as a network administrator easier. A Windows NT deployment that used to require five domains and a handful of resource domains now, with appropriate OUs and group management, requires only one domain in Windows 2000.

To facilitate the structure of administration that may exist in multidomain Windows NT 4 environments, and as a by-product of its structure and security implementation, Active Directory enables administration of subsets of objects to be delegated, with fine-grained control enabled for certain subsets or containers of objects (for example, all users in a given OU). Furthermore, fine-grained permissions can be based on attributes rather than on the object as a whole (for example, authority to change an office location attribute for all users in a given OU, but not authority to change other user attributes such as passwords or telephone numbers).

These capabilities are all the result of Active Directory services' security implementation. Security implementation is not only reasonably simple and straightforward, it is also powerful and flexible, and as a result, highly administrator-friendly.

**Tip**   Secure your domain controllers both electronically and physically. Because domain controllers contain the Active Directory information repository, they should be treated as mission-critical and organizational secret-holding servers. One good way to electronically secure them is to allow only administrators to log on interactively to the console of a domain controller. This keeps would-be traitors from getting through the front door regardless of the security you have inside. Physically securing your domain controllers is important, too, and I discuss some strategies for doing so later in this chapter.

## Object and Attribute Security

As you know, everything stored in Active Directory is represented as an object, and every object contains a set of attributes. Every object in Active Directory is secured based on Windows 2000 security descriptors. Each object's security descriptor has a DACL associated with it that protects permissions to the object. However, Active Directory takes access to and administration of objects one step further—each *attribute* for each object in Active Directory can be configured for different permissions. This enables object attributes to be configured for different permissions.

Object security settings can be configured in any of the following ways:

- Security settings can apply to the entire object, including all of its attributes.
- Security settings can apply to a group of attributes, defined by property sets within the object itself.
- Security settings can apply to an individual attribute of the object.

The best and most efficient security scenario involves setting permissions at the highest point in the object hierarchy as possible, and then making exceptions for groups within that hierarchy. The most efficient approach to setting policies or DACL permissions is to apply them to a large group (say, an entire OU) and then configure exceptions to those general policies and permissions. Often, such an approach to policy and permission settings can save an administrator lots of work. The default permission for the creator of an object is read/write access to all properties of the object.

**Caution**   Remember the golden rule of policy settings in Windows 2000: denying access overrules allowing access. This is similar to the overriding "No Access" rule in Windows NT. For example, if you deny a large group—let's say sales OU members—read/write access to an object and then make exceptions for a nested group or subgroup—for example, sales OU administrators that allow read/write access to the object—the exception won't stick. That's because the members of the subgroup are members of a larger group that has been denied access. Remember this when making exception settings; it can save you a whole bunch of headaches in the troubleshooting process. One way to avoid this situation is to *start* with the enabling permissions, and then make restrictive exceptions for subgroups using the Deny access permissions.

Another useful approach is setting permissions on a given property set, which is a grouping of object attributes that apply to all objects of a particular type. The configuration of property sets (which attributes belong to which property set) is customized by modifying the schema. For more information on working with the schema, see Chapter 14, "Administratively Leveraging Active Directory Services."

## Inheritance

Active Directory handles permission settings on a container object differently than it handles permissions on objects within that container. Container objects can also have fine-grained access control applied to them, but the effect of certain permission requirements affects all objects within the container. For example, if you set permission requirements on the creation of objects such as users in a given OU container, you can designate who has permission to create new users in a given OU. By doing so, you can effectively delegate—and control—who has the capability to create users in a given OU. This marriage of security and delegation is explored further in Chapter 9, "Managing Active Directory Services."

Associated with the concept of placing particular access rights on a container is how objects that are created within a container (which can be either subcontainers or, in the case of an object that can contain no other objects, *leaf* objects) inherit access right settings. There are two kinds of access control inheritance: dynamic inheritance and static inheritance.

With dynamic inheritance, an object's access control settings are dynamically determined each time a query on the object is performed by computing the collective access rights of its own permissions and all cumulative permissions of its parent objects throughout the directory. While this approach provides a certain degree of flexibility, the obvious problem with this is that each attempted query results in significant computational overhead, since the permissions of all parents of a given object must be calculated.

With static inheritance, the permissions for a given object are calculated only once—at the time the object is created—at which time the cumulative permissions for the parent or container object are merged with the object's default permissions to create the access control settings for the object. After such calculation of access rights, all queries determine the permission settings of that object by calculating access rights at that object only. The advantage of this approach is that queries can be performed with much less computational overhead and with much more efficiency. (You only evaluate the object itself for permissions, rather than having to evaluate and compute permissions for all its parent objects.) The trade-off, however, is that permissions applied to a parent object or objects after the creation of an object do not automatically flow down to a child object; if such permission inheritance is required after the creation of a given object, that inheritance of permissions must be manually propagated down the container hierarchy.

Windows 2000 implements a form of static inheritance called *Create Time inheritance*. With Create Time inheritance, the access control information that flows from the parent object to child objects can be defined, but after the creation of the object (and the configured inheritance of access rights at creation time), any changes to parent object access rights must be specifically propagated by the administrator.

### Password Security

If there is one object attribute that is most sensitive to security, it is the user's password. In any Active Directory deployment, if the security of a user's username and password is breached, all sorts of damage or loss can occur. Windows 2000 and Active Directory have been designed to minimize this risk by making password storage as secure as possible.

Passwords are not stored directly in Active Directory. Instead, the password attribute of user objects is an encrypted string that is derived from the password. Administrators can choose from several algorithms to encrypt passwords. Decryption of this password-derived encryption string requires a system key, and an administrator can protect a system by choosing where it is stored (such as on some sort of removable media).

Note also that access to a user object's password attribute is never granted to any users other than the owner of the password. (Administrators are unable to access password attributes.) To facilitate authentication of or changes to passwords, Windows 2000 allows only processes with the Trusted Computer Base privilege—a privilege granted only to processes running in the security context of the Local Security Authority (LSA)—to read or change the password attributes.

## Directory Database Security

Active Directory secures its information repository by handling queries in a special fashion. Rather than securing its object and object attributes by placing only Windows 2000 DACLs on the objects and object attributes, Active Directory services takes its database security further by disallowing users and applications from gaining direct access to the information repository. Active Directory requires that queries against its information repository be routed through the supported Active Directory Service Interfaces (ADSI) application programming interfaces (API) calls, which connect to the *Directory Service Agent* (DSA). The DSA then executes the query on the user's or application's behalf. The DSA is a protected process that is integrated with the domain controller's primary security process—the LSA.

The DSA executes the query using a mechanism called *impersonation*. With impersonation, Active Directory uses the security credentials (the security token) of the querying entity and has the DSA make the query to the Active Directory object or objects necessary to satisfy the query. If the security credentials of the querying entity are not sufficient to satisfy the query, the DSA does not provide the requested information.

Because only the DSA can gain access to the physical information store and because the DSA is integrated with the LSA, the Active Directory information repository is kept at "arm's length" from any queries, which ensures that the directory and its objects remain secure.

# Understanding the Windows 2000 Security Infrastructure

Now that Windows 2000 security primitives and basic Active Directory security concepts have been covered, the discussion can turn to how Windows 2000 creates a network-capable security infrastructure that is robust, scalable, and capable of being considered a secure and distributed enterprise-class directory service solution. As mentioned previously in this chapter, a distinction must be made between the security implementation (which uses SIDs and DACLs) and Windows 2000 security protocols (such as Kerberos and NTLM). The security implementation has already been explained in this chapter with the coverage of Windows 2000 security and Active Directory security. But all of the security offered by Windows 2000 and Active Directory is nullified if security information cannot be secured as it traverses the network. Such secure transit of security information is achieved through the primary security protocol: the Kerberos protocol.

Remember if you will the analogy I discussed earlier in this chapter that compared the security implementation in Windows 2000 to a system of padlocks and combinations. Recall that an object's DACL is like a padlock, a user's token is like a combination, and a security protocol is like the delivery person who delivers the combination used to unlock the padlock.

Windows 2000 provides the following security protocols:

- Kerberos V5
- NTLM
- Digital certificates (which map to a Windows 2000 user account)
- Secure Sockets Layer/Transport Layer Security (SSL/TLS)

There is good reason for so many protocols; each of these security protocols are appropriate for different situations:

- **Kerberos V5** protocol is appropriate for most Windows 2000 logon and authentication situations, and is the default authentication method for Windows 2000.

- **NTLM** is provided mainly for backward compatibility with deployments running Windows NT 4 and earlier, as well as computers running Windows 3.11. NTLM is also used to authenticate logons between stand-alone Windows 2000 computers (that is, Windows 2000 computers that are not participating in a Windows 2000 domain).

- **Digital certificates** are appropriate for use with a PKI deployment and are especially useful for authentication of outside users to your organization's Windows 2000 and Active Directory deployment. The use of PKI authentication, with its digital certificates and Certificate Authorities, will become more prevalent as the deployment of PKI in corporations, organizations, and the Internet becomes a more common occurrence.

- **SSL/TLS** is appropriate for connection-oriented security, such as access to Web-based resources on an intranet or the Internet.

The creation of a security infrastructure like the Windows 2000 security infrastructure creates lots of otherwise unavailable capabilities. In fact, the security infrastructure in Windows 2000 may be the single most important engine behind the enterprise-class directory service-based features of Windows 2000. With its deployment, the idea of one big network (essentially, the absorption of corporate networks into the Internet) with highly and completely secured sections (such as a corporation's network boundaries) can become a reality. Perhaps this won't happen overnight, but with the standards compliance, scalability, and robust security of Windows 2000, the foundations are there especially with the availability of the PKI.

For starters, though, let's concentrate on how you can use the security protocols in Windows 2000 to create a secure environment within your organization's network infrastructure. Creating that environment starts with understanding how the Windows 2000 security infrastructure operates, and that starts with understanding the first step in any network environment: logon.

## Logon, Authentication, and Authorization

Logon, authentication, and authorization are all very distinct events, but the distinctions among them are often lost in the blur of getting onto the network. These three events— logon, authentication, and authorization—form the basis on which nearly all security events occur. Understanding the difference between each is important to understanding the way Windows 2000 implements security and how Kerberos and other security protocols function.

### Logon

Logging on to a Windows 2000 distributed network environment is a process we generally take for granted; you enter your username and password, and if you don't mistype anything, you're granted access to the system. However, what's going on behind the scenes is more complicated, and it's necessary to understand the behind-the-scenes details of the logon process to understand the operational details of authentication.

When you log on to a Windows 2000 computer, you present a username and password to the interactive logon screen. Interactive logon is handled by Winlogon, which runs in a shared process with the LSA. When you log on, you are actually authenticating your logon information with the LSA on the Windows 2000 computer at which you type in your credentials. If your logon credentials specify that your user account is based on the local computer, Winlogon passes your credentials to LSA, which compares those credentials to accounts located on the local machine. If your logon credentials specify membership in a Windows 2000 domain, Winlogon passes your credentials to the LSA, which then checks with a domain controller to ensure that your username and password are the same as those stored in Active Directory. If they are, you are authenticated. Notice that when your credentials specify a Windows 2000 domain, the LSA is not directly authenticating you; rather, it is checking with Active Directory to ensure your credentials are valid. It is important to understand that the LSA on the Windows 2000 computer you're logging onto doesn't authenticate you itself, but rather it uses Active Directory to do so and *trusts* Active Directory's response.

As a result, logon at any Windows 2000 computer is the same. You don't have to maintain an account on the individual Windows 2000 computer as long as that computer is a member of a Windows 2000 domain, you have a valid user account in the Windows 2000 domain or forest, and you have credentials that allow you to log on to that computer. Regardless of where the logon credentials reside, as long as the LSA on the Windows 2000 computer can trust the credentials you provide, you can log on to the computer (or the domain or forest, as appropriate). The LSA then caches your credentials for use whenever you attempt to authorize use of an object throughout the course of your logon session. Those credentials are cached in volatile memory and flushed upon logoff for security reasons.

One of the primary benefits of the Windows 2000 logon approach, which is made possible by the Winlogon/LSA authorization steps outlined, is that you need to log on only once to access all the network resources you are authorized to use. The alternative is that you log on to a Windows computer and then re-enter your username and password every time you need to use a network resource, which can be very inconvenient. With this single sign-on approach of Windows 2000 and the implementation of the open standard Kerberos security protocol, all network resource permissions are based on your Windows 2000 user account. Therefore, all attempts to access network resources subsequent to your logging on use the credentials you supplied at logon. With the centralized security infrastructure of Windows 2000 and the integration of Kerberos V5, single sign-on can become a reality. Other contributing factors that make single sign-on a big deal are discussed later in this chapter in the "Understanding Public Key Infrastructure" section.

## Authentication

Authentication is the process of proving that you are who you say you are, or in more technical terms, the process of authenticating your identity. In Windows 2000, this process generally consists of providing a username and the corresponding password.

## Authorization

Logon occurs once per logon session (kind of self-evident, I know). Authentication in Windows 2000 also generally happens once per logon session, though under certain circumstances it can happen more than once per logon session. Authorization, on the other hand, occurs frequently during any given logon session; in fact, it occurs every time a user attempts to access a secured object or resource.

Authorization is not the same as authentication. Authentication is the process of proving your identity, while authorization is the process of determining whether you (the authenticated you) have sufficient permissions to access a given object. Authorization is determined by comparing a security principal's access rights against the security descriptors of a given object. If the security principal (such as a user) is authorized to use the object in the way it requests, the requested use of the object is permitted. In Windows 2000, the Windows 2000 security subsystem determines whether a given query has authorization to carry out its requested task (such as reading the attribute of an Active Directory object).

## Understanding the Kerberos Protocol

The Kerberos protocol provides a secure means of mutual authentication between two nodes—generally a client and a server. Sitting between this duo, Kerberos becomes the necessary third party that's trusted by both members of the duo (the client and the server). In an authentication transaction, the Kerberos protocol acts as a sort of trust escrow that enables both client and server to securely conduct their network transactions. This three-party approach is where Kerberos got its name; Kerberos (Cerberus for you Roman mythology fans) was the three-headed dog that guarded the entrance to Hades.

The Kerberos protocol is divided into three services. The first service authenticates users at logon (Authentication Service [AS] Exchange); the second service provides time-sensitive session keys, or tickets, with which clients can authenticate themselves to network servers (Ticket Granting Service [TGS] Exchange); and the third service facilitates the interaction between a ticket-holding client and the server to which the ticket provides access (Client/Server [CS] Exchange). Before I explain the details of how each of these services operates, however, some additional information about the basic premises on which the Kerberos protocol functions needs to be presented.

### Kerberos Basics

The Kerberos protocol operates on the premise of a secret that is shared by only two entities; if two (and only two) computers share that secret, each can verify the other's identity by determining whether the other computer knows the secret.

The Kerberos protocol also functions on the premise that the network over which such validation is occurring is not secure. It presumes that users are sitting on the wire, listening to data going back and forth and attempting to gain unauthorized access to resources based on what information can be gleaned from monitoring network traffic. Therefore, the Kerberos protocol takes great steps to ensure that users of its protocol (both clients and servers) are protected against such rogue users.

The *Key Distribution Center* (KDC) is the computer service that employs the Kerberos protocol as the third-party escrow in the secured authentication transaction. The KDC is a service that runs on all Windows 2000 domain controllers; it is fundamental to Windows 2000 security. A Kerberos service also runs on all Windows 2000 computers, both clients and servers, enabling them to partake in Kerberos-enabled authentication activities.

As mentioned previously, the Kerberos protocol operates on the premise of a shared secret; the Kerberos protocol implements this shared secret as a session key that enables holders of that session key to encrypt or decrypt data. Since that session key (which can also be considered an encryption/decryption key) is held by only two entities, data encrypted with the session key on one entity (the client) can be decrypted only by the other key holder, the server. The importance of these session keys is realized when they are used to prove that the holders of the keys (the client and server) are who they say they are. The process by which this occurs is explained in the next few sections.

The Kerberos protocol is a bit of a slippery protocol to understand. To help facilitate the process of understanding it, I've boiled the basics down into several bulleted lists and provided an illustration in Figure 8-1.

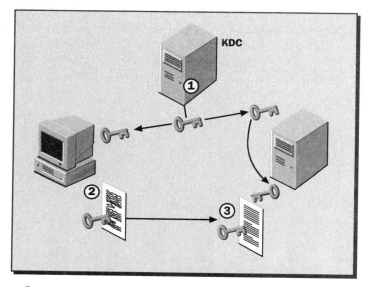

① KDC provides a unique key to a client and server that want to communicate in a secure way.

② Client encrypts information with the unique key.

③ Server uses its copy of the key to decrypt information sent by the client. Since only this client and this server share the unique key (their "secret") both are assured that the data is safe and genuine.

**Figure 8-1.** *Kerberos Basics.*

Kerberos involves three computers:

- The client
- The server
- The KDC (the trusted escrow officer in the security transaction)

The Kerberos protocol consists of three basic services:

- AS Exchange (used at initial logon, at which time a ticket granting ticket is obtained)

- TGS Exchange (which provides time-sensitive session keys for use by client)
- CS Exchange (a client/server exchange in which TGS session keys are used)

The following are Kerberos facts:

- Kerberos operates on the premise of a shared secret.
- The KDC runs on all domain controllers.
- KDC security information is integrated with Active Directory.

As the processes and steps involved with Kerberos authentication are explained, I'll continue to use this boiled-down approach to make sure things are clear.

## Kerberos Authentication with AS Exchange

The Kerberos protocol provides a better approach to authentication than just throwing usernames and passwords across a network. As you can imagine, submitting your username and password in an unsecured network environment is, well, not a secure way of doing things. Since the KDC is *the* trusted authority in a Windows 2000 deployment, all other servers and resources in a given Windows 2000 domain can operate on the premise that once you've authenticated yourself to the KDC, that's good enough authentication for them (the servers and other resources). This is somewhat akin to going to a carnival, paying a cover price at the gate to get a ticket-stamp placed on your hand, and then gaining admittance to all the rides you want by simply showing your ticket-stamped hand. Ride operators trust that the ticket-stamp you have on your hand authenticates that you paid the cover price. They *trust* the ticket-stamp and as a result *admit* you onto the rides.

When you first log on to a Windows 2000 network, you receive something like a ticket-stamp. It's called a ticket granting ticket (TGT). Figure 8-2 shows how the process occurs.

1. The password typed in at logon is converted to an encryption key by the Kerberos client software running on the client, and the encryption key is packaged with a local timestamp that is encrypted with the user's *long-term key*. (The long-term key, which is derived from a user's password, is stored in Active Directory as part of the user object.) This encrypted timestamp is called *pre-authentication data*.

2. The encryption key (derived from the password) and the pre-authentication data are sent to the KDC in the form of a KRB_AS_REQ message, using Transmission Control Protocol (TCP) on port 88 of the KDC's Internet Protocol (IP) address.

3. The KDC—which resides on a domain controller—receives the message, decrypts the pre-authentication data by retrieving the user's long-term key from Active Directory, and then evaluates the timestamp. If the timestamp passes, the KDC can be assured that the request is timely and that the user has knowledge of the account's long-term key; to the KDC, the client is authenticated. To pass means that the timestamp is within a specified time interval, which is set by default to five minutes of local or timeserver time.

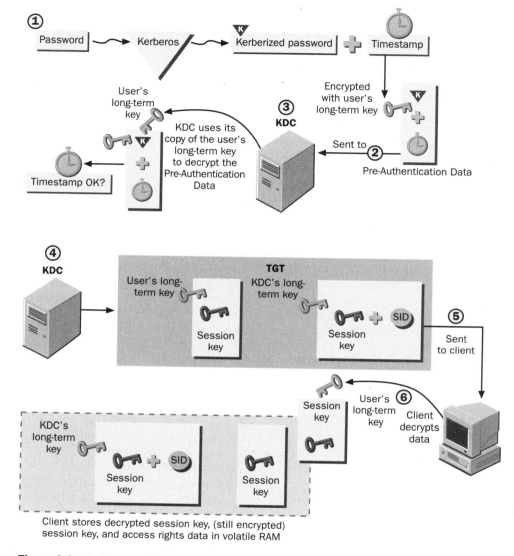

**Figure 8-2.** *Kerberos authentication with AS Exchange.*

4.  The KDC creates a unique session key and encrypts it with the user's long-term key. The KDC then creates a copy of the unique session key, adds access rights information about the user in the form of a security token, and encrypts

all that data with its *own* long-term key. This collection of data constitutes the TGT. If this process is taking place in a multidomain environment, the KDC checks the Global Catalog for any groups to which the user might belong and adds any it finds to the security token.

5.  The KDC sends the session key (encrypted with the user's long-term key) and the TGT (encrypted with the KDC's long-term key) back to the client in the form of a KRB_AS_REP message, using TCP on port 88 of the KDC's IP address.

6.  The client decrypts the session key (encrypted with the user's long-term key) and stores both the session key and the encrypted TGT in a volatile cache that is destroyed upon logoff.

At this point, the client has a TGT and is ready to request access to various servers or resources located throughout the Windows 2000 forest. The client is *authenticated*. From this point forward, all exchanges with Windows 2000 servers or other Windows 2000 computers, including domain controllers, are performed using this session key and the TGT.

One point to note about step 1: the user's password undergoes a *one-way hash* before it is passed as the encryption key to the KDC. A one-way hash, as its name suggests, is a one-way encryption that is not decryptable. When the hashed password reaches the KDC (which *is* Active Directory), the KDC performs the same hash algorithm on the user's password (because the KDC, through Active Directory, has access to the password). If the hash results in the same encryption key as was provided by the client, the KDC can be assured that the password is correct. Note that this enables the password to be unambiguously verified *without* transmitting the password over the wire.

### KDC Interaction with TGS Exchange

Once authenticated—that is, once they have a TGT—clients can request access to Kerberized resources (resources that are secured using the Kerberos protocol).

> **Note**   TGTs are not valid indefinitely. You've noticed that timestamps are involved in many of the encrypted items going back and forth between the KDC and the client; this enables the Kerberos protocol to keep reinventing new session keys. By inventing new session keys and invalidating old ones, the Kerberos protocol is better equipped to keep attackers further at bay. Security attackers can't grab a network exchange, work on cracking it for a few days, and then come back and use it on the network; it'll be invalid. TGTs are no exception; though configurable, the default setting for the expiration of a TGT is eight hours—a common time frame associated with logon sessions.

Once a user logs on, authenticates with a KDC and receives its TGT, it's ready to request access to Kerberized resources. Figure 8-3 and steps 1 through 5 show how this process works:

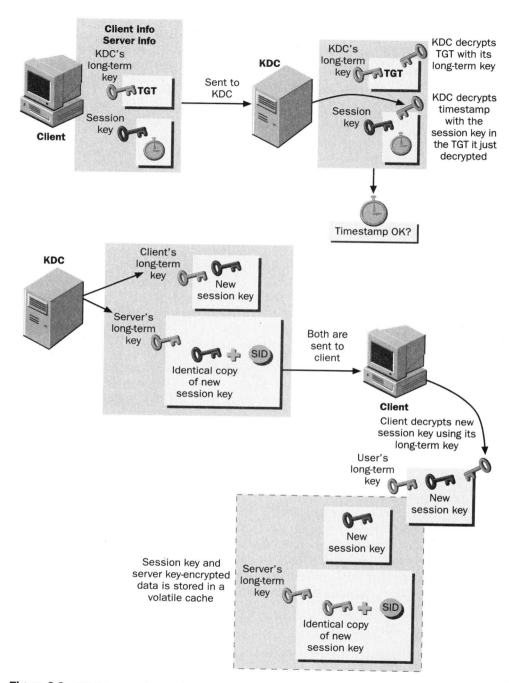

**Figure 8-3.** *KDC interaction with TGS Exchange.*

1. The client sends a service request to the KDC in the form of a KRB_TGS_REQ message. The contents of the message include the name of the client (Client1), the name of the server (Server1), a timestamp encrypted with the session key (obtained at the end of the AS Exchange), and the TGT.

2. The KDC decrypts the TGT (which it can do because the TGT is encrypted with the KDC's long-term key), and uses the enclosed session key to decrypt the timestamp submitted with the message. If the TGT and timestamp are valid, the KDC goes to the next step.

3. The KDC creates two copies of a brand-new session key. This new session key will be used later in the CS Exchange that occurs between the client and the server.

4. The KDC encrypts one copy of the brand-new session key with the client's long-term key. The KDC then packages the second copy of the new session key with the client's security token, and encrypts the entire package with the server's long-term key. The KDC then returns the client key-encrypted session key, as well as the server key-encrypted data package (which includes a copy of the session key as well as the client's security token) back to the client, in the form of a KRB_TGS_REP message, using TCP on port 88 of the KDC's IP address.

5. The client receives the KRB_TGS_REP message, decrypts its copy of the session key (with its own long-term key), and stores the decrypted session key as well as the server-key-encrypted package in a volatile cache that is destroyed at logoff.

There are a few items worth noting about the TGS Exchange. First of all, no passwords are traversing the wire in this exchange. That means exposure to would-be attackers is minimized because, even if they were to capture a sequence of packets, there would be no passwords to extract.

Next, the timestamp mentioned in step 1 is often called an *authenticator*, but rather than add further mental computational overhead to the process of understanding TGS Exchange, I've called it a timestamp throughout this discussion. It's possible, but unlikely, that authenticators other than a timestamp could be used.

And finally, once the KDC provides the client with the KRB_TGS_REP message (and its contents), the KDC steps out of the picture. This is important from an efficiency and performance standpoint; once a client gets a ticket to access resources on a server (which is what this sequence does), the need to contact and interact with a domain controller is completed. With NTLM, client contact with a server required the server to in turn contact a domain controller to authenticate the credentials of the client; such inefficiencies are not part of the Kerberos security protocol.

Once the client gets this ticket from the KDC, it can contact the server directly through a CS Exchange.

### Client/Server Interaction with CS Exchange

With a TGS ticket in cache, a client is ready to gain access to the requested server's resources, but it must first establish a session with the target server and, through Kerberos-specified steps, present the authority with which it claims access rights to said resources. These steps are collectively called the CS Exchange.

The CS Exchange, as the client/server acronym prefix implies, involves only the client and its targeted server. (To clarify and to help with the explanation of this exchange, I've renamed the "brand-new session key" I mentioned in the previous section. In this section, it's called the "client-server session key".) Figure 8-4 and steps 1 through 5 show how the CS Exchange works.

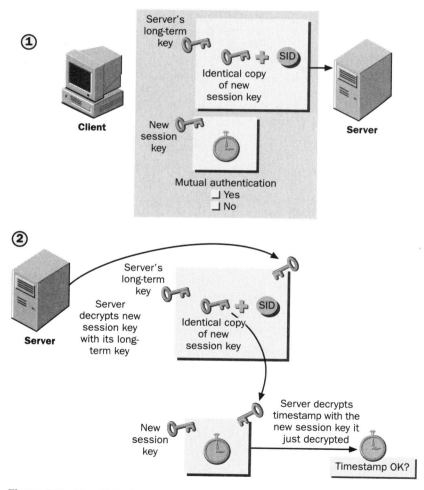

**Figure 8-4.** *The CS Exchange.*

1. The client creates an information package to send to the server; this package consists of a timestamp encrypted with the client/server session key, the ticket received from the TGS Exchange (which is encrypted with the server's long-term key), and a flag that indicates whether the client wants *mutual authentication*. The client puts this package into a KRB_AP_REQ message and sends it to the server.

2. The server decrypts the ticket (which only the server can do, since the ticket is encrypted in the server's long-term session key), which contains the client's security token. The server checks the validity of the timestamp, and then checks whether the client is requesting mutual authentication. If mutual authentication is not requested, the process proceeds to step 5.

3. If mutual authentication is requested, the server extracts the timestamp, packages it with another identifying piece of data, encrypts it with the client/server session key, and sends it back to the client in the form of a KRB_AP_REP message. By placing an additional piece of identifying data in the message, the server assures the client that the server's long-term key was used to decrypt the client/server session key, and that the decrypted session key was then used to encrypt data and send it back. By requiring the additional piece of identifying data, this mutual authentication process precludes attackers from impersonating the server by grabbing the KRB_AP_REQ message and simply sending it back (without the additional piece of identifying data).

4. If mutual authentication is requested, the client receives the KRB_AP_REQ message and decrypts the returned timestamp and additional piece of identifying data. The client can thus be assured that the server is authentic.

5. Authentication is complete, and the connection is established.

This process of a client and server exchanging information in a shared-secret manner, with the KDC as the "escrow officer" that authenticates the identity of both client and server, occurs whenever a Windows 2000 client needs to gain access to a Windows 2000 server. As such, these steps have taken the place of NTLM authentication procedures in a pure Windows 2000 environment or an environment where all clients are capable of Kerberos authentication.

## Kerberos Implementation Specifics

With the basics of the Kerberos protocol explained and the steps of its three exchanges enumerated, some of the finer and more specific implementation features and capabilities of the Kerberos protocol can be discussed. These features, as you can imagine in a book about Active Directory services, are often the result of the Windows 2000 security infrastructure's tight integration with Active Directory services.

### Standards

The Windows 2000 implementation of Kerberos adheres to the Internet Engineering Task Force (IETF) Request for Comments (RFC) 1510, which provides implementation recommendations for the Kerberos authentication protocol. While Windows 2000 implements the RFC 1510 recommendations, it also extends the recommendations in certain places. Where appropriate, Windows 2000 uses alternative implementation methods. For example, since Active Directory services has a specific replication implementation, Windows 2000 does not use RFC 1510's replication protocol. RFC 1510 also recommends using User Datagram Protocol (UDP) to submit Kerberos messages, but UDP is appropriate only when the data package can fit into a single datagram, which equates to 1500 bytes on an Ethernet. Since security tokens in Windows 2000 can be much larger than 1500 bytes, TCP is a better transport mechanism than UDP, and therefore TCP is used instead of UDP for Kerberos messages.

**Note** In Windows 2000, the Windows 2000 domain is equivalent to a Kerberos *realm*.

### Implementation

Like all security protocols in Windows 2000, the Kerberos protocol is implemented as a security support provider—which means that it's implemented as a dynamic link library (DLL) that is supplied with Windows 2000—and it is loaded by the LSA when the system boots. NTLM is also loaded upon system bootup; however, the Kerberos protocol is always the first security protocol chosen.

The KDC is implemented on every domain controller as a single process that runs in the process space of the LSA, even though the KDC's two services—the AS Exchange and the TGS Exchange—provide logically different functions. The user account, or security principal, that the KDC uses is called krbtgt; this account cannot be deleted from Active Directory. Just like the clients and servers that use the KDC, the KDC itself derives its long-term key and session keys from its password.

### Features and Benefits

The Kerberos protocol is a superior security protocol to NTLM. The following list describes many of the features and benefits of the Kerberos protocol. It also presents compelling reasons why the Kerberos protocol is the default security protocol for Windows 2000 and why you should consider making the Kerberos protocol the only authentication protocol in your Windows 2000/Active Directory deployment.

- The Kerberos protocol provides faster authentication and creates less ongoing authentication load on domain controllers than NTLM.

- Windows 2000 implements extensions to the Kerberos protocol that enable support of authentication based on public/private key pairs, which are the building blocks of a public key infrastructure. PKI is discussed in more detail in the next section.

- Since the Kerberos protocol implements a symmetric shared-key secret (vs. asymmetric keys, as found in PKI), which means that encryption and decryption are not extremely expensive to use for encrypting bulk data, the client/server session key can also be used to encrypt data transmitted back and forth across the client/server connection.

- The KDC is involved only in AS Exchange and TGS Exchange; the CS Exchange involves only the client and server. Though the steps outlined in the earlier sections explain this, it's an important point to reiterate because it enables the Kerberos protocol to scale efficiently.

- The KDC doesn't track tickets; it just watches for attack-like activity. This enables the Kerberos protocol and the KDC to provide superior performance.

### Customization

An administrator can configure and customize some features of the KDC and the Kerberos protocol so that the Kerberos protocol will better fit your deployment's requirements. Configuration of the Kerberos protocol is done at the domain level, providing further policy flexibility in the domain structure of your Windows 2000 deployment. You must be a member of the Domain Administrators group to modify Kerberos settings. These modifications include the following:

- **Allow forwardable tickets:** Allowing forwardable tickets enables servers to request TGS tickets when their services require that a user-initiated application or request access another server. Essentially, the server acts and makes requests on the client's behalf. Forwardable tickets require a forwardable TGT, which the client requests in the AS Exchange. With Group Policy, forwarding ticket settings can also be configured for individual servers and groups.

- **Allow renewable tickets:** Allowing renewable tickets enables clients to renew Kerberos tickets to avoid ticket expiration during a given connection or logon session. Note that TGS tickets are necessary only at the beginning of a server connection; and therefore, once a client is authenticated the connection won't be interrupted even if the TGT ticket expires, since the session will already have been established.

- **Setting maximum ticket age:**  Setting the maximum ticket age specifies the amount of time a TGT ticket is valid. The default value is eight hours.

- **Setting maximum ticket renewal age:** Setting the maximum ticket renewal age specifies the maximum ticket age at which a granted ticket can be renewed and after which renewal is revoked and a new ticket must be obtained.

- **Setting maximum proxy ticket age:** Setting the maximum proxy ticket age specifies the maximum time that a proxy ticket is valid. Proxy tickets are used for back-end servers and are passed to the front-end server that will initiate connections to the back-end server (on the client's request). Proxy tickets allow for secured multitiered application implementations.

- **Forcibly log off users when tickets expire:** Configuring the Kerberos protocol to forcibly log off users when their TGT ticket expires is self-explanatory.

**Real World**

You can increase your Active Directory deployment's security and authentication performance by making the Kerberos protocol the only security protocol in your Windows 2000 deployment. If you do this, you can even map UNIX-based Kerberos credentials to Active Directory user accounts. You'll also need to upgrade all of your clients to support Kerberos authentication. If you aren't using Windows 2000 on all your clients, you can upgrade Windows 95, Windows 98, and Windows NT 4 Server and Workstation computers to the Distributed Security Client. The Distributed Security Client software is available free from *http://www.microsoft.com* and includes Kerberos V5 security software.

## Understanding Public Key Infrastructure

With the widespread acceptance of the Internet and its effect on our computing environments, new security requirements are being placed on enterprise networks. In an effort to provide IT professionals with the tools necessary to adapt to and account for this shift into network openness and connectivity, Windows 2000 includes the tools necessary to deploy a PKI in your organization.

A PKI is just a collection of capabilities that are built into a given network deployment. Taken together, these capabilities enable administrators or other IT professionals to build a secure network authentication system based on public key technology. This collection of components is not too terribly long. The elements of a PKI are as follows:

- Digital certificates
- Certificate services
- Policies to manage the distribution and administration of certificates
- Additionally, to support the use of Smart Cards, which are becoming increasingly popular, PKI can also include Smart Card support.

Implied in this short list of PKI requirements, however, is the capability of the network environment to manage the distribution of certificates and their corresponding public keys. In order for PKI to be anything more than a good idea, a centralized location (preferably a centralized and distributed information store) must exist to manage the retrieval and storage of certificates, which are certificate service publications. As you might have guessed, that centralized repository is available with the advent of Active Directory. And to further integrate with Windows 2000 and Active Directory, a PKI using digital certificates can map the users of such digital certificates to Windows 2000 user accounts in Active Directory.

### PKI Basics

A PKI operates on a handful of basic premises. You need to understand these basic premises to understand how certificate services provide the foundation on which a PKI is created. Rather than begin with a bunch of presumptions about the simple requirements of certificate services, without which later explanations would be foggy at best, let's start from the beginning.

Basic security over a shared medium, such as today's corporate or organization network environment, starts with encryption. Encryption is the process of scrambling data before sending it over a shared medium, such as the corporate network or the Internet. Scrambling data before sending it over the network makes it much more difficult for would-be listeners to read the data than if it were in plain text. In order for authorized recipients to understand the encrypted data, however, they must be able to decrypt it, so the sender and the receiver of data must somehow agree on how to encrypt and then decrypt data. Data is scrambled, or encrypted, with something called a key (such as a session key that's used in the Kerberos authentication process). There are two types of keys in encryption technology: *symmetric keys* and *asymmetric keys*.

Symmetric keys are just what you would expect them to be; they are identical. Symmetric keys are similar to house keys, in that multiple keys to your house are identical, and any copy of the house key can be used to lock or unlock your house's front door. The Kerberos protocol session keys are an example of symmetric keys used in encryption and identity validation.

Asymmetric keys are not identical. When asymmetric keys are used in encryption key technology, two keys form a key pair. As such, if one key is used to encrypt data, the other key must be used to decrypt that data. Asymmetric keys are somewhat similar to the keys that are used to open safety deposit boxes at your local bank; you keep one key to your safety deposit box in your possession, and the bank keeps another key to your box that is not identical to your key. Both keys must be used to unlock the box. With asymmetric key pairs, one key is generally a public key (often made public by being published in some central repository such as Active Directory). The other key is called the private key, and it must be secured such that no one but its owner has access to it. Asymmetric keys in cryptography are generally referred to as a key pair.

With key pairs (asymmetric encryption technology), if one key is used to encrypt data, the corresponding key is used to decrypt the data. Either key can encrypt or decrypt, but the corresponding key is required to perform the opposite function (decrypting or encrypting, respectively). If the key that decrypts the data is not available, then the encrypted data will remain in its unreadable, encrypted state, and is therefore useless. This use of one of the keys to encrypt and the other (corresponding) key to decrypt is the foundation of certificate services.

In this key-pair system, it's no big deal if someone has your public key; as far as you're concerned, they can encrypt all the data they want with your public key because doing so doesn't threaten any of your sensitive data. However, keeping your private key secure is imperative. How do you keep your private key secure on a shared medium? Never send it out. Private keys are never transmitted across a shared medium, whereas public keys can be sent to anyone who wants them.

## Digital Certificates

Public and private keys alone do not provide sufficient protection against attacks in the shared network environment of today's enterprise networks and the Internet. What if an attacker attempts to infiltrate your network environment by using your public key (which is, by definition, available) to impersonate a server with which you're communicating? You believe that you're communicating with Server1, but in fact someone is intercepting the data and impersonating Server1 with their own data. How do you protect yourself against something like this? PKI provides protection against this kind of attack through the implementation of digital signatures, digital envelopes, and digital certificates—a veritable digital post office.

## The Digital Post Office

The problem with using public and private keys alone is that with any given communication with a server, you can't be assured that you're really communicating with the server that you think you're communicating with. Someone could be *spoofing* the information, or making it appear as though you're exchanging information with your favorite file server, when in fact you're exchanging information with some hacker's file server who intends to take your information and do all sorts of bad things with it. How would you know if such bad things are happening on your network? You wouldn't, unless the data was signed in a way that allowed you to verify, unquestionably, that the server you're communicating with (your favorite file server, in this example) is actually the server you think it is. This is a job for the digital post office.

The process of encryption and the security that a digital post office can provide are often compared to the process of sending a letter. Included in this analogy is a comparison of a secured network delivery to a delivery going through a post office. There are three technologies included in this digital post office:

- Digital envelopes
- Digital signatures
- Digital certificates

## Digital envelopes

Digital envelopes are actually already familiar. To say that you put information in a digital envelope is another way of saying that data has been encrypted for secure transmission across the network using someone's public key. You can equate using digital envelopes to using privacy envelopes to send letters and checks to friends and bill collectors (that is, envelopes that are not see-through).

## Digital signatures

Digital signatures are a bit of a variation on the encryption theme, because they aren't used to scramble information. Instead, as the name implies, a digital signature is used to digitally sign a piece of data, thereby confirming the identity of the sender of the data. Digital signatures leverage the public/private key relationship and take advantage of public key availability, in a very smart approach to authorship verification. The following example illustrates how digital signatures work.

Jack wants to send Ronald a message. (Perhaps the message is about an ongoing discussion they're having over which of them makes the best hamburger.) Jack not only wants to encrypt the message, but he also wants Ronald to be able to verify that Jack sent the message. Jack includes a string—the digital signature—in his message to Ronald that is encrypted with his (Jack's) private key. Remember: either the private key or the public key can encrypt data, the other key provides the opposite function. Ronald uses Jack's public key to decrypt the signature and thereby verifies Jack's identity as the sender of the message.

Why does this work? Because only Jack has access to Jack's private key, and the relationship between Jack's private key and public key is such that verification of Jack's digital signature will be successful only if it is actually generated (and encrypted) by Jack's private key. All public keys are available to everyone. They have to be—otherwise, no one would be able to send encrypted data to anyone else. Ronald therefore has easy access to Jack's public key and can verify the digital signature. Notice that during this entire process, Jack's private key is never sent over the wire, yet he can uniquely sign (place a digital signature in) messages that are, thereby, verifiably sent by him.

## Digital certificates

Digital certificates are one of the primary elements of a PKI and are used to verify a user's identity. With digital envelopes and digital signatures, there is a fundamental assumption that all parties are who they say they are. But what about spoofing, where a user attempts to impersonate another user? A given user may have a public/private key pair that identifies the user, but how can you verify their identity? With digital certificates and a trusted Certificate Authority (CA), you can be assured that the server is not being spoofed. This trust relationship between the client, server, and trusted entity (the CA in this case) is similar to the trust relationship involved with the Kerberos protocol, in which the client and server trust the KDC as authenticator of the client (and server).

The difference between using digital certificates with a CA and using simply the Kerberos protocol with its KDC is that CAs can be used when the client or server (or both) does not belong to the KDC's realm—such as a Windows 2000 domain (or trusted domain). Digital certificates and a trusted CA, therefore, can provide a Kerberos-like trusted third-party environment for users outside your network's security borders.

The relationship between digital certificates and CAs goes even further: a CA is the creator and issuer of encryption keys, which are the basis of security in any digital certificate. The function of a digital certificate is to validate the identity of a given user, and a digital certificate contains a complete set of information about its owner, including the entity's public key. The CA is also the issuer of digital certificates (and therefore, the creator of the public/private key pair, the public key half of which is included in each user's digital certificate).

For digital certificates to be of any real value, all parties must trust the issuer (the CA) of these digital certificates. To use the phrase most commonly heard when discussing digital certificates, the issuer of the digital certificates must be a mutually trusted entity, just like the KDC in the Kerberos protocol must be trusted by the client and server involved in a Kerberos-based authentication. On the Internet, one example of a CA is VeriSign. In Windows 2000, Microsoft provides Microsoft Certificate Server givng you the capability to create (and therefore, control and manage) your own PKI.

Digital certificates generally follow the X.509 standard, which was developed at the IETF as the public key infrastructure (PKIX) recommendation. SSL digital certificates are also X.509 certificates, which means they meet standardization criteria for electronic certificates as set forth in the X.509 standard. An X.509 certificate (and thus all SSL digital certificates) contains the following fields:

- Version
- Serial number
- Signature algorithm ID
- Issuer name
- Validity period
- Subject user name
- Subject public key information
- Issuer unique ID
- Subject unique identifier
- Extensions
- Signature on the above fields

Note that SSL/TLS certificates also conform to the X.509 standard. When certificate services are implemented in an Active Directory or PKI deployment, Windows 2000 administrators can use Active Directory services administration tools to map external users (users who present their digital certificates) to one or more Windows 2000 user accounts for the application of access rights (permissions) to enterprise resources. Windows 2000 then uses the Subject field (the Subject user name listed above) to identify the user associated with the certificate. With such identification, Windows 2000 and Microsoft Certificate Server can map that identified user to a user account stored in Active Directory.

Just like Kerberos tickets, digital certificates are subject to expiration and rejection, so just because an entity gets a certificate, that doesn't mean that the entity is free to roam forever with their authenticated identification. Just like a drivers license or student ID card, digital certificates can expire, and they can be revoked by the issuer.

## Certificate Services

In a Windows 2000 deployment, you can operate—and thereby manage and control policies for—your own certificate services. As you might imagine, certificate services are integrated with Active Directory, and they contribute significantly to the ways in which Active Directory secures your enterprise's environment, the information repository managed by Active Directory, and other network resources.

Certificate services are based on a CA. A CA is an application that implements certificate services by issuing, managing, and revoking digital certificates that are based on the X.509 standard.

**Note**   When Microsoft Certificate Server is integrated with Active Directory services, it is considered an Enterprise certification authority. It is possible to deploy Microsoft Certificate Server on a computer that does not depend on Active Directory for its information store and publication of pertinent certificate information; in this case, the deployment of Microsoft Certificate Server in Windows 2000 is considered a stand-alone certification authority.

By enabling organizations to be their own CA, Windows 2000 enables organizations to avoid dependence on an outside CA. Doing so provides the capability for organizations to create customizable, manageable strong security solutions that can be tailored to an organization's needs. When compared to using an external CA, Microsoft Certificate Server gives an organization more autonomy over the issuance, requirements, and revocation of digital certificates. There are plenty of reasons why such autonomy is useful. These reasons include the following capabilities of Microsoft Certificate Server:

- Component architecture
- Flexibility
- Scalability
- Abstraction from specific key validation techniques
- Industry standard implementation

These features enable Microsoft Certificate Server's capability to provide a robust, scalable, and customizable PKI. Understanding how these features do so is important to understanding how Active Directory can further secure your Windows 2000 deployment.

### Component Architecture

Just like Windows 2000, Certificate Server has been engineered with a component architecture that enables customization of certain aspects of its functionality without having to build an entirely new program with each required customization. Certificate Server's component architecture is like a bookshelf that comes with adjustable shelf-holders and shelves. Similar to that customizable bookshelf, Certificate Server's architecture comes with customizable components such as the server engine and exit modules. Unlike a bookshelf that comes with glue and screws and a limited number of shelves that can't be moved, the component-based bookshelf allows you to customize it to your needs and adjust it as your needs change.

Like a bookshelf made up of adjustable components, the Certificate Server's architecture consists of a handful of components. These include:

- The intermediary
- The server engine
- The server database
- A component group that handles certificate activity
- Exit modules

The *intermediary* is like an interface, or transmission format front-end, for Certificate Server. For example, Microsoft Internet Information Server (IIS) is an intermediary for HTTP-based certificate requests. The intermediary, in abstract terms, comprises two components. The first component is the intermediary application that acts on behalf of clients that want certificate services. The second component, called the Certificate Server Client Interface, handles communication between the intermediary application and Certificate Server's server engine.

The *server engine* is the core of Certificate Server's component-based architecture. The server engine handles and redirects requests, from initial contact through certificate generation. At each stage of the process, the server engine interacts with all components to make sure all necessary procedures are carried out appropriately.

The *server database* contains certificate information and keeps a log of all certificates that have been issued. Microsoft Certificate Server is integrated with Active Directory services, which means that the server database component of Microsoft Certificate Server immediately gains all of the robustness, security, scalability, and distribution features that are inherently available with Active Directory. The server database component—that is, the Active Directory information repository—also maintains Certificate Revocation Lists (CRLs). With the logging, administrators can keep detailed information about certificates that were requested, rejected, authenticated, and otherwise handled by Certificate Server. Active Directory also maintains a status queue of all pending certificate processes.

The "component group" doesn't have a proper name, but it enables a Microsoft Certificate Server deployment to extensively customize the *issuance, creation,* and *authentication* process of digital certificates.

- **Issuance:** The issuance of digital certificates can be customized by customizing the policy module. A policy module is a set of rules that determine how digital certificates are issued, renewed, and revoked. Whenever a request is received by Microsoft Certificate Server, it is passed to the policy module for validation and is thereby either approved or revoked. By customizing the policy module, an organization can customize the policies by which digital certificates are issued, renewed, or revoked.

- **Creation:** The creation of digital certificates is a process that requires the cooperation of the policy module and extension handlers. Extension handlers set customized additions, or fields, on a digital certificate. With the addition of extension handlers, digital certificates can be customized to have additional information, which is created with extension handlers and subsequently parsed by the policy module to create a customized digital certificate solution.

- **Authentication:** Authentication is abstracted from Microsoft Certificate Server. Microsoft Certificate Server doesn't handle the process of key authentication; the authentication process is passed on to the cryptographic service provider or providers (CSPs) installed on the system and configured to handle key validation. Windows 2000 comes with a number of CSPs, including RSA (developed by Ronald Rivest, Adi Shamir and Leonard Adleman, and the name is a combination of the first letters of their last names), Diffie-Hellman (developed by Whitfield Diffie and Martin Hellman), and DSS (developed by the National Security Agency and adopted by the United States government as its digital signature standard). The abstraction of authentication means that Microsoft Certificate Server doesn't do any authenticating on its own; it instead relies on a customizable module accessed through the CryptoAPI.

*Exit modules* handle the publication of certificates and the publication of CRLs. In Windows 2000, Microsoft Certificate Server has an exit module that publishes CRLs in Active Directory services. There can be more than one exit module installed and running on Microsoft Certificate Server, and by default, Microsoft Certificate Server will notify each exit module whenever a certificate or CRL is issued. Exit modules can be written in the Component Object Model (COM) interface, allowing them to notify any entity or directory of the publication of a certificate or CRL. This entity could also be a database—perhaps an accounting database that charges customers based on their use of a site.

## Flexibility

Microsoft Certificate Server has a great deal of flexibility built into its architecture. Organizations can take advantage of this flexibility in many ways. For example, an online auto parts distributor might set up terms with the stores to which it ships its products; with Microsoft Certificate Server, the distributor could require that credit terms be submitted through e-mail to the accounting department. After accounting has authorized a certain line of credit, the store might be issued a digital certificate, which allows the store into a secured section of the distributor's Web site, where online orders can be placed up to the store's credit limit. By implementing Microsoft Certificate Server, the distributor can place its own requirements for how certificates are issued, and if a store falls out of grace with the accounting department, the distributor can easily revoke that store's digital certificate. This independence and internal management of certificates allow the distributor lots of flexibility with how it implements and uses Microsoft Certificate Server.

## Scalability

Certificate Server is scalable because it is integrated with Active Directory and therefore inherits the Active Directory scalability features.

## Key Validation Abstraction

Key validation techniques define how keys are implemented with regard to validating a user's identity. As mentioned earlier, Microsoft Certificate Server employs the CryptoAPI. The CryptoAPI is modular because it has replaceable components. These components, known as CSPs actually perform the cryptographic functionality. This ability to replace the "engine" that encrypts the data means that an organization can get the level of cryptographic sophistication appropriate for its needs.

Microsoft Certificate Server relies on the CryptoAPI, and thereby relies on the CSP being implemented on Certificate Server, to handle the management of keys. Because Certificate Server is isolated from handling keys, the keys are as secure as the CSP being implemented on the system. This CSP could be anything from standard software modules to hardware-based key generation devices such as FORTEZZA cards. The result is that Microsoft Certificate Server can be as secure as an organization needs it to be, based on replaceable encryption components.

### Industry Standards

Microsoft Certificate Server issues certificates based on the X.509 version 1.0 and 3.0 digital certificate standard specifications. In addition to this standard, Certificate Server accepts certificate requests based on the PKCS #10 request standard.

## Certificate Service Operation

As part of the PKI, any certificate service must perform three primary functions in its certificate handling:

- Accept certificate requests
- Process certificate requests
- Maintain Certificate Authority status

The following sections explain how Microsoft Certificate Server performs these tasks, which can help you deploy a PKI based on Active Directory that's tailored to your organization's needs.

### Accepting Certificate Requests

Microsoft Certificate Server accepts certificate requests from client (or servers) that wish to use Certificate Server as the identifying authority for secure communication over shared mediums such as the Internet. The process of issuing a certificate to an entity, whether that's a client or a server, is called *enrollment*; when a client has been issued a digital certificate from Certificate Server, certificate enrollment for that client has taken place.

### Processing Certificate Requests

From the user's perspective, the process just happens, and depending on whether the user is a client or a Web server administrator, the certificate is automatically installed on the computer or returned as a saved file. For Microsoft Certificate Server, there's more going on. The processing of a certificate request actually has a few steps to it.

- **Receiving the request:** The certificate request is received by the intermediary and sent in the industry standard PKCS #10 format to Microsoft Certificate Server's server engine.
- **Approving the request:** The server engine passes the request to the policy module, which processes the request and determines whether the request is approved (and sets optional properties in the certificate, if applicable).
- **Creating the certificate:** If the policy module approves the certificate request, the server engine creates a complete digital certificate based on the request (and any optional properties set by the policy module, if applicable) and signs the certificate with its (Microsoft Certificate Server's) private key.

- **Publishing the certificate:** When certificate creation is complete, the server engine stores the completed certificate and notifies the intermediary. At this point, any exit modules that have been installed are also notified through an issuance event. This notification allows exit modules to further process the issuance of the certificate (not the certificate itself), such as publishing the certificate to Active Directory. Once the exit modules have been notified, the intermediary is provided with the certificate, which it passes on to the client.

### Maintaining CA Status

The process of maintaining CA status is a bit more involved than the other primary Certificate Service functions and thus requires a longer explanation.

A CA is a certificate issuing and maintenance entity, such as VeriSign or a Microsoft Certificate Server deployment. A CA has the authority and capability to authenticate the identity of any client or server that has been issued one of its (the Certificate Authority's) certificates.

The CA is the mutually trusted third party that is responsible for validating that an entity (client or server) is who it says it is. CAs also issue a certificate that is specific to them, but this certificate works a little differently than certificates they issue for clients and servers. This CA certificate is the key that enables entities to confirm the signatures a CA puts on any of its issued certificates; this approach is similar to how a Kerberos KDC encrypts TGTs it issues with its own (the KDC's) ticket, enabling the KDC to subsequently verify its validity.

A certificate server that issues certificates is also a CA. (It must be a CA if you want others to trust the certificates it issues.) A CA creates a certificate for itself and makes that certificate publicly available, thereby allowing users (clients or servers) to validate the authenticity of certificates it has issued. This process of validation occurs by using the CA's publicly available certificate (which contains the CA's public key) to decrypt and thereby validate the signature the CA puts on its issued certificates.

The somewhat confusing part of this client-server relationship comes with client-validation or server-validation of a CA. Figure 8-5 and steps 1 through 3 show this process.

1. When a client attempts to access a network server based on a digital certificate, it requests a copy of that server's digital certificate.

2. Because the client also wants to confirm the validity of the certificate, the client locates the central certificate store and gets a copy of the certificate that belongs to the CA that issued the server's certificate. That central certificate store is Active Directory if the CA is Microsoft Certificate Server.

3. With the public key included in the CA's certificate, the client decrypts the signature on the server's certificate and thereby validates the identity of the server to which the client is connecting. Why is the server's identity validated? Because the digital signature on the server's certificate has been encrypted with the CA's private key; if that digital signature can be verified (decrypted) with the CA's public key, then that verifies the certificate is valid because the client and server trust the CA.

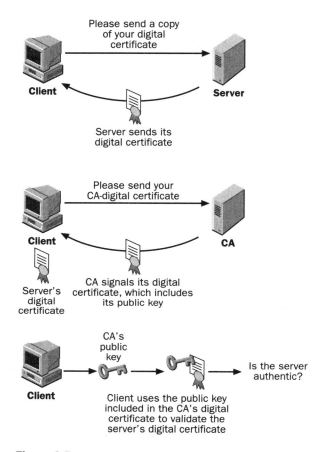

**Figure 8-5.** *Maintaining CA status.*

## Policies

If you deploy Microsoft Certificate Server in your enterprise (vs. using third-party certificate services) and thereby create a PKI within your organization, you can implement policies for certificates that fit your organization's security needs.

Policies can shape the requirements that are placed on decisions, such as the requirements for a given user to receive a certificate. (Does the user have to appear in person to make the application?) Other policies—such as revocation of certificates (a list of which is published for public access in the form of a Certificate Revocation List, or CRL), renewal procedures, and expiration periods—can also be implemented.

## Smart Card Support

Smart Card support is becoming more prevalent as shared network resources need to be secured from some users (both inside and outside an organization) but accessed by other users. Smart Cards are security devices that come in card form and are approximately the size of a PCMCIA card.

Windows 2000 Server and Windows 2000 Advanced Server support the use of Smart Card logon. Smart Cards maintain X.509 certificates in their memory, which when used in conjunction with a Smart Card reader and Windows 2000, enables logon to deviate from the standard username/password pair. Generally, Smart Cards require that a user type a certain PIN number, which in conjunction with the Smart Card itself and the X.509 digital certificate contained therein, enables a user to be authenticated in a PKI. Kerberos standards–permitted extensions are also implemented for Smart Card interaction on Windows 2000, enabling users to authenticate to the KDC using Smart Card technology.

# Understanding SSL/TLS

Another form of security available with Windows 2000 and Active Directory services is Secure Sockets Layer (SSL). The SSL 3.0 standard, which defines how SSL should be implemented, is the basis for another security standard, called Transport Layer Security (TLS). TLS was ratified by the IETF in RFC 2246. While TLS 1.0 differs slightly from SSL 3.0, a TLS server can securely communicate with an SSL client, and vice versa. From this point forward, the term SSL will be used to jointly mean SSL and TLS.

SSL differs from its approach to providing security in a Windows 2000 environment; primarily, SSL can be used to enable users *outside* a given organization to create a secure channel with servers *in* the organization. This capability is particularly useful for Web applications, such as electronic commerce applications, and is most often implemented for Internet information services.

SSL is a piece of software that sits between TCP and the application layer. When enabled, SSL provides a secure communication channel between a user and a server by implementing RSA data security encryption. SSL is implemented through the use of a DLL called schannel.dll. Invocation of SSL is transparent to users; when SSL is needed for a given connection, it is automatically implemented without user intervention.

SSL provides three important functions:

- SSL authenticates that data is being sent to its intended server and that the server is secure.
- SSL encrypts data as it travels between a client and a server.
- SSL ensures that data received by the server hasn't been tampered with along the way.

## SSL Sessions

In basic terms, an SSL session is an encrypted line of communication between a client and the server. However, the process of getting an encrypted communication line that only the client and server can understand requires a bit of work. This process is the bedrock of today's electronic security, and SSL shares its encryption roots with the likes of the Kerberos protocol and digital certificates.

SSL works on the basis of an asymmetric, or a public/private, key pair. Using digital certificates does not change the premise on which private and public keys operate. One can easily decrypt digital certificates from a particular digital certificate issuing authority by using the issuer's widely available public key. But to encrypt a certificate without the issuer's private key (that is, to create a forged certificate that will work with a certificate issuer's widely available public key) is not feasible because of the complex mathematical nature of encryption encoding.

The following steps explain what happens during an SSL session:

1. The client establishes a connection to the server.
2. The server sends its digital certificate along with its public key.
3. The client and the server negotiate encryption depth—40 bit or 128 bit. Due to export laws, 128-bit encryption is available only within the U.S. and Canada.
4. The client randomly generates a session key and encrypts the session key with the server's public key. The session key—which has been encrypted with the server's public key—can be decrypted only with the server's private key, so the session key is secure as it is transmitted over the wire.
5. The server decrypts the session key, and a unique secure communications channel is established between the client and server, because all data will be encrypted or decrypted with the randomly generated session key.

You might have noticed that there are a lot of similarities between this sequence of events and the events that occur in a Kerberos authentication session and in a PKI-enabled digital certificate verification exchange. Notice that in SSL sessions, as with Kerberos sessions and PKI exchanges, no private keys were ever transmitted over the network. Also notice that session keys are randomly generated. The breadth of available randomized keys is so immense that correctly guessing the session key is computationally unfeasible, which goes a long way in thwarting attacks from rogue users listening to the shared-medium wire.

If a given server is configured to require a client certificate (in the previous example, only a server certificate was required), the following steps are added to the process:

1. The server requests a digital certificate from the client.
2. The client sends its digital certificate along with its public key.

With client certificate authentication, three items must be taken into consideration, all of which are mainly concerned with the ability of the protocol (SSL) and the server to handle client certificates:

- The protocol must be able to handle server and client certificates, which includes the appropriate responses and replies. SSL 2.0 does not have the ability to handle client certificates; SSL 3.0 does.
- The client must be able to handle the exchange of certificates, including verification of server certificates and the presentation, storage, and management of its own certificate, when requested.
- The server must be able to handle certificate requests and verifications and, just as importantly, map client certificates to ACLs on the server.

The use of SSL security doesn't come for free: implementation of SSL, with its data encryption and use of digital certificates, puts additional load on the server's CPU and adds to the communication traffic between the client and the server. While NTFS user permission security also introduces some processing overhead, the impact of NTFS security is minimal. Because SSL's impact on CPU and bandwidth performance is not negligible, it should be carefully evaluated during the planning phase of any Windows 2000 security deployment.

# Security and Active Directory Deployments

Many of Active Directory services' features are direct results of the tight integration between Active Directory and Windows 2000 security. The following sections explain how Active Directory deployments make use of the security features available as a result of the integration of the Windows 2000 security subsystem and Active Directory.

## Security and Domain Trusts

Windows 2000 domains create transitive trusts between the parent and child domains in a domain tree, and the root domain in each domain tree create transitive trusts with other root domains in the forest. These transitive trusts that each parent-child pair of domains in a given Windows 2000 domain hierarchy establishes are Kerberos trusts.

Windows 2000 allows clients that have been provided with a TGT in one domain to use that TGT as proof of authentication for access to resources in other Windows 2000 domains in the forest. This is possible because Windows 2000 domains establish transitive trust relationships with other domains in the tree or forest. Specifically, each parent domain shares an interdomain session key with its child domain; this interdomain session key enables referral tickets to be encrypted and passed back and forth for authentication purposes between these two domains. It is this chain of interdomain keys that enable users in one domain within the tree hierarchy to establish connections with resources in other domains in the tree hierarchy.

Figure 8-6 and the following steps should illustrate how the trust relationships work. Consider a Windows 2000 domain tree hierarchy that consists of four domains, A, B, C, and S. A is the domain at the top of the hierarchy, B is its child, and C is a child of B. Domain S is also a child of A. Given this hierarchy, imagine that a user in domain C wants to gain access to a server in domain S. The following would occur:

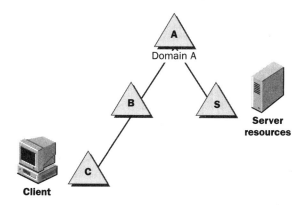

**Figure 8-6.** *Security and Domain Trusts.*

1. The client sends an access request (a TGS request) to a KDC in its own domain—domain C.

2. The KDC in domain C figures out that the server to which the client wants to gain access resides in domain S. In response, the KDC in domain C passes a *referral ticket* to the client. The referral ticket is actually a TGT encrypted with the interdomain session key that the KDC in domain C shares with the KDCs in domain B. By sending this referral ticket back to the client, the KDC in domain C is referring the client to the KDC in domain B.

3. The client receives the referral ticket and submits the request to the KDC in the referred domain—domain B.

4. The KDC in domain B figures out that the server to which the client wants to gain access resides in domain S. The KDC in domain B responds by sending a referral ticket (encrypted with the interdomain session key it shares with domain *A*) back to the client, referring the client to domain A.

5. The client receives the referral ticket and submits the request to the KDC in the referred domain; this time, it's domain A.

6. The KDC in domain A figures out the server is in domain S. The KDC in domain A sends the client a referral ticket (a TGT) that points to the KDC in domain S. This referral ticket has been encrypted with the interdomain session key that domain A shares with domain S. The KDC in domain A shares a session ticket with domain S because there is a direct parent-child domain relationship between domains A and S.

7.   The client gets the referral and submits a request to the KDC in domain S, which can then finally create the session keys and TGS messages necessary to enable the client to establish a CS Exchange with the server in domain S.

This process is really involved, and as you may have guessed, you take a performance hit every time an interdomain referral is made. You might be thinking that it would be a lot easier and save more time if each domain simply established trust relationships with all other domains in the forest (that is, created and maintained session keys for every domain in the forest). That wouldn't be such a good solution because one of the requirements of Windows 2000 and Active Directory is that they scale to very large organizations. The maintenance involved in creating and tracking all those domain-to-domain keys would hinder its scalability.

Recall from Chapter 3, however, that you can create a cross-link trust between two domains that do not have a parent-child relationship and essentially cut through the referral process involved in "walking" the domain tree. As you might have guessed, creating a cross-link trust between domains instructs these domains to create and establish an interdomain session key and to share that key between their domains. This sharing enables single-step referrals from one domain to the (cross-connected) next possible.

## Physical Security

One part of security that absolutely cannot be overlooked in an Active Directory deployment is the matter of physical security in the network and in the organization's physical structure. Simply put, you can have all the security protocols in the world securing your network transactions , but if you don't take steps to secure your servers and your wiring closets, you're opening up your deployment to the possibility of a serious breach in security.

One reason that you need to physically secure your Windows 2000 computers—and especially all of your domain controllers—is that you must protect keys used in Kerberos authentication sessions—session keys as well as the more coveted long-term keys.

If you have deployed a PKI and used Microsoft Certificate Server as your CA—thereby integrating the storage of public and *private* keys into Active Directory—you have another element of security to be concerned with in your deployment—protecting the private keys kept in Active Directory. As was mentioned in an earlier section, private keys unlock encrypted data in an asymmetric (public/private) key environment. If you aren't taking steps to secure each replication and partition of your Active Directory deployment, you're putting the security of those private keys at risk.

OK, so enough with the doomsday, fire-and-brimstone warnings about securing your physical servers. Now it's time for some recommendations as to how you can go about implementing physical security in your Active Directory—and Windows 2000—distributed network environment.

### Equipment Room Lockdown

The first step you should take is to secure your equipment rooms. These are the rooms in which your routers and switches reside and in which important servers such as domain controllers are often placed. These rooms are generally scattered throughout your organization's buildings, campus, or floors—whichever the case may be. Securing these rooms means putting locks on the doors. Plenty of manufacturers make numerically coded locking mechanisms. With these mechanisms, you punch in a code and the door unlocks. Fumbling with a padlock can be a bit cumbersome, not to mention it makes your equipment room wiring closet look like some sort of garden tool shed. And if your CIO sees that the $500,000 worth of networking equipment and wiring the company has purchased is being secured with a $3 padlock, he or she might seriously question your judgment. In the grand scheme of things, $50 on a decent lock is a small price to pay to secure your equipment room and impress the CIO.

If you've placed your servers—whether they're Windows 2000 domain controllers, Windows 2000 Advanced Server clusters, or IIS Web farms—in a different location than your wiring or equipment room, use locks there as well. You can disperse the combinations to the locks for these rooms (which, just like passwords, should be changed periodically) among appropriate administrators, further securing the room. If an administrator leaves or is let go (that's the nice term for *fired*), make it a point to change the locks right away. You don't have to distrust an administrator to take this step; changing the locks is just a precaution.

Remember that certain forms of malicious mischief or even worse—something like a tap into your Ethernet network to capture data with a sniffer—don't require direct access to your servers. Though network connections don't guarantee access to your data, especially with the way that the Kerberos protocol uses session keys and encryption to electronically tighten the security on Windows 2000 resources, keeping your equipment room safe from bad-doers (or those in your company who believe they can fix their problems by modifying where their network tap is plugged into) should be part of your security plan.

### Server Security

Not all servers are conveniently located in some numeric–keypad lockable equipment room; some of them are in areas that aren't so easily secured. Many enterprise-sized servers have lockable cabinets. If you have a server like this, and if further security is desirable, throw a padlock on the server. The casual thief won't be prepared to deal with such obstacles, and that alone could save you a few thousand dollars or more in drives, RAM, or processors and the time needed to replace all of this equipment.

Another means of protecting your servers (domain controllers or others) is to disable or actually disconnect your servers' floppy disk drives. Make sure to do this to your domain controller. If there's no floppy disk drive on the server, it's hard to boot from it. It's also hard to introduce a virus from a floppy disk if the floppy disk drive isn't connected to the server.

Most servers these days also can be booted from a CD. Once your server has been loaded with Windows 2000 Server or Advanced Server (presuming a new install from a CD), you should disable the Boot From CD option in the BIOS and then password-protect the BIOS.

> **Tip**   You can boot from a CD and get right into the installation process.

## Net Tap Protection

There is the possibility that hackers who are interested in getting to your data could tap into your network by splicing a network cable and listen to what's going back and forth over the wire. A lot can be discovered about a network by listening to what floats through the wiring of the infrastructure, but the eavesdropper would need equipment that can either store all the data or know what data to filter out. The eavesdropper also needs the proper tools to quickly splice and repair the wire and the tap. The Kerberos protocol protects against such eavesdropping, which is a compelling reason to make the Kerberos protocol the only security protocol in the deployment. However, such eavesdropping could still do damage—not all data that a Kerberos-authenticated user pulls from any given server is necessarily encrypted. Eavesdropping could pose an attack threat. While such eavesdropping is not a common occurrence, if it's going to happen, it will happen on a network that uses copper cabling.

Why copper? Because with the right tools, an eavesdropper can cut, splice, tap into, and then repair a copper wire, such as CAT 5, within the course of a minute or so. Depending on where the cut was made, a user could have a minute of outage or an entire subnet could have the minute of outage, but in the time it takes to call the system administrator to fix or look into the problem, network connectivity would return. All would be back to normal, with one exception: the person who created the network tap is gathering and analyzing every packet going over the wire.

There are two ways to protect yourself from this intrusion: encrypt the data you send over the network, or use fiber-optic cable to cable unsecured areas.

### Encrypting Your Network Data

When you encrypt the data you send over the wire to protect it from eavesdroppers, consider the international implications of doing so. Make sure you follows the U.S. government's exportation and encryption laws and guidelines.

Encrypting the data you send over the network may require special encryption software. That is, you might have to put some of the unassuming features of the Routing and Remote Access Software (RRAS) of Windows 2000 to special use. You should make RRAS and its Virtual Private Network capabilities your encryption software. RRAS can be used to secure LAN environments by encrypting data that goes over the local network. In short, you can create a Point-to-Point Tunneling Protocol (PPTP) tunnel between two subnets that might be transmitting particularly sensitive information, and by sending all data through RRAS servers on either end (with the "encrypt transmitted data" choice selected), you can encrypt data as it traverses part of the physical LAN infrastructure.

### Using Fiber-Optic Cable

The means by which fiber transmits data from one node to the other requires specific parameters and communication protocols. Luckily, fiber-optic cable doesn't take well to being spliced or tapped. This is good news to those who need secure access or secure extensions to their network, but whose network cabling must go through areas in which physical security is unsatisfactory.

For example, if two sections of your network are divided by a street that runs between buildings, your organization may have the rights to run cabling between the buildings, but what you probably don't have is the right to limit access to the conduit running between the buildings—a conduit that may be located in a utility easement of some sort.

If your organization deals with secrets (whether trade, defense, or others) that must electronically pass between these buildings (and therefore through the accessible easement under the street) and if you use copper wiring, the conduit through which your network cabling runs can be a compromising area of your deployment's security. If conspirators working against you were able to get to that conduit and tap into your copper wiring, they could capture every packet going across that link and do whatever they wanted with the data—like use all sorts of off-site processing power to crack whatever encryption you've placed on your data. How do you avoid such compromising cabling? Use fiber in the conduit. It's more expensive than copper, but it isn't nearly as susceptible to tapping.

There are other obvious benefits of fiber: fiber enables longer runs, offers higher throughput (with proper hardware on either end of the connection), and is less sensitive to electrical disturbance.

### Physical Security—The Bottom Line

While all of these physical security measures might sound like overkill or paranoia, keep this in mind: just because you're paranoid doesn't mean someone isn't after you (or in this case, after your servers).

# Chapter 9
# Managing Active Directory Services

When any deployment is put into service, whether it is a Microsoft Windows 2000/Active Directory services deployment, a router deployment, or an application deployment, administrators lean back in their chairs, take a deep breath and a sip of coffee, and then start managing the deployment. Management goes hand in hand with a deployment and often starts even before the deployment is completed. Clearly, then, you need information about managing Active Directory services.

This chapter provides you with the Active Directory services management information you need and provides a comprehensive treatment of issues specific to Active Directory management, such as managing replication traffic, performing backups, and managing flexible single-master operation (FSMO) roles. However, many administrators need even more than this Active Directory–specific information; they need to administer the Windows 2000 deployment as a whole, not just Active Directory services. For that reason, I've included information on other administrative tricks and technologies that administrators will hopefully find useful—information like a Group Policy overview, explanations about Windows 2000 command-line utilities, and more. By presenting Active Directory services management information and explaining Windows 2000 management techniques, I hope this chapter will help the jack-of-all-administration manage a Windows 2000 and Active Directory deployment knowledgeably and effectively.

This chapter consists of three primary sections:

- **Everyday Management:** This section covers day-to-day management tasks, such as adding users and creating computer accounts. Though this might sound mundane, the bulk of an administrator's time is spent performing these types of tasks, and the table you'll find in this section that specifies which interface can be used for a given task is a great candidate for repeated referencing. This section starts out with tables that map familiar tasks to their respective Windows 2000 interfaces, explains primary Windows 2000/Active Directory services snap-ins, and concludes with explanations of promoting servers to Active Directory domain controllers, delegating administrative duties, and backing up and restoring Active Directory.

- **Advanced Management:** Tasks that might be performed by specialized groups in your organization are addressed in this section. This section contains explanations of what I'll call enterprise tasks, which are tasks that require an overall view of the health of the enterprise Active Directory services deployment, such as replication configuration and management of FSMO roles. This section also contains information about Group Policy, which is something that policy administrators will be interested in perhaps more than Active Directory administrators. However, Group Policy is important to understand, so its explanation in this book is a must.

- **Command-Line Management:** Windows 2000 has more command-line capabilities than any version of Microsoft Windows NT. This is a sensible approach because lots of administrators find it much easier and faster to administer a deployment from the command line (myself included). No mouse-clicking, no property-sheet-navigating—just quick, parameter-enhanced commands that speed your efforts to run the organization from a small, powerful, character-based interface. In fact, one of the primary tools you'll use to administer Active Directory services is a command-line utility—Ntdsutil. There are many others, and you'll learn about the most prevalent utilities in this final section of the chapter.

## Everyday Management

Everyday management tasks are the common tasks that administrators who work with a Windows 2000/Active Directory services deployment handle on a daily basis. Windows 2000 introduces a new way of performing these tasks, which is a reflection of Microsoft's efforts to make it easier for administrators to do their job by providing centralized administration tools.

Management tasks in Windows 2000 are achieved largely through the use of Microsoft Management Console (MMC) snap-ins. The best way to understand the MMC and its snap-ins is to compare them to a Nintendo system like the Nintendo 64. With a Nintendo system, you have the Nintendo box itself and then you go out and buy cartridges for your favorite game, which you subsequently slip into the Nintendo box and play for hours on end. Without the game cartridge, the Nintendo box just sits there and for the most part is an empty shell. Put a game cartridge into it, however, and it turns into something you can use. The MMC is similar in that you have the shell (the MMC itself) and you load or add snap-ins to communicate with whichever Windows 2000 component you need to administer. For example, if you need to administer your deployment's users and groups, you load the Active Directory Users And Computers snap-in.

**Note** You can have more than one snap-in loaded into the MMC at any given time, and you can even save favorite snap-ins for easy retrieval, just like you save favorites in a Web browser.

When the designers of Windows 2000 took aim at centralizing its administration, they made sure that administrators could easily slip from one administrative interface to the other—something that the MMC and its snap-ins goes a long way in facilitating. Almost everything in Windows 2000 is administered with a snap-in, and all those snap-ins adhere to rigid design and implementation standards geared toward ensuring that similar tasks are carried out with similar steps. This design approach enables administrators who are familiar with a snap-in associated with a particular Windows 2000 component to quickly adapt to administering other Windows 2000 components (or services, or applications). For example, in almost every snap-in in Windows 2000, you can right-click objects to get shortcut menus, so if you right-click a user in the Active Directory Users And Computers snap-in, you get a shortcut menu, as Figure 9-1 illustrates.

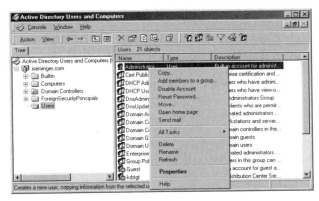

**Figure 9-1.** *Right-clicking a user in the Active Directory Users And Computers snap-in results in the appearance of a shortcut menu.*

If you right-click a snap-in name, you will get a shortcut menu (appropriate for that snap-in) as well, as shown in Figure 9-2.

This consistency of behavior among snap-ins isn't exclusive to Active Directory snap-ins; you'll find it in essentially every snap-in that you can load in Windows 2000. The previous example is just one way in which the design requirements for Windows 2000 snap-ins are geared toward providing a consistent administrative experience for administrators. For administrators, that means learning how to perform the tasks they need to perform just got a lot easier, and it means the way they perform those tasks will be a lot more consistent. Snap-ins are discussed further in the "Using Active Directory Services Snap-Ins" section later in this chapter.

In addition to providing snap-ins, Windows 2000 offers a handful of other ways to carry out administrative tasks, including scripting, programming, and command-line utilities.

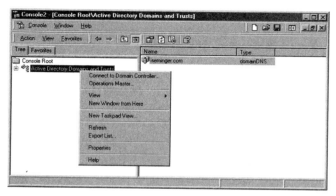

**Figure 9-2.** *Right-clicking the Active Directory Domains And Trusts snap-in generates a shortcut menu also.*

## Mapping Windows NT Tasks to Windows 2000 Interfaces

Many administrators are familiar with the way administrative tasks were carried out in Windows NT 4.0, and the new way of performing similar tasks in Windows 2000 might require some getting used to. Knowing how the tasks you commonly performed with Windows NT are carried out in Windows 2000 can provide you with a big head start on your Windows 2000 administrative effort. Table 9-1 maps Windows NT 4.0 administrative tasks and interfaces to Windows 2000 tasks and interfaces.

**Table 9-1.  How to perform familiar Windows NT tasks in Windows 2000.**

| Task | Windows NT 4.0 | Windows 2000 |
| --- | --- | --- |
| Deploy a domain controller | Windows setup | Active Directory Wizard (dcpromo.exe) |
| Manage user accounts | User Manager | Active Directory Users And Computers snap-in |
| Manage groups | User Manager | Active Directory Users And Computers snap-in |
| Manage account policy | User Manager | Group Policy |
| Manage audit policy | User Manager | Group Policy |
| Add computer accounts | Server Manager | Active Directory Users And Computers snap-in |
| Manage computer accounts | Server Manager | Active Directory Users And Computers snap-in |
| Set policies for users and computers in a site | System Policy Editor | Group Policy (accessed through Active Directory Sites And Services snap-in) |
| Set policies for users and computers in a domain | System Policy Editor | Group Policy (accessed through Active Directory Users And Computers snap-in) |

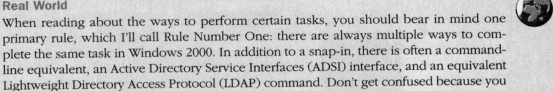

**Real World**

When reading about the ways to perform certain tasks, you should bear in mind one primary rule, which I'll call Rule Number One: there are always multiple ways to complete the same task in Windows 2000. In addition to a snap-in, there is often a command-line equivalent, an Active Directory Service Interfaces (ADSI) interface, and an equivalent Lightweight Directory Access Protocol (LDAP) command. Don't get confused because you thought that you added a user using the snap-in rather than the command-line equivalent; you can use either approach, or you can use other methods. This chapter shows you the most commonly used approach to achieving a task, but that doesn't mean the approach shown is the only way to do it. Use the approach you are most comfortable with, but realize you can probably perform the same task in other ways as well.

You'll probably notice (if you haven't already) that Rule Number One applies to almost any action or task you perform in any Windows operating system, not just in Windows 2000.

## Promoting Windows 2000 Servers to Domain Controllers

The process involved in promoting a Windows 2000 Server computer to a domain controller and thereby making it part of an Active Directory services deployment is fortunately very straightforward. Microsoft has provided an installation wizard, aptly called the Active Directory Installation wizard, to guide you through the process of promoting a Windows 2000 server to a domain controller. Although this process is straightforward, it's at the heart of deploying Active Directory services. Simply put, you can't have Active Directory services in your Windows 2000 environment until you promote a Windows 2000 server to a domain controller.

The following steps walk you through the process of using the Active Directory Installation wizard to promote a server to a domain controller. You can choose options throughout your process that are different than the options shown in these steps, depending on your deployment.

1.  Launch the Configure Your Server application, which is found in the Administrative Tools program group. Click the Start button, point to Programs, then point to Administrative Tools and click on Configure Your Server. When the the Windows 2000 Configure Your Server window appears, in the left pane, click Active Directory. The Windows 2000 Configure Your Server dialog box should look like Figure 9-3.

2.  Scroll down in the Configure Your Server dialog box. Click the link shown in Figure 9-4 to start the Active Directory Installation wizard.

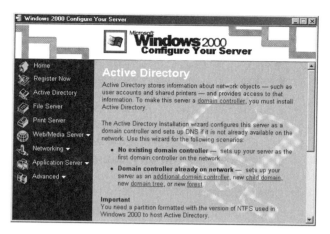

**Figure 9-3.** *The Windows 2000 Configure Your Server dialog box.*

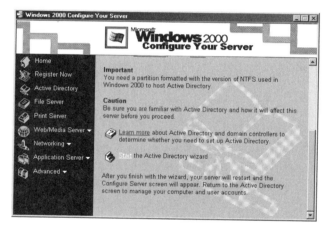

**Figure 9-4.** *The Start The Active Directory Wizard link.*

When you click the link, Windows 2000 greets you with the Active Directory Installation wizard welcome screen, as shown in Figure 9-5.

3. Click Next in the welcome screen. You're presented with the first of a progression of wizard screens that walk you through the first part of the server promotion process, solicit input that directs the wizard to take appropriate actions, and provide you with choices based on your input. The Domain Controller Type screen, shown in Figure 9-6, enables you to make a server a domain controller for a new domain or to make it another domain controller in an existing domain. In this example, I selected the first option.

**Figure 9-5.** *The welcome screen of the Active Directory Installation wizard.*

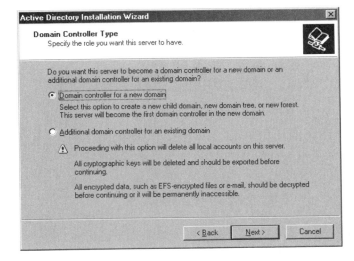

**Figure 9-6.** *The Domain Controller Type screen.*

4.   Click Next to display the Create Tree Or Child Domain screen. In this screen, you choose whether to create a new domain tree or a child domain in an existing tree. I selected the Create A New Domain Tree option, as shown in Figure 9-7.

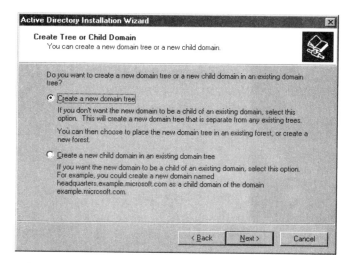

**Figure 9-7.** *The Create Tree Or Child Domain screen.*

5.  Click Next to display the Create Or Join Forest screen, as shown in Figure 9-8. Here you choose whether to create a new forest or to place a new domain tree into an existing forest. I selected the Create A New Forest Of Domain Trees option.

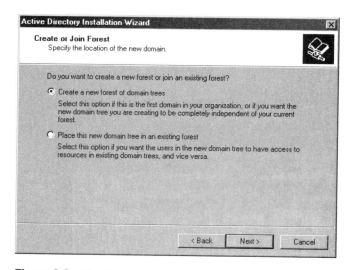

**Figure 9-8.** *The Create Or Join Forest screen.*

6.  Click Next to display the New Domain Name screen, as shown in Figure 9-9. Here you can type the DNS name.

7.  Click Next again to display the NetBIOS Domain Name screen, as shown in Figure 9-10. Here you can enter the corresponding NetBIOS name for the domain you're creating.

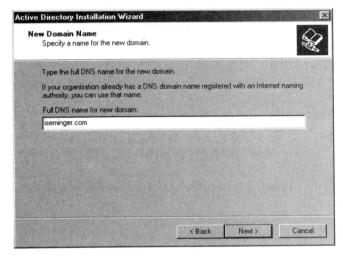

**Figure 9-9.** *The New Domain Name screen.*

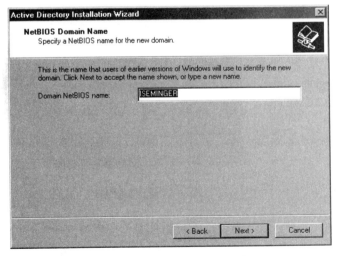

**Figure 9-10.** *The NetBIOS Domain Name screen.*

8.  Click Next to display the Database And Log Locations screen, as shown in Figure 9-11. Here you provide a location for the database and log files. Remember that it's best, for performance purposes, to use separate partitions

for the directory information store (the ntds.dit file) and the log file, even though the default locations provided are on the same partition as your Windows 2000 installation. (This is necessary because Windows 2000 has no way of ensuring that you have additional hard disks available for these files.)

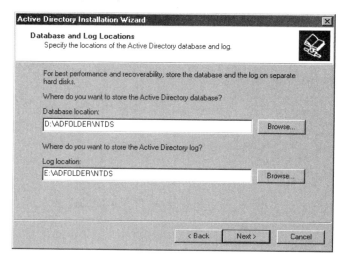

**Figure 9-11.** *The Database And Log Locations screen.*

9.  Click Next to display the Shared System Volume screen, as shown in Figure 9-12. This screen is similar to the Database And Log Locations screen. Here you choose where to place the shared system volume, which is often within the Windows 2000 installation directory.

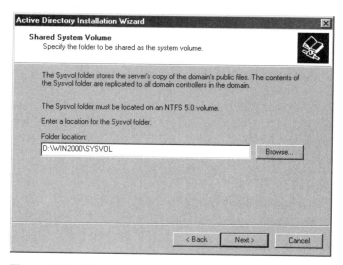

**Figure 9-12.** *The Shared System Volume screen.*

10. Click Next. The wizard attempts to connect to the DNS server handling your domain to determine whether it supports dynamic updates. If it cannot locate the DNS server, you're presented with an information message similar to the one shown in Figure 9-13.

**Figure 9-13.** *The information message that appears when the wizard cannot connect to the specified DNS server.*

In this situation, simply click OK, and the Configure DNS screen appears, as shown in Figure 9-14. This screen provides you with the opportunity to install Windows 2000 DNS as part of the installation process.

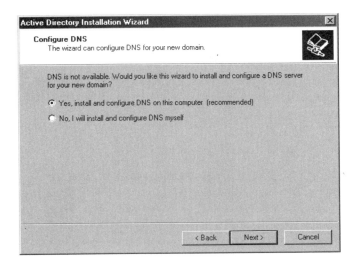

**Figure 9-14.** *The Configure DNS screen.*

11. Select Yes and click Next to display the Permissions screen, as shown in Figure 9-15. This screen deals with access permissions that pertain to server applications that perform access rights lookups in a certain fashion, such as the Microsoft Routing and Remote Access Service (RRAS). The screen presents the choice to make permissions settings weaker and thereby backward compatible or to make them compatible with only Windows 2000.

**More Info**   For more information about issues associated with RRAS servers, check out the "Transitioning RRAS Servers" section in Chapter 11, "Upgrading to Active Directory Services."

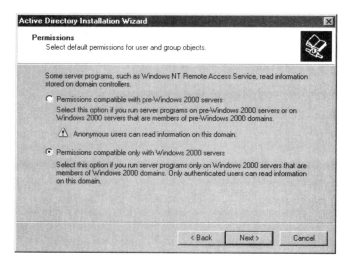

**Figure 9-15.** *The Permissions screen.*

12. Click Next to display the Directory Services Restore Mode Administrator Password screen, as shown in Figure 9-16. Here you provide a password to assign to the local computer's administrator account (vs. an Active Directory services administrators group account). This account will be necessary if you need to put the soon-to-be domain controller into Directory Services Restore Mode. See the "Performing Active Directory Services Backups and Restores" section later in this chapter for more information.

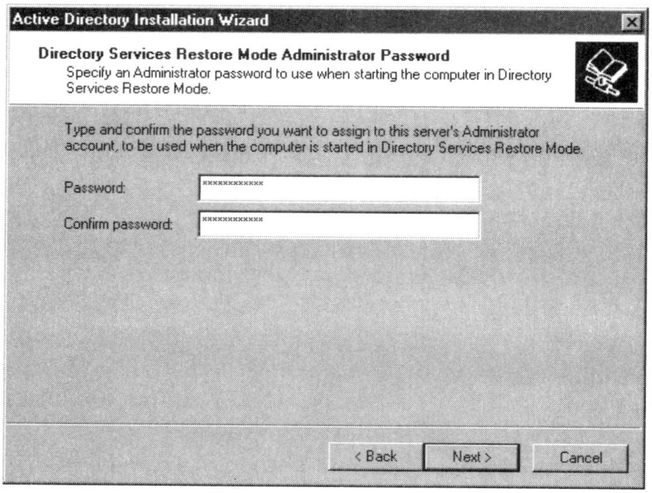

**Figure 9-16.** *The Directory Services Restore Mode Administrator Password screen.*

13.   Click Next to display the Summary screen, as shown in Figure 9-17. This screen summarizes the choices you have made. If you wish to change any of your choices, simply click Back until you reach the screen containing the choice you wish to change, and then click Next until you return to the Summary screen.

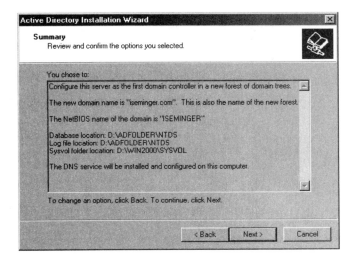

**Figure 9-17.** *The Summary screen.*

14.   After you are sure of your choices, click Next to begin installing Active Directory services on the local computer. As the installation process proceeds, which can take some time, the wizard provides you with information regarding its progress in the installation of Active Directory services. A typical information screen is shown in Figure 9-18.

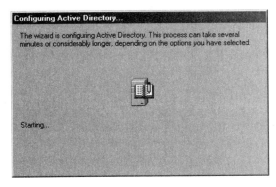

**Figure 9-18.** *An information screen keeps you apprised of Active Directory installation status.*

15. When the process is completed, the wizard presents you with the Completing The Active Directory Installation Wizard dialog box, shown in Figure 9-19, that informs you of the successful completion.

**Figure 9-19.** *The Completing The Active Directory Installation Wizard screen.*

16. Click Finish, and Windows 2000 then prompts you to restart your computer so that the installation of Active Directory services can take effect, as shown in Figure 9-20.

**Figure 9-20.** *After you click Finish, you will be prompted to restart your computer.*

And that's it. Once you restart your computer, it's officially an Active Directory services domain controller and you officially have an Active Directory services deployment. Of course, you'll quickly install another domain controller to add to the domain for fault tolerance purposes, right?

## Using Active Directory Services Snap-Ins

The primary user interface for Active Directory services consists of four MMC snap-ins, each of which is targeted at specific tasks associated with the management of Active Directory services. The snap-ins make up a group of administrative interfaces that have been developed to work within the MMC, and they all have a similar look and feel. Creating snap-ins with a similar look and feel allows users to take advantage of their familiarity with one snap-in and use that familiarity to help make other Windows 2000 administrative activities easier. The four primary snap-ins used to administer Active Directory services are as follows:

- Active Directory Users and Computers
- Active Directory Sites and Services
- Active Directory Domains and Trusts
- Active Directory Schema

You can manage your Active Directory services deployment from any Windows 2000 computer, whether the computer is a domain controller or (better yet) a Windows 2000 Professional computer that has the Windows 2000 Administrative Tools installed on it. Windows 2000 Administrative Tools are used to install snap-ins onto a Windows 2000 Professional computer that otherwise would not have such snap-ins, such as the snap-ins associated with managing Active Directory services.

There are a few ways you can ensure that snap-ins associated with Windows 2000 Administrative Tools are available to administrators responsible for managing various components of Active Directory services:

- Assign the associated snap-ins (individually or as part of the Windows 2000 Administrative Tools) to a group of administrators.
- Publish the associated snap-ins (individually or as a group) so that they will be available to a group of administrators or from a group of computers.
- Install the Windows 2000 Administrative Tools on the Windows 2000 Professional computer from which administration of Active Directory services is going to take place.

To assign or publish the associated snap-ins and thereby ensure that the snap-ins will be available to administrators responsible for managing Active Directory services, you can use Group Policy, IntelliMirror, or both. For more information about Group Policy, see the "Windows 2000 Group Policy" section later in this chapter, and for more information about IntelliMirror, see Chapter 14, "Administratively Leveraging Active Directory Services."

### Installing Administrative Tools

To install the Windows 2000 Administrative Tools onto a Windows 2000 Professional computer, use the Windows 2000 Administration Tools Setup wizard. This wizard walks you through the process of installing the Windows 2000 Administration Tools suite on a Windows 2000 Professional computer. To invoke the wizard, follow these steps:

1. Insert a Windows 2000 Server or Windows 2000 Advanced Server CD into your CD drive, go to the \i386 directory, and start the adminpak.msi program. The Windows Installer launches, and after a few moments the welcome screen of the Windows 2000 Administration Tools Setup wizard appears, as displayed in Figure 9-21.

**Figure 9-21.** *The welcome screen of the Windows 2000 Administration Tools Setup wizard.*

2. Click Next to start the installation. The installation might take a few minutes, and you will see some information screens reporting installation progress. When the installation is complete, the Completing The Windows 2000 Administration Tools Setup Wizard screen will appear.

3. After installation, the Windows 2000 Administrative Tools can be found by clicking the Start button, pointing to Programs, and then pointing to the Administrative Tools program group.

**More Info**  As an administrator, you're likely to spend a fair amount of time working with the four main Active Directory snap-ins, but you will almost certainly also spend time using command line–based tools, such as Ntdsutil. For more information on command-line utilities and how to use them, as well as how to get the most out of using the command line (cmd.exe) in Windows 2000, check out the "Command-Line Management" section later in this chapter.

---

**Caution**   You should administer Active Directory services and its domain controllers from a remote workstation and leave the domain controllers locked up and secure from access. If you're traipsing in and out of your supposedly secure environment on a daily basis to administer the Active Directory services deployment on the domain controllers themselves, your domain controllers are probably less secure than if you were to leave that locked room alone and administer Active Directory from your Windows 2000 Professional computer. Remember that all Windows 2000 domain controllers have sensitive data on them and require more security than Windows NT domain controllers. For more information and harping about your deployment security, check out Chapter 8, "Active Directory Services and Security."

---

## Loading a Snap-In into the MMC

Loading a snap-in into the MMC is a fairly straightforward task. Depending on the services or applications you have installed on the Windows 2000 computer from which you plan on administering Active Directory services, you could have a few available snap-ins or a whole bunch of them. To load a snap-in into the MMC, follow these steps:

1.   Start the MMC by clicking the Start button, clicking Run, typing MMC into the Open text box, and clicking OK. The MMC console appears, as shown in Figure 9-22.

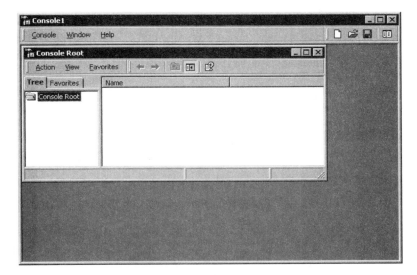

**Figure 9-22.** *The MMC console.*

2.   Click Add/Remove Snap-In in the Console menu, and then click Add in the Add/Remove Snap-In dialog box. Figure 9-23 shows what your screen should look like when you add a snap-in to your MMC. (Note that in this figure, the Console Root window inside the Console window has been maximized.)

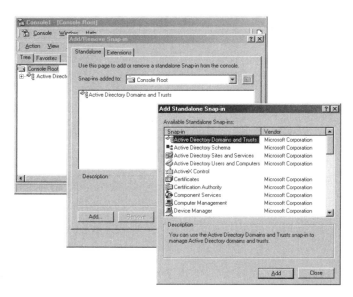

**Figure 9-23.** *Adding a snap-in to the MMC.*

3. From there, you simply choose the snap-in you want to load into the MMC console you're working on and click Add. To install more snap-ins, simply repeat this step and then start administering. For management of Active Directory services, of course, you'll likely be loading the four Active Directory services snap-ins discussed in the following sections.

If you are running Windows 2000 Server or Windows 2000 Advanced Server, you can also access snap-ins directly from the Administrative Tools program group. To do so, click the Start button, point to Programs, and then point to the Administrative Tools group. When selecting Active Directory snap-ins or any other snap-ins with this method, you circumvent the process of adding the snap-ins by using the Add/Remove Snap-In menu command.

## Active Directory Users And Computers Snap-In

Much of the time you spend managing Active Directory services will be done using the Active Directory Users And Computers snap-in. Its interface covers most of the common day-to-day tasks associated with Active Directory, as you'll learn throughout the course of using it. Figure 9-24 shows the Active Directory Users And Computers snap-in.

**Note**   If you want to manage users or groups that are associated with a single computer, such as a stand-alone Windows 2000 Server computer, rather than managing users or groups associated with Active Directory services, use the Local Users And Groups snap-in.

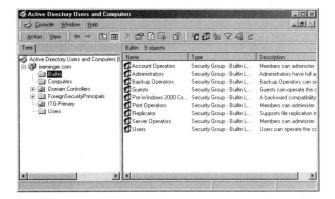

**Figure 9-24.** *The Active Directory Users And Computers snap-in.*

When you need to manage any of the objects found in the Active Directory Users A

nd Computers snap-in, right-click the object and choose the appropriate management task. For example, if you needed to manage data associated with a particular user, you would invoke the Properties dialog box for a user by right-clicking the user in the right-hand pane of the Active Directory Users And Computers snap-in and then clicking Properties, as shown in Figure 9-25.

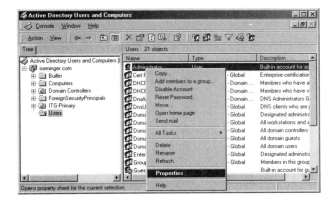

**Figure 9-25.** *Managing users with the Active Directory Users And Computers snap-in.*

Although this is just one example of how to manage objects with just one Active Directory snap-in, it's important to understand that all management of users in all Active Directory snap-ins is performed the same way. This is precisely Microsoft's goal in providing the centralized and consistent administrative interfaces found in Windows 2000; once you're familiar with performing one type of administrative task using Windows 2000 administrative tools, your ability to quickly perform other administrative tasks is nearly guaranteed. This section and the other sections on snap-ins that follow focus on show-ing you the interfaces you'll encounter when creating objects—but these interfaces are very similar to the interfaces used for managing such objects. Therefore, you should read the rest of the sections on snap-ins while keeping in mind that management of both pre-existing and newly created objects is performed similar to the manner shown in the previous example of managing a user.

But let's get back to the Active Directory Users And Computers snap-in. There are a num-ber of tasks that administrators commonly perform with the Active Directory Users And Computers snap-in. The following sections walk you through the most commonly per-formed tasks.

### Adding a User

To add a user to a given container, such as an organizational unit (OU) or a domain, follow these steps:

1.  Select the container in the left pane of the Active Directory Users And Comput-ers snap-in, right-click that container, point to New, and then click User in the submenu that appears, as shown in Figure 9-26.

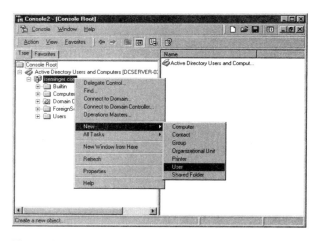

**Figure 9-26.** *The first step in adding a new user.*

2.  In the New Object - User dialog box that appears, enter the new user's name, logon name, and domain, as shown in Figure 9-27.

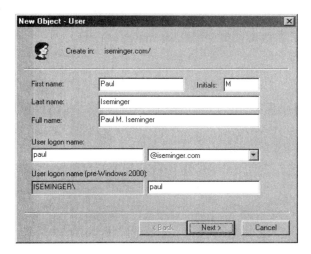

**Figure 9-27.** *The New Object - User dialog box.*

3.  Click Next, enter the user's password, and choose from various other options, as shown in Figure 9-28.

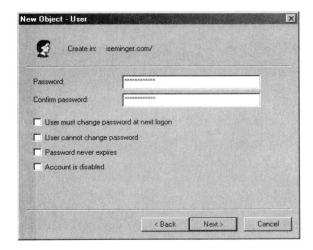

**Figure 9-28.** *Entering a new user's password.*

4.   Click Next to see the summary screen, as shown in Figure 9-29. If you need to change anything, click Back, make the change, and click Next until you return to the summary screen. Click Finish to create the new user.

**Figure 9-29.** *The summary screen.*

Of course, you can always initiate this process using the toolbar supplied with the Active Directory Users And Computers snap-in. Figure 9-30 shows the Add User button you can click on the snap-in toolbar to initiate the process of adding a new user.

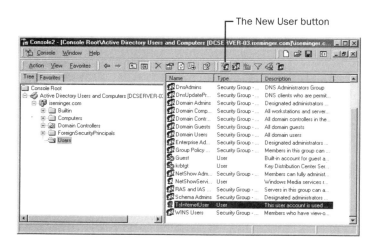

**Figure 9-30.** *The Add User button on the Active Directory Users And Computers snap-in toolbar.*

## Adding a Computer

To add a computer to a given container, such as an OU or a domain, follow these steps:

1. Select the container in the left pane of the Active Directory Users And Computers snap-in, right-click that container, point to New, and then click Computer in the submenu that appears, as shown in Figure 9-31.

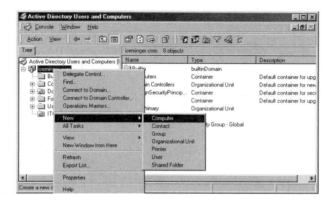

**Figure 9-31.** *The first step in adding a new computer.*

2. In the New Object - Computer dialog box that appears, type the new computer's name, as shown in Figure 9-32.

**Figure 9-32.** *The New Object - Computer dialog box.*

3. Click Next, and if the new computer is to be a managed computer, select the check box and type the GUID. Figure 9-33 shows this dialog box.

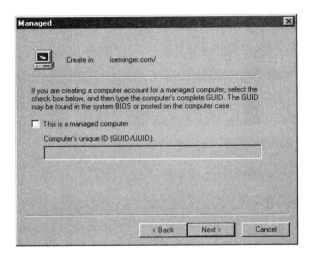

**Figure 9-33.** *The Managed dialog box.*

4. Click Next to see the summary screen, as shown in Figure 9-34. If you need to change anything, click Back, make the change, and click Next until you return to the summary screen. Click Finish to create the new computer.

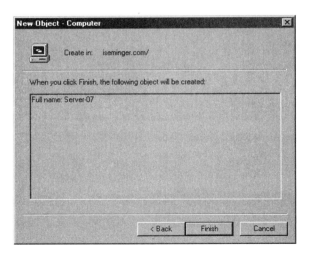

**Figure 9-34.** *The summary screen.*

## Adding a Group

To add a group to a given container, follow these steps:

1. Select the container in the left pane of the Active Directory Users And Computers snap-in, right-click that container, point to New, and then click Group in the submenu that appears, as shown in Figure 9-35.

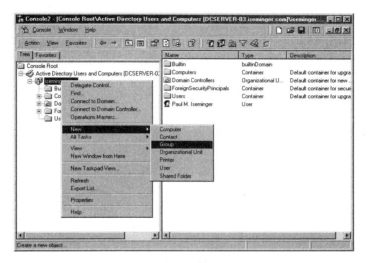

**Figure 9-35.** *The first step in adding a group.*

2. In the New Object - Group dialog box that appears, type the new group's name, and then select the scope and type, as shown in Figure 9-36.

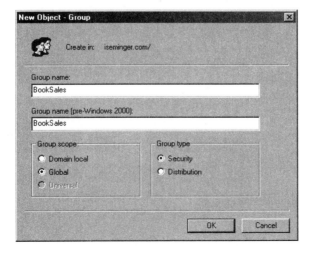

**Figure 9-36.** *The New Object - Group dialog box.*

3. Once you click OK, the group is created. If you need to change anything, you can modify the properties of the group just as you modify many other objects in Active Directory services; right-click the objects and then click Properties from the shortcut menu that appears.

### Adding an OU

To add an OU to a domain or to nest an OU within an existing OU, follow these steps:

1. Select the container (domain or OU) in the left pane of the Active Directory Users And Computers snap-in, right-click that container, point to New, and then click Organizational Unit in the submenu that appears, as shown in Figure 9-37. In this example, I create a new OU called ITG-Primary. (Remember that OUs are supposed to map to your IT structure—if you don't remember, consult Chapter 7, "Planning an Active Directory Services Deployment.")

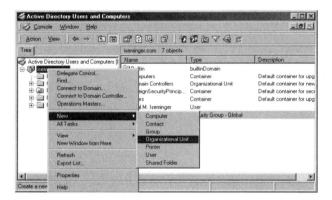

**Figure 9-37.** *The first step in adding an OU.*

2. In the New Object - Organizational Unit dialog box that appears, shown in Figure 9-38, type the OU's name and click OK to create the new OU.

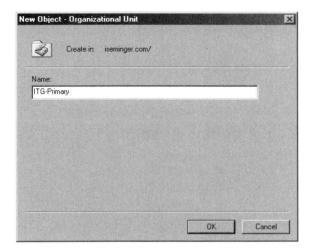

**Figure 9-38.** *The New Object - Organizational Unit screen.*

## Adding Printers and Shared Folders to Active Directory Services

As an administrator, you must specify the printers and shared folders you want to expose to users when they search Active Directory services for such objects. To enable administrators or users (with appropriate privilege) to add a printer to Active Directory services, follow these steps:

1. Select the container (domain or OU) in the left pane of the Active Directory Users And Computers snap-in, right-click that container, point to New, and then click Printer in the submenu that appears, as shown in Figure 9-39.

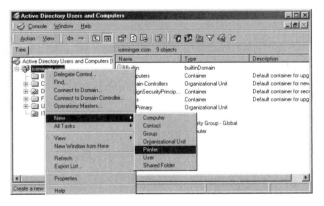

**Figure 9-39.** *The first step in adding a printer.*

2. In the New Object - Printer dialog box that appears, shown in Figure 9-40, type the printer's network path and click OK to add the printer.

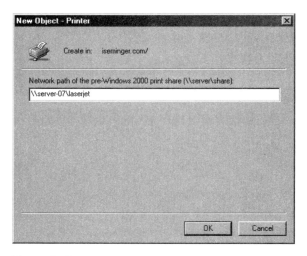

**Figure 9-40.** *The New Object - Printer dialog box.*

To add a file share to Active Directory services, enabling users in your organization to search the directory for the file share, follow these steps:

1. Select the container (domain or OU) in the left pane of the Active Directory Users And Computers snap-in, right-click that container, point to New, and then click Shared Folder in the submenu that appears, as shown in Figure 9-41.

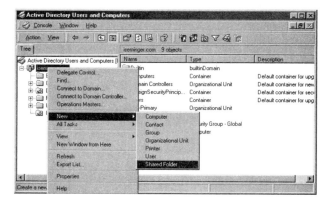

**Figure 9-41.** *The first step in adding a shared folder.*

2. In the New Object - Shared Folder dialog box that appears, shown in Figure 9-42, type the shared folder's name and network path and click OK to add the shared folder.

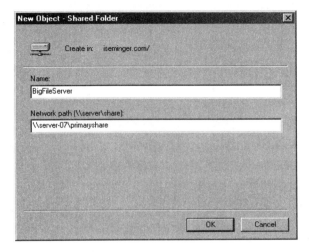

**Figure 9-42.** *The New Object - Shared Folder dialog box.*

**Note** If you implement Microsoft distributed file system (Dfs) in your Windows 2000/Active Directory environment, Active Directory automates the handling of the Dfs share. For more information about Dfs and Active Directory services, see Chapter 14, "Administratively Leveraging Active Directory Services."

### Moving Objects Between Containers

Moving objects between containers such as OUs or security groups is simple. With the Active Directory Users And Computers snap-in, moving objects between containers is as easy as selecting the objects and then clicking Move in the selected items' shortcut menu (displayed when you right-click the selected objects). Just follow these steps to move the collection of objects we just finished creating in the previous few sections into the OU, ITG-Primary, that we also just created.

1. In the right pane of the Active Directory Users And Computers snap-in, select the objects you wish to move, as shown in Figure 9-43.

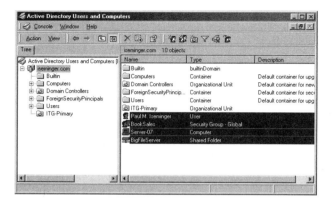

**Figure 9-43.** *The first step in moving objects between containers.*

2. Right-click the selected objects, and select Move from the shortcut menu, as shown in Figure 9-44.

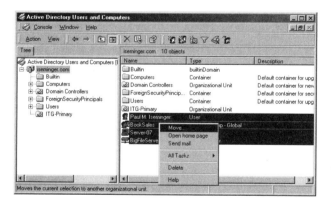

**Figure 9-44.** *Selecting Move from the shortcut menu.*

3. In the Move dialog box that appears, select the container into which you want to move the objects, as shown in Figure 9-45.

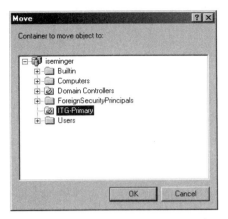

**Figure 9-45.** *The Move dialog box.*

4.  Now select the new container in the left pane of the Active Directory Users And Computers snap-in, and notice that the objects you moved appear in the right-hand pane, as shown in Figure 9-46.

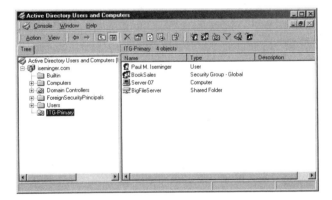

**Figure 9-46.** *The objects have been moved into the new container.*

## Active Directory Sites And Services Snap-In

Use the Active Directory Sites And Services snap-in to manage sites and services such as replication strategies for your deployment. You will likely use the Active Directory Sites And Services snap-in less frequently than the Active Directory Users And Computers snap-in. Figure 9-47 illustrates the Active Directory Sites And Services snap-in.

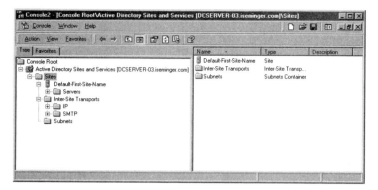

**Figure 9-47.** *The Active Directory Sites And Services snap-in.*

There are a few common tasks that you'll likely need to perform using the Active Directory Sites And Services snap-in, among which is the creation (and management, and modification) of sites. The following section explains how to use the Active Directory Sites And Services snap-in to create a site.

### Creating a Site

Active Directory services defines a site as a collection of IP subnets that are well connected, which means the IP subnets in the collection are connected at LAN speeds or greater. To create or modify a site using the Active Directory Sites And Services snap-in, follow these steps:

1. Right-click the Sites folder and then click New Site in the shortcut menu, as shown in Figure 9-48.

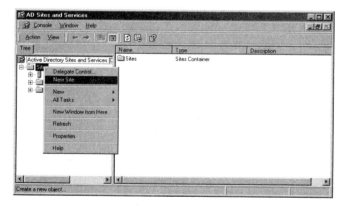

**Figure 9-48.** *Creating a new site with the Active Directory Sites And Services snap-in.*

2.  In the New Object - Site dialog box that appears, type the name of the site you want to create, as displayed in Figure 9-49.

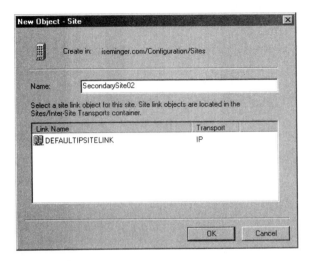

**Figure 9-49.** *The New Object - Site dialog box.*

3.  Click OK to display an information dialog box that informs you that there's more configuration to be done before the site will really be up and running, as displayed in Figure 9-50.

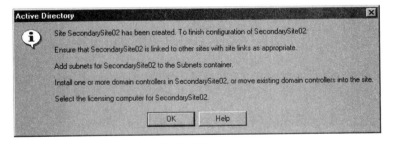

**Figure 9-50.** *There's more to do with a site than just create it; you must provide additional parameters and specify which servers and other objects in your deployment reside in that site.*

You must provide a site link that connects the site you just created to other sites in your deployment, and you must associate a cost with that site link. The following steps outline the process associated with creating a site link and assigning it a cost.

1. Using the Active Directory Sites And Services snap-in, expand the Inter-Site Transports folder, choose the transport your site link will use (probably IP), right-click the transport (IP in this instance), and choose New Site Link from the shortcut menu, as shown in Figure 9-51.

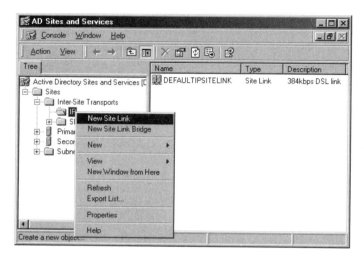

**Figure 9-51.** *The first step in creating a new site link.*

2. In the New Object - Site Link dialog box that appears, you specify basic information about the site link, such as its name and the sites that it connects (if you only have two sites, the site link will, of course, connect those sites), as shown in Figure 9-52.

3. Click OK to return to the Active Directory Sites And Services snap-in, and the new site link is visible in the appropriate subfolder (IP or SMTP) of the Inter-Site Transports folder. Figure 9-53 shows the site link I created in the previous step.

4. You must configure the site link's properties to complete the site link creation process. The configuration of a new site link is done in a property page that's accessed by right-clicking the site in the Active Directory Sites And Services snap-in, and choosing Properties from the shortcut menu, as shown in Figure 9-54 on page 224. The steps used to modify an existing site link (such as the default site link provided by Active Directory services, creatively called DEFAULTIPSITELINK) are the same as these new site link configuration steps.

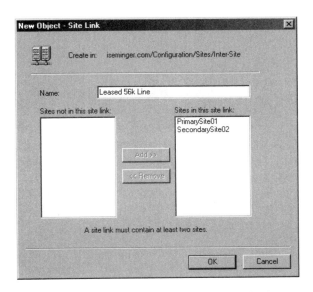

**Figure 9-52.** *The New Object - Site Link dialog box.*

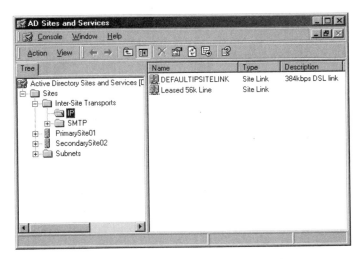

**Figure 9-53.** *The new site link shows up in the appropriate transport subfolder of the Inter-Site Transports folder.*

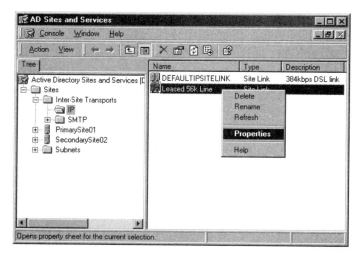

**Figure 9-54.** *Configuring the new site link requires extra steps.*

5. In the site link's property sheet that appears, you can configure the cost associated with the site link and specify the frequency with which Active Directory replication should occur between sites, as shown in Figure 9-55. More information about appropriate cost values is provided later in this section.

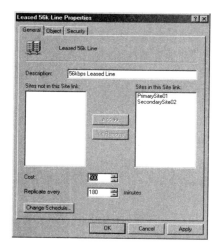

**Figure 9-55.** *Specifying the cost associated with a cost link is done after the site link is created.*

6.   You can also associate a schedule with the site link. Active Directory services uses site link schedule information to schedule replication traffic between sites. To specify a schedule, click the Change Schedule button located in the bottom left corner of the site link's property sheet. You are presented with a dialog box similar to that shown in Figure 9-56.

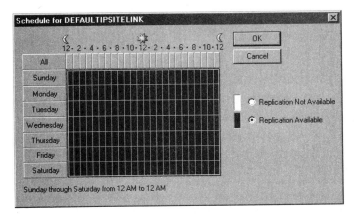

**Figure 9-56.** *The schedule associated with a site link.*

7.   To create a block of time during which you do not want replication traffic to use the site link, simply select that time block by dragging over the time blocks identified in the Schedule dialog box and then select the Replication Not Available option button to the right of the schedule block, as demonstrated in Figure 9-57.

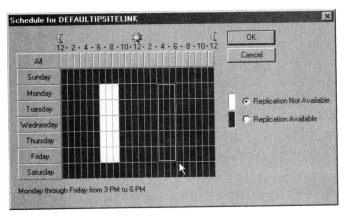

**Figure 9-57.** *Specifying time blocks to keep replication traffic from taking up site link bandwidth during a specified time period.*

Costs can be based on the actual monetary cost of transmitting data, such as per-use charges, or they can be based on availability of the bandwidth, such as the availability of a slow 56 kilobits per second (kbps) link that fills up quickly (because there isn't a lot of bandwidth on it to go around). The recommended settings for particular WAN connections, based on these considerations, are as follows:

| WAN Connection | Recommended Cost Setting |
| --- | --- |
| International link | 5,000 |
| Branch office link | 1,000 |
| 56-kbps link | 500 |
| 384-kbps xDSL link | 100 |
| T1 or greater backbone link | 1 |

Note that these are guidelines, which means you can associate whatever cost-assignment scheme you would like to your sites. Realize, however, that Active Directory services uses site-link cost as a major factor in determining its replication topology. For more information about how Active Directory services automatically creates its replication strategy (and what you can do to modify it), see the "Managing Replication Strategies" section, which is found in the "Advanced Management" section later in this chapter.

**Planning** The Knowledge Consistency Checker (KCC) uses site-link cost information in addition to other information, such as site-link schedules and any latency associated with such site-link schedules, to create its replication topology in the form of a least-cost spanning tree. That means that if a given site can use two links and the costs of using those links add up to 50 or can use another site link with a cost of 100, the KCC will choose the least-cost site-link combination to route Active Directory replication traffic if scheduling constraints are equal. You should take this feature into consideration when designating the cost metric of each site link.

### Assigning a Subnet to the Site

You also have to define a subnet to associate with your created site. At this point, the issues involved in creating the sites get a little murky (or at least complex—and if you don't know IP quite well, murky and complex tend to be synonymous).

To assign a subnet to a site, follow these steps:

1. Right-click the Subnets folder, and then click New Subnet in the shortcut menu, as shown in Figure 9-58.

2. In the New Object - Subnet dialog box that appears, you define the site by IP subnet address and corresponding subnet mask, as shown in Figure 9-59. After you click OK, Active Directory services transforms your input into the *www.xxx.yyy.zzz/mm* format. (No, you probably aren't going to be familiar with that format, nor should you be.) Knowing what to enter in this dialog box

is much easier if you can read binary and understand what Active Directory is actually asking for. The sidebar that follows Figure 9-59, "Reading Binary and Creating Active Directory Services Sites," should help you do both. Once you have appropriately entered your IP subnet address and subnet mask, Active Directory creates the site, and the replication traffic configuration (as well as other site-based decisions Active Directory services uses site information to make) can make the most appropriate use of your sites, the locations of your domain controllers, and the site-based location of domain controller services.

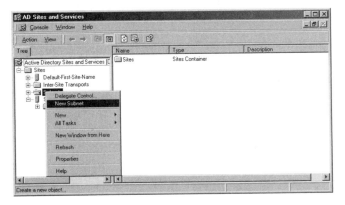

**Figure 9-58.**  *The first step in creating a new subnet.*

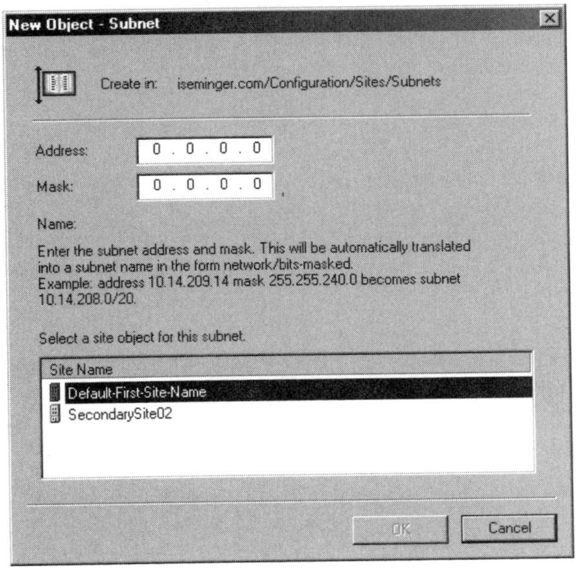

**Figure 9-59.**  *The New Object - Subnet dialog box.*

## Reading Binary and Creating Active Directory Services Sites

Understanding the explanation associated with creating an Active Directory services site is an exercise in reading binary, and that's a language most people don't speak on a daily basis. If you want to ensure you understand what Active Directory services is asking for in the New Object - Subnet dialog box, you can translate the subnet address and the mask into binary and derive the appropriate input.

Here's an example. If you have a subnet with an IP address (when masked) of 254.14.252.0, the subnet has the following binary IP address:

```
11111110.00001110.11111100.00000000
```

The confusing part of this configuration requirement is that the IP address of your *subnet* (not just one client on the subnet) should be discussed in conjunction with your subnet mask (and that isn't very clear from the New Object - Subnet dialog box). In this example, the assumption is that you have the following network mask:

```
11111111.11111111.11111100.00000000
```

That means, in more common (decimal) terms, you have a network mask of 255.255.252.0.

Let's do a quick translation from decimal into binary. The binary version is derived from adding the following values for each bit position, based on whether the bit is set to 1, for each octet. (An octet is the period-delimited set of eight bits.)

```
   0       0       0       0     0     0     0     0
 [128]   [64]    [32]    [16]   [8]   [4]   [2]   [1]
```

In our example, the first octet is the following:

```
11111110
```

So, we add the values for the bit positions as follows:

```
128 + 64 + 32 + 16 + 8 + 4 + 2
```

The last value—the decimal 1 (which happens to be the decimal addition value as well as the binary value to which the bit is set—in this case of doing arithmetic, we're looking at its decimal addition value)—isn't added because the bit in that position of the octet is set to zero. When we add all those values together, we get 254, which is the value of the first octet in the 254.14.252.0 address. Other numbers can be generated similarly; in fact (or of course, depending on your level of experience with reading binary), any value between 0 and 255 can be generated by a combination of eight bits. Add one more bit, and you double the numbers that can be generated by the combination of bits. (Nine bits has 512 different combinations, 10 bits has 1024, and so on.)

Therefore, if your subnet mask is 255.255.252.0, your mask (of 1s) is the following:

```
11111111.11111111.11111100.00000000
```

Because the 252 equates to setting the first six bits in its octet to 1, in decimal terms it equates to 128 + 64 + 32 + 16 + 8 + 4.

How does this apply to the *www.xxx.yyy.zzz/mm* format that the New Object - Subnet dialog box uses? Simple—you have to count the number of bits set to 1 in your subnet mask (starting from the *left* of the series of octets), and that number is the *mm* that Active Directory wants after the forward slash (/). In our example, that means 8 (the first octet is all 1s) + 8 (the second octet is the same as the first) + 6 (in the third octet, six bits are set to 1)—for a grand total of 22.

The good news is that this kind of number translation isn't an everyday occurrence; once you get your sites configured and entered into Active Directory, you have to modify them only when your network's physical topology changes (or if IP address assignments change). Good thing, wouldn't you say?

### Active Directory Domains And Trusts Snap-In

Like the other Active Directory services snap-ins, the Active Directory Domains And Trusts snap-in is named to directly reflect the activities and administrative tasks you perform with it; with this snap-in, you manage Active Directory domains and any trusts you need to establish with other (interforest) domains. Figure 9-60 illustrates the Active Directory Domains And Trusts snap-in:

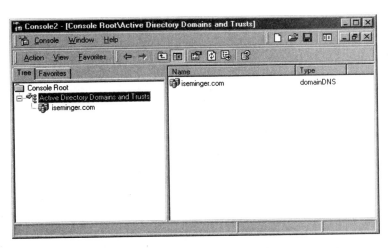

**Figure 9-60.** *The Active Directory Domains And Trusts snap-in.*

The following sections explain some of the management tasks most commonly performed with the Active Directory Domains And Trusts snap-in.

### Adding a Trust

To add an explicit one-way trust between two domains, follow these steps:

1. Right-click a domain in the left pane of the Active Directory Domains And Trusts snap-in, and then click Properties in the shortcut menu that appears, as shown in Figure 9-61.

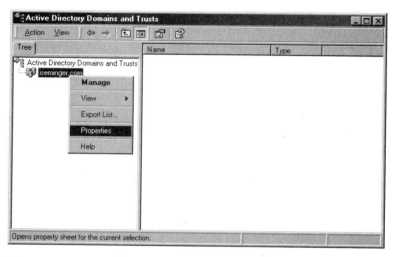

**Figure 9-61.** *Creating a new trust with the Active Directory Domains And Trusts snap-in.*

2. The selected domain's property sheet appears. The Trusts property page is where you manage trusts and is shown in Figure 9-62.

   You can choose either to add a domain that the selected domain should trust or to add a domain that trusts the selected domain. Determine which explicit one-way trust you want to create, and then click the Add button next to the appropriate box.

3. When you click either Add button, the Add Trusted Domain dialog box appears. Here you provide the appropriate password for the trusted (or trusting) domain, as shown in Figure 9-63.

**Note** All domains in a given forest have transitive trust relationships and do not require that administrators explicitly create trusts between them. This process of creating a domain trust, therefore, is appropriate for creating a trust between domains that reside in different forests (or between a Windows 2000 domain and a Windows NT domain).

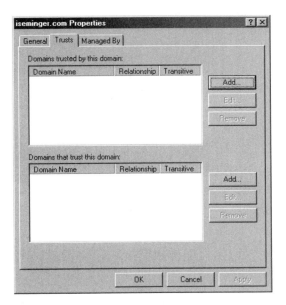

**Figure 9-62.** *The Trusts property page for the selected domain.*

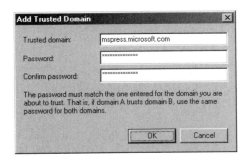

**Figure 9-63.** *The Add Trusted Domain dialog box.*

## Switching to Native Mode

As I've mentioned a couple of times already in this book (and will mention again in upcoming chapters), you should make the switch to native mode as quickly as your deployment requirements allow.

To switch a domain to native mode, follow these steps:

1. Right-click the domain that you want to switch from mixed mode to native mode in the left pane of the Active Directory Domains and Trusts snap-in, and then click Properties in the shortcut menu that appears. (This is the same selection you make to add a trust, as explained in the previous section.)

2. The domain's Property sheet appears, as shown in Figure 9-64. On the General property page, click the Change Mode button, and the domain is switched. It's important to realize that this is a one-way switch; once you switch the domain to native mode, you cannot switch it back to mixed mode.

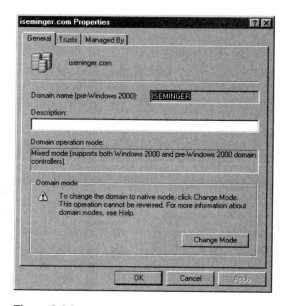

**Figure 9-64.** *Use the General property page to switch from mixed mode to native mode.*

**More Info**  For more information about switching to native mode and the advantages switching to native mode provides, see the "Switch to Native Mode" section in Chapter 11, "Upgrading to Active Directory Services."

## Active Directory Schema Snap-In

The Active Directory Schema snap-in is the tool you can use to manage Active Directory schema classes and attributes. To have access to the Active Directory Schema snap-in, you must install the Windows 2000 Administrative Tools (located in the adminpak.msi file) on the computer from which you want to manage the schema, even if that computer is already a Windows 2000 domain controller. (For information about how to install Windows 2000 Administrative Tools, consult the beginning of the "Using Active Directory Services Snap-Ins" section.) After you load the Active Directory Schema snap-in and launch the MMC, you see the window shown in Figure 9-65.

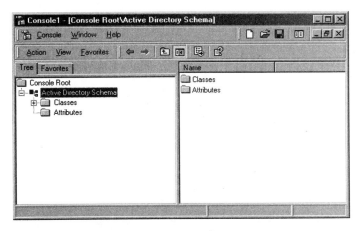

**Figure 9-65.** *The Active Directory Schema snap-in.*

The following sections explain management tasks performed with the Active Directory Schema snap-in.

**Caution**   You take the stability of your Active Directory deployment in your own hands when you begin administering objects in the schema. You should use extreme caution when performing an administrative task involving changes to any Active Directory schema objects, such as adding or (especially) deleting schema objects.

### Adding a Class Object

To create a schema class object, follow these steps:

1.  Right-click the Classes container in the left pane of the Active Directory Schema snap-in, and then click Create Class in the shortcut menu that appears, as Figure 9-66 illustrates.

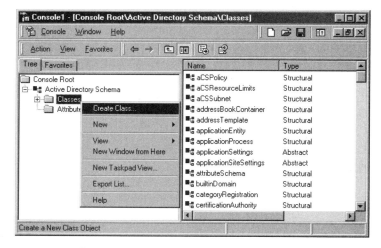

**Figure 9-66.** *Adding a new class object to the schema using the Active Directory Schema snap-in.*

Alternatively, you can add an extra step to the creation process if you'd like. (I don't know why you would, but you should know that you can.) Simply right-click the class container, click New on the shortcut menu, and then click Class.

2. You're presented with a warning about the seriousness (and permanence) of creating schema objects (whether classes or attributes), as shown in Figure 9-67. Click OK to proceed.

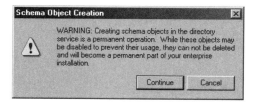

**Figure 9-67.** *You are warned about the permanence of creating a schema object.*

3. In the Create New Schema Class dialog box, you must enter information about the schema class you are creating, as shown in Figure 9-68. Note that I've used a bogus Object ID (OID) in this example; you will need to provide a real and appropriate OID for each schema class object you create. You also provide a common name and LDAP name for your schema class. (Again, these should be planned, real, and appropriate based on your schema class creation plan.) If the object has a parent class, specify it in the Parent Class list box, and then choose the class type from the drop-down menu.

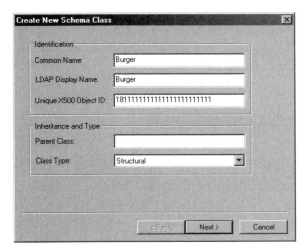

**Figure 9-68.** *The Create New Schema Class dialog box.*

---

**More Info**  For more information about OIDs and the many issues surrounding making changes or additions to the schema, see Chapter 10, "Working with the Active Directory Services Schema."

4.  Click Next to display the Create New Schema Class dialog box, which enables you to specify the mandatory and optional attributes that make up the class, as shown in Figure 9-69. To add attributes, click the Add button next to either the mandatory or optional box, as appropriate. When you click either Add button, you see the Select Schema Object dialog box shown in Figure 9-70, which lets you choose attributes to add to your new schema class object.

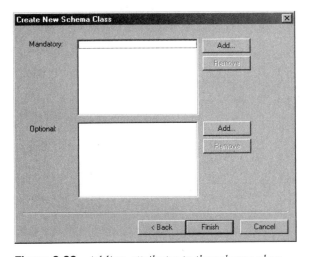

**Figure 9-69.** *Adding attributes to the schema class.*

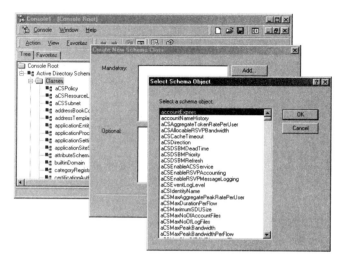

**Figure 9-70.** *Choosing attributes from the list of available attributes to add to the new schema class.*

5. When you add attributes, the Create New Schema Class dialog box displays the attributes in their corresponding (mandatory and optional) boxes, as shown in Figure 9-71. When you've completed adding the attributes you want associated with the class object, click Finish and the object is created.

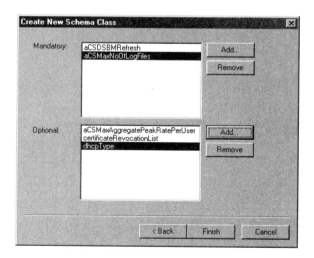

**Figure 9-71.** *Newly added attributes are displayed in the Create New Schema Class dialog box.*

6.  Once you choose attributes, they show up in the Create New Schema Class dialog box; when you're done choosing attributes, click Finish to create the class.

### Adding an Attribute Object

To create a schema attribute object, follow these steps:

1.  Right-click the Attributes container in the left pane of the Active Directory Schema snap-in, and then click Create Attribute in the shortcut menu that appears, as shown in Figure 9-72.

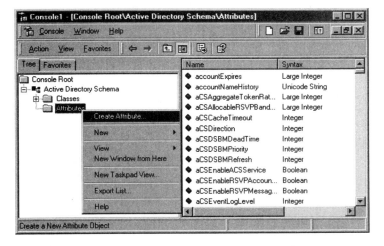

**Figure 9-72.** *Adding a new attribute object to the schema.*

Just as with the creation of a schema class object, you can add an extra step to the creation process if you'd like. (I still don't know why you would, but you *can*.) Simply right-click the attributes container, click New on the shortcut menu, and then click Attribute.

2.  You are presented with the same warning about the seriousness and permanence of creating schema objects as shown in Figure 9-67. Click Continue, and the Create New Attribute dialog box appears, as shown in Figure 9-73.

3.  Once you complete the information and click OK, the attribute is created.

    After creating the new attribute, you must associate it with a particular class to make that attribute meaningful (or more precisely, to have that attribute used). Adding an attribute to a class is explained in the next section. After you associate that attribute with a class or classes, you must create instances of that class or those classes for your newly created attribute to become visible (that is, used) in your Active Directory services deployment.

**Figure 9-73.** *The Create New Attribute dialog box.*

### Adding a New Attribute to a Schema Class

The process of adding a new attribute to an existing schema class (which, of course, is the only way to add an attribute to a class since you can't add an attribute to a class that doesn't exist!) is straightforward. Follow these steps:

1.  Right-click the class you wish to add the attribute to, and then click Properties in the shortcut menu, as shown in Figure 9-74.

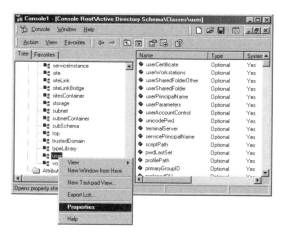

**Figure 9-74.** *Viewing the properties of a schema class object.*

2.  On the Properties sheet that appears, click the Attributes property page, as shown in Figure 9-75.

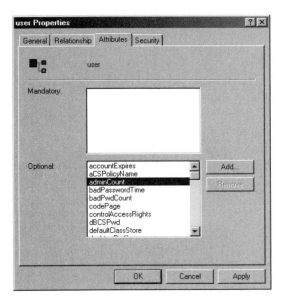

**Figure 9-75.** *The Attributes property page of the object's Properties sheet.*

3. Click the Add button to display the Select Schema Object dialog box, as shown in Figure 9-76. Select the object that you want to add the attribute to, and click OK.

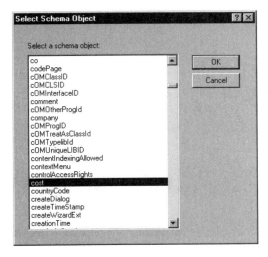

**Figure 9-76.** *The Select Schema Object dialog box.*

There might be constraints (such as permission requirements) associated with changes made to a particular class object, such as the addition or deletion of the object's attributes or of the entire class object itself. This is especially likely if the class object is an object that is provided with Active Directory services as part of the base schema.

> **More Info** For a thorough rundown of the schema, its objects, and the constraints associated with them, check out Chapter 10, "Working with the Active Directory Services Schema."

### Viewing Information About a Class Attribute

There's all sorts of information available about a given schema class and its attributes. To get information about such objects using the Active Directory Schema snap-in, right-click the object in the Active Directory Schema snap-in and then click Properties, as shown in Figure 9-74. You can view all sorts of information, including object relationships, security, and all the other properties we have discussed thus far, by examining all the tabs of the property sheet for the selected object.

### Including an Attribute in the Global Catalog

Perhaps you've created a few schema classes and associated appropriate attributes with them and now you want some of those associated attributes to be propagated to the Global Catalog—just as the attributes of all those built-in schema classes are propagated in the Global Catalog. To replicate attributes to the Global Catalog, follow these steps:

1. Right-click the attribute in the Active Directory Schema snap-in, and click Properties on the shortcut menu, as shown in Figure 9-77.

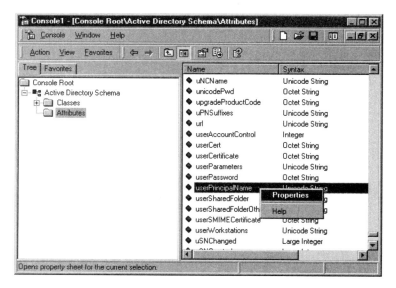

**Figure 9-77.** *Viewing the properties of a schema attribute object.*

2.   The Properties sheet for the selected attribute appears. Toward the bottom of the Properties sheet, there is a check box enabling you to replicate this attribute in the Global Catalog, as shown in Figure 9-78.

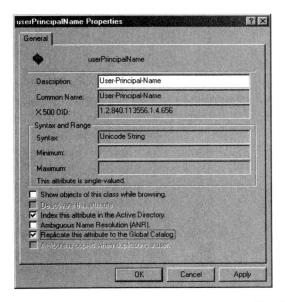

**Figure 9-78.** *Selecting the check box that enables the attribute to be replicated to the Global Catalog.*

## Delegating Administration

The snap-ins that come with Windows 2000 and Active Directory services have delegation of authority built into them, making the process associated with such delegation much easier on administrators than it otherwise might be. Windows 2000 has the Delegation Of Control wizard, which walks administrators through the process of delegating administration for commonly delegated tasks. If necessary, the wizard can be modified to enable control to be delegated with customized delegation settings.

This section illustrates how to use the Delegation Of Control wizard. You'll likely have to modify the steps and the selections shown based on your organization's needs (as you will have to do with many of the procedures shown in this chapter). However, the examples in this section and the rest of this chapter should help familiarize you with the steps you need to take to perform various tasks and thereby make it easy for you to use the tools within your own deployment.

1.   The Delegation Of Control wizard is invoked through the Active Directory Users And Computers snap-in. The container that is selected when you initiate the Delegation Of Control wizard is the container over which you delegate

control. For example, if you right-click a given OU and then click Delegate
Control in its shortcut menu, the Delegation Of Control wizard enables you to
delegate control for that selected container, as shown in Figure 9-79.

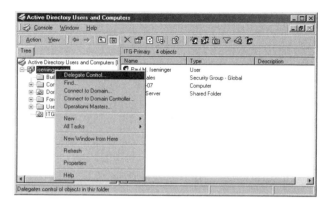

**Figure 9-79.** *Invoking the Delegation Of Control wizard from the Active Directory
Users And Computers snap-in.*

2. The welcome screen of the Delegation Of Control wizard appears, as shown in
Figure 9-80.

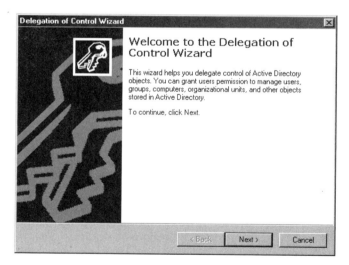

**Figure 9-80.** *The welcome screen of the Delegation Of Control wizard.*

3. Click Next to display the Users Or Groups screen, as shown in Figure 9-81. (It
will be empty until you add users or groups.) Here you choose the user or
group to whom you want to delegate control.

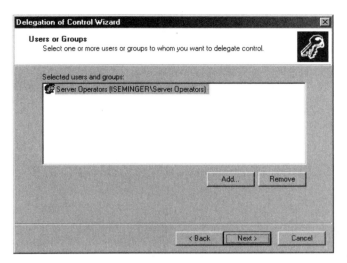

**Figure 9-81.** *The Users Or Groups screen of the Delegation Of Control wizard.*

4.   Click Add to display the Select Users, Computers, Or Groups dialog box, as shown in Figure 9-82. Here you actually add the users or groups to whom you want to delegate control. Choose the users or groups, and then click OK.

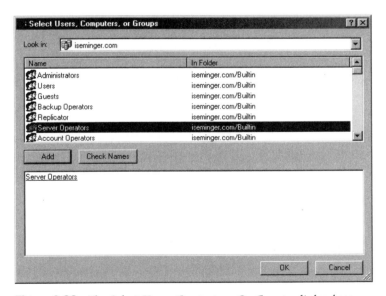

**Figure 9-82.** *The Select Users, Computers, Or Groups dialog box.*

5.   The wizard returns you to the Users Or Groups screen, where the users, or groups to whom you chose to delegate control are displayed, as shown in Figure 9-81.

6. Click Next to display the Tasks To Delegate screen, as shown in Figure 9-83. Here you must specify the tasks (the object types) over which you want control and delegate them to the users or groups specified in Step 4. You can choose from commonly delegated tasks, or you can customize the tasks you want to delegate. The wizard provides a list of common tasks to delegate, or you can choose specific objects over which you want to delegate control by choosing the Create A Custom Task To Delegate option button and clicking Next. The Active Directory Object Type screen will appear if you choose to create a custom task, and this screen is shown in Figure 9-84.

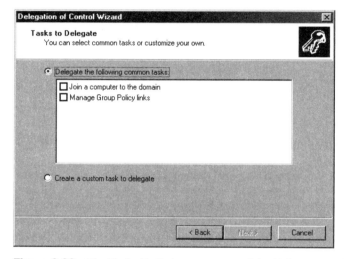

**Figure 9-83.** *The Tasks To Delegate screen of the Delegation Of Control wizard.*

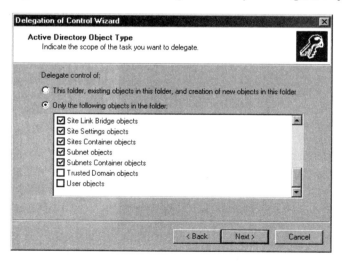

**Figure 9-84.** *The Active Directory Object Type screen of the Delegation Of Control wizard.*

7. Once you have specified the task over which you want to delegate control, click Next to display the Permissions screen, as shown in Figure 9-85. Here you must specify the specific permissions you are granting to the delegated group.

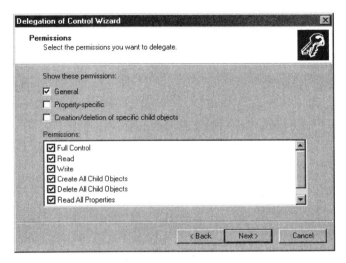

**Figure 9-85.** *The Permissions screen of the Delegation Of Control wizard.*

8. Click Next to display the Completing The Delegation Of Control Wizard screen, as shown in Figure 9-86. This screen contains a summary of the choices you've made.

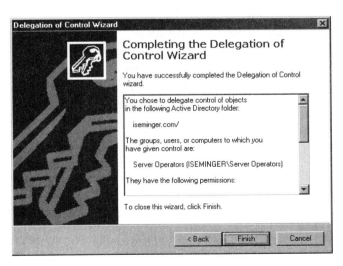

**Figure 9-86.** *The Completing The Delegation Of Control Wizard screen.*

**Real World**

You can augment the delegation of control by creating customized MMC consoles, saving them, and distributing them to appropriate administrators. This approach can greatly ease administration. Since these customized consoles aren't tied to a lot of data, they aren't very large and can therefore easily be sent in e-mail. To save a certain configuration for an MMC console, simply arrange the settings as you want them, click Console, and then click Save. The configuration is saved as the file name you provide, with the .msc extension appended. If you want to ensure that the settings aren't changed, you can configure the .msc console file permissions as read-only.

## Performing Active Directory Services Backups and Restores

Backing up your data is like putting gas into your car; if you don't do it consistently, you're eventually going to get stuck somewhere unpleasant. Backing up is a basic part of administration, and if you don't do it, you're endangering the ongoing health and uptime of your deployment.

Windows 2000 comes with a suite of backup tools that can be launched from the command line by typing ntbackup or from the Windows 2000 System Tools group by clicking Backup. Figure 9-87 shows the welcome screen you see with the Windows 2000 Backup and Recovery Tools.

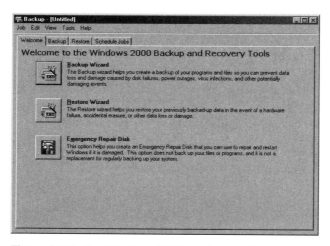

**Figure 9-87.** *The Windows 2000 Backup and Recovery Tools welcome screen.*

The Windows 2000 Backup and Recovery Tools suite provides a Backup wizard that guides you through the process of backing up your data and can help you decide what type of backup fits best with the selections you make during this process. If you want to back up Active Directory services, however, only one backup method enables you to back up the Active Directory information repository and its associated files: Normal backup of the System State data.

A handful of Windows 2000 Backup and Recovery Tools features make the backing up of Active Directory services and related information an administrator-friendly process.

- Backups can be performed on a domain controller while the domain controller remains on line.
- The System State data backed up in association with Active Directory services enables the entire domain controller's state (and thereby the entire domain's Active Directory services state) to be restored from the backup. You do not need to perform separate backup operations for Active Directory information and system status information.
- Backup can be performed with batch files or scripting, or it can be scheduled with the interface provided in Windows 2000 Backup and Recovery Tools.
- Active Directory services (and the domain controller's associated System State data) can be backed up to any removable media or to a file.

The *System State data* is a collection of settings and files that enable the Windows 2000 Server computer to be placed in exactly the state it was in when the backup was performed. If you don't include the System State data during a given Active Directory services backup, inconsistencies with the Windows 2000 operating system and your Active Directory snapshot could lead to instability or data inconsistency—all of which is avoided by tying the Windows 2000 System State data to an Active Directory backup. System State data consists of the following:

- System startup files
- The system registry
- The computer's COM+ class registration database
- File Replication Services
- Certificate Server, if installed
- DNS, if installed
- The Active Directory services information repository

---

**Note**   You cannot restore an Active Directory services backup without restoring System State data.

## Performing a Backup

Performing the backup of Active Directory services (every week at least, please!) is very straightforward. Performing the backup consists of launching the Windows 2000 Backup and Restore Tools as explained previously, clicking the Backup wizard button, and then following the wizard through the following steps:

1. Click Start, then Programs, then Accessories, then System Tools, and then Backup. In the Backup dialog box that appears, click the Backup wizard button. The standard wizard welcome screen appears, as shown in Figure 9-88.

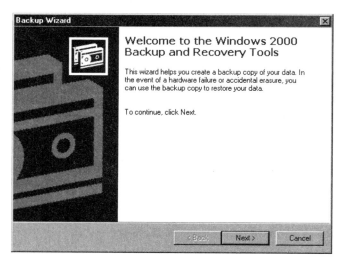

**Figure 9-88.** *The welcome screen of the Windows 2000 Backup wizard.*

2.  Click Next to display the What To Back Up screen, as shown in Figure 9-89. Here you select the data you want to back up. You must click Only Back Up The System State Data to back up your Active Directory information store.

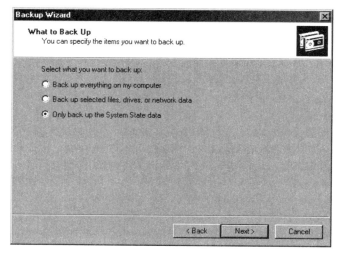

**Figure 9-89.** *The What To Back Up screen of the Windows 2000 Backup wizard.*

3.  Click Next to display the Where To Store The Backup screen, as shown in Figure 9-90. Here you specify the location of the backup file, which can be an installed backup medium such as tape, CD-R, CD-RW or a file.

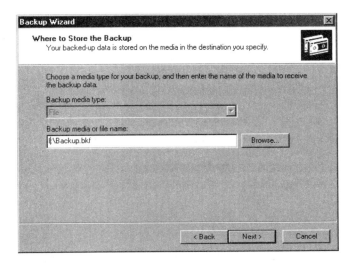

**Figure 9-90.** *The Where To Store The Backup screen of the Windows 2000 Backup wizard.*

4.   Click Next to display the Completing The Backup Wizard screen, as shown in Figure 9-91. This screen displays a summary of your backup choices.

**Figure 9-91.** *The Completing The Backup Wizard screen.*

5.   If that's all the configuring you want to do, you can initiate the backup by clicking Finish. However, some advanced settings are worth noting and are pertinent to Active Directory services. You can access these advanced settings by clicking the Advanced button.

6. Click the Advanced button. The Type Of Backup screen appears, as shown in Figure 9-92. Here you can specify the type of backup to be performed. Remember that you must choose Normal backup when backing up Active Directory services.

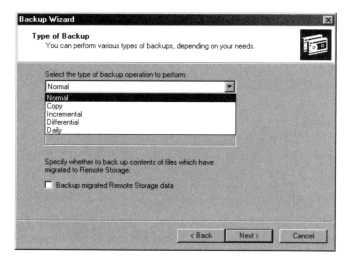

**Figure 9-92.** *The Type Of Backup screen.*

7. Click Next to display the How To Back Up screen, as shown in Figure 9-93. Here choose whether or not you want to verify the backed up data after it's been written to the backup destination.

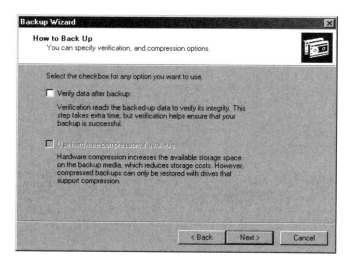

**Figure 9-93.** *The How To Back Up screen.*

8. Click Next to display the Media Options screen, as shown in Figure 9-94. Here you choose whether you want the backup to append data to the medium or overwrite it.

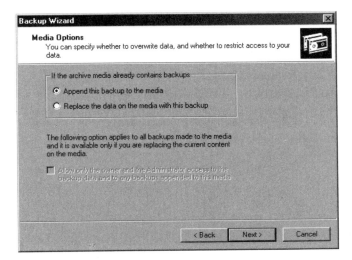

**Figure 9-94.** *The Media Options screen.*

9. Click Next to display the Backup Label screen, as shown in Figure 9-95. Here you provide a label for the backup itself and for the media as desired.

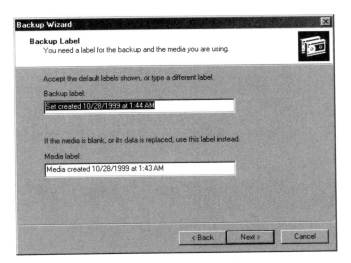

**Figure 9-95.** *The Backup Label screen.*

10. Click Next to display the When To Back Up screen, as shown in Figure 9-96. Here you choose whether to perform the backup immediately or to schedule it for later execution, and enter a schedule. When the process is completed, the Backup wizard sends you back to the Completing The Backup Wizard screen shown in Figure 9-91.

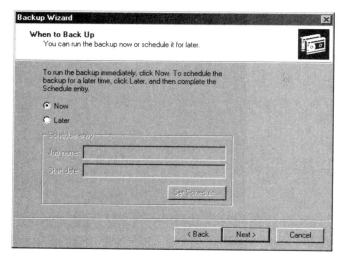

**Figure 9-96.** *The When To Back Up screen.*

11. If you've chosen to back up immediately, after you click Finish you can watch the backup happen in the Backup screen, as shown in Figure 9-97.

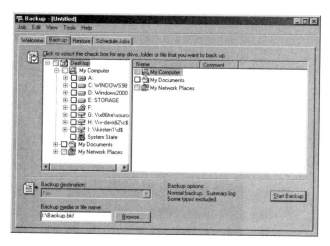

**Figure 9-97.** *Monitoring backup status in the Backup screen.*

> **Caution**   With the backup utility (in Windows 2000 Backup and Restore Tools) provided with Windows 2000, you can perform backups on only the local computer, which means you'll have to be at the physically secured domain controller to do so. There will certainly be third-party backup programs that will enable administrators to perform remote backups.

### Performing a Restore

When you need to restore Active Directory services (hopefully *not* every week!), you need to perform the following steps:

1. Remove (delete) all references in the Active Directory Sites And Services snap-in to the domain controller being restored.

2. Determine whether you will perform an authoritative restore or a nonauthoritative restore. Authoritative and nonauthoritative restores are explained in the paragraphs following this list.

3. If necessary, reinstall Windows 2000 Server on the computer.

4. Load Windows 2000 on the computer in Directory Services Restore Mode by pressing F8 at startup and choosing Directory Services Restore Mode.

5. While the computer is in Directory Services Restore Mode, perform the restore using the Restore wizard in Windows 2000 Backup and Restore Tools.

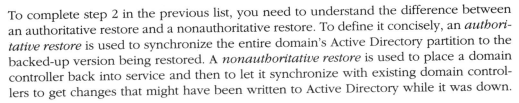

> **Caution**   You must be an administrator on the *local system* to perform a restoration of Active Directory services. That means you have to log on with an account on the local system (not in Active Directory) that has administrator privileges in order to successfully perform an Active Directory services restore.

To complete step 2 in the previous list, you need to understand the difference between an authoritative restore and a nonauthoritative restore. To define it concisely, an *authoritative restore* is used to synchronize the entire domain's Active Directory partition to the backed-up version being restored. A *nonauthoritative restore* is used to place a domain controller back into service and then to let it synchronize with existing domain controllers to get changes that might have been written to Active Directory while it was down.

By default, the restore process in the Restore wizard included as part of the Windows 2000 Backup and Restore Tools performs a nonauthoritative restore. If you want to perform a nonauthoritative restore, you must simply follow the steps outlined in the previous list, and once the restored domain controller synchronizes with existing domain controllers, its restore is complete.

To perform an authoritative restore, you must take additional steps. Once you have performed the restore in Directory Services Restore Mode, leave the computer in that mode and use the Ntdsutil command-line utility to mark as authoritative either part of the restored directory partition or the entire directory partition. Performing an authoritative restore for part of the directory is useful if a particular object or container is inadvertently deleted, but you should use such restores with caution and reluctance. For example, the following commands could be typed at the command prompt to specify an authoritative restore for only the Sales OU in the *corp.iseminger.com* domain:

```
D:\>ntdsutil
ntdsutil: authoritative restore
Restore Subtree OU=Sales,DC=corp,DC=Iseminger,DC=COM
```

If you want to get information about the options available with the Ntdsutil command-line utility, type a question mark (?) at the authoritative restore: prompt. The following Help information appears:

```
authoritative restore: ?

?                            - Print this help information
Help                         - Print this help information
Quit                         - Return to the prior menu
Restore database             - Authoritatively restore entire …
Restore database verinc %d   - … and override version increase
Restore subtree %s           - Authoritatively restore a subtree
Restore subtree %s verinc %d - … and override version increase
```

**More Info**   There's all sorts of information about Ntdsutil in the final section of this chapter, including information about its options and parameters.

Once you've completed the authoritative restore, you can reboot the computer and bring it on line in Standard Mode (without pressing F8 at startup to choose options). At that point, all other domain controllers in the restored domain controller's domain will synchronize their entire directory tree or a specified subset with the restored version. (You used Ntdsutil to specify whether the authoritative restore should be performed for all or part of the tree, remember?)

It's important to restate that authoritative restores should be used only in drastic situations; since Active Directory services is a multimaster directory service, you can avoid such restore requirements. In most circumstances, a nonauthoritative restore (which includes the subsequent synchronization of the restored domain controller with existing domain controllers) will be the only restore you'll need to perform. Use the authoritative restore option only in dire circumstances.

## Advanced Management

Some management tasks are less commonly performed and are generally the responsibility of senior IT staff members with advanced skills. Some of these advanced management tasks, such as specifying the kinds of applications or settings over which users have control, require that policies be made on a corporate basis and must be carried out through the network-enabled capabilities of tools such as Active Directory services. Other advanced management tasks simply require more sophistication on the administrator's part than everyday management tasks require or at least a more advanced skills set than some administrators (perhaps those who must only reset passwords or add computer accounts) might have.

There could be all sorts of advanced management issues in a given organization. Configuring a router to enable Resource Reservation Protocol (RSVP) signaling could be considered an advanced management task, but such a task isn't directly associated with Active Directory services. Other administrative tasks, such as defining new schema classes and implementing associated user interfaces (display specifiers) to access such advanced schema capabilities, are too dependent on individual implementations to properly explain here and therefore are better suited for dedicated books or treatments. In this section, the advanced management tasks being addressed are general enough that they can be explained in a straightforward fashion, but they are tasks that you can perform or familiarize yourself with and then modify as appropriate for your deployment.

## Managing Replication Strategies

Active Directory services automatically takes care of most replication concerns for Active Directory information by creating a connection topology that's housed in the Configuration container and that enables Active Directory information to make the best use possible of network connections. After you create sites and specify site links and their associated costs, Active Directory creates a virtual map of your sites (and their interconnections) and directs Active Directory replication traffic according to prescribed intersite and intrasite algorithms.

However, there are some Active Directory replication facts an administrator should know about to have a complete understanding of the way Active Directory services (automatically) handles replication. The following is a list of the issues and technologies an administrator should understand when considering Active Directory replication strategies:

- The KCC
- Bridgehead servers
- Manual designations

These issues and technologies will be discussed in the sections that follow.

---

**Planning**   Realize that as an administrator you do not have to do anything for Active Directory services to create an optimized replication strategy for your enterprise. Replication topology is created automatically, and the automated selections Active Directory services makes for your deployment's replication strategy function just fine without any intervention by you. The following sections present situations in which you might want to make modifications to that automatically created process.

## The KCC

The KCC is a process that runs on every domain controller and is responsible for creating the replication topology for an Active Directory deployment and implementing the replication strategy—such as the routes and connections used to replicate Active Directory information between domain controllers and between sites—for the entire deployment. The KCC is responsible for evaluating sites and site links, site-link costs and schedules, available domain controllers, and other factors; and it automatically creates the replication strategy (topology) for your deployment. By default, the KCC process runs every 15 minutes, and each time it runs, the entire replication topology is reconsidered. Replication partners, connections, site information, site-link information, subnet settings within a given site, bridgehead servers, and other settings are analyzed; the appropriate settings (perhaps without any changes from the previous analysis) are put in place; and the replication topology is thereby re-created.

During its analysis of sites and site links, the KCC automatically designates which domain controllers replicate to each other and how updated information is replicated between sites. Figure 9-98 illustrates how replication data is handled during both intrasite replication (when data is being sent within a site) and intersite replication (when data is being sent across site links to another site). You might recognize this illustration from Chapter 7, "Planning an Active Directory Services Deployment."

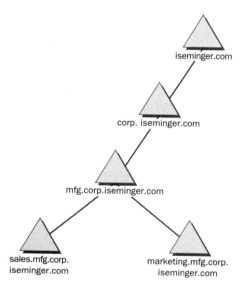

**Figure 9-98.** *How intrasite replication traffic is handled compared to how intersite replication traffic is handled.*

As you can see from the table, replication data sent between sites is compressed before it is transmitted in order to conserve site-link (WAN) bandwidth. Another strategy the KCC uses to conserve site-link bandwidth is the use of bridgehead servers. Bridgehead servers are explained in the following section.

The important fact to remember about the KCC is that its activity is automatic and doesn't require any intervention from the administrator. There's nothing to manage, nothing to configure, and nothing to schedule (outside of site-link use) for the KCC to perform its tasks. However, you can modify how the KCC implements replication traffic transmissions by making manual designations.

**Note**   Domain controllers have built-in safeguards to prevent replication data from updating continuously throughout the enterprise. These safeguards are based on the use of Update Sequence Numbers (USNs) for updates. See Chapter 5, "More Active Directory Services Architecture," for more information on USNs.

## Bridgehead Servers

When Active Directory replication traffic is transmitted between two sites, the KCC uses all means possible to ensure that the site-link bandwidth used for the replication data is kept to a minimum. One strategy is to compress the data before it is sent over the site link, and another involves the use of what is called a bridgehead server. A *bridgehead server* is a single domain controller in each site that receives all intersite replication data. After receiving replication updates from another site, the bridgehead server disseminates the replication data to other domain controllers within its site, thereby reducing the replication traffic that must cross the site link.

To better understand how this process works, consider the following sequence of illustrations. In Figure 9-99, you'll see two sites in a sample Active Directory services deployment. Each site has multiple domain controllers, and each site has one bridgehead server designated by the KCC.

At certain intervals (the length of which are based on settings in the site-link schedule and which are 3 hours unless otherwise configured), the bridgehead server in Site 2 polls the bridgehead server in Site 1 for any updates it might require. If the bridgehead server in Site 1 determines that it has updated Active Directory data, it compresses the replication information and sends it to the bridgehead server in Site 2, as illustrated in Figure 9-100.

Notice that the bridgehead server is polling for changes as opposed to being notified of replication changes. Polling is used with all bridgehead servers. This is a superior approach to replicating updates; with push replication (the inferior choice), it is difficult for a source domain controller to know what replication data is needed by the destination domain controller. With pull replication (the better implementation and the implementation used in Active Directory services), the destination domain controller knows which replication information to request (for example, "Send me all data that has a USN higher than $x$").

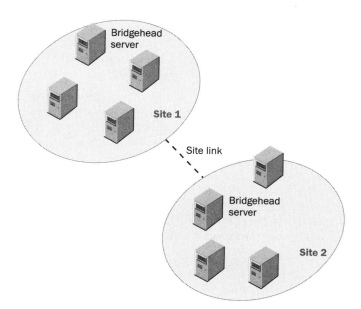

**Figure 9-99.** *Two sites in an Active Directory deployment, with multiple domain controllers and one bridgehead server in each site.*

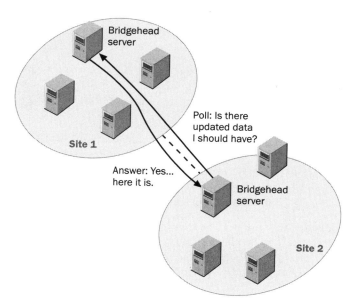

**Figure 9-100.** *The bridgehead server polls the bridgehead server in another site for updated data, and if it is appropriate to do so, the data is transmitted.*

Since domain controllers within a site are well connected (and are generally more up-to-date since their replication isn't constrained by site-link schedules), notifications are used to indicate that an update is available. After the domain controller's replication partners are notified, they can pull necessary replication data.

Once the bridgehead server has received all the replication data, it proceeds to disseminate the replication data to the rest of the domain controllers in its site, without compressing the information, as illustrated in Figure 9-101.

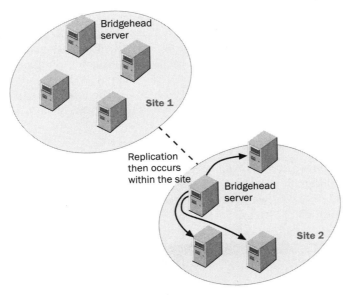

**Figure 9-101.** *Once the bridgehead server has received the updated information from the bridgehead server in another site, it replicates the information to other domain controllers in its own site.*

You might want the KCC to use a specific domain controller as the preferred bridgehead server for a given site. If this is the case, you need to manually designate the domain controller to serve as the bridgehead server.

## Manual Designation

You already have some part in creating the Active Directory replication strategy; you define sites and site links and associate schedules and costs with those site links. As previously mentioned, the KCC uses that information to generate its replication strategy. However, you might want to further control the replication strategy. For example, you might want to specify one or more domain controllers in your site as preferred bridgehead servers or specify a domain controller's immediate replication partner or partners. When you manually designate more than one domain controller as preferred bridgehead servers, the KCC automatically chooses one of them as the site's bridgehead server.

Manual designation can be done in a number of ways. (This sounds familiar, doesn't it?) The graphical user interface you use to make changes to the replication strategy is the Active Directory Sites And Services snap-in, but you can also make replication-based designations with command-line utilities, such as the Repadmin utility provided in the Windows 2000 Resource Kit. Realize, however, that by manually designating one or more particular domain controllers as preferred bridgehead servers, you limit the capability of the KCC to provide bridgehead server failover to another domain controller if your preferred bridgehead server or servers go off line. When the automatically designated bridgehead server is unavailable, the KCC automatically selects another domain controller to perform bridgehead server operations. If you manually designate one or more domain controllers as bridgehead servers and none of your manually designated bridgehead servers are available, replication will not occur to that site. The KCC instead logs an error message (viewable through Event Viewer) that states that you have designated bridgehead servers and that none of them are available.

To designate a server as a bridgehead server, follow these steps:

1. In the Active Directory Sites And Services snap-in, expand the site for which you want to designate a preferred bridgehead server, expand its Servers container, right-click the server you want to designate as a preferred bridgehead server, and then click Properties, as shown in Figure 9-102.

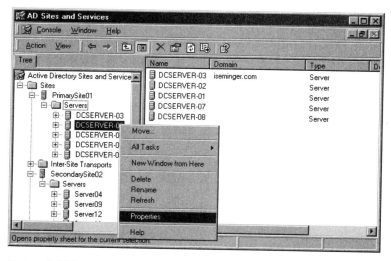

**Figure 9-102.** *Choosing Properties in the target domain controller's shortcut menu in the Active Directory Sites And Services snap-in.*

3. The domain controller's property sheet should appear. Choose the transport for which you want the domain controller to be a preferred bridgehead server and click Add, as shown in Figure 9-103.

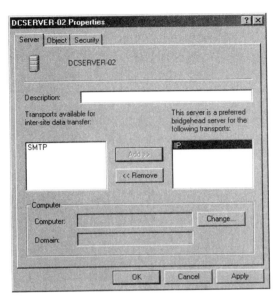

**Figure 9-103.** *Selecting the transport for which you want your domain controller to be a preferred bridgehead server.*

## Windows 2000 Group Policy

Windows 2000 provides an extended and comprehensive infrastructure for managing user, group, and computer policies in a Windows 2000 and Active Directory services environment. This infrastructure is built around Windows 2000 Group Policy and includes the concept of configurable, assignable, and nestable instances of Group Policy settings known as Group Policy objects, or GPOs, for yet another three-letter acronym (TLA).

Group Policy is enabled by Active Directory services rather than being part of the Active Directory services infrastructure. However, Group Policy needed to be explained in this book because the same administrators who are responsible for managing Active Directory services will likely be responsible for managing Group Policy, or at the very least, Active Directory administrators will be expected to be familiar with Group Policy.

Simply put, Group Policy enables administrators to centrally manage and control Windows 2000 desktops.

Group Policy has settings that administrators can specify or control, the collection of which governs the user's experience at a Windows 2000 computer. When an administrator defines a collection of these settings, they are saved in a GPO. Once these settings are defined and saved—thereby becoming a GPO—they can be applied to relevant objects that Windows 2000 uses to organize its environment, such as users or organizational units. There is a vast collection of settings that can be applied, and you can assign more than one GPO to the same group. For example, say that you define one GPO that requires the screen size of users' workstations to be set to 800 by 600 and then you define another GPO that requires the users' passwords to be at least eight characters in length. You could apply both GPOs to a given group, resulting in workstations with 800 by 600 screens and user passwords that were at least eight characters in length.

Group Policy has a couple of operational dimensions that you should understand. Group Policy objects can apply to an Active Directory container such as an OU, which defines the administrative border of the GPO and effectively bounds its authority. (Call this the authority dimension.) Group Policy also has a collection of Group Policy settings, enabling you to define how the GPO affects the objects that reside within the GPO's administrative scope (call this the settings dimension).

### Group Policy Scope

The scope of GPOs can be defined by any of the following Active Directory containers:

- Domains
- OUs
- Sites

When you specify the scope of a GPO, you can specify whether certain security groups within the site, domain, or OU are excluded. GPOs can flow down a hierarchy in such a way that if you specify a GPO for a given OU, you can have that GPO apply to all nested GPOs. Thus, you can specify one GPO as high in the hierarchy as possible and, in so doing, enable that GPO to apply to all objects farther down the hierarchy. At each level of the hierarchy, you can specify whether a particular GPO applies to the container (an OU, for example) over which you have administrative control. (You must, however, have sufficient access rights to do so.)

There could be instances in which inherited GPOs conflict with a GPO you want to specify for a given container. To address this situation, Group Policy enables administrators to specify whether a particular GPO inherits settings from GPOs defined higher in the hierarchy or whether a given GPO overrides such settings. Active Directory enforces GPOs in the following order:

1. Site-based GPOs
2. Domain-based GPOs
3. OU-based GPOs

For example, if a certain setting is defined in a GPO with a scope of a certain site and that setting is also defined in a GPO whose scope is an OU within that site, the setting in the site-based GPO overrides the setting defined in the OU-based GPO.

**Planning**  If you want to define a GPO whose scope encompasses a container that is beneath other containers that also have GPOs applied to them, you can set your GPO to override inherited settings. Of course, overriding inherited settings is subject to access restrictions; with appropriate access rights, you can also specify that settings in a given GPO cannot be overridden. Therefore, if you want to ensure that a given policy applies to your entire enterprise, you should ensure that it's set at the site level and that its settings cannot be overridden.

## Group Policy Settings

Group Policy settings are based on the following objects:

- **Computers:** Group Policy settings that are based on computers (or groups of computers, such as all computers in a specified OU, site, or domain) restrict the behavior of a computer, regardless of which user is logged on. You can set restrictions such as assigned and published applications, security settings, or printers.

- **Users or groups:**  Group Policy settings that are based on groups follow users or group members to any Windows 2000 computer that they use. For example, if a user named Paul is assigned a particular application through a GPO assigned to his OU—whether the GPO is enforced based on his individual user account or enforced based on a group to which he belongs—that application will appear on any Windows 2000 computer Paul uses, as long as that computer is within the GPO's scope (Paul's OU). In this example, the administrative boundary is the OU, and the GPO applies to (is enforced based on) his user account (or his group membership).

Group Policy is configured and administered through the Active Directory Users And Computers snap-in. To create a GPO Group Policy Object, follow these steps:

1. Right-click the object in the Active Directory Users And Computers snap-in that represents the scope you want the GPO to have, and then choose Properties from the shortcut menu. The property sheet for the object appear, as shown in Figure 9-104.

2. From the Group Policy property page, you can create new GPOs for use in the container, apply an existing GPO to the container, or perform other administrative tasks associated with Group Policy. If you click Add to create a new GPO or Edit to edit an existing GPO, the Group Policy snap-in is launched, as shown in Figure 9-105.

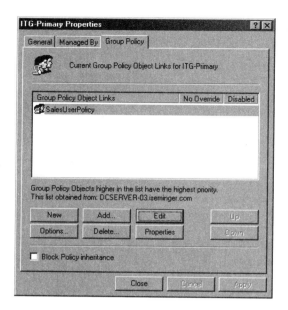

**Figure 9-104.** *Clicking Properties in the shortcut menu of a Container object brings up the object's properties and is the first step in creating a GPO.*

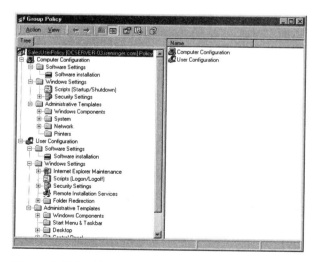

**Figure 9-105.** *The Group Policy snap-in.*

3.  Choose the Group Policy settings you want to include in the new GPO. There are a lot of settings to choose from, but as mentioned previously, policy settings

are based on computers or users. The best way to familiarize yourself with all these settings is to look through each one and consider how each setting could be beneficial to your organization. You should ensure that you have a justification whenever you decide to apply a Group Policy setting—just like you should ensure you have a justification when you add a domain to your Active Directory deployment plan. Creating and enforcing policies just for the sake of using the cool new Group Policy interface probably isn't justification enough (although, admittedly, it is compelling).

**More Info**   Group Policy is most effective when coupled with the use of IntelliMirror and Remote Installation Services, both of which are included with Windows 2000 and enabled by Active Directory services. Chapter 14, "Administratively Leveraging Active Directory Services," goes into detail about IntelliMirror and Remote Installation Services.

## Managing FSMO Roles

Part of your initial planning for your Active Directory services deployment is the placement of Active Directory FSMO roles. FSMO roles are explained in detail in Chapter 4, "Active Directory Services Scalability Architecture," but let's quickly recap the FSMO roles an administrator must manage and their coverage.

As you might recall, there are five FSMO roles in Active Directory, and each of these five FSMO roles falls into one of two categories: forestwide roles or domainwide roles. Forestwide roles require only one FSMO master throughout the entire forest, while domainwide FSMO roles require that one Windows 2000 domain controller hold the FSMO role for each domain. Here's a quick recap of which FSMO roles fall into which category:

- **Forestwide FSMO roles:** Schema Master, Domain Naming Master
- **Domainwide FSMO roles:** RID Master, PDC Emulator, Infrastructure Master

Part of the management of these FSMO roles includes ensuring that there is only one role holder for each FSMO role in each category. That means that for each forestwide FSMO role, *only* one domain controller in the entire forest can hold the role. For each domainwide FSMO role, *only* one domain controller in each domain can hold the role. Again, you cannot have more than one domain controller in any forest holding the same forestwide FSMO role, and you cannot have more than one domain controller in any given domain holding the same FSMO role.

Generally, once you plan and place your FSMO role holders, there won't be much reason to reassign those roles to other domain controllers. You should place your forestwide FSMO role holders in your primary site and place the domainwide FSMO role holders in the site that contains the majority of objects for a given domain. For example, if the manufacturing domain is housed primarily in Ireland, which happens to be Site 2 in your Active Directory site configuration, the domain-based FSMO role holders should be physically located in Site 2 (Ireland). For replication purposes, it's best to have all domain-based FSMO role holders in the same site, and it's better yet to ensure FSMO role holders direct replication partners.

When you install the first domain controller for a given forest, that domain controller is assigned as the role holder for all five FSMO roles. When domains are added to a forest, the first domain controller for a given domain is assigned all three domainwide FSMO roles. You must manually transfer FSMO roles to different domain controllers, if appropriate, to change that default setting. Determining whether it is appropriate to transfer an FSMO role to a different domain controller should be based on how much redundancy is built into your network and the number of domain controllers you have. The general rule in computing is that it's good to minimize the impact of a single point of failure. This leads to the conclusion that assigning FSMO roles to different domain controllers is the best approach if such dispersing of FSMO roles is possible (and if other considerations, such as whether the CPU on a given domain controller can handle the relatively low overhead associated with maintaining an FSMO role allow it). That's a good general rule to follow with FSMO roles, but there's an exception to the rule you should keep in mind. The RID Master and PDC Emulator roles should be held by the same domain controller unless the load on the domain controller mandates that you assign these roles to different computers.

**Planning**   Normally, the Infrastructure Master should not be placed on a Global Catalog domain controller because of the Windows 2000 implementation of cross-domain object references. (Cross-domain object references in the domain won't be updated in this scenario.) If all domain controllers are Global Catalog domain controllers, however, it doesn't matter which domain controller is the Infrastructure Master.

When an FSMO role holder goes off line for a short period, it generally does not produce a noticeable effect. However, in the case of hardware failures or other events that might require an FSMO role holder to be off line for an extended period, you might have to transfer the role to another domain controller. This should be a last resort; if possible, let the existing FSMO role holder come back on line. If FSMO roles must be transferred, you can perform the role transfer through the appropriate snap-ins or through the command line.

The graphical interface you use to manage FSMO roles depends on the FSMO role being managed. The following is a list of the roles and their corresponding snap-ins:

- Schema Master is managed with the Active Directory Schema snap-in.
- Domain Naming Master is managed with the Active Directory Domains And Trusts snap-in.
- Domain-based roles are all managed with the Active Directory Users And Computers snap-in.

You can view and manage FSMO roles from the Active Directory snap-ins in several ways:

- In the left pane of the Active Directory Schema snap-in, right-click Active Directory Schema, and then choose Operations Master in the shortcut menu, as shown in Figure 9-106. The Change Schema Master dialog box, as shown in Figure 9-107, is then displayed.

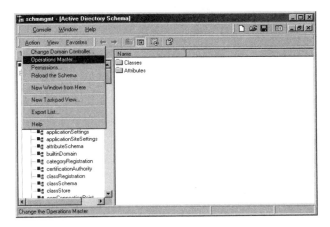

**Figure 9-106.** *The shortcut menu shown when right-clicking the Active Directory Schema snap-in.*

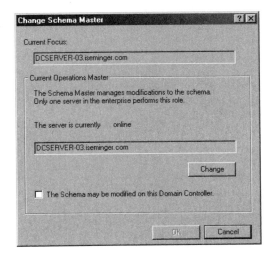

**Figure 9-107.** *The Change Schema Master dialog box.*

- In the left pane of the Active Directory Domains And Trusts snap-in, right-click Active Directory Domains And Trusts and choose Operations Master from the shortcut menu, as shown in Figure 9-108. Figure 9-109 shows the Change Operations Master dialog box that appears. This dialog box can be used for viewing and changing the Domain Naming Master Operations Master role.

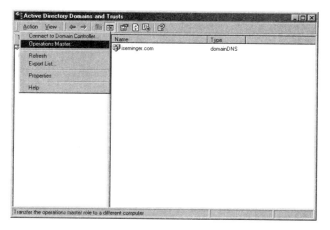

**Figure 9-108.** *The shortcut menu shown when right-clicking the Active Directory Domains And Trusts snap-in.*

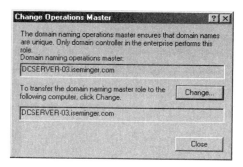

**Figure 9-109.** *The Change Operations Master dialog box.*

- In the left pane of the Active Directory Users And Computers snap-in, right-click Active Directory Users And Computers and choose Operations Master from the shortcut menu. Figure 9-110 shows the one of the three tabs of the Operations Master dialog box that appears.

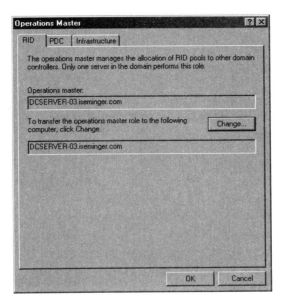

**Figure 9-110.** *The RID tab of the Operations Master dialog box.*

**Note**   Before you can change the FSMO role holder, you must connect to the server to which you want to transfer the FSMO role. You can connect to the server using the Ntdsutil utility.

You can also manage FSMO roles with the Ntdsutil command-line utility. To do so, type ntdsutil at the command line and then type roles. The syntax used when managing roles with the Ntdsutil utility is the following:

```
D:\>ntdsutil
ntdsutil: roles
fsmo maintenance: ?

?                              - Print this help information
Connections                    - Connect to a specific domain
                                 controller
Help                           - Print this help information
Quit                           - Return to the prior menu
Seize domain naming master     - Overwrite domain role on
                                 Connected server
Seize infrastructure master    - Overwrite infrastructure role
                                 on connected server
Seize PDC                      - Overwrite PDC role on
                                 connected server
Seize RID master               - Overwrite RID role on
                                 connected server
```

*(continued)*

*(continued)*

```
Seize schema master              - Overwrite schema role on
                                   connected server
Select operation target          - Select sites, servers, domains,
                                   Roles and Naming Contexts
Transfer domain naming master    - Make connected server the domain
                                   naming master
Transfer infrastructure master   - Make connected server the
                                   infrastructure master
Transfer PDC                     - Make connected server the PDC
Transfer RID master              - Make connected server the RID
                                   Master
Transfer schema master           - Make connected server the schema
                                   Master

fsmo maintenance:
```

The transferring of roles is a fairly quick and simple operation when the existing FSMO role holder (and target FSMO role holder) is on line. However, if the existing FSMO role holder is not on line, as might be the case in a severe hardware failure, you might need to *seize* the FSMO role. Seizing an FSMO role should be a last resort.

> **Note** You must have proper access rights to perform FSMO role transfers. By default, you must be a member of the Schema Administrators group to transfer the Schema Master FSMO role. To transfer the Domain Naming Master FSMO role, you must be a member of the Enterprise Administrators group, and to transfer domain-based FSMO roles, you must be a member of the appropriate Domain Administrators group. Of course, the capability to delegate is pervasive in Active Directory services, so you can delegate the authority to change a corresponding FSMO role if you are a member of one of these groups.

To perform an FSMO role seizure from the command line, use Ntdsutil. To seize the Schema Master, RID Master, or Domain Naming Master, you *must* use Ntdsutil.

> **More Info** For a thorough explanation of each of the FSMO roles in Active Directory services, see Chapter 4, "Active Directory Services Scalability Architecture."

# Command-Line Management

The number of utilities available in Windows from the command line has actually increased with the release of Windows 2000. Although this increase in command line–based utilities might sound odd for an operating system that is deeply rooted in its user interface, it's actually quite logical: administrators like to use the command line.

Of course, if you haven't used the command line much, this might be something that takes a little getting used to. But once you become accustomed to using the command line and begin to use its much faster commands for performing common tasks, you'll feel lost without it—and faster, more efficient, and more effective *with* it.

## Getting the Most out of the Command Line

Since Windows 2000 makes extensive administrative use of the command line, you might as well get comfortable with it. The following sections explain how to customize the command line and offer some shortcuts to make the command-line interface much more user friendly and easier to navigate.

### Customizing the Command Line

You can perform a few optimizations to the Windows 2000 command line (often referred to as the command prompt) that make it much easier to use and more administrator friendly. Adjusting the settings—such as changing the color scheme, adjusting the colors, increasing the command history buffer, and so on—is simple, but it makes working with the command line unbelievably easier.

These settings modifications are just tricks that have worked for a long time in Windows NT and continue to work in Windows 2000, but they're so useful that you'll find yourself at a loss when sitting in front of a command line for which the settings are not applied. I use every one of these settings as soon as I sit in front of a command line—they're that useful.

Figure 9-111 shows the command-line interface as it is presented by Windows 2000 (without any modifications). Although this isn't a color screen shot, notice that the command characters are a little dull and notice the lack of a horizontal scroll bar.

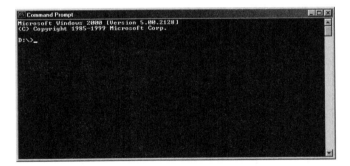

**Figure 9-111.** *An unconfigured command line and its bland settings.*

When you click the leftmost end of the title bar, you get the application menu, from which the command-line configuration parameters are available. Figure 9-112 displays the application menu you get when clicking the appropriate side (left side) of the title bar.

**Figure 9-112.** *Clicking the left side of the title bar brings up the command line's application menu.*

In the command line's application menu, click Properties. You are then presented with a property sheet that enables you to configure the command line. There are configuration settings you can make in each of the property pages, as I'll point out below.

---

**Planning**   The way in which you configure these settings to launch the command line should be the way you intend to launch your command line on a regular basis. Since this configuration information is associated with a shortcut, if you configure the command line for one shortcut, get things just the way you like them, and then launch the command line from a different shortcut, your settings are lost. The best way to avoid this possible inconsistency is to select the way you generally launch the command line (mine is by pressing Windows logo key+R, typing cmd, and then pressing ENTER), make configuration settings, and then launch the command line in that manner from that point forward.

The first property page is the Options property page. Figure 9-113 displays the Windows 2000 command line's Options property page.

I make the following modifications to the Options page:

- In the Command History frame, I increase the command history to 100 by setting Buffer Size to 100. This means that I can easily recall the last 100 commands I entered.

- In the Edit Options frame, I enable QuickEdit mode and Insert mode. QuickEdit mode enables you to drag the contents of a command line with your right mouse button and, upon right-clicking again, to copy the selected contents to the Clipboard. Insert mode enables you to copy contents of the Clipboard (which might have been copied from an earlier command-line command) and move them to the command line.

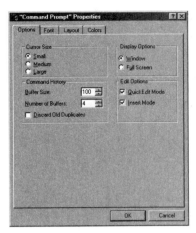

**Figure 9-113.** *The Options property page of the Command Line's property sheet.*

The second page of the Windows 2000 command line's property sheet is the Font page. You can modify any of these font settings and see if the outcome is more to your liking than the default settings, but I generally leave all these alone. No changes you make here will materially affect the advantages found in making changes to the other command-line property pages.

The third page of the command-line's property sheet is the Layout page. Figure 9-114 displays the Windows 2000 command line's Layout page.

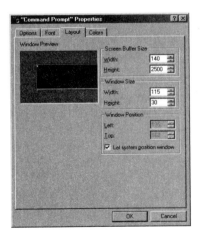

**Figure 9-114.** *The Layout page of the Command Line's property sheet.*

This is where you really get the command-line interface to work the way you want it to. I make the following modifications to the Layout page:

- In the Screen Buffer Size frame, I increase the width of the buffer to 140 and the height to 2500. Making these modifications keeps you from losing the command prompt's output. Without this modification, when more than 300 lines are output the information disappears beyond the top of the Command-Line window and you can't scroll back farther than 300 lines to see the information again—and 300 lines go quickly. With these new settings, you can scroll 2,500 lines up and 140 characters to the right. And if you have a mouse with a wheel, you can use that wheel to scroll back up through the buffer.

- In the Windows Size frame, I change the width of the actual Command-Line window to 115 and the height to 30. The changes you decide to make to these two settings will depend entirely on how you choose to work, and the screen-size settings of your Windows environment will play a part. I have my screen area set to 1152 by 864; on a 21-inch monitor, 115-characters-wide by 30-characters-high is perfect (for me). You can play with these settings to get the combination that works best for you.

**Note** To check or modify your screen-size settings, right-click anywhere in the Windows desktop, click Properties, and then click the Settings page. The settings are displayed below the Desktop area slider. If you aren't an administrator on your local computer, you might not be able to modify the screen-size settings.

The fourth page of the command-line property sheet is the Colors page. Figure 9-115 displays the Windows 2000 command line's Colors property page.

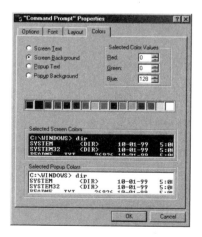

**Figure 9-115.** *The Colors page of the Command Line's property sheet.*

I'd show you the custom interface we just created, but the gray scale book illustration would not do the comparison justice. I make the following modifications to the Colors property sheet:

- For Screen Background, I choose navy blue instead of leaving it set to black. (Click the Screen Background option button, and the rest of the property sheet's settings will apply to the screen background.) Navy blue is the second box from the left in the color bar and is the selected box in Figure 9-115.
- For Screen Text, I choose white instead of the dirty-gray color that's chosen by default. This combination of a navy-blue background and white text is much easier on my eyes. You might have a selection of colors you like better; you can customize the appearance of the command line to fit your liking.

As soon as you click OK, the command line asks you whether you want to apply the property changes you just made to the current window only or to modify the shortcut from which you launched your Command-Line window. (If you choose the former option, the changes will disappear as soon as you close the command-line session; if you choose the latter option, your changes will stick with the shortcut you used.)

You can contrast the default command-line interface shown in Figure 9-111 with the customized command-line interface you just created.

Of course, the customizations I like to make to the command line when I'm working might not be great for you. Armed with the easily accessible customization information included in this section, though, you'll hopefully find a way to make the command line a management tool that works and appears how you want it to.

## Command-Line Shortcuts

Command-line shortcuts are perhaps little known, but they are quite useful. Once you're familiar with these command-line shortcuts, you'll likely find yourself using them quite often and wondering how you functioned before you knew about their existence (which is similar to how you probably felt about e-mail and the Internet).

| Shortcut Key | Description |
| --- | --- |
| UP ARROW | Displays the previous command. Pressing UP ARROW repeatedly steps backward through the command buffer one command at a time. Same as pressing F5. |
| DOWN ARROW | Displays the next command (in the command buffer). |
| LEFT ARROW | Moves left one space in the command without erasing existing characters. |
| RIGHT ARROW | Each time this key is pressed, one character from the previously executed or selected command is displayed. |

*(continued)*

*(continued)*

| Shortcut Key | Description |
| --- | --- |
| F1 | Each time this key is pressed, one character from the previous command is typed and the cursor is moved to the next position to the right. Same as using the RIGHT ARROW key. |
| F2 | Copies the previous command, up to a specified character. |
| F3 | Displays the command holding the most recent position in the command buffer. |
| F4 | Deletes all characters between the cursor and the next instance (to the right) of the specified character. Deletes characters up to (but not including) the specified character. |
| F5 | Displays the previous command. Same as the UP ARROW key. |
| F7 | Displays a listing of the command buffer, through which you can navigate with the UP ARROW and DOWN ARROW keys, the HOME and END keys, and the PAGE UP and PAGE DOWN keys. |
| F8 | Cycles repeatedly upward through the command buffer. |
| F9 | Enables selection of a command from its numbered position in the command buffer. |

There are some Windows 2000 user-interface shortcuts that are accessible from the keyboard that can be real time-savers as well. The following listing provides some of the most commonly used shortcuts:

| Key Combination | Result |
| --- | --- |
| Windows logo key+R | Displays the Run command |
| Windows logo key+E | Launches Windows Explorer |
| Windows logo key+F | Launches a dialog box that enables you to find files |
| CTRL+SHIFT+ESC | Opens the Windows Task Manager |
| CTRL+ESC | Opens the Start menu (same as clicking the Start button) |

Some of the commonly used utilities in Active Directory services also have short executable names that reside in the path, which enable you to launch the utilities by simply typing their executable name at either the command line or in the Run dialog box. Those commonly used utilities and their shortcuts are the following:

| Command | Description |
| --- | --- |
| Cmd | Opens an instance of the command line |
| Eventvwr | Launches the Windows 2000 Event Viewer snap-in (a great first step in any troubleshooting session) |
| Mmc | Opens the MMC as a blank shell (no snap-ins loaded) |
| Perfmon | Launches the Windows 2000 Performance snap-in (formerly known as Performance Monitor) |
| Winmsd | Launches the System Information snap-in |
| Winver | Launches the Windows Version Information window |

### Command-Line Syntax

The command line can certainly do more than what I've outlined in the previous paragraphs. The shortcuts I've explained can be really useful for administrators, but it's nice to know that more Help information for the command line is available. To get (cmd.exe) context-sensitive help, simply type cmd /? at the command prompt, and Windows 2000 will display its help information one screen at a time.

## Active Directory Services Command-Line Utilities

One of the primary tools you'll use to manage Active Directory services is a command-line based utility: Ntdsutil. The utility is multifaceted, has extensive submenus, and in general is the equivalent of a handful of utilities that all just happen to be rolled up into one neat executable file.

General Windows 2000 management makes extensive use of the command line by using such utilities as Net * (a long collection of network-based commands, such as Net use), Ipconfig, Ping, Route, and the standard suite of navigational commands that most people use when working with the command line (such as Dir, Cd, Xcopy, Rd, Pushd, Netstat, and others). While these commands are useful, this section is going to target the more complex commands that administrators will likely use to manage Active Directory services from the command line. The commands covered in this section are as follows:

- Ntdsutil
- LDIFDE
- Runas

The final command, Runas, is new with Windows 2000 and is not specifically tied to Active Directory services, but I've talked to administrators who wanted to, but couldn't, do in previous versions of Windows what Runas is capable of doing. Runas could be extremely useful to administrators in their day-to-day management, and for that reason, it's included here.

### The Ntdsutil Utility

The primary command-line utility used to manage Active Directory services is the Ntdsutil utility. This utility enables many of the administrative tasks and is the only administrative interface for some Active Directory tasks. You should get used to using Ntdsutil.

Ntdsutil is complex, and it sometimes can be difficult to envision the utility as a whole because of its extensive set of submenus. This section provides you with a printed version of the Help information for Ntdsutil and its subcommands, which hopefully will be a little more approachable than the online version.

Navigating Ntdsutil isn't all that difficult, but it's easy to get lost because of the utility's submenus. The rule to keep in mind is that when you type **q** (for quit), you get dropped into the next highest submenu group in the utility. For example, if you type Ntdsutil at the command line (and press ENTER), you are put into the main Ntdsutil menu structure.

If you then type **ROLES** (and press ENTER), you jump into the FSMO Roles submenu. At this point, if you type **Q** (and press ENTER), you are dropped back to the main Ntdsutil menu structure.

Reproduced below is the Help information that appears between each submenu, which will hopefully clarify the submenu structure. The first set of Help information is the main Ntdsutil menu. I'll go through each of its submenu groups (such as Authoritative restore) in turn.

```
D:\>ntdsutil
ntdsutil: ?

?                              - Print this help information
Authoritative restore          - Authoritatively restore the DIT
                                 database
Domain management              - Prepare for new domain creation
Files                          - Manage NTDS database files
Help                           - Print this help information
IPDeny List                    - Manage LDAP IP Deny List
LDAP policies                  - Manage LDAP protocol policies
Metadata cleanup               - Clean up objects of decommissioned
                                 servers
Popups %s                      - (en/dis)able popups with "on" or
                                 "off"
Quit                           - Quit the utility
Roles                          - Manage NTDS role owner tokens
Security account management    - Manage Security Account Database -
                                 Duplicate SID Cleanup
Semantic database analysis     - Semantic Checker


ntdsutil: authoritative restore
authoritative restore: ?

?                              - Print this help information
Help                           - Print this help information
Quit                           - Return to the prior menu
Restore database               - Authoritatively restore entire
                                 database
Restore database verinc %d     - ... and override version increase
Restore subtree %s             - Authoritatively restore a subtree
Restore subtree %s verinc %d   - ... and override version increase


ntdsutil: domain management
domain management: ?

?                              - Print this help information
Connections                    - Connect to a specific domain
                                 controller
```

```
Help                          - Print this help information
List                          - List known Naming Contexts
Precreate %s %s               - Precreate CR for domain %s1 (a DN)
                                allowing server %s2 (a full DNS
                                name) to dcpromo

Quit                          - Return to the prior menu
Select operation target       - Select sites, servers, domains,
                                Roles and Naming Contexts
```

```
ntdsutil: files
file maintenance: ?
```

```
?                             - Print this help information
Compact to %s                 - Compact DB to specified directory
Header                        - Dump the Jet database header
Help                          - Print this help information
Info                          - Return information about DS files
Integrity                     - Perform Jet integrity check
Move DB to %s                 - Move DB to specified directory
Move logs to %s               - Move log files to specified
                                directory

Quit                          - Return to the prior menu
Recover                       - Perform soft database recovery
Repair                        - Perform database repair - YOU CAN
                                LOSE DATA

Set path backup %s            - Set online backup directory path
Set path DB %s                - Set DB file path
Set path logs %s              - Set logging directory path
Set path working dir %s       - Set NTDS working directory path
```

```
ntdsutil: ipdeny list
IP Deny List: ?
```

```
?                             - Print this help information
Add %s %s                     - Add IP address as
                                <Address> <Mask>
                                Use "NODE" as mask for single node.
                                Examples: add 172.32.12.34 NODE
                                          add 172.34.44.0
                                              255.255.255.0

Cancel                        - Cancel the changes made
Commit                        - Commit the changes made to the server
Connections                   - Connect to a specific domain
                                controller

Delete %d                     - Delete an entry with given index.
Help                          - Print this help information
Quit                          - Return to the prior menu
```

*(continued)*

*(continued)*

```
Show                             - Show current list of IP addresses
                                   on list
Test %s                          - Test an IP address against the
                                   Current list



ntdsutil: ldap policies
ldap policy: ?

?                                - Print this help information
Cancel Changes                   - Cancel the changes made
Commit Changes                   - Commit the changes made to the
                                   server
Connections                      - Connect to a specific domain
                                   controller
Help                             - Print this help information
List                             - Lists supported policies on
                                   the server
Quit                             - Return to the prior menu
Set %s to %s                     - Sets the policy value
Show Values                      - Show values of policies



ntdsutil: metadata cleanup
metadata cleanup: ?

?                                - Print this help information
Connections                      - Connect to a specific domain
                                   controller
Help                             - Print this help information
Quit                             - Return to the prior menu
Remove selected domain           - Remove DS objects for selected
                                   domain
Remove selected Naming Context   - Remove DS objects for selected
                                   Naming Context
Remove selected server           - Remove DS objects for selected
                                   server
Select operation target          - Select sites, servers, domains,
                                   Roles and Naming Contexts



ntdsutil: roles
fsmo maintenance: ?

?                                - Print this help information
Connections                      - Connect to a specific domain
                                   controller
Help                             - Print this help information
Quit                             - Return to the prior menu
```

```
Seize domain naming master       - Overwrite domain role on
                                   connected server
Seize infrastructure master      - Overwrite infrastructure role
                                   on connected server
Seize PDC                        - Overwrite PDC role on connected
                                   server
Seize RID master                 - Overwrite RID role on connected
                                   server
Seize schema master              - Overwrite schema role on
                                   connected server
Select operation target          - Select sites, servers, domains,
                                   roles and Naming Contexts
Transfer domain naming master    - Make connected server the domain
                                   naming master
Transfer infrastructure master - Make connected server the
                                   infrastructure master
Transfer PDC                     - Make connected server the PDC
Transfer RID master              - Make connected server the RID
                                   master
Transfer schema master           - Make connected server the
                                   schema master


ntdsutil: security account management
Security Account Maintenance: ?

?                                - Print this help information
Check Duplicate SID              - Check SAM database for any
                                   duplicate SID.  Won't Clean them
Cleanup Duplicate SID            - Check SAM database for any
                                   duplicate SID and Clean them up
Connect to server %s             - Connect to server, Net Bios Name
                                   or DNS host name
Help                             - Print this help information
Log File %s                      - Specify log file name, otherwise
                                   the default is dupsid.log
Quit                             - Return to the prior menu


ntdsutil: semantic database analysis
semantic checker: ?

?                                - Print this help information
Get %d                           - Get record info with given DNT
Go                               - Start Semantic Checker With No
                                   Fixup
Go Fixup                         - Start Semantic Checker with
                                   Fixup
Help                             - Print this help information
Quit                             - Return to the prior menu
Verbose %s                       - Turn verbose mode on/off
```

Note that some of the submenus (such as Domain management) have items that have submenus themselves (such as Connections). As you gain experience performing the daily Active Directory services management tasks, you'll find that Ntdsutil is an invaluable utility, and it won't take long for you to feel at home working with it.

## The LDIFDE Utility

The LDIFDE utility is used for performing bulk, script-based object imports into (and exports from) the Active Directory services database. You can export all sorts of objects, such as user accounts, OUs, groups, and many others.

**More Info** The format in which LDIFDE imports and exports data is based on an Internet Engineering Task Force (IETF) recommendation. For more information on the LDIF standard, consult the IETF Web site at *http://www.ietf.org*.

Following this paragraph is a listing of the online Help information for the LDIFDE utility. I've found that having Help information on paper assists in understanding how to use a given technology or tool, so I thought you might also benefit from having it in front of you. You'll see this information again in Chapter 12, "Migrating to Active Directory Services."

```
LDIF Directory Exchange

General Parameters
==================
-i                 Turn on Import Mode (The default is Export)
-f filename        Input or Output filename
-s servername      The server to bind to (Default to DC of logged in
                   Domain)
-c FromDN ToDN     Replace occurences of FromDN to ToDN
-v                 Turn on Verbose Mode
-j                 Log File Location
-t                 Port Number (default = 389)
-u                 Use Unicode format
-?                 Help


Export Specific
===============
-d RootDN          The root of the LDAP search (Default to Naming
                   Context)
-r Filter          LDAP search filter (Default to "(objectClass=*)")
-p SearchScope     Search Scope (Base/OneLevel/Subtree)
-l list            List of attributes (comma separated) to look for
                   in an LDAP search
-o list            List of attributes (comma separated) to omit from
                   input.
-g                 Disable Paged Search.
-m                 Enable the SAM logic on export.
-n                 Do not export binary values
```

```
Import
======
-k                      The import will go on ignoring 'Constraint
                        Violation' and 'Object Already Exists' errors
-y                      The import will use lazy commit for better
                        performance

Credentials Establishment
=========================
Note that if no credentials is specified, LDIFDE will bind as the
currently logged on user, using SSPI.

-a UserDN [Password | *]            Simple authentication
-b UserName Domain [Password | *]   SSPI bind method

Example: Simple import of current domain
    ldifde -i -f INPUT.LDF

Example: Simple export of current domain
    ldifde -f OUTPUT.LDF

Example: Export of specific domain with credentials
    ldifde -m -f OUTPUT.LDF
            -b USERNAME DOMAINNAME *
            -s SERVERNAME
            -d "cn=users,DC=DOMAINNAME,DC=Microsoft,DC=Com"
            -r "(objectClass=user)"
```

**More Info**   You can find more information about using LDIFDE, including an example of its usage, in Chapter 12, "Migrating to Active Directory Services."

## The Runas Utility

Using Runas enables administrators to avoid having to log off and log back on to a computer when they need to perform an administrative task requiring broader administrative credentials than the currently logged on user's credentials. With Runas, the associated program is run based on the credentials provided in the runas command, regardless of the credentials associated with the currently logged on user.

The Runas utility can be especially useful for administrators who work on Windows 2000 computers throughout the enterprise (perhaps making visits to workstations or servers) and need to run a given command based on their administrative rights (their administrator account) rather than on the account of the user who's currently logged on, but who do not want to disrupt the server or workstation (as logging off would do).

The following Runas Help information is the same thing you see when you type runas /? at the command line:

```
D:\>runas /?
RUNAS USAGE:
```

*(continued)*

*(continued)*
```
RUNAS [/profile] [/env] [/netonly] /user:<UserName> program

    /profile       if the user's profile needs to be loaded
    /env           to use current environment instead of user's.
    /netonly       use if the credentials specified are for
                   remote access only.
    /user          <UserName> should be in form USER@DOMAIN or
                   DOMAIN\USER
    program        command line for EXE.  See below for examples

Examples:
> runas /profile /user:mymachine\administrator cmd
> runas /profile /env /user:mydomain\admin
      "mmc %windir%\system32\dsa.msc"
> runas /env /user:user@domain.mycompany.com
      "notepad \"my file.txt\""

NOTE:  Enter user's password only when prompted.
NOTE:  USER@DOMAIN is not compatible with /netonly.
```

## Conclusion

Most administrators spend lots of their waking hours working away in the administrative trenches of Active Directory services, and that means using the management interfaces provided by Windows 2000. While some of the management tasks are everyday tasks, some of them are advanced, and others are available only from the command line, Microsoft has made every effort to make the administrative burden lighter by creating a common interface by which administrators can manage their Active Directory services deployments. By becoming familiar with these tasks and ways to complete them, you become better prepared to manage Active Directory deployments—which is the whole idea of a book like this, isn't it?

Throughout this chapter, you've seen a lot of screen shots, and that was by design. By providing lots of visual information about Active Directory services and how to manage it, I've helped you become better prepared to manage your own deployments and to approach management tasks with familiarity and a good sense of how the Windows 2000 Active Directory services interface works. Such familiarity and knowledge will hopefully put you ahead of the pack.

This chapter also provided you with some shortcuts and tips to make management easier by saving keystrokes or configuring the interface with which you manage Windows 2000 to work better for you. Even a few modifications here and there—such as in the command line—can make you more productive and effective, and they can even make what will surely become common tasks easier to manage.

# Chapter 10
# Working with the Active Directory Services Schema

Active Directory services is a powerful computing tool. Without any modification, Active Directory provides all the directory services most organizations will ever need; administrators can simply use existing Active Directory objects and attributes, and users can go about their merry using ways. But there's more to Active Directory than the objects and attributes included on the Microsoft Windows 2000 CD. The Active Directory services schema can be extended to include objects and attributes tailored to an organization's or application's needs.

Understanding how the Active Directory services schema works is a necessary part of the Windows 2000 administrator's repertoire. *Extending* the schema is a different animal altogether; schema extension and other types of schema modification are complex processes that require significant planning and can have implications throughout your enterprise deployment of Windows 2000 and Active Directory. Certainly, before you administer the schema or even consider extending it, you need to have a firm grasp on how it functions and how Active Directory objects are derived from the schema's contents.

## Understanding the Schema

The schema can be considered the collection of templates from which all objects and attributes in Active Directory services are derived. Simply put, if an instance of an object exists in Active Directory, it was derived from an object template found in the schema. (A more technical term for an object template is an object class.) If that were all that you needed to know about the schema, working with the schema would be pretty straightforward and simple. It's neither, and you need to know more before you dig in.

In more technical language, the schema is the namespace for a given forest that contains the universe of objects that can be stored in Active Directory services. As such, the schema enforces the rules that govern both the content and the structure of an Active Directory implementation. Two of the concepts referred to in this definition require further explanation:

- Namespace
- Content and structure enforcement

Before jumping into the discussion of those two concepts, I need to briefly mention a couple of facts about the schema that you should keep in mind as you read this chapter. Windows 2000 ships with a base schema, sometimes called the base *directory information tree* (DIT), which provides all the objects and attributes necessary for Windows 2000, including the objects and attributes necessary for its services, for its basic configuration (including the configuration of users and groups), and for all of its features to start working right out of the box. When you add users to your organization in a Windows 2000 deployment, you're simply creating additional instances of already-existing base schema classes (class objects). When you consider extending the schema, you are considering creating additional objects in the schema because the base schema doesn't address the particular need your organization has for a particular type of object.

## The Schema Namespace

As you recall from Chapter 6, a namespace is a context within which all names must be unambiguously resolvable. Given this definition, there can be a number of different uses for a namespace. You can have a Domain Name System (DNS) namespace such as the Internet (in which all names, such as *www.microsoft.com*, are unambiguously resolvable), you can have a namespace for the Microsoft Management Console (MMC) (in which all snap-in names are unambiguously resolvable), and you can have a Windows Internet Naming Service (WINS) (which happens to be flat, and all names are unambiguously resolvable). Some such namespaces are hierarchical, and some (WINS, for example) are flat. Hierarchical namespaces can be partitioned into individual naming contexts, whereas flat namespaces cannot. This enables a hierarchical namespace to scale much better than a flat namespace. A good comparison between a partitioned (hierarchical) namespace and an unpartitioned (flat) namespace is the comparison between DNS and WINS, respectively.

The schema is an individual namespace and its own naming context. It interacts with other namespaces (such as a domain's Active Directory services partition), and it governs how other namespaces are structured and populated with objects, but it is a namespace and can be identified separately from other namespaces that might reside on a given domain controller. (In the next several paragraphs, I explain how there can be multiple namespaces on a given domain controller.)

Domain controllers in an Active Directory services deployment maintain a copy of the Active Directory partition associated with the Windows 2000 domain to which they belong—you probably know that by now. These domain partitions are namespaces because within a domain, all names must be unambiguously resolvable. A domain partition namespace is part of the larger forestwide namespace; because a Windows 2000 forest uses a hierarchical approach to its namespace (which mirrors to the way the forest's namespace fits within the DNS hierarchy), each level of the hierarchy is a namespace as well. I know this is confusing and can make understanding namespaces and naming contexts difficult, but that's how a namespace hierarchy works. Remember that this namespace concept is kind of like the concept of a family. Each generation, or level, of the family is its own namespace within the larger hierarchical namespace of the family tree. For example, you wouldn't have two John Does in the same generation of a family, but you can have a John Doe father (in one level of the namespace hierarchy) and a John Doe son (in the next lowest level of the namespace hierarchy). Because their names are appended with *senior* and *junior,* in the entire family hierarchy both names are unambiguously resolvable.

In addition to maintaining a copy of its domain's Windows 2000 partition, each domain controller in a Windows 2000 environment maintains a copy of the schema, as well as another namespace called the configuration namespace. That's a total of at least three namespaces that each domain controller maintains. Sometimes these namespaces are referred to as naming contexts, as partitions, or by some other name that isn't quite as accurate as it should be. This book won't confuse you by doing such nasty things—these entities are namespaces, and that's what they'll be called throughout this discussion.

The *domain partition namespace* on a given domain controller contains the Active Directory services objects associated with the domain to which the domain controller belongs. This is simply a partition (based on Windows 2000 domains, as you remember) of the complete forest-based directory.

The *configuration namespace* is a forestwide namespace that contains information about the physical configuration of the entire enterprise. Domain controllers use the configuration namespace to maintain information about sites (such as their subnet addresses and subnet masks, as well as their physical wide area network [WAN] link characteristics and replication requirement information), about the Windows 2000 domain hierarchy, and about other configuration information. A domain controller uses its collection of objects and the information contained in the configuration namespace to get a "view" of the entire enterprise and to appropriately establish replication and referral partners.

The *schema namespace* holds the object and attribute templates that govern the instantiation of (the creation of instances of) all the classes of objects and attributes for any given domain partition namespace. This governing of object and attribute instantiation equates to content and structure enforcement for the forestwide directory, which brings us to the next section.

## Content and Structure Enforcement

The schema is a collection of *classes* and *attributes;* classes consist of schema class objects (known as *classSchema* objects), and attributes consist of schema attribute objects (known as *attributeSchema* objects).

The collection of these two kinds of schema objects in the schema dictates the possible content of objects in an Active Directory services deployment; that is, it imposes and enforces the rules that control the content (objects that can be created) and structure (object-to-object relationships) of an Active Directory deployment. The following sections explain these two types of schema objects and detail how they interoperate. The first section discusses schema class objects (*classSchema* objects); the next section examines schema attribute objects (*attributeSchema* objects).

## Schema Class Objects

All schema class (*classSchema*) objects in the directory are derived from one *superclass* (an overriding or parent class)—the *classSchema* object class. When one instance of a *classSchema* object (for example, an object called User) is instantiated to populate an Active Directory services implementation, that instantiated object becomes an object in Active Directory (whose properties and attributes are defined by the schema class from which it was instantiated). To put it a little differently, a *classSchema* object is a generic template from which more specific templates are created (such as one called User). Those specific templates enable administrators to create concrete objects that can populate an Active Directory implementation (such as a user object whose name attribute is JohnDoe).

Therefore, the process by which concrete Active Directory services objects (such as a user object with a name attribute of JohnDoe) are brought into being is the following:

1.  We start with the generic template—the *classSchema* object.
2.  Then we create (or Microsoft creates for use in the base DIT) more specific templates that reside in the schema—which we call schema classes—based on the *classSchema* object. An example of a schema class is the User *classSchema* object.
3.  Finally we instantiate Active Directory objects based on the population of schema classes that have been created in the schema. For example, we can create a user object (based on the User schema class) with a name attribute of JohnDoe.

To put it into one sentence, a schema class is a template from which Active Directory services objects are derived. All objects that you'll ever see created in an Active Directory deployment are derived from a defined schema class.

Schema classes are defined by their attributes. Attributes that are assigned to any given schema class are instances of the *attributeSchema* object, just as any class in the schema is an instance of the *classSchema* object. Schema classes are also defined by what I'll call their *genealogy constraints*. Each schema class has a combination of the following attributes:

- Mandatory class attributes (*mustContain* attributes)
- Optional class attributes (*mayContain* attributes)

In addition to those attributes, each schema class incorporates the following into its definition:

- Valid parents of the schema class (its genealogy constraints)

The collective designation of each of these attributes and its genealogy constraints defines each schema class. Keep in mind that schema classes have only attributes that are *mustContain* attributes or *mayContain* attributes; there is no middle ground in terms of the types of attributes that are assignable to a schema class. Also, remember that a classSchema object's attribute is either *mustContain* or *mayContain*; it cannot be both. Keep in mind, too, that genealogy constraints are not technically attributes; they are constraints. (This distinction becomes important later in this chapter, when attributes are defined.) A listing of all the *classSchema* objects included in the base DIT is provided later in this chapter, in the section titled "The Base Schema."

## Schema Attribute Objects

Schema attributes are like any other attribute you can imagine in that they describe the object with which they are associated. In fact, you can even take that a step further and state that the list of attributes for a given object (if that list of attributes is complete enough) actually *defines* the object with which it is associated. The relationship between schema *attributeSchema* objects and the schema *classSchema* objects they describe is no different.

The attributes in the schema comprise the universe of attributes from which all schema class object properties are derived. That is, the list of available schema attribute objects—each of which is derived from the *attributeSchema* class—is a comprehensive list, so if you want to assign a particular attribute to a *classSchema* object that you're creating, you first must ensure that the attribute is among the list of schema attributes.

Compare the attributes of a schema class with the attributes of a person—you have height, weight, hair color, name, shoe size, and finger count—all of which are properties of the person, and the sum of which actually define that particular person (class). When some sort of directory of persons is created (perhaps for a gym class), certain properties of these persons are recorded in that directory to create an appropriate listing. Those properties might include mandatory information such as name, height, weight, and shoe size, and they might contain some optional properties such as hair color. Some available properties might not be used at all, such as finger count. (Maybe it isn't relevant to the gym class.)

Schema attributes and the properties recorded for the gym class are similar in nature; however, they operate a little differently. One common misconception is that attributes are single values, like a shoe size or a finger count. They are not; an attribute object consists of a number of different fields that very specifically define the attribute and its characteristics. This is necessary; some attributes might be string values (like a name), while other attributes might be binary values (like an address handle), but all of them might have other associated configuration characteristics (such as a syntax definition characteristic) in addition to the attribute's value itself.

An important fact about schema attribute objects is that they are defined separately from all the schema class objects. So conceptually, if there are 190 schema class objects in the base DIT for Active Directory services and 900 or so schema attribute objects in the base DIT, each of these "lists" of schema objects (schema class objects and schema attribute objects) is defined differently, and any schema attribute object can be applied to multiple schema class objects. A listing of all of the schema attribute objects available in the base DIT is provided later in this chapter, in the section titled "The Base Schema."

### Syntax Objects

An attribute of all *attributeSchema* objects that's important to understand is the *attributeSyntax* attribute. Simply put, the syntax of a given *attributeSchema* object dictates the syntax of the *attributeSchema* attribute, such as whether it's an integer, a string, and so forth. There are two primary facts that you should keep in mind with regard to syntax objects in Active Directory services:

- Syntax objects don't appear directly in Active Directory.
- You can't add new syntaxes.

Syntax objects in Active Directory services adhere to various standards and naming and numbering conventions that have been established by various naming authorities or standards bodies. Some of the naming conventions and guidelines might seem odd or counterintuitive, but there are reasons for the various naming conventions (which are beyond the scope of this book). Contributing to the complexity of syntax naming conventions is the fact that more than one standard is being observed, which means that there must be a mapping of one type of syntax to the naming conventions or requirements to multiple standards. In practice, this mapping of syntaxes and associated complexity isn't too big of a deal for a couple of reasons. First, the available syntaxes are thorough and well defined, which means you don't have to define them yourself (you can't), so you can simply live with the existing syntaxes and go about your administering of Active Directory services. Second, if you're going to be creating new objects and therefore using syntaxes, you'll have to do a bunch of planning anyway, so the additional considerations you'll have to give to syntaxes will be only part of the planning you'll be doing.

The following list includes all 23 of the syntax objects that are available for Active Directory services, as well as a concise definition for each syntax object. Note that some of the syntax objects adhere to standards. This standards adherence dictates the naming conventions these syntax objects use.

***AccessPointDN***: An X.400 syntax distinguished name.

***Boolean***: Specifies either a TRUE or FALSE value.

***CaseExactString***: A case-sensitive general-string character set.

***CaseIgnoreString***: A case-insensitive teletex character set.

***DirectoryString***: A case-insensitive Unicode string.

***DN***: A string containing a distinguished name.

***DNWithBinary***: An *OctetString* syntax object containing a binary value and a distinguished name. Active Directory services ensures that the distinguished name is current.

**DNWithString:** An *OctetString* syntax object containing a string value and a distinguished name. Active Directory services ensures that the distinguished name is current.

**Enumeration:** A syntax defined by the International Telecommunications Union (ITU). The Enumeration syntax is treated as an integer in Active Directory.

**GeneralizedTime:** A time string in the format defined by the Abstract Syntax Notation One (ASN.1) standard. For more information, check out the International Organization for Standardization (ISO) 8601 standard and the ITU's X.680 standard.

**IA5String:** A case-sensitive International Alphabet 5 (IA5) character set.

**Integer:** A 32-bit integer.

**INTEGER8:** A large integer. Use for 64-bit values.

**NumericString:** A string that contains digits.

**NTSecurityDescriptor:** An *OctetString* containing a security descriptor.

**OctetString:** An array of bytes. Use *OctetString* to store binary data.

**OID:** A string containing object identifiers (OIDs). (OIDs are strings that contain digits and periods.)

**ORName:** An X.400 syntax.

**PresentationAddress:** A string used for storing ISO presentation addresses.

**PrintableString:** A case-sensitive string containing a printable character set.

**ReplicaLink:** Used only by Active Directory.

**Sid:** An *OctetString* containing a security identifier (SID). Use this syntax only for the storage of SID values.

**UTCTime:** Another (different) time string format defined by the ASN.1 standard. For more information, check out the ISO 8601 and ITU X.680 standards.

## Object Interaction Clarified

It's easy to get lost in all the implementation details, but hopefully, the examples and the review of the way schema objects interact that are provided in this section will serve to really cement your understanding of the way the schema works.

There are two separate lists of objects in the schema—one containing schema class objects and one containing schema attribute objects. Schema class objects—or *classSchema* objects—are the templates by which Active Directory objects are created. The properties that define all these Active Directory object templates are the schema attribute objects—or *attributeSchema* objects. Any attribute that a *classSchema* object uses is selected from the existing list of defined schema attributes (that is, *attributeSchema* objects that have already been created).

Schema class objects are defined by their mandatory attributes, optional attributes, and genealogy constraints. Schema attribute objects are defined by their "attribute attributes," as well as by the syntax objects that constrain the format of many of those attribute attributes (such as whether it's a string or a Boolean value).

An example of how all these classes of objects and their attributes interoperate is in order. Hopefully, the following example might hit a little closer to home than stuffy explanations of vague and intangible objects. (I know it does for me.) The example is based on the idea of a hamburger and a cheeseburger you might buy in a restaurant. In this example, we can call a hamburger and a cheeseburger instances of the *classSchema* schema object. Both the hamburger and the cheeseburger are therefore considered object classes.

A hamburger has a certain set of *mustContain* attributes:

- Buns
- Patty

A hamburger also has a certain set of *mayContain* attributes:

- Ketchup
- Mustard
- Lettuce
- Pickles
- Onions

There might be other *mayContain* attributes in your deployment of a hamburger, but in this example, we're working with the most common hamburger attributes (as determined by me). Notice that none of the attributes that are in the *mustContain* list are in the *mayContain* list; these lists are exclusive of each other for any given attribute.

Keep in mind that each of these attributes has its own defining characteristics and configuration parameters (buns—round, made of wheat, cooked for a while, and so forth) but represents an individual attribute in terms of the hamburger object.

Additionally, realize that these attributes, when put together into this collection and grouped in this way, create something discrete—the definition of a hamburger object, in this particular case. Although what we have is a collection of attributes, this special collection takes on a life of its own. However, talking about hamburgers and what they're made of won't get you very far if what you want is a real hamburger—until you have your own hamburger deployment, you don't have a concrete object. Once you take the definition of this hamburger class, with each of the class's *mustContain* attributes and some (or all) of its *mayContain* attributes, and actually create a hamburger object, you have a real hamburger. This is exactly how it works with Active Directory services' User class as well. You have the class definition included in the base DIT with Active Directory, but that isn't a concrete object yet—once you put together the attributes (that is, specify values for the object's attributes, such as a user's name), you have a real user object.

What about the cheeseburger? Good question. It's a lot like a hamburger, and it shares some of the same attributes. How does this relate to the schema and Active Directory services? Almost perfectly. Let's take a look at the attributes of a cheeseburger.

A cheeseburger has the following set of *mustContain* attributes:

- Buns
- Patty
- Cheese

Yes, two of these three attributes are also in the list of hamburger attributes, but we're defining a cheeseburger. A cheeseburger also has a certain set of *mayContain* attributes:

- Ketchup
- Mustard
- Lettuce
- Pickles
- Onions

Because this object has been defined with its collection of *mustContain* and *mayContain* attributes and because it has a unique name in this imaginary namespace, it represents a unique object. In fact, the cheeseburger could even have the exact same sets of *mustContain* and *mayContain* attributes as the hamburger, but with its different name, it becomes a discrete and unique object. If you create a cheeseburger object with all of its *mustContain* attributes (buns, patty, and cheese) and any of its *mayContain* attributes, you have an instance of the cheeseburger class.

Now let's make a comparison between the Active Directory schema and a restaurant. There are three important comparisons to draw in order to see just how this hamburger to cheeseburger comparison maps almost exactly to the Active Directory services schema. The most obvious similarity is that attributes from both the hamburger and Active Directory services are pulled from a common pool of available attributes. In the following list, the elements of a schema are compared to the elements of a restaurant:

- The entire restaurant equates to the entire schema (restaurant = schema).
- The menu items equate to schema class objects (menu item = *classSchema* object).
- Available restaurant ingredients equate to schema attribute objects (ingredient = *attributeSchema* object).

These comparisons make understanding the schema and how all of its objects and attributes work together a little easier. To further clarify how the schema works, let's get more specific with our restaurant to schema analogy. We'll begin by comparing the way ingredients are tracked and used in a restaurant to the way attributes are listed and used in the schema. The restaurant has a list of raw ingredients that it keeps separate from its list of menu items, and many of those ingredients actually go into more than one menu item. Likewise, the schema contains numerous *attributeSchema* objects, which are listed separately from the *classSchema* objects, and a given *attributeSchema* object can be assigned to more than one *classSchema* object.

The next important observation to make when comparing this to Active Directory services and the schema is to see how syntax works into the picture:

- Syntax objects equate to food group membership (syntax = food group).

This is a bit of a stretch: because it's somewhat difficult to nail down a definition of syntax, it's not easy to make a comparison between a syntax object and an everyday item or concept. But here goes. Food groups are categories into which all the ingredients in our imaginary restaurant can be placed. (For example, cheese is in the dairy group and lettuce is in the fruits/vegetables group.) Food groups aren't viewable concrete objects in the restaurant. In addition, food groups don't define the ingredients associated with them—you can say that ketchup is part of the fruit/vegetable food group, but that doesn't define ketchup. Similarly, syntax objects aren't viewable objects in the schema. And the syntax of an attribute does not define the attribute. You can point to a name attribute and say that its syntax is that of a string, but saying the syntax is a string doesn't define the name attribute. Also, if one of our restaurant ingredients isn't a member of the (exactly) four food groups, it isn't eligible to be on the list of ingredients—just as attributes (and thereby, classes) aren't allowed to have syntaxes outside the available syntax objects.

And finally we'll add one more element to our restaurant to schema comparison—one that has to do with the genealogy constraint. (As you remember, the genealogy constraint pertains to schema class objects, and it defines which objects can be parents of an object.)

- Genealogy constraints equate to menu group placement (genealogy = menu group).

Let's say the restaurant's menu is divided into various menu groups, which we can also call parent listings, or menu item containers. These parent listings include burgers, salads, side orders, beverages, and desserts. Every menu item that the restaurant offers must fall under one of these parent listings. Thus, these parent listings, or menu item *containers,* dictate the structure of the menu items that the restaurant offers. All menu items fall in one of their parent listings—burgers, salads, side orders, beverages, or desserts. This requirement—or constraint—dictates and maintains the structure of the overall food directory for the restaurant.

It's important to note that ingredient items (attributes) aren't listed on the menu—they don't have to be because they're the ingredients that, when ordered in various and specific ways, actually *comprise* the menu items (object classes).

Note that there are lots of ingredients (attributes) and that those ingredients could make up more menu items (object classes) than the restaurant offers. The restaurant has to determine whether the collection of menu items (object classes) meets its needs. If not, the restaurant can create more menu items by either using its existing ingredient list or by expanding its ingredient list and then creating new menu items. As you've probably guessed, this is just how you extend the schema—first you determine whether the existing attribute list is sufficient to create your new object class. If so, create the new class, and if not, you first create the new attribute and then create the new class. Extending the schema is covered in detail later in this chapter in a section aptly called "Extending the Schema."

So in any given restaurant, you have a bunch of ingredients (attributes) and a fair number of menu items (class objects), each of which falls under a particular menu group (genealogy constraint). The next section goes into detail about what the Windows 2000 base DIT is serving up.

# The Base Schema

Windows 2000 ships with a base schema that provides all the schema class objects and schema attribute objects necessary for a full-featured, fully capable Active Directory services deployment. The objects provided with the base schema, or base DIT, will enable IT professionals to perform most any task that they need to do with their Active Directory deployment.

Windows 2000 differentiates between the schema objects in the base DIT and all other schema objects through a convention that groups each type in a different category. Category 1 schema objects are all schema objects (classes and attributes) that ship with Windows 2000 and are part of the base DIT. Category 2 schema objects are everything else—that is, Category 2 objects are objects that have been created and added to the schema subsequent to the deployment of the base DIT.

The following sections list the schema class objects (*classSchema* objects) and the schema attribute objects (*attributeSchema* objects) included in the base DIT.

## Base DIT Class Listing

For those of you who care to count, there are almost 200 schema class objects provided by Windows 2000 in the base DIT. An alphabetical listing of the classes Windows 2000 includes in its base DIT is available in Appendix A. Take a look.

## Base DIT Class Hierarchy

While the alphabetical DIT class listing is great for a technical reference, it doesn't show the hierarchy that these classes form. The hierarchical listing shows subclasses and superclasses; that is, it shows which classes have classes derived from them and what those classes are. Appendix B illustrates the class hierarchy in the base DIT. Because some classes can have multiple parents, some classes are listed more than once. Such duplicate entries (upon second appearance) are set in italic.

There are a couple of classes that you need to be familiar with to understand the structure of the schema: the *Top* class and the *Lost-And-Found* class.

The *Top* class is a special class that sits at the top of the schema class hierarchy. Because it occupies that position in the hierarchy, it is a superclass of all classes that exist in the schema. Since classes inherit attributes from all superclasses, it logically follows that all classes in the schema inherit attributes from the *Top* class. The following is a list of the attributes of the *Top* class:

- Instance-Type
- NT-Security-Descriptor
- Object-Category
- Object-Class

Since all classes (and objects created from these classes) inherit these attributes, whenever a schema class object is created for inclusion in the schema, these attributes must be considered and defined. The *Instance-Type* and *Object-Class* attributes will not provide a default value; administrators must provide values for these attributes prior to completing the creation of any schema class object. The *NT-Security-Descriptor* and *Object-Category* attributes both use default values that are based on other (mandatory) configuration parameters of the schema class object itself.

The *Lost-And-Found* class is a holding place for objects that have been orphaned from the schema hierarchy. Orphaning occurs when objects are deleted, moved, or otherwise "lost" when replication between domain controllers occurs.

## Base DIT Attribute Listing

As mentioned previously, the Active Directory services schema keeps separate lists of objects and attributes, just as a restaurant keeps separate lists of ingredients and menu items. They are separate items, yet they are interdependent. Appendix C contains a list of the *attributeSchema* objects that are supplied in the base DIT for Windows 2000.

For those of you who care to count, there are more than 900 attributes provided by Windows 2000 in the base DIT. That's a lot of ingredients to draw from, whether you're attempting to modify or extend an existing class with additional attributes, or you're cooking up an entire operating system.

### Managing the Schema

The schema is managed through the Active Directory Schema snap-in or through the various Windows 2000 command-line utilities. The Active Directory Schema snap-in and the management utilities included in Windows 2000 are explained in detail in Chapter 9, "Managing Active Directory Services."

# Extending the Schema

Extending the schema is not a trivial event. Extending the schema is somewhat akin to replacing a 2000-node switch or making a change in your backbone transmission medium: it's mission critical, it requires planning, and it should be done only if the existing setup simply does not work for your organization. But if you plan and deploy your schema extension properly, it can work like a charm and provide all sorts of great computing improvements—just like a replaced switch or backbone medium can provide all sorts of benefits as long as the replacement process is planned and carried out with care.

With the warning aside, I'll acknowledge that there are probably plenty of reasons to extend the schema. There are as many reasons to extend the schema as there are types of companies and organizations in the world. Extension of the schema shouldn't be taken lightly, but it shouldn't necessarily be shunned. It should be scrutinized, and if it still is necessary, it should then be well planned. For example, products or services could be created as classes. A manufacturing company could create new attributes that are common to its products, compile them into classes representing the various products, and do all sorts of tracking, sales monitoring, or who knows what with them.

Since class objects, attributes, and the base DIT that comes with Windows 2000 have already been defined and explained in detail, you already know about objects and attributes and their availability in the base DIT. What you may not know is that from an application's perspective, extending the schema (such as developing an application that extends the schema during its installation process) can be a great feature-enabling endeavor. When a software company touts its application as being "directory enabled," that means the application has been built with the capability to read Active Directory services objects (and their attributes) or has the capability to create schema objects such as classes and attributes. All these capabilities enable the application to directly interact with Active Directory. That means the schema can be extended with applications that use the schema to provide extended capabilities.

Creating schema classes is a complicated process, so before you try it, you should make sure you've exhausted all your other options. The following is a list of the steps you should take before you try to create schema classes:

1. **Examine the existing schema**   Make sure that you're familiar with all the existing classes and attributes and that none of the classes—or any of the available attributes that could be added to modify existing classes—can meet your needs. The next few steps are variations on this theme but should be considered in the order presented.

2. **Try to modify an existing class**   Try to find a class you could modify to meet your needs rather than extending the schema. Sometimes adding a previously unavailable attribute (from the list of available attributes) or adding a

new possible parent to an existing class can create the functionality that your organization needs—and modifying a class does not require the planning involved with creating a new class. This is a good option when one additional attribute could add the functionality you need. For example, you could add a *SalesGoal* attribute to a User object.

3. **Try to create a new subclass.** A subclass is simply a class that is derived from another class (a superclass). The subclass inherits all of the attributes of the original superclass, plus whatever attributes you specify. Creating a subclass is easier than creating a class from scratch because the dependencies and logical consistencies involved with creating a class from scratch are already in place.

4. **Try to create a new attribute.** Often the functionality you need is almost available with a certain class or subclass, but there's just one attribute that's missing. The creation of an attribute is less involved than the creation of a new class.

If none of those options can meet your needs, you probably need to extend the schema by creating a new class.

**Caution**   Don't derive a subclass of the User class because user management will become too messy. If you create a subclass of the User class and then put users into that class, there's no way to "return" them to the standard (original) User class, nor is there any way to delete the subclass.

## *classSchema* Configuration Parameters

The base DIT included with Windows 2000 comes with more than 190 schema class objects ready for use in your organization's Active Directory services deployment. If those included schema class objects don't fit your organization's needs and you want to create new ones, you need to be familiar with the configuration parameters that define all schema class objects.

Since all schema class objects are derived from the same object class (*classSchema*), they share configuration parameters that dictate the way that Active Directory services and the schema treat them (in terms of indexing, identification, and other functions). Note that these configuration parameters are different from any *attributeSchema* attributes that might be applied to the object you eventually create; in the restaurant to schema comparison, configuration parameters would be comparable to the "name, price, and location on the menu" information about the menu item rather than to its ingredients.

Each schema class object that serves as an object template in the schema is an instance of the *classSchema* class, and each has the following collection of configuration parameters associated with it:

*cn*: Descriptive relative distinguished name of the class. Stands for *common name*.

*lDAPDisplayName*: Name used by Lightweight Directory Access Protocol (LDAP) clients to identify the class.

*schemaIDGUID*: Globally unique identifier (GUID) that uniquely identifies the class.

***adminDisplayName:*** Display name of the class used for administrative tools.

***governsID:*** Object identifier (OID) that uniquely identifies the class. You must obtain a unique OID for and assign a unique OID to every schema class you create. See the section entitled "Object Identifiers" later in this chapter for more information about OIDs and their requirements.

***rDNAttID:*** Type of relative distinguished name used by instances of the class.

***mustContain:*** List of mandatory (*mustContain*) attributes for instances of the class. This differs from the previous entry in that once created, this configuration parameter can be changed.

***systemMustContain:*** List of mandatory (*mustContain*) attributes for instances of the class. Note that once created, this configuration parameter cannot be changed.

***mayContain:*** List of optional (*mayContain*) attributes for instances of the class. This differs from the previous entry in that once created, this configuration parameter can be changed.

***systemMayContain:*** List of optional (*mayContain*) attributes for instances of the class. Note that once created, this configuration parameter cannot be changed.

***possSuperiors:*** List of classes that can be the class's parents (possible superiors) in the directory hierarchy. This differs from the previous entry in that once created, this configuration parameter can be changed.

***systemPossSuperiors:*** List of classes that can be the class's parents (system possible superiors) in the directory hierarchy. Note that once created, this configuration parameter cannot be changed.

***objectClassCategory:*** Integer value specifying the class type. The following is a list of the valid class types:

      0 = 88 Class

      1 = Structural

      2 = Abstract

      3 = Auxiliary

More information about class types is provided later in this chapter, in the section entitled "Class Types."

***subClassOf:*** Identifies the class from which instances of this object class inherit attributes.

***auxiliaryClass:*** Auxiliary classes from which the class inherits *mayContain* and *mustContain* attributes. This differs from the previous entry in that once created, this configuration parameter can be changed.

***systemAuxiliaryClass:*** Auxiliary classes from which the class inherits *mayContain* and *mustContain* attributes. Note that once created, this configuration parameter cannot be changed.

***defaultObjectCategory:*** Specifies the default category of the class; used if no class is specified. More information on class categories is provided later in this chapter.

***defaultHidingValue***: Boolean value that specifies default value of the *showInAdvancedViewOnly* configuration parameter of the object class (*showInAdvanced ViewOnly* is a special configuration parameter used for hiding the object from administrative tools, used to keep the UI from getting cluttered.) When TRUE, the object is hidden from administrative snap-ins.

***systemOnly***: Specifies whether only the system can create and modify instances of the class.

***defaultSecurityDescriptor***: Default security descriptor assigned to new instances of the class if no security descriptor is specified.

***isDefunct***: Boolean value that indicates whether the class is defunct.

***description***: Text description of the class. Used by administrative applications.

***objectClass***: Specifies the class of the object. This is always *classSchema*.

***nTSecurityDescriptor***: Security descriptor of the class.

## Creating New Schema Class Objects

If you need to extend the schema by creating new schema class objects, be aware of several issues before doing so. Just knowing the *classSchema* object characteristics outlined in the previous section is not enough; there are planning considerations to incorporate into the object creation process and additional definitions you need to understand before you start creating new *classSchema* objects. These issues and planning considerations are the following:

- Obtaining OIDs for your new class from the appropriate agency
- Choosing an appropriate class type
- Understanding the impact your class's location in the hierarchy has on inheritance
- Understanding the system checks that occur upon class creation

Each of these issues is discussed individually in the following sections, and you should make sure that your planning process addresses each of them. Some of them are obviously important, and some have requirements that seem less important (such as securing a guaranteed unique OID)—but they are all important. Skipping any of the following steps can lead to grief down the deployment road—and as we all know, such grief generally comes at the most inopportune time.

### Object Identifiers

Object identifiers are globally unique numeric identifiers that uniquely identify any object created either privately (as in your organization) or publicly (as in objects created by Microsoft for inclusion in Windows 2000). OIDs are managed and handed out by issuing authorities and are based on a numeric tree structure that enables logical and hierarchical distribution of OID numbers and value ranges.

Even if your deployment is private and sealed off from the rest of the world with three-foot-thick cement walls, you need to get your OIDs from the appropriate international (or local, depending on your location) naming authority because creating a new class has universal implications. Do not make up your own OIDs.

The following is an example of one of Microsoft's OIDs:

1.2.840.113556.1.5.4

As previously mentioned, there's a specific numeric and hierarchical structure to OIDs that is created by the dots separating the groups of numbers. The following paragraphs break down the sample OID and explain its hierarchy.

[**1**.2.840.113556.1.5.4] The leading dot-delimited section of the OID (**1**. in this example) designates the root authority, which in this case is the International Organization for Standardization (ISO)—no, the acronym isn't incorrect and in fact isn't an acronym. It's derived from the Greek word *isos* (meaning *equal*). ISO is a worldwide federation of national standards bodies, with representation from approximately 130 countries.

[1.**2**.840.113556.1.5.4] The second dot-delimited section (**2**. in this example) is delegated by ISO to various national standards bodies; in the case of the example being used, the 1. means ISO, and the 2. prefix and its subordinate hierarchies have been delegated to the American National Standards Institute (ANSI). ISO has delegated other numbers to other national registration authorities such as AFNOR (France), BSI (United Kingdom), DIN (Germany), JISC (Japan), and so forth.

[1.2.**840**.113556.1.5.4] ANSI has assigned the value 840 in the third dot-delimited section of the OID hierarchy to the United States of America.

[1.2.840.**113556**.1.5.4] The United States has assigned the value 113556 in the fourth dot-delimited section of the numeric OID hierarchy (and, thereby, any numeric structure below it) to Microsoft. The value in the fourth section is the same in all the OIDs created by a given organization, so any OID that starts with 1.2.840.113556 has been created by Microsoft—thus, the OID's assignment, as outlined, comes first from ISO, then from ANSI, and then from the United States to Microsoft. Microsoft has created an internal structure for using its hierarchy of OID numbers, just as an organization might create a DNS hierarchy once it receives a name. For example, Microsoft's domain hierarchy begins with *microsoft.com,* and subdomains such as *msdn.microsoft.com* and even *mspress.microsoft.com* can be created under the root domain because both of these domains fall within the Microsoft-owned *microsoft.com* DNS hierarchy.

[1.2.840.113556.**1**.5.4] Microsoft has assigned the value 1 in the fifth dot-delimited section of its OID hierarchy to represent its directory service, which is Active Directory. However, there are a number of objects that require OIDs in Active Directory, including both class objects *and* attribute objects, so there are further OID assignments to be made.

[1.2.840.113556.1.**5**.4] Microsoft has designated that the value 5 in the sixth dot-delimited section of its OID hierarchy be used for directory service classes.

[1.2.840.113556.1.5.<u>4</u>] And finally, in the last dot-delimited section of the numeric OID hierarchy that has been assigned to Microsoft, Microsoft has designated the value 4 to represent the unique class called Builtin-Domain.

As you can see, there is quite a bit of planning that goes into the assignment and use of OIDs. If your organization needs to create classes (or attributes, for that matter), it must go through the steps involved in getting an OID hierarchy assigned to it and then take steps to ensure that its OID hierarchy is structured logically.

There are a couple of approaches you can take to get the OIDs you need to create your own objects:

- Contact the ISO Name Registration Authority (NRA) for your region.
- Use the OIDGEN utility.

### How to Contact Your ISO Name Registration Authority

Contacting the ISO NRA for your region is the best way to go about getting OIDs for your organization. One reason why this is such a good approach is that it's a one-time event; once you have your root OID, you can create as many OIDs in your organization's subordinate OID hierarchy as you need. There's usually a fee associated with getting an OID from your NRA, so be prepared for that. If your organization is in the United States, you can get the fee schedule and procedure information for obtaining your OID root by going to the following Web page and clicking the appropriate links:

- http://www.ansi.org/public/services/reg_org.html

If you're outside the United States, you can find out about the Name Registration Authority for your country or region by checking out the ISO Web site. The following Web page contains a list of ISO member bodies and provides links to their Web sites:

- http://www.iso.ch/members/index.html

### The OIDGEN Utility

The less preferred way of getting OIDs for your organization's custom-created schema objects is to use the OIDGEN utility, which is available with the Windows 2000 Resource Kit. To create OIDs, the OIDGEN utility uses a combination of the OID tree assigned to Microsoft (by ANSI) and a GUID that is created each time the application is run (once per OID request). This combination ensures that the OIDs the OIDGEN utility creates adhere to the ISO standard and that they are unique.

When the OIDGEN utility is run, it creates two base OIDs, an *Attribute Base OID* and a *Class Base OID*. You need to run this utility only once per OID request; once you run the utility and obtain your base OIDs for classes and attributes, you can (and should) maintain an OID hierarchy that properly manages internal OID assignments under each of the two base OIDs.

Once you generate these base OIDs, you can request to register them with Microsoft. Do so by sending an e-mail message to oids@microsoft.com with pertinent and complete information in the body of the message.

## Class Types

When creating a *classSchema* object, you must choose a class type for it, as one of the mandatory configuration parameters of *classSchema* objects is *objectClassCategory*. (For more information on the configuration parameters of *classSchema* objects, see the "*classSchema* Configuration Parameters" section earlier in this chapter.) There are four types of classes from which you can choose, and of those four, three—the structural, abstract, and auxiliary class types—are valid class types for new schema class objects. When used properly, the right combination of abstract, auxiliary, and structural classes can create a useful and manageable schema object collection and can make any subsequent extensions to the schema much easier than they might otherwise be.

A *structural* class is the only type of class from which instances can be derived for object instantiation in Active Directory services. A structural class can be derived from either an abstract class or another structural class. Use the structural class when you want the object you're creating—such as a *CupHolder* object or a *Products* object—to populate your Active Directory implementation. The other two usable class types are useful in helping you prepare your structural class. The structural class type is specified during the creation of an object by setting the object's *objectClassCategory* configuration parameter value to 1.

A class that is designated as an *abstract* class is a template that you can use to create a framework of attributes that apply to any of the class's subclasses, which can be structural, auxiliary, or even other abstract classes. In fact, auxiliary classes (explained next) can be derived from only abstract classes. All subclasses of an abstract class inherit all mandatory and optional attributes of the abstract class, plus any attributes that are defined in the subclass itself. An abstract class is somewhat similar to the idea of a neighborhood, in that you could start with the idea of developing a neighborhood (with attributes such as zoning requirements, house size constraints, street sizes, and others) and then create houses, parks, stores, and streets. These houses, parks, stores, and streets all have their own attributes and also inherit all the attributes of the neighborhood, and thereby actually create the neighborhood based on the inherited and defined attributes of the neighborhood. The abstract class type is specified during the creation of an object by setting the object's *objectClassCategory* configuration parameter value to 2.

An *auxiliary* class is used to group attributes that you want to be applied (as a group) to any given structural class. As mentioned previously, auxiliary classes cannot be instantiated in Active Directory services and can be derived from only abstract classes. An auxiliary class is kind of like the fries and pop you get when you order a combination meal at your local burger joint. You can choose a specific meal, but you always have auxiliary fries and a pop thrown in with it. (For this to be a perfect analogy, the burger restaurant would have to let you get fries or a pop *only* when you order a meal since auxiliary classes cannot be instantiated in Active Directory.) In this example, the combo meal would be an abstract class, the fries and pop (of varying sizes and flavors) would be auxiliary classes, and specific combo meals themselves (like a BigCheeseburger meal) would be structural classes. The auxiliary class type is specified during the creation of an object by setting the object's *objectClassCategory* configuration parameter value to 3. To help clarify the idea of an abstract class, consider Figure 10-1.

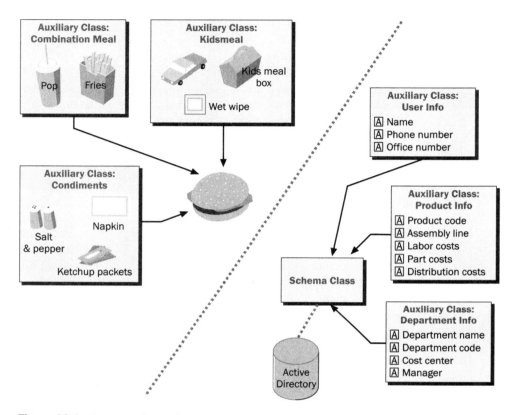

**Figure 10-1.** *How auxiliary classes work in Active Directory services and in the drive-through.*

When class type is not specified in a class's *objectClassCategory* configuration parameter, the class is treated as an *88* class. The 88 class type is an earlier type inherited from the 1993 X.500 standard. Don't define any new classes you create as 88 classes. When an object's class type is not specified, the object's *objectClassCategory* configuration parameter value is set to 0 to designate an 88 class.

## Inheritance

Inheritance inevitably occurs whenever a schema class object is created. The previous section alluded to the way inheritance functions when a schema class is created. This section addresses it directly.

Simply put, an object inherits all attributes—both *mustContain* attributes and *mayContain* attributes—from every parent in its schema class hierarchy. To put it another way (using some terminology you can use at Active Directory parties), each subclass inherits all attributes from every superclass in its directory hierarchy. The two sentences say exactly the same thing: one uses the terms *subclass* and *superclass;* the other just uses the more commonplace term (*parent*). If attributes are added to a class in the hierarchy subsequent to its creation, all subclasses inherit the newly added attributes (except *mustContain* attributes, as explained in the following section) once the schema cache is updated.

## System Checks

Whenever an attempt is made to extend the schema by creating a new object, Active Directory services performs system checks to ensure that the creation of the object (with its attribute characteristics and genealogy constraints) doesn't endanger the integrity of the directory. The two types of system checks that are performed are consistency checks and safety checks.

### Consistency Checks

To ensure that the schema can maintain internal consistency, Active Directory services performs consistency checks whenever classes or attributes are modified or created. When an attribute is created or modified, Active Directory checks to ensure that all of the following attribute requirements are met:

- Value of *governsID* is unique.
- Value of *lDAPDisplayName* is valid and unique.
- Value of *schemaIDGUID* is unique.
- Value of *rDNAttID* has its syntax set as *string* (Unicode).
- Classes in *subClassOf* follow the following rules of the class-type hierarchy:
  - Abstract classes can inherit from only other abstract classes.
  - Auxiliary classes cannot inherit from structural classes.
  - Structural classes cannot inherit from auxiliary classes.
  - Classes defined in *subClassOf, systemAuxiliaryClass, auxiliaryClass, systemPossSuperiors,* and *possSuperiors* exist as schema objects.
  - Attributes defined in *systemMayContain, mayContain, systemMustContain,* and *mustContain* exist as schema objects. (You can't specify attributes here presuming that you'll create them afterward—the consistency check won't pass.)
  - Classes in *systemAuxiliaryClass, auxiliaryClass, systemPossSuperiors*, and *possSuperiors* have their *objectClassCategory* value set to 0 or 3 (indicating an 88 class and an auxiliary class, respectively).

Active Directory also performs the following consistency checks for attribute modifications (but not for attribute creations):

- Value of *attributeID* is unique.
- Value of *mAPIID* is unique (if specified).
- Value of *rangeLower* is smaller than value of *rangeUpper* (if specified).

- Values for *attributeSyntax* and *oMSyntax* match. See the table on page 311 for the correct matching syntax.
- Value of *linkID* is unique (if specified).

The following table lists the syntax-matching requirements that must be met when Active Directory services performs consistency checks. Note that the information in the following tables is specific to creating schema objects and fairly nitty-gritty technical, so you might feel lost and these entries might seem arcane if you aren't familiar with creating schema objects.

| attributeSyntax | oMObjectClass |
|---|---|
| 2.5.5.1 | \x2B0C0287731C00854A |
| 2.5.5.7 | \x56060102050B1D for ORName.<br>\x2A864886F7140101010B for DNWithBinary.<br>Default is ORName if no *oMObjectClass* is specified. |
| 2.5.5.13 | \x2B0C0287731C00855C |
| 2.5.5.14 | \x2B0C0287731C00853E for AccessPointDN.<br>\x2A864886F7140101010C for DNWithString.<br>Default is Access-Point if no *oMObjectClass* is specified. |

**More Info** If you want more information about the relationship between the *attributeSyntax* and the *oMObjectClass* configuration parameters, check out the *Active Directory Developer's Reference Library,* available at bookstores everywhere from Microsoft Press. Or you can go to MSDN Online's Internet-accessible technical library, found at the following address:

· *http://msdn.microsoft.com/library*

### Safety Checks

Active Directory services performs safety checks to ensure that modification of the schema by one person or application does not break another application. Since multiple applications and users share the same schema, these safety checks are imperative. The following list explains the safety checks performed by Active Directory upon any attempted modification or creation of a schema object:

- *mustContain* attributes cannot be added to a class.
- *mustContain*, *mayContain*, and *possSuperiors* attributes cannot be deleted.
- *rangeLower* and *rangeUpper* values cannot be changed on base DIT attributes.
- *attributeSecurityGUID* cannot be changed on base DIT objects.
- *lDAPDisplayName* cannot be changed on base DIT objects.
- *defaultObjectCategory* cannot be changed for base DIT objects.
- *objectCategory* cannot be changed for instances of a base DIT object.
- Base DIT objects cannot be deactivated.

**Note**   Both the consistency and safety checks occur when any schema object is modified or created, whether the object is a *classSchema* object or an *attributeSchema* object.

## Schema Object Creation Process

Once all the issues outlined in the previous parts of the "Creating New Schema Class Objects" section have been addressed or at least considered, and you've planned your approach to creating classes or attributes, you can move ahead with creating the new schema class object. An important feature of Active Directory services is that schema updates are dynamic; you can start using the objects you create immediately after their creation, without having to reboot or to stop and restart the directory service.

There are some ordered steps you should follow when going through the creation process for your schema objects and a number of different tools that you can use to create the schema objects. First, the steps:

**Step 1:** Determine how you want to extend the schema. Generally, schema extensions fall into one or more of the following categories:

- Modifying or creating classes
- Modifying or creating attributes
- Deactivating custom-made classes or attributes

**Step 2:** Ensure you have proper permissions to extend the schema. You must be logged on as a member of the Schema Administrators group to do so.

**Step 3:** Ensure you're targeting the domain controller holding the Schema Master flexible single-master operation (FSMO) role. Schema changes can be made on only the Schema Master FSMO role holder.

**Step 4:** Remove the schema-locking registry entry (the safety interlock) on the Schema Master FSMO role holder, enabling schema changes to occur. The registry entry you must change (or create if it isn't present on the Schema Master FSMO role holder) is

*HKLM\System\CurrentControlSet\Services\NTDS\Parameters\Schema Update Allowed*

and the value must be nonzero to enable schema changes. If you use the Active Directory Schema snap-in, this registry modification is done automatically.

**Step 5:** Modify or create your schema attributes first. (Make sure you've planned your approach, scrutinized your reasoning for making changes, and chosen values for each attribute you plan to modify or create.)

**Step 6:** Modify or create your schema classes next. (Make sure you've planned your approach, scrutinized your reasoning for making changes, and chosen values for each class you plan to modify or create.)

**Step 7:** Add attributes to your created (or modified) classes.

**Step 8:** If you need to have the information propagated to the rest of the domains' domain controllers in less than 5 minutes, force a schema update. For more information about schema updates and why 5 minutes is the magic time window, check out the section titled "The Schema Cache" later in this chapter.

**Step 9:** Reengage the schema's safety interlock by setting its registry value to 0.

There are several ways you can go about implementing steps 5 and 6 (creating or modifying attributes or classes) of the schema object creation process. The following list describes the means by which schema objects can be created or modified:

- Through the Windows 2000 user interface, with the Active Directory Schema snap-in. The Active Directory Schema snap-in is not listed with default snap-ins. This is by design—making schema modifications is a serious event. More information about how to find the Active Directory Schema snap-in and a detailed explanation of the Active Directory Schema snap-in are provided in Chapter 9, "Managing Active Directory Services."

- Programmatically (with your programming language of choice, including Microsoft Visual Basic and C/C++), using Active Directory Service Interfaces (ADSI).

- Through scripting, using Windows Scripting Host (WSH) capabilities that are built into Windows 2000 in conjunction with the two command-line tools LDIFDE and CSVDE. More information about how to use LDIFDE and CSVDE is provided in Chapter 9, "Managing Active Directory Services."

**More Info** If you want more information about programmatically extending the Active Directory services schema, check out the *Active Directory Developer's Reference Library,* available at bookstores everywhere from Microsoft Press. Or you can go to MSDN Online's Internet-accessible technical library, found at the following address:

*http://msdn.microsoft.com/library*

### *attributeSchema* Object Configuration Parameters

Configuration parameters of *attributeSchema* objects function the same way that configuration parameters of *classSchema* objects function. Many of these attribute configuration parameters are similar to class configuration parameters—any object, whether it's an object class or an attribute, needs to have configuration information, like a name, associated with it. Such association is done through an *attributeSchema* object's various configuration parameters.

All attributes that populate the schema are instances of one special schema class—the *attributeSchema* class. The following list defines the configuration parameters that any schema attribute object (any instance of the *attributeSchema* class) has:

***cn*:** Descriptive relative distinguished name of the attribute.

***lDAPDisplayName*:** Name used by LDAP clients to identify the attribute.

***schemaIDGUID*:** GUID that uniquely identifies the attribute.

***adminDisplayName*:** Display name of the attribute used for administrative tools.

***attributeID*:** OID that uniquely identifies the attribute. You must obtain a unique OID for and assign a unique OID to every schema attribute you create. See the section entitled "Object Identifiers" earlier in this chapter for more information about OIDs and their requirements.

***attributeSecurityGUID*:** Used by the system to identify the attribute.

***attributeSyntax*:** Syntax of the attribute, in the form of an OID. Must correspond with *oMSyntax*; see the table later in this section for more details.

***oMSyntax*:** Syntax of the attribute, as defined by the X/Open Object Model specification. Must correspond with *attributeSyntax*; see the table later in this section for more details.

***oMObjectClass*:** Specifies the binary value that describes the type of the attribute.

***rangeLower*:** Lower range (value) allowed for the value of the attribute.

***rangeUpper*:** Upper range (value) allowed for the value of the attribute.

***isSingleValued*:** Indicates whether the attribute is single valued or multivalued. More information on single valued and multivalued attributes is provided later in this chapter.

***searchFlags*:** Determines the indexing characteristics of the attribute.

***isMemberOfPartialAttributeSet*:** Boolean value specifying whether the attribute is replicated to the Global Catalog. TRUE indicates that the attribute is replicated to the Global Catalog.

***linkID*:** Specifies (when this value is a pointer) whether the attribute is part of a link-pair. A link-pair can be either a forward link or a back link. More information on links is provided later in this section.

***systemFlags*:** System-specific flags determine whether certain operations can be performed on the attribute, such as deleting the attribute, renaming it, moving it, limited moves, and so forth.

***systemOnly*:** Specifies whether users can modify the attribute.

***mAPIID*:** Integer by which MAPI clients identify the attribute.

***isDefunct*:** Boolean value that indicates whether the attribute is defunct.

***description*:** Text description of the attribute.

***objectClass*:** Specifies the class of the object. This is always *attributeSchema*.

***nTSecurityDescriptor*:** Security descriptor of the attribute.

For those of you who were counting, that's a total of 22 object attributes that are involved in the creation of a schema attribute object (yes, attributes of the attribute, or more technically, configuration parameters). However, not all of these configuration parameters are mandatory. The following lists specify which configuration parameters are mandatory (*mustContain*) and which are optional (*mayContain*).

Mandatory (*mustContain*) configuration parameters for schema attribute objects are:

- *cn*
- *objectClass*
- *attributeID*
- *attributeSyntax*
- *oMSyntax*
- *schemaIDGUID*
- *nTSecurityDescriptor*
- *isSingleValued*
- *lDAPDisplayName*

Optional (*mayContain*) schema attribute object configuration parameters are:

- *rangeLower*
- *rangeUpper*
- *isMemberOfPartialReplicaSet*
- *searchFlags*

As you can see, there are nine *mustContain* configuration parameters (for any given *attributeSchema* object) and four *mayContain* configuration parameters. If we wanted to make an analogy between these mandatory and optional configuration parameters and something from everyday life, we could use the schema attribute/gym class property comparison we made previously. Remember that students in our fictional gym class have properties—like shoe size—associated with them and that these properties are like schema attributes. These properties also have properties associated with them. For example, the shoe size property has an upper and a lower bound (somewhere between 5 and 19, presumably) and maybe some optional properties (such as narrow or wide, as in a shoe size of 12 narrow). Configuration parameters are like these properties of properties.

A special relationship exists between the *attributeSyntax* and *oMObjectClass* configuration parameters. These two configuration parameters both specify an attribute's syntax—they just have different forms. When you create an attribute, you must ensure that the two configuration parameters contain values that are specifying the same type of syntax.

| oMSyntax | attribute-Syntax | Explanation |
|---|---|---|
| **Boolean** | | |
| 1 | 2.5.5.8 | Boolean.<br>For queries that include attributes of Boolean syntax in a filter, you must specify TRUE or FALSE (for example, myboolattr=TRUE). |
| **Integer** | | |
| 2 | 2.5.5.9 | 32-bit integer. |
| **OctetString** | | |
| 4 | 2.5.5.10 | Array of bytes.<br>Use *OctetString* to store binary data. |
| **INTEGER8** | | |
| 65 | 2.5.5.16 | Large integer.<br>Use for 64-bit values. |
| **ObjectSecurityDescriptor** | | |
| 66 | 2.5.5.15 | *OctetString* containing a security descriptor. |
| **DN** | | |
| 127 | 2.5.5.1 | String containing a DN.<br>The *oMObjectClass* is the following value: \x2B0C0287731C00854A<br>Use this string syntax to store distinguished names that you want kept up-to-date by Active Directory. When an attribute of DN syntax is created with a valid distinguished name, Active Directory treats the attribute as a reference to the object represented by the distinguished name that was set. If the referenced object is renamed or moved, Active Directory ensures that the attribute reflects the change. If the attribute is reset with a new distinguished name, the attribute is referenced to the object represented by the new distinguished name.<br>This string syntax can also be used for linked distinguished names. Back links must be of DN syntax. Forward links can be of DN syntax (as well as DNWithString, DNWithBinary, AccessPointDN, or ORName syntax). Linked attributes must have a *linkID* defined. See the description of *linkID* earlier in this section.<br>For queries that include attributes of DN syntax in a filter, you must specify full distinguished names—wildcard characters (for example, cn=foo*) are not supported for filters on attributes with DN syntax. |

*(continued)*

*(continued)*

| oMSyntax | attribute-Syntax | Explanation |
|---|---|---|
| **DNWithOctetString** | | |
| 127 | 2.5.5.7 | *OctetString* containing a binary value and a distinguished name. Active Directory keeps the distinguished name up-to-date.<br>The *oMObjectClass* is the following value:<br>\x2A864886F7140101010B<br>*DNWithOctetString* has the following format:<br>*B:CharCount:binaryvalue:ObjectDN*<br>Such that *CharCount* = the count of hex digits in *binaryvalue*, *binaryvalue* = the hex digit representation of the binary value stored, and *ObjectDN* = the distinguished name of an object referenced by this attribute.<br>Active Directory maintains the *ObjectDN* portion so that it contains the current distinguished name of the object originally specified when the value was created. |
| **ORName** | | |
| 127 | 2.5.5.7 | From X.400<br>The *oMObjectClass* is the following value: \x56060102050B1D |
| **CaseExactString** | | |
| 27 | 2.5.5.3 | String: General-String character set, case sensitive.<br>Use this string syntax for attributes that should contain characters from only the General-String character set.<br>Active Directory does not currently enforce the General-String character set restriction on attributes of *CaseExactString* syntax; however, future versions may enforce it. Therefore, if you use attributes of *CaseExactString* syntax, you should use characters from only the General-String character set. |
| **DirectoryString** | | |
| 64 | 2.5.5.12 | String: Unicode, case insensitive.<br>Use this string syntax if the attribute must be capable of containing strings supporting the full range of the Unicode character set and if the attribute does not require case sensitivity. When Active Directory performs comparisons against attributes of this syntax (such as evaluating a query), it performs case-insensitive comparisons. |
| **GeneralizedTime** | | |
| 24 | 2.5.5.11 | *GeneralizedTime* is a time string format defined by ASN.1 standards. See ISO 8601 and ITU X.680 for more information. Use this syntax for storing time values in *GeneralizedTime* format. |
| **IA5String** | | |
| 22 | 2.5.5.5 | String: IA5 character set, case sensitive. Use this string syntax for attributes that should contain characters from only the IA5 character set.<br>Active Directory does not currently enforce the IA5 character set restriction on attributes of IA5String syntax; however, future versions may enforce it. Therefore, if you use attributes of IA5String syntax, you should use characters from only the IA5 character set. |

| oMSyntax | attribute-Syntax | Explanation |
|---|---|---|
| **NumericString** | | |
| 18 | 2.5.5.6 | String containing digits.<br>    Active Directory does not currently enforce the digit restriction on attributes of *NumericString* syntax; however, future versions may enforce it. Therefore, if you use attributes of *NumericString* syntax, you should use only digits. |
| **OID** | | |
| 6 | 2.5.5.2 | String for containing OIDs. The OID is a string containing digits (0–9) and decimal points (.). |
| **UTCTime** | | |
| 23 | 2.5.5.11 | *UTCTime* is a time string format defined by ASN.1 standards. See ISO 8601 and ITU X.680 for more information. Use this syntax for storing time values in *UTCTime* format. |
| **CaseIgnoreString** | | |
| 0 | 2.5.5.4 | String: teletex character set, case insensitive. Use this string syntax for attributes that should contain characters from only the teletex character set.<br>    Active Directory does not currently enforce the teletex character set restriction on attributes of *CaseIgnoreString* syntax; however, future versions may enforce it. Therefore, if you use attributes of *CaseIgnoreString* syntax, you should use characters from only the teletex character set. |
| **AccessPointDN** | | |
| 127 | 2.5.5.14 | From X.400<br>The *oMObjectClass* is the following value: \x2B0C0287731C00853E |
| **PresentationAddress** | | |
| 127 | 2.5.5.13 | String for containing Open Systems Interconnection (OSI) presentation addresses.<br>    The *oMObjectClass* is the following value: \x2B0C0287731C00855C<br>    See Requests for Comments (RFCs) 2252 and 1278 for more information. |
| **PrintableString** | | |
| 19 | 2.5.5.5 | String: Printable character set, case sensitive. Use this string syntax for attributes that should contain characters from only the Printable character set.<br>    Active Directory does not currently enforce the Printable character set restriction on attributes of PrintableString syntax; however, future versions may enforce it. Therefore, if you use attributes of *PrintableString* syntax, you should use characters from only the Printable character set. |

*(continued)*

*(continued)*

| oMSyntax | attribute-Syntax | Explanation |
|---|---|---|
| **DNWithString** | | |
| 127 | 2.5.5.14 | *OctetString* containing a string value and a distinguished name. Active Directory keeps the distinguished name up-to-date.<br>The *oMObjectClass* is the following value:<br>\x2A864886F7140101010C<br>DNWithString has the following format:<br>*S:CharCount:stringvalue:ObjectDN*<br>Such that *CharCount* = the count of characters in *stringvalue*, *stringvalue* = the string value stored, and *ObjectDN* = the distinguished name of an object referenced by this attribute.<br>Active Directory maintains the *ObjectDN* portion so that it contains the current distinguished name of the object originally specified when the value was created. |
| **Enumeration** | | |
| 10 | 2.5.5.9 | Defined by the ITU. Treated as an integer in Active Directory. |
| **ReplicaLink** | | |
| 127 | 2.5.5.10 | System only.<br>Used by Active Directory. The *oMObjectClass* is the following value:<br>\x2A864886F71401010106<br>If the attribute needs to store a binary value, use *OctetString*. If the attribute needs to store a linked distinguished name, use DN, DNWithString, or DNWithBinary depending on your needs. |
| **Sid** | | |
| 4 | 2.5.5.17 | *OctetString* containing a security identifier (SID). Use this syntax to store SID values only. |

# Creating New Schema Attribute Objects

Creating a new attribute is not quite as involved as creating a new schema class; there are no hierarchical issues or inheritance implications to consider with attributes because their hierarchy is flat. (That is, there is no hierarchy.) However, creating a new attribute does have implications, and there are issues you need to be aware of before you create the attribute. These issues, which should simply be considered part of the planning process involved with extending the schema, can have a significant impact on your new attribute's usefulness. The issues are outlined in the following sections.

## Multivalued Attributes

Attributes can represent either a single value or multiple values. Attributes that have their *isSingleValued* configuration parameter set to FALSE have the capability of containing multiple values.

In the Active Directory Schema snap-in, attributes that are capable of having multiple values are considered multivalued. The important fact to keep in mind if you create a multivalued attribute is that there is no implicit (or guaranteed) ordering of the multiple values, which means that values specified first, second, and third aren't guaranteed to be returned in that order. Also, there is no guarantee that Active Directory services will return multiple values in the same order when multiple queries against the attribute are made. In short, don't depend on any consistent query-response ordering of multiple values in a multivalued attribute because there isn't any guarantee of it.

### Indexing Attributes

You can specify that the attribute you create will be indexed when it is associated with a given class object. The benefit of indexing an attribute is that attributes you specify to be indexed are kept in an index used by Active Directory to search for objects, so queries concerning an object containing an indexed attribute are resolved much faster than without an index (as the index is searched first).

You should follow some guidelines when determining whether to specify that an attribute is indexed. Indexed attributes should be single valued because indexing multivalued attributes increases the amount of time it takes to update an index and resolve queries and increases the storage requirements of an index. Indexed attributes should also be unique.

## Deactivating Classes and Attributes

Simply put, you can't delete an object class or an attribute; you can only deactivate it. Furthermore, you cannot deactivate any attributes or classes that are part of the Windows 2000 base DIT (Category 1 schema objects). That means you can deactivate only custom-created classes or attributes, such as schema objects added by your organization's IT department or schema objects added during an application's installation. When you deactivate a schema class or attribute, you essentially make it invisible to users and administrators in your organization (except for the existing, nondeleted *instances* of the class), but you can't entirely delete a class once it's created.

The process of deactivating a schema class object is simple and is easily done from the Active Directory Schema snap-in. (You can also do this using any other method used to modify or add objects to the schema.) To deactivate a schema class object, do the following:

- Set its *isDefunct* configuration parameter value to TRUE. (Its syntax is Boolean.)

As with any modification to the schema, Active Directory performs certain consistency and safety checks whenever an attempt to deactivate an object is made. As you might suspect, Active Directory ensures that the class being deactivated is not a superclass of an existing (nondefunct) schema class object, an auxiliary class used by an existing class, or in the *possSuperiors* configuration parameter of any existing class. For schema attribute objects, Active Directory ensures that an attribute that is being deactivated is not a member of the *mustContain* or *mayContain* configuration parameter of any existing class. If any of these consistency or safety checks fails, the attempt to deactivate the object fails.

When an object is deactivated, Active Directory services does not delete any instances of deactivated objects. Instances of the object continue to exist (and can be searched for) in Active Directory until they are deleted by an administrator or another user with proper permissions. Although instances of a deactivated class continue to exist, any attempt to create a new instance of the class will fail, and the failure will be the same failure you would get if the object never existed.

## Resurrecting Classes and Attributes

Deactivated classes and attributes can be resurrected at any time. The process is simple and intuitive: simply set the *isDefunct* configuration parameter for the class or attribute to FALSE. Again, and as with any modification to any schema object, Active Directory services performs safety and consistency checks to ensure that the modification does not threaten the consistency and integrity of the directory.

Note that deactivated objects cannot be modified except to change their *isDefunct* configuration parameter to FALSE.

## The Schema Cache

The schema is stored on the hard disk of every domain controller in the organization. For performance reasons, however, domain controllers also keep a copy of the schema in memory (which enables domain controllers to access the schema much faster than if they had only a hard disk–based version of it). The version of the schema that is kept in memory is called the *schema cache*.

Whenever a schema update occurs, the updated information is first added to the on-disk copy of the schema. While any such update is occurring, the schema cache services any queries that require the schema to be checked. Five minutes after any change is made to the on-disk copy of the schema (such as an object creation or attribute modification), the schema cache is refreshed. If another update to the schema occurs before the 5-minute interval is reached, the timing begins again, such that the schema cache is updated only after 5 minutes of schema-change inactivity.

The 5-minute delay between schema updates and refreshes of the schema cache can make it appear as though schema changes weren't applied, even though they indeed were applied. That's because the schema cache, which services queries, has no knowledge of schema modifications until it is updated by the modified on-disk copy of the schema.

To avoid this 5-minute delay problem, you can manually trigger a schema cache update, which prompts the schema cache to immediately refresh its schema information from the on-disk version. The way that this update occurs is that the schema cache begins to build a "secondary" schema cache from the on-disk image of the schema, while the "primary" schema cache is still servicing any queries. Once the update is complete, the primary schema cache (which is now old) is destroyed and the new (formerly secondary) version of the schema cache begins servicing schema queries.

Note that until the schema cache update is fully completed, the schema cache that services queries won't have the updated version; just because you initiate a schema cache update doesn't mean that a query submitted a second later will respond with the updated information. You must wait until the schema has been completely refreshed from the on-disk version before schema modification will be evident.

## Conclusion

The Active Directory services schema is the collection of class and attribute objects. A class object is really just a named collection of attribute objects that represent a concrete object, such as a user. The base DIT, which is the set of class and attribute objects that comes with Active Directory services, is a fully functional and well-rounded set of objects, which you likely will never need to expand. If you do find that your organization could benefit from the creation or modification of schema objects, you should ensure that proper planning goes into such decisions because making modifications is not a trivial task, and it can have implications for your entire Active Directory services deployment.

Schema objects and associated administration is a fairly complex and technical undertaking, and some of the parameters and information associated with the schema can be arcane and sometimes downright perplexing. However, extension of the schema can result in powerful information management capabilities.

# Chapter 11
# Upgrading to Active Directory Services

A lot of companies are running Microsoft Windows NT as their primary network operating system (NOS), and many of these companies are considering upgrading to Microsoft Windows 2000 for their NOS. Presumably, if you administer or own a network with Windows NT as your primary NOS, you too are considering an upgrade to Windows 2000—or you are spellbound by the intricate plot of this technical reference. If you are thinking of making the switch, you'll want some direction or information about the issues involved with moving a Windows NT 3.51 or 4.0 deployment to Windows 2000. (Upgrades to Windows 2000 from earlier versions of Windows NT are not supported.) This chapter outlines the issues you'll need to consider, the challenges you'll certainly face, and the options to choose from during your upgrade decision-making process.

**Note** You can upgrade to Windows 2000 from Windows NT versions 3.51 and 4.0, but not from Windows NT versions 3.1 and 3.5. If you are using these earlier versions, upgrade to either Windows NT version 3.51 or 4.0 and then to Windows 2000.

Creating your personalized Active Directory services deployment plan is the first step in any upgrade to Windows 2000. Chapter 7, "Planning an Active Directory Services Deployment," showed you how to create this plan. However, common IT information requirements dictate that before you can complete your plan you will need to learn more about the issues surrounding an upgrade, such as whether to perform an in-place upgrade or a restructure, which domain controllers to upgrade, how to provide for backward compatibility, and how certain services will be affected by the upgrade—all of which is explained in this chapter. How can you learn about this new and complex technology and create and implement an upgrade at the same time without losing your sanity? Well, I recommend that you read both Chapter 7 and this chapter and, after careful consideration of their content and recommendations, begin developing your deployment and upgrade plan. There's no way around it: deploying Active Directory services, as either a fresh installation or an upgrade, requires a significant amount of information and planning. A successful deployment also requires feedback from the same groups from which you solicit feedback when planning a new deployment. (See Chapter 7, "Planning an Active Directory Services Deployment" for more details on gathering feedback.) Creating a plan is the most important step of any Windows 2000 deployment.

If you are considering an upgrade from a Windows NT environment, half of the issues you'll have to address relate to your existing Windows NT deployment, the details of which are known only to your organization. The remaining issues relate to the new Windows 2000 features. You'll first need to learn what's available and then decide which features are important to your deployment. Since I don't know about your Windows NT deployment or which Windows 2000 features you find irresistible, I'll have to make some assumptions and educated guesses to guide you through this upgrade. To make this advice applicable to your deployment, I'll ask that you refer to a list you'll make (at my behest) near the beginning of this chapter. At various points throughout the chapter, you'll be adding to the list and revising your scribbling, so keep that notepad handy.

## Understanding Your Upgrade Options

There are three ways to upgrade from Windows NT 3.51 and 4.0 to Windows 2000. You can upgrade your Windows NT environment; you can completely restructure it; or you can do some combination of the two.

- **In-place upgrade of your Windows NT environment:** With an in-place upgrade, your user domains remain largely unchanged. You simply place the existing domains into a DNS-based domain hierarchy. Generally speaking, an in-place upgrade is the easiest route to deploying Windows 2000 and poses the least risk of disruption.

- **Restructuring of your Windows NT environment:** A restructuring is a complete redesign of your domain structure in an effort to provide the best forest and domain hierarchy possible for your Windows 2000 environment. Restructuring allows you to conform to the naming and planning recommendations outlined in Chapter 7. It also creates a very clean Windows 2000 environment that enables your deployment to take full advantage of Windows 2000 features and guidelines.

- **Combination upgrade:** There's no reason why you can't combine an upgrade and a restructuring if that's what suits your needs. You might consider this option if, for example, part of your environment has domains that are ready for a transition to Windows 2000 and other domains that would be easier to manage if consolidated into one large domain. The combination upgrade is likely to be the most common option for those with Windows NT environments.

Of course, there are advantages and disadvantages to each approach, but the two most significant differences between an in-place upgrade and a restructuring are: an in-place upgrade maintains your existing domain structure, and a restructuring results in more administrative overhead and requires more resources, such as computers and time.

Regardless of which approach you choose, certain steps are the same. To get your Windows NT environment fully transitioned to a Windows 2000 environment, you must:

1.  Create a forest plan, which includes domain trees.

2.  Map out your sites and site links, and consider them throughout the process.

3.  Create an ideal domain plan that is independent of your transition and based on the recommendations outlined in Chapter 7.

4.  Outline and prioritize your upgrade goals.

5.  Compare your upgrade goals to the type of upgrade process (upgrade and restructuring). This chapter will help guide the comparison.

6.  Review your domain plan and modify if necessary. (Exclude resource domains in this step; they're covered in the next step.)

7.  Create a resource domain strategy with the aim of consolidating these domains into organizational units (OUs).

8.  Create an OU strategy that maps to your IT staff's organizational structure.

9.  Combine your resource domain strategy and your OU strategy.

10.  Review your forest plan, domain plan, site plan, and OU plan. The focus of the review should be a comparison of each plan to your prioritized upgrade goals. Then decide which upgrade option is best (has the most agreeable set of trade-offs) for your environment.

11.  Notice that these 10 steps, which need to be done sequentially, begin with forest and domain planning. You should have gone through most of the Windows 2000 Active Directory services structure planning before you begin determining which upgrade path is most appropriate for your organization. If you haven't read Chapter 7, "Planning an Active Directory Services Deployment," you should head back there and do so.

Even planning a new Windows 2000 Active Directory services deployment requires that you consider your organization's unique requirements; having to transition an existing Windows NT environment only adds to the list of unique requirements. These requirements, which come from circumstances or issues unique to your existing Windows NT deployment, will determine which transition approach is best for you. The next section outlines what those circumstances might be and gets you pointed in the right upgrade direction.

## Upgrade or Restructure: Choosing the Right Path

The decision-making process of your Windows NT transition is often fraught with trade-offs. Trade-offs are inevitable in a Windows 2000 transition; these trade-offs do not necessarily affect the availability of Windows 2000 features or capabilities, but almost certainly affect the amount of administrative overhead required.

Below is a list of questions that can quickly guide you toward the most appropriate upgrade option. While the following questions are fairly subjective, the goal is to lead you to a solid objective decision regarding which upgrade option is best for you. Give careful consideration to the issues raised in these questions, and then determine the technical justifications (based on your existing deployment) for your answers. It's a good idea to jot down your answers and, alongside them, quick explanations and some technical justification (which will be specific to your deployment) for each answer.

### Does your Windows NT domain structure function well?

The answer to this is somewhat subjective; but one way to gauge its functionality is to measure how much administrative headache is associated with infrastructure activity (versus day-to-day standard administrative activities). Other factors to measure are how complex, messy, and unsatisfactory your current domain plan is. Another thing to look at when rating your domain structure is the alignment of your domains. To do so, refer to planning considerations outlined in Chapter 7. Another way of asking this question is: Are you happy with your current domain structure? Happiness, of course, is an equally subjective state of affairs.

*If you answered YES:* You're on your way to an upgrade.

*If you answered NO:* You're leaning toward a restructure.

### Does your Windows NT domain structure function reasonably well?

You might not be tickled pink with your current Windows NT domain structure, but if you think it works reasonably well and that a few changes here and there might get you to the tickled pink stage, the following guidelines apply.

*If you answered YES:* You're a good candidate for a combination upgrade.

*If you answered NO:* You're well on your way toward restructuring.

### Can your production environment endure possible upgrade pains?

*Production environment* is just a nifty term for the computing environment in which your users carry out their day-to-day activities (as compared to a test lab, where outages or problems don't affect the day-to-day routine of the organization). It's important that your IT staff determine your production environment's ability to withstand the glitches and setbacks that can occur during the upgrade process, such as transition time that can be associated with moving or upgrading accounts, or changes in administrative operations that may slow response times to common network administrative issues. You can take steps to minimize the impact of upgrading to Windows 2000, and those steps (which vary for each deployment) should certainly be taken at every opportunity. Steps to take to minimize potential problems include running tests of your deployment plan in a lab and monitoring its impact. Another way to minimize disruptions to production is to perform domain controller upgrades and administratively transition domains or OUs at night when most users are gone. A third way to prevent downtime is to upgrade small domains first. Remember to record problems that occurred during these initial domain upgrades, and adjust your deployment plan to avoid future impacts. Regardless of how many preventative measures you take, you run the risk that users will feel the impact of the upgrade process. However, your consideration of the question posed in this section can impact how much test lab time and deployment staging your upgrade is going to require. If this issue isn't that important to you, you may choose to minimize the costs and time associated with the related preventative measures. If you determine this issue is a big concern, you'll probably want all administrators involved to be part of the test lab process so that they're familiar with the plan and the process, you'll want to schedule upgrades at night, and so forth.

Some production environments simply cannot risk any interruption in service, not even a hiccup during the upgrade process. I'm not referring to an environment where in response to an upgrade snafu the IT person says, "Gee, this temporary resource access delay is a real inconvenience. I think I'll go get another doughnut." I'm talking about the kind of environment where every minute counts and the IT person's response to the same delay would be to scream, "Code Red! Call in every administrator we have! We're losing three million dollars a minute!" If you sleep with your pager clipped to your ear, you're probably working in the "Code Red" environment and can't risk any interruption in service during the upgrade process.

*If you answered YES:* You're a good candidate for an in-place upgrade.

*If you answered NO:* Seriously consider creating a parallel, pristine Windows 2000 environment that you can get running and test. To avoid any interruption to production, move user accounts to the new environment in the dead of night (or some other unobtrusive time).

### Does your current domain structure make you lose sleep at night?

*If you answered YES:* You probably need to restructure.

## Tallying the Results

Tally your answers to the first three questions to determine the transition path that most closely fits your organization's Windows NT environment.

If you answered *YES* to two or more of the first three questions, you can probably begin the process of transitioning to Windows 2000 with an in-place upgrade of your existing Windows NT environment.

If you answered *NO* to two or more of the first three questions, you'll first want to restructure your current Windows NT environment and then move your organization from the existing Windows NT environment to the Windows 2000 deployment. Once you've moved to the new deployment, decommission the Windows NT deployment and reassign its resources. For example, you'll want to reassign your Backup Domain Controllers (BDCs) to Windows 2000 domain controllers.

If you answered *YES* to the fourth question, well, you probably need to restructure.

You shouldn't make any final decisions regarding transition path until you've read about and weighed the costs and benefits of each path. Later in this chapter, I discuss the drawbacks associated with each approach. The following sections outline the steps to take for an in-place upgrade and for a restructuring of your domain environment.

# Upgrading from a Windows NT Environment

Of the two options, upgrading is the simpler and safer transition to Windows 2000.

The administrative burden associated with transitioning to Windows 2000 is greatly reduced with an upgrade because the trust settings and accounts in existing Windows NT domains are preserved. Whereas restructuring starts from scratch and requires accounts to be moved or cloned, upgrading leaves those security and account settings in place and simply upgrades them to Active Directory services as part of the Active Directory deployment.

Upgrading an existing Windows NT deployment preserves the following:

- User accounts and corresponding passwords
- Established one-way trust relationships between existing and upgraded domains
- Visibility of the domain and its resources to downlevel clients

These can be compelling reasons to choose an upgrade over a restructuring. Upgrade is a good option, especially if the administrative staff does not have the available resources or the skills to perform the effort-intensive steps necessary to restructure.

**Real World**

You don't have to wait until your Active Directory services infrastructure is in place before you upgrade desktops (to Windows 2000 Professional) or member servers (to Windows 2000 Server, Windows 2000 Advanced Server, or Windows 2000 Datacenter Server). Although certain Windows 2000 features won't be available until Active Directory services are available, gating the rollout of desktops and servers based on Active Directory isn't necessary. Avoiding such a hold-up can keep the organization's transition to Windows 2000 rolling.

## The Upgrade Process

Once you've determined that your organization would be best served by performing an in-place upgrade or a combination upgrade and restructure—in which case the upgrade as a whole is the first phase of the process—you need to follow a certain set of steps to get you from the decision process to a Windows 2000 Active Directory services environment. The following steps should help you create an appropriate upgrade process. Keep in mind that your organization might have special considerations that will require additional steps. For example, you might want to identify groups within your organization to consult before the upgrade commences. The seven steps listed below, which are discussed after the list, will get your Active Directory deployment up and running.

1. Scrutinize your existing domain structure.
2. Provide for rollback to the Windows NT environment.
3. Force a synchronization of all BDCs.
4. Upgrade the Primary Domain Controller (PDC).

5. Upgrade BDCs.

6. Transition associated resource domains.

7. Switch to native mode.

Repeat these steps for each account domain in your Windows NT environment. The best method is to begin with a domain that has fewer users (thereby minimizing any impact on early-stage upgrades). The experience you gain upgrading the smaller domains will enable you to minimize the negative impact of the upgrade process on your larger domains.

While these steps might appear straightforward, each has associated caveats that warrant further discussion. The following sections address each step.

### Scrutinize Your Existing Domain Structure

As part of your requisite upgrade task, plan the order by which you will upgrade the domains in your existing Windows NT environment. Here are some guidelines to consider when developing that plan:

- **Upgrade account domains first.** If you're going to leave all your domains intact—including both account domains and resource domains—you should begin by upgrading account domains. Doing so enables users in those domains to take advantage of Windows 2000 features as soon as possible. Also, to do any domain consolidation, the domain into which you will move your account and resource domains must exist, and it must be upgraded to Windows 2000. By the way, you might not be consolidating account domains, but you should be consolidating resource domains.

- **Upgrade smaller domains first.** I've mentioned this before, but I want to make sure you understand this point. By upgrading smaller domains, which presumably are domains that contain fewer users, you can limit to the fewest number of users any potential impacts your upgrade process might have. Another advantage of upgrading smaller domains first is that you will undoubtedly gain some useful experience with the first few upgrades; that experience can help subsequent domain upgrades go smoother.

Remember that at this point you have already created your forest plan, domain plan, OU plan, and site topology plan. Therefore, this scrutinization of your existing domain structure is being done to determine the best approach to upgrading the various domains in your Windows NT environment. You should ensure that your approach to upgrading coincides with the domain and forest plan that you created during Chapter 7. Specifically, you need to remember the following requirement:

- The first Windows 2000 Active Directory services domain you create will be the root of the forest.

If you are performing an upgrade but have chosen for some good reason to create a dedicated root domain, you should create that Windows 2000 domain prior to upgrading any of your existing Windows NT domains to Windows 2000.

> **More Info** For more information about your root domain, and whether to use an existing domain or a dedicated domain for your forest root, see Chapter 7, "Planning an Active Directory Services Deployment."

Another issue to consider when scrutinizing your existing domain structure is the association of resource domains with larger, user account domains. How do they make the transition to (absorption by) larger Windows 2000 domains that are acting as OUs? Before you begin upgrading any resource domains, read the upcoming section entitled "Transition Resource Domains."

> **Caution** To avoid the need to delete or modify domains down the road, scrutinize your domain tree plan before you begin upgrading domains and placing them into the Windows 2000 DNS-based domain hierarchy. Modifying domains is not a simple task, especially when they are situated midway in a Windows 2000 domain hierarchy. Make sure your domain plan is solid, has been scrutinized by appropriate groups, and provides for future growth in ways that avoid the need for future domain-based changes before moving ahead with domain upgrades.

### Provide for Rollback to the Windows NT Environment

For most deployments, it's imperative to be able to undo (roll back) an upgrade if problems come up during the transition. Before you proceed with your upgrade plan, have a rollback plan in place.

There are a handful of things you can do to ensure rollback capability during the course of your upgrade. They are:

- **Perform a complete backup.** Part of your rollback plan should include the creation of a complete backup of domain-based information (such as the user account database and the Security Account Manager [SAM]) just before the PDC is upgraded.

- **Create a spare BDC, and then take it offline during the PDC upgrade.** You can ensure rollback is possible by creating a spare BDC and synchronizing it with the PDC when the rest of the BDCs are being forced to synchronize. After synchronization, take the spare BDC offline, place it in a secure area, and keep it disconnected from the network. This creates an image of the domain-based information as it is just before you upgrade the PDC. If necessary, you could put the domain back into its pre-upgrade state by bringing the BDC online and promoting it to PDC.

- **Ensure each domain has at least one BDC.** This protects the domain from becoming orphaned. If a catastrophic, unrecoverable error occurs during the process of upgrading the PDC, you can promote the BDC and the domain can continue to function. There are other valid reasons to retain a Windows NT BDC before a Windows 2000 upgrade. See the section entitled "Switch to Native Mode" for further discussion.

## Force a Synchronization of All BDCs

The first step in the upgrade of a Windows NT domain to a Windows 2000 domain is the upgrading of the PDC to Windows 2000 Server. However, before upgrading the PDC you must check that all BDCs have current domain-based information and that this information is replicated. Therefore, you must force all BDCs to synchronize with the PDC.

## Upgrade the PDC

Once all BDCs are synchronized, you can begin the upgrade process and get the PDC upgraded to Windows 2000. Once the upgrade process is completed, the Windows 2000 installation process recognizes that the computer on which the upgrade is being performed is a PDC, and the Active Directory Installation wizard (DCPromo.exe) is automatically launched. You are then presented with the following list of options:

- Create the first tree in a new forest
- Create a new tree in an existing forest
- Create a replica of an existing domain
- Create a child domain

Once you've made your choice, the Active Directory Installation wizard installs Active Directory services on a computer running Windows 2000 Server. This installation turns the computer into a domain controller. The entire contents of the Windows NT account database, as well as the SAM, are converted into Active Directory objects and brought into the Active Directory information store. When run on a PDC, the Active Directory Installation wizard has additional implications for this newly upgraded Windows 2000 computer.

- The upgraded computer automatically assumes the PDC Emulator FSMO role.
- New security principals can continue to be created on the upgraded computer and get replicated to other domain controllers, including BDCs, as appropriate.
- Windows NT BDCs continue to replicate their information to the upgraded computer.
- Failed authentication requests are forwarded to the upgraded computer before being failed.
- The domain is officially operating in mixed mode.

Once the Windows 2000 Server is online and acting as the PDC Emulator (and as a Windows 2000 domain controller), Active Directory services is used to store all existing domain-based information, as well as any new information added to the domain subsequent to its placement into service. To Windows 2000 servers (and any directory-enabled clients), the PDC Emulator appears as a Windows 2000 domain controller and as holder of the PDC Emulator FSMO, with all associated characteristics. To Windows NT BDCs and downlevel clients, the PDC Emulator exposes its Active Directory information repository as a flat store during replication and synchronization, thereby appearing as a Windows NT PDC.

As alluded to earlier in this section, if the Windows 2000 computer acting as the PDC Emulator becomes disabled or otherwise goes offline, it *can* be replaced by means of the standard process used to promote a Windows NT BDC computer to PDC.

> **More Info** The FSMO roles delegated to domain controllers in a Windows 2000 Active Directory environment, including the PDC Emulator FSMO role, are explained in detail in Chapter 4, "Active Directory Services Scalability Architecture." Administrative information, such as how to change FSMO role ownership, is provided in Chapter 9, "Managing Active Directory Services."

### Upgrade BDCs

The next step in the process is to upgrade remaining BDCs to Windows 2000.

As you may recall from Chapter 8, "Active Directory Services and Security," Windows 2000 domain controllers, which all upgraded Windows NT BDCs become, require more stringent security than their predecessors. For this reason, it's good practice to review the physical security in place for your BDCs when you upgrade them to Windows 2000. If they're sitting in your break rooms next to the coffee pot, you should probably move them to more secure locations prior to their upgrade.

> **Caution** Some applications must run on a BDC to function properly. This requirement is generally a function of the application's need to have certain security-based access to resources or accounts that are only available if the application is running on a BDC (or a PDC). If you have such an application, you must ensure that the application will run properly under Windows 2000. If it cannot and the application is mission-critical, you will need to maintain at least one BDC in your Windows 2000 domain, which precludes you from switching the domain to native mode. Check with the application vendor, or test the application in your lab for proper functionality on Windows 2000 before switching to native mode.

### Transition Resource Domains

If you are going to upgrade all your resource domains in-place (rather than transition them into OUs within an existing or upgraded account domain), consider the following guideline.

> **Best Practice** Resource domains that stand to get the most out of Windows 2000 features should be upgraded first. For example, if you plan to deploy Microsoft IntelliMirror or Remote OS Installation as part of your overall change and configuration management strategy, it stands to reason that you should first enable these features for as many computer accounts as possible. These accounts probably reside in your largest resource domains. Since IntelliMirror and Remote OS Installation depend on Active Directory services, the most efficient way to take great advantage of Active Directory's administrative features is to give the highest upgrade priority to resource domains with the largest account bases.

---

**More Info**  Microsoft's Change and Configuration Management initiative, which includes IntelliMirror and Remote OS Installation, are explained in detail in Chapter 14, "Administratively Leveraging Active Directory Services."

---

If you are going to consolidate some of your resource domains into other existing resource domains, upgrade the target resource domains first. The best policy for consolidating or collapsing domains is to begin with upgrading the target domain, or the domain into which other domains are going to be placed. Then if necessary, upgrade the domains that are going to be retired, or simply upgrade the domain controllers in those retired domains and specify that they join their respective target domains.

If you're going to follow the recommendations outlined in Chapter 7 and restructure your resource domains as OUs in target domains—perhaps into an existing account domain that you've recently upgraded from your Windows NT environment—consult the section entitled "Transitioning Resource Domains into OUs" later in this chapter.

## Switch to Native Mode

Switching from mixed mode to native mode is the final step in upgrading a domain from a Windows NT environment to a Windows 2000 Active Directory services environment. While it's best to switch to native mode as soon as possible, it's not necessary to do so immediately. In fact, it might be months or even longer before you switch to native mode. As you probably suspect, there are trade-offs and other mitigating circumstances to consider before switching. I hope that you won't wait long because there are material advantages to making the switch as soon as possible. What, you ask, are the advantages to switching to native mode? The advantages to having a Windows 2000 Active Directory deployment functioning in native mode are:

- Multimaster replication is enabled throughout the entire domain, enabling updates to occur on any domain controller rather than only on the PDC Emulator.
- Universal and Domain Local Groups are enabled.
- Group nesting is enabled.
- All local groups on the PDC Emulator computer are turned into domain local groups.

Certain circumstances might dictate that you defer switching your Windows 2000 domain to native mode. The following list explains the primary reasons to keep your deployment in mixed mode.

- **To maintain one or more BDCs in your domain:** This might be due to having an application that must run on a Windows NT BDC to function properly. Once you switch to native mode, you can no longer add Windows NT BDCs to the domain.

- **To maintain Windows NT rollback capability:** This might remain a requirement because of technical, managerial, or political reasons. Regardless of the reason, if you need the capability to roll back to Windows NT domains, you need to maintain at least one BDC in your domain. As already discussed, switching to native mode requires that all DCs are upgraded to Windows 2000. For example, if just one domain controller BDC is not upgraded, you can't switch to native mode.

- **To physically secure your BDCs:** Physical security of Windows 2000 domain controllers is a must. It's even more of a priority for Windows 2000 than it is for Windows NT BDCs. If you can't secure a given Windows 2000 domain controller, you shouldn't upgrade it.

Although you can switch your Windows 2000 Active Directory services deployment to native mode once all of your domain controllers have been upgraded, you are not required to have all (or any, for that matter) member servers upgraded to Windows 2000 to do so. You can have Windows NT or Windows 9x computers participating in the domain and still switch to native mode, as long as all domain controllers have been upgraded.

Switching to native mode is as simple as clicking a user interface–based button or flipping a software switch. You can do this by navigating to the Active Directory Domains And Trusts snap-in, right-clicking the domain you want to switch to native mode, and choosing Properties from the Context menu that appears. You'll see the General property sheet, as displayed in Figure 11-1.

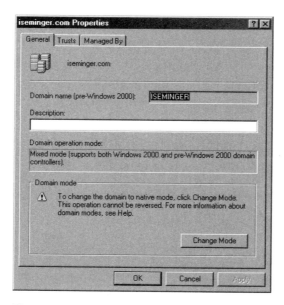

**Figure 11-1.** *Flipping the software switch to begin functioning in native mode.*

As you can see, there is a frame near the bottom of the property sheet called Change domain mode. Inside this frame is a Change Mode button. Click it, and you switch the domain in question to native mode.

> **Caution**   You can switch *to* native mode, but because of the differences between how Windows 2000 and Windows NT domain controllers store data, Windows 2000 does not allow you to switch *back*. Make the switch to native mode with care.

## Upgrading Additional Domains

Many of the steps outlined in the previous sections discuss tasks or recommendations associated with upgrading a single domain. Once you've upgraded one of your Windows NT domains, continue the process until all domains are upgraded Windows 2000. Upgrade each domain using the same scrutiny under which you placed the first domain.

As you upgrade existing domains into the Active Directory services forest, the Active Directory information store expands incrementally. Although the Active Directory information store is partitioned, enterprisewide data (such as Global Catalog, schema, and configuration container information) begins to get replicated throughout the enterprise. Eventually, the default replication schedule, the schedule specifically configured by the administrator, floods the enterprise domain structure and all global information will have reached every domain controller in the enterprise.

## Transitioning LAN Manager Replication to File Replication Services (FRS)

There is one issue concerning the Windows NT LAN Manager Replication Service (LMRepl) and Windows 2000 that you need to know about: Windows 2000 doesn't support the LMRepl. Windows 2000 replaced LMRepl with a revamped but incompatible version of the service called File Replication Services (FRS).

LMRepl is often used in Windows NT to replicate logon scripts from one Windows NT domain controller to another. While LMRepl doesn't need domain controllers to replicate logon scripts, replicating logon scripts is a common use of LMRepl, and therefore needs to be addressed. The problem with using it this way is that LMRepl won't function in a Windows 2000 mixed mode domain or a native mode domain. This means that if you have replication partners that need to be upgraded, you have to generate a plan to upgrade the replication functionality that LMRepl was providing to FRS.

You have at least the two following options:

- Move the replication information housed in the export directory to the System Volume (SYSVOL) of a Windows 2000 domain controller. In this configuration, FRS will automatically replicate the information to all other domain controllers in the domain using multimaster replication.

- Leave the replication information housed in the export directory on a computer running Windows NT Server, and upgrade this computer only after all other import computers have been upgraded. Import directories can accept imported data from LMRepl; they just can't export. Upgrade your export computer last, and then transition to FRS.

Regardless of which option you choose, and even if you come up with your own solution, you should structure your strategy so that the server hosting the export directory is the last replication-involved computer to be upgraded. If you run into a situation in which the PDC is the computer hosting the export directory, you should select a new export server and reconfigure LMRepl because, as you know, the PDC must be the first Windows NT domain controller that gets upgraded.

## Transitioning Routing and Remote Access Service (RRAS) Servers

Because of the way that the Routing and Remote Access Service (RRAS) process checks for RRAS properties, a Windows NT RRAS Server operating in an Active Directory services environment creates a security situation that requires administrators to choose whether or not to loosen the Windows 2000 security associated with Windows NT 4.0 RRAS Servers. The best way to avoid this problem is to upgrade the Windows NT RRAS Server to Windows 2000 early in the upgrade process.

When RRAS runs on a given Windows NT computer, it runs as LocalSystem, and because it runs as LocalSystem it logs on to the computer with NULL credentials (no username or password). Active Directory services will not accept object attribute querying with NULL credentials. When a RRAS Server contacts a Windows 2000 domain controller to get information about a user's RRAS properties, Active Directory services denies the query. This can result in inconsistent behavior: If the RRAS happens to contact (or receives a response from) a Windows NT BDC in a mixed-mode domain, RRAS will be able to gather its requested information and continue servicing clients. However, if that same query happens to contact a Windows 2000 domain controller in that same mixed-mode domain, the Windows 2000 domain controller will reject the request.

Exceptions that negate this security issue are the following:

- If the RRAS Server is running on a BDC, it has local access to the SAM and therefore doesn't introduce the security problems outlined earlier.
- Security has been relaxed in your Windows 2000 Active Directory deployment by allowing everyone account permissions to read any property on any user object. This setting is enabled during the Active Directory Installation wizard's Weaken The Permissions option.

For anyone who is even mildly security-minded, the best approaches are to either run RRAS on a BDC or upgrade the RRAS Server to Windows 2000 very early on in the domain upgrade process.

# Restructuring a Windows NT Environment

Restructuring a Windows NT deployment is a significant undertaking.

If you have decided to restructure your deployment, you have determined that nothing about your existing Windows NT domain structure could contribute to a well-functioning Windows 2000 Active Directory deployment. In this case, you will create a *pristine forest*, which is a Windows 2000 domain environment that is deployed essentially as a shell forest and domain hierarchy. This environment, designed by you, has the ideal structure into which you will move incrementally your existing user, computer, and resource base. To conceptualize your newly created pristine forest with its domain hierarchy completely prepared, step back and look at its logical structure and say, "Wow, that's a great looking Windows 2000 forest and domain plan. It's going to be perfect for our organization. Now all it needs are a user base and computing resources."

Once you've finished gloating over your pristine forest, you can turn your attention to your existing Windows NT domain structure, at which point you'll probably think, "Man, now I have to transition all these users and resources from this Windows NT environment to the pristine forest. Good thing I have a detailed plan that enables me to know specifically where each user account and computing resource will be placed in the pristine forest, and that Microsoft has provided tools that will make the transition easier for me."

**Note**  Of course, you can create a pristine forest on the same physical network as your Windows NT environment; the division between the two deployments (the existing Windows NT deployment and the pristine Windows 2000 deployment) is logical, not physical.

## Understanding Restructuring

Let's look at the process of restructuring from a slightly different perspective. This new perspective will help provide insights to the restructure plan and implementation processes, and show how to use existing tools and methods to make the restructure plan and processes as easy as possible.

When you create a Windows 2000 deployment from scratch (without considering an existing Windows NT deployment), you go through the steps outlined in Chapter 7, "Planning an Active Directory Services Deployment." Once you have your plan, you create the root domain and then additional domains. In the course of creating additional domains, construct the DNS-based hierarchical domain structure. Once that is completed (or even during the course of its completion), you begin populating the domains with users, resources, and OUs, based on your deployment plan and as appropriate.

Now imagine that this Windows 2000 environment you created from scratch grows or changes over time. This growth may require you to make some organizational changes to the deployment. Perhaps, as the result of a domain being restructured or retired, or new domains being created, you have to move users or resources from one domain to another.

How do the steps taken to implement those organizational changes differ from the steps taken to restructure? The primary difference is that instead of populating the new domains with users and resources based on your deployment plan, you are populating the restructured but pristine (in effect, new) domains with users from an existing Windows NT deployment. You are *moving* or *cloning* users and resources, instead of *creating* them. The point is that once the new domain structure plan has been created and the new Windows 2000 environment is in place, the process of placing users and placing resources are very similar to each other. In fact, they're only different in terms of how you populate your pristine (new) domains.

The reason this similarity is important is that Microsoft has created a set of tools that enable organizational changes (either in an existing Windows 2000 environment or during the process of a restructure) to be made with ease. These tools, which are described in detail in Chapter 13, "Making Postdeployment Organizational Changes," take advantage of two restructure-based capabilities built into Windows 2000 to make the administrative task of restructuring much easier.

The two capabilities built into Windows 2000 that enable restructuring are:

- **The capability to move security principals between domains:** With Windows 2000, security principals can be moved between domains (including domains that aren't even in the same forest) and still retain their *SIDhistory*. With SIDhistory, the moved users retain the SID in their security tokens, in spite of the fact that they reside in an entirely different domain after the move. A user also retains all access to resources associated with the domain account from which the user is being moved. The reason this is such a nice feature is because SIDs are based on the domain the account resides in, and creating a new account creates a completely new SID. Resource access control lists (ACLs) are based on SIDs. Without SIDhistory, a user account moved from one domain to another would lose all previously set access rights to resources throughout the enterprise, creating the huge administrative burden of resetting access rights for every user moved between domains.

- **The capability to move domain controllers between domains:** This is a feature because Windows 2000 domain controllers can be moved from one domain to another without requiring that the operating system be completely reinstalled. This feature reduces administrative overhead for many reasons, including the fact that settings and applications (or services) no longer have to be reinstalled from scratch, as they would if moving domain controllers between domains required that the operating system be completely reinstalled.

While these restructure enablers make the process of organizational changes and restructuring much easier (and, in reality, possible) for administrators, there are still steps and tasks that administrators must complete to prepare for a smooth transition from the existing Windows NT deployment into the pristine Windows 2000 forest. The process for transitioning users and resources from your Windows NT deployment to your pristine Windows 2000 forest will likely follow these steps:

1. **Plan and deploy your pristine forest.** This effort should coincide with the planning steps you completed based on information in Chapter 7, "Planning an Active Directory Services Deployment." Create the pristine forest, and switch it to native mode.

2. **Plan the transition of groups, users, and resources into the pristine forest.** This includes mapping groups, users, and resources from your existing Windows NT environment into target domains in the pristine forest. Note that global groups in a given domain will need to follow their user (member) base. Complete this mapping plan before you begin any part of the transition process.

3. **Establish trust relationships with your resource domains.** For the target domain, or the domain into which you are transitioning users, establish appropriate one-way trust relationships with each resource domain needed in order to maintain resource access. This step is necessary so that users moved to the pristine forest can maintain access to resources held in the not-yet-transitioned resource domains.

4. **Clone Windows NT global groups into the pristine forest.** Since resource access in Windows NT is generally based on global group membership, you need to ensure that those groups are transitioned to the pristine forest's target domain. Windows 2000 provides a cloning tool called ClonePrincipal that greatly simplifies this task. ClonePrincipal is explained in detail in Chapter 13, "Making Postdeployment Organizational Changes."

5. **Clone users into the pristine forest.** The next step is actually cloning the users (the previous step only cloned global groups). Your mapping plan (explained in step 1) will provide you with the necessary guidance. You should clone a few users first and check that their access to resources is intact before cloning the bulk of the Windows NT domain's user base.

6. **Retire the Windows NT domain.** Test to ensure that the transition has been successfully completed and that resource access is functioning properly. Then retire and dismantle the Windows NT domain. If necessary, you can reinstate the BDCs as Windows 2000 domain controllers in another domain (such as the domain to which you have transitioned the users), provided adequate physical security for the new domain controllers is available.

As you probably noticed, a number of new utilities are available for Windows 2000 deployments that enable the transitioning of objects (such as users, computers, domain controllers, and associated security settings) from one domain to another. These include:

- ClonePrincipal (available in the Windows 2000 Resource Kit)
- Netdom (available in the Windows 2000 Resource Kit)
- SIDhistory (more a capability than a tool or a utility)

## Transitioning Resource Domains into OUs

There's enough difference between making post-deployment organizational changes to OUs and transitioning Windows NT resource domains into OUs to merit explaining resource domain transitions separately.

As you remember from Chapter 7, "Planning an Active Directory Services Deployment," your OU structure should mirror your IT administrative structure. This step in the upgrade process requires that you consider the administration of each resource domain, as well as which users are primarily using the resources located in the resource domain, and migrate the resource domain accordingly. Since you'll have already created your OU plan (Chapter 7 planning steps should have been completed before you began this process), transitioning resource domains is simply a matter of deciding into which OU the resources in each resource domain should be placed.

This process, of course, will require that you consider the site topology. Check to see that users and their frequently used resources reside in the same site. Since OUs are easy to change after they've been structured, you don't need to get things perfect the first time around (though you should strive to do so). The following items outline the steps involved with transitioning a given resource domain into an OU in a target Windows 2000 domain. Before taking these steps, you should have completed the planning steps outlined in Chapter 7.

1. **Plan the transition of groups and resources into the OU.** This includes mapping the resource domain's groups into the appropriate OU. If the resource domain is being transitioned into a single OU (a 1:1 mapping), this step will be simple. If the resource domain is being divided among multiple groups, complete a mapping plan before beginning the transition process that shows which resources are going to which OU.

2. **Establish trust relationships with domains outside the target forest.** If you have domains (whether Windows NT or Windows 2000 domains) residing outside the target OU's forest and users in these domains require access to those external resources, you will need to establish appropriate one-way trust relationships with those domains. If you have a copy of the Windows 2000 Resource Kit, you can use the Netdom utility to easily identify existing trust relationships.

3. **Clone Windows NT global groups into the target OU.** Since resource access in Windows NT is generally based on global group membership, you need to ensure that those groups are transitioned to the OU's target domain. If you have a copy of the Windows 2000 Resource Kit, you can use a cloning tool called ClonePrincipal, which greatly simplifies this task.

4. **Upgrade BDCs to Windows 2000, and then demote them.** Note that this step requires you to upgrade the PDC to Windows 2000 and run the resource domain in mixed mode. (PDCs must be upgraded before BDCs.) This step enables you to transition the resource domain's BDCs (and the PDC) into the

new OU. If necessary, you can transition them to the new OU as domain controllers for the domain in which the OU resides, or simply turn them into member servers.

5. **Transition resources into the OU.** In this step, you begin moving servers into the OU. Begin by cloning a few servers to test that access to the OU's resources is intact. If you are satisfied with the results, clone the remaining resources.

6. **Retire the resource domain.** Before you retire and dismantle the resource domain, test to ensure that the transition has been completed successfully and that resource access is functioning properly.

# Conclusion

As you've gathered, quite a bit of planning and a number of steps are involved with upgrading an existing Windows NT environment to a Windows 2000 Active Directory services environment. You can choose from two distinct paths to complete the process. You can do an in-place upgrade and maintain your existing domain structure, or you can use the transition to Windows 2000 as an opportunity to restructure your domains. The third option is simply a combination of the two; you do an in-place upgrade and then modify some of the domains (such as resource domains) in order to take better advantage of Windows 2000 enhanced features and capabilities.

Many of the issues related to restructuring are nearly identical to issues related to making post-deployment changes to an existing Windows 2000 deployment, and restructuring can take advantage of the tools Microsoft has made available to ease the administrative burden associated with such undertakings. These tools were also built to assist with Windows NT upgrades and make these transitions easier and less disruptive to a production environment.

Whether you're doing an in-place upgrade or a restructure, the steps and processes outlined in this chapter augment the planning steps required before any upgrade can occur. Planning steps are explained in Chapter 7, "Planning an Active Directory Services Deployment."

# Chapter 12
# Migrating to
# Active Directory Services

Directory services exist in many different forms. Some directory services are specialized for particular tasks or applications, such as e-mail, while others, such as Active Directory services and Novell's Novell Directory Services (NDS), are comprehensive directory services designed for network computing. Directory services exist for other reasons too—some might be particular to a given organization or line of business. In addition to these many reasons for having directory services, there is directory consolidation, one of Active Directory services' primary goals. Directory consolidation wouldn't be possible if Active Directory services weren't able to absorb other directories. Fortunately it can, and in fact, it provides tools that make directory consolidation easy on the administrator.

This chapter discusses migrating from a couple of specific directory services to Active Directory services, and then rounds out the discussion of migration with an explanation of a Microsoft-provided command-line tool that enables you to migrate from any Lightweight Directory Access Protocol (LDAP)–compliant directory. Specifically, this chapter covers the following scenarios:

- Migrating from a Novell NDS tree or the NetWare bindery with the forthcoming tool from Microsoft, the Microsoft Directory Synchronization Service (MSDSS)
- Migrating from Microsoft Exchange Server 5.5 with the Active Directory Connector (ADC)
- Migrating from any LDAP-compliant directory with the command line–based LDIFDE utility

As with any migration or deployment effort, with your migration to Active Directory services you need to ensure that you've planned the steps and tasks necessary to ensure a smooth transition from the old way of doing things to the new. Such planning requires that you scrutinize the existing structure—such as your NDS or bindery deployment, your Exchange Server deployment, or your existing directory—and determine how to manage the change that will occur with the migration. This should consist of two separate considerations:

- How administrative responsibilities will change after migration
- How you will manage and perform the migration

In other parts of the book, I have recommended that you develop a plan before you attempt to make any significant changes to your network. This chapter is no different. I strongly recommend that you have a migration plan in place, weigh the costs and benefits of performing the migration, and then reconsider and make any necessary modifications to the plan *before* you begin the migration. Although the information provided in this chapter should help you form your plan, the steps outlined in the following discussions presume that you have created your plan, including provisions that ensure the migration process will have the least impact as possible on production-environment users.

## Migrating from Novell NDS

At press time, Microsoft is in the process of completing a directory synchronization tool called Microsoft Directory Synchronization Service (MSDSS). Rather than provide you with an explanation of what *might* be available when MSDSS is actually released, I'm going to point you to an online source that I update regularly and thereby provide you with what is available when MSDSS is actually released. The following link takes you to the Web site:

> *http://www.iseminger.com/books/adtr*

MSDSS is based on DirSync technology, itself an Internet Engineering Task Force (IETF) Internet Draft (I-D) for which the IETF is (at press time) soliciting feedback from the industry. MSDSS will be capable of doing more than migrating a Novell NDS deployment (which is explained in the "DirSync" section later in this chapter), but explaining exactly what MSDSS is capable of is better saved for a released version. Check the Web site; I'll provide a thorough explanation of MSDSS and update other book-related information as information becomes available.

## Migrating from Exchange Server

Active Directory services is capable of synchronizing with the Exchange Server 5.5 information repository (which is also considered a directory service). Many of the concepts associated with Exchange Server and its directory will be familiar to you; Active Directory is based on the Exchange Server database, though the two code paths forked early in the development of Microsoft Windows 2000 and Active Directory now has some architectural differences that are appropriate for an enterprise directory service that serves an entire network.

When discussing a migration from Exchange Server 5.5 to Active Directory services, it's perhaps more appropriate to call such a migration a *synchronization*. The Exchange Server directory is still maintained in its own information store once the migration is complete, and data that is shared (or synchronized) between Exchange Server and Active Directory is replicated in a way similar to the way data is replicated among domain controllers in a Windows 2000 (multimaster) domain. With Exchange Server Platinum—

the successor to Exchange Server 5.5—the integration of Exchange Server and Active Directory services is seamless and the process of moving from Exchange Server to Active Directory can truly be considered a migration; there is no longer a separate information store for Exchange Server—its absorption by Active Directory is complete.

This section first provides details on integrating Exchange Server 5.5 with Active Directory. The section then discusses migrating from Exchange Server Platinum.

## Active Directory Services and Exchange Server 5.5

Microsoft provides a tool called the Active Directory Connector (ADC) to facilitate replicating information between Active Directory and Exchange Server 5.5. This tool enables you to replicate information between Exchange Server 5.5 and Active Directory services in either direction (from Active Directory to Exchange Server, or vice versa).

**Note**   To synchronize data between Exchange Server 5.5 and Active Directory services, you need to have Exchange Server 5.5 Service Pack 1 or later.

There is no need to immediately synchronize Active Directory services and Exchange Server when you upgrade your Exchange Server computers to Windows 2000, because Exchange Server continues to function just as it did before the upgrade. As such, you can plan and coordinate the connection between Exchange Server and Active Directory when appropriate administrative resources are available, and after you and your IT staff have been properly trained to handle changes associated with the synchronization.

Exchange Server deployments in your organization are likely handled by an administrative staff that is separate from the one that manages your Active Directory infrastructure. When creating a plan to migrate from Exchange Server to Active Directory services, you must ensure that both administrative teams or departments share in the planning and deployment phases of the migration. When planning the migration, include ample time for both administrative teams to review the plan, make comments or recommendations, and then review each other's input.

### Active Directory Connector

Synchronization between Exchange Server and Active Directory services is achieved through the ADC, which is provided on the Windows 2000 Server CD (in the Valuadd\Mgmt\ADC folder). ADC is not installed or configured as part of the Windows 2000 Server or Active Directory services setup, so you must install ADC separately. There are two components that must be installed:

- The service component
- The Active Directory Connector Management tool

The service component is installed once on the Windows 2000 server that will be connecting to the server running Exchange Server. You should install the service component on a Windows 2000 Server computer acting as a domain controller.

The Active Directory Connector Management tool is the management interface that enables administration of the synchronized directories, and like most MMC snap-ins, it can be installed on multiple computers for convenient management. When installed, ADC Management can be accessed in the Administrative Tools group of the Programs menu.

ADC manages synchronization (replication of data between Active Directory and the Exchange Server deployment, actually) through connection agreements. A *connection agreement* is the control mechanism through which you define the objects to be replicated, the direction of the replication, the replication schedule, and the method of authentication used during replication. ADC can manage multiple connection agreements, providing you with fine-grained control over what information is replicated and when it is replicated. For example, you could configure one connection agreement to continuously update information from Exchange Server to Active Directory and another agreement to move information in the opposite direction (Active Directory to Exchange Server) once a day.

There is a special type of connection agreement, called a *Primary Connection Agreement* that can create new objects in the destination directory as well as replicate information about existing ones. You should have only one Primary Connection Agreement per Exchange Server/Active Directory pair to avoid creating duplicate objects in the destination directory.

## Setting Up a Connection Agreement

When you set up connection agreements, you will need to make several decisions.

### Direction of Replication

First you will need to make a decision about the direction of replication. You can replicate from Active Directory to Exchange Server, from Exchange Server to Active Directory, or in both directions. Your decision will be influenced more by administrative considerations than by technical considerations; if your organization is large and distributed, the Active Directory administrator group and mail administrator group are likely in different parts of your organization and different locations. Both groups may want to retain control over their information, so you might want to set up two-way replication to accommodate both groups. In smaller organizations, however, one-way replication will likely be sufficient.

Also, if you deploy Exchange Server Platinum, your decision is made for you. Exchange Server Platinum is managed from Active Directory interfaces and is completely integrated with Active Directory services. (No replication is necessary; Exchange Server Platinum uses the same information repository as Active Directory services.) Managing Exchange Server 5.5 from Active Directory interfaces subsequent to an Exchange Server/Active Directory ADC configuration can help you prepare for that scenario.

### Schedule of Replication

In addition to making decisions about the direction of replication, you will need to plan the schedule of replication. In a small network, you might be able to replicate data whenever it changes, using one connection agreement. More likely, though, you will need to schedule replication at certain times and possibly divide replication activities among multiple connection agreements, in which case you should consider the following issues:

- **Number of users or mailboxes:** If there are more than 500 mailboxes, it's recommended that you divide the objects among several connection agreements that perform replication at different times.

- **Frequency of change:** If your data changes every day and the changes are expected to be propagated quickly, you should schedule replication to occur frequently. If changes are less common or there is not a strict need for immediacy, you can schedule replication to occur less often and thereby introduce less network traffic and computational load on the servers running Exchange Server and on Active Directory servers.

- **Other connection agreement schedules:** If you have multiple connection agreements, you should avoid overlaps in replication schedules to minimize the impact that replication will have on performance.

A good approach to dividing up replication activities is to mirror your Active Directory organizational structure in Exchange Server: create recipient containers in Exchange Server that match Active Directory organizational units (OUs), place users from a given OU in the container that maps to the OU, and then create a connection agreement for each OU.

### Authentication Method

When setting up connection agreements, you also need to decide which method of authentication your connection agreements will use to make the connection. Exchange Server can use Secure Sockets Layer (SSL) encryption for such connections. Although SSL can slightly impact the time associated with completing the replication process, you should use this option when replicating to a server outside your organization. The combinations of authentication methods and their security capabilities are summarized in the following table:

**Authentication Methods and Their Security**

| Encryption | Basic (Clear Text) | Windows Challenge/Response |
|---|---|---|
| **Not encrypted** | Password sent unencrypted | Password not sent |
| | Other authentication information sent unencrypted | Other authentication information sent unencrypted |
| **SSL encryption** | Password and information sent | Password not sent |
| | Entire channel is encrypted | Entire channel is encrypted |

The connection uses an account that you specify when you configure the connection agreement. The account you specify needs to have permission to read from both Exchange Server and Active Directory and permission to write to the destination directory.

### Attributes to Be Replicated

You configure the attributes to be replicated using a *Policy*. A Policy contains configuration options that are shared among all connection agreements and are specific to Exchange Server. A full explanation of Exchange Server and its policies are beyond the scope of this book.

## Deletions

One final decision you need to make when setting up connection agreements and planning replication concerns the way deletions are handled. In the connection agreement, there are two options for handling deletions.

If you are replicating from Active Directory to Exchange Server, you can configure the connection agreement to perform one of the following actions during replication in the case of a deletion in Active Directory:

- **Delete the Exchange Server mailbox:** This option removes the mailbox from Exchange Server if the corresponding user is removed from Active Directory.

- **Keep the Exchange Server mailbox and store the deletion list in the temporary .csv file:** This option appends deletion information to a comma-delimited text file. The file can be found in %SystemRoot%\System32\MSADC\<*Connection Agreement name*>\ex55.csv.

If you are replicating from Exchange Server to Active Directory, you can configure the connection agreement to perform one of the following actions during replication in the case of a deletion in Exchange Server:

- **Delete the Windows account:** This option removes the user account if it is removed in Exchange Server.

- **Keep the Windows account and store the deletion list in the temporary .ldf file:** This option appends deletion information to an LDIF file. The file can be found in %SystemRoot%\System32\MSADC\<*Connection Agreement name*>\Win2000.ldf.

## A Sample Exchange Server Migration

To put all of this together, let's walk through a simple and fictitious scenario that shows how one company, the now infamous Iseminger.com, implemented Active Directory services and Exchange Server in its Windows 2000 environment. Just to make sure there are no misconceptions about the purpose of this example, let me state that it is provided only to illustrate the relationship between Exchange Server and Active Directory and should not be considered a model by which to build your Active Directory plan or, for that matter, a sophisticated Exchange Server replication scheme. For information about building your Active Directory deployment plan, consult Chapter 7, "Planning an Active Directory Services Deployment."

Back to the example. Iseminger.com has a large central office with several hundred people and two branch offices with about 50 people each. Its network environment is based on Microsoft Windows NT 4.0, with a server running Microsoft Exchange Server 5.5 (with Service Pack 1 applied, of course) deployed at the main office and at each branch. The branch offices have wide area network (WAN) connections to the main office, and e-mail was routed to the main office for connectivity to the Internet. The client workstations at the main office are running Windows NT 4.0 Workstation, and the branch offices have a mix of Microsoft Windows 95–based and Microsoft Windows 98–based workstations.

The administrators decided to upgrade their servers to Windows 2000 Server as soon as possible to take advantage of its many benefits, and they decided to upgrade the computers running Windows NT 4.0 Workstation to Windows 2000 Professional for the same reasons. The branch offices would use Windows 98 and Windows 95 until they received new computers (which were scheduled to arrive within the next few months) to enable the transition to Windows 2000 Professional. Since the Platinum release of Exchange Server wasn't available when they chose to perform the upgrade, they planned to use ADC to synchronize Active Directory with Exchange Server 5.5. In the branch offices, the administrators decided to replicate from branch office Exchange Server computers to the Active Directory information store in an effort to more easily manage the Exchange Server accounts in each branch office. In the main office, replication would occur from Active Directory to Exchange Server in an effort to simplify management of main office accounts.

The administrators at the main office upgraded the servers and workstations to Windows 2000 and began setting up their information in Active Directory. Meanwhile, the administrators at the branch offices installed the latest service packs to their Windows-based workstations to ensure interoperability with the Windows 2000 deployment. Once the plans were made and revised, and the upgrades and deployments were completed, ADC was installed on one of the Windows 2000 domain controller computers. Changes were made to the Exchange Server hierarchy to match the structural organization created with the Active Directory services deployment, and a one-way connection agreement was configured to send information to the Exchange Server computer. Since the replication traffic would traverse network cabling that resided in only the main office building, encryption was deemed unnecessary for the connection. (Although because plenty of bandwidth was available, the choice was contested by the security-minded personnel, who lost because the other administrators put the issue to a vote when the security folks were out getting doughnuts.) The connection agreement was set up as a Primary Connection Agreement to enable new user accounts that were added to Active Directory to be added to Exchange Server automatically. User account properties didn't change very often, so replication was set up to occur once each night.

At the branch offices, the Exchange Server computers were configured with a two-way connection agreement with the aforementioned domain controller at the main office. The connection used SSL encryption to protect data. (The security folks made sure they were in attendance for this vote.) An immediate synchronization was performed to move the data to the Active Directory information store, and the connection agreement was set up to replicate on a per-event basis. A branch office administrator could now enter a new account that would then immediately be transferred to the main office. Administrators at the main office would therefore have to assign permissions only to resources located in the main office.

## Integration of Exchange Server Platinum and Active Directory Services

Exchange Server Platinum removes the requirement for different information stores that existed in Active Directory/Exchange Server deployments and completely integrates with

Active Directory services. This integration of Exchange Server and Active Directory services provides several distinct administrative advantages:

- **Improved replication:** By integrating with Active Directory services, Exchange Server takes advantage of the existing network infrastructure and benefits from the more efficient approach to replication that Active Directory implements. (Active Directory services replicates only changed data rather than entire sets of data.)

- **Better security:** Exchange Server Platinum inherits the fine-grained, attribute-level resource control inherent in all Active Directory objects.

- **Simplified administration:** Exchange Server Platinum (as well as almost everything else associated with Windows 2000) can be managed with a single tool: MMC. You can also manage with a full replica of the directory, reducing ownership cost.

- **Better scalability:** Exchange Server Platinum can scale with Active Directory, which can scale to the largest enterprise.

- **Extensible schema:** Administrators can add new attributes to objects associated with Exchange Server, capitalizing on their experience with Active Directory schema management.

- **Common programming interface:** Active Directory Service Interfaces (ADSI) provides a single Component Object Model (COM) interface for writing scripts or developing applications, which can work equally well with Exchange Server Platinum and Active Directory services.

In Exchange Server Platinum, there are two main types of information that will be stored in the Active Directory services information repository:

- Recipient information
- Configuration information

## Recipient Information

Recipient information stored by Active Directory services and used by Exchange Server Platinum includes the following entities:

- Mailboxes
- Distribution Lists
- Custom Recipients

A *Mailbox* is simply a User object that has an e-mail address. Information that determines to which server the mail should be routed is stored as part of the User object. In Exchange Server Platinum and the current version of Exchange Server, users are considered part of a domain rather than part of a site. If a user moves to a different part of the company, you can make the appropriate administrative changes by simply updating the user information in Active Directory to indicate where the mail should be routed.

The *Distribution List* is a new object in Active Directory that represents Exchange Distribution Lists. These objects enable you to group users in any way necessary, across groups or organizations.

A *Custom Recipient* represents a user who does not have a Windows account in your Windows 2000 deployment. Such users are represented by an e-mail-enabled Contact object. In practice, any object in Active Directory can be a recipient. The schema class object of the class must be modified to include the Exchange-Recipient Auxiliary class, which enables the schema class object to store information that enables Exchange Server to properly route the mail. For example, with this capability, you could set up your server as a mail recipient, thereby enabling users to send e-mail directly to the server to report problems or request information. The e-mail would be routed to the administrator, but users would not need to know the administrator's e-mail address.

## Configuration Information

The second type of information used by Exchange Server Platinum is configuration information. A Configuration container is created in Active Directory that houses Exchange Server Platinum configuration information. The Configuration container contains various subcontainers that organize the information.

One subcontainer of particular interest is the *Sites container*. Within the Sites container are objects representing every Active Directory site, which in turn have containers for such things as connectors, monitors, protocols, and servers. With the integration of Exchange Server Platinum and Active Directory, there is one unified definition of sites. As you remember from Chapter 7, "Planning an Active Directory Services Deployment," sites are defined as a group of Internet Protocol (IP) subnets that are connected at local area network (LAN) speeds or higher. Exchange Server Platinum uses site information to automatically optimize its messaging topology.

## Moving to Exchange Server Platinum

When you install Exchange Server Platinum, it adds new classes and attributes to the Active Directory schema. To support these new schema classes and attributes, Exchange Server Platinum adds extensions to the functionality of the Directory Services Administration snap-in and provides additional snap-ins for managing Exchange Server Platinum–specific information.

User objects will be migrated to Active Directory, and any Exchange Server object that has a primary Windows account is merged with the Active Directory object representing it. Other objects become new objects in Active Directory.

Existing Exchange Server 4.0 and 5.*x* clients can continue to operate without being upgraded. For example, an Exchange Server 5.5 client will be automatically redirected to connect with Active Directory—though Exchange Server 4.0 and 5.0 clients will need to have the latest service pack installed to facilitate the redirection.

# Migrating from Other Directory Services

For every directory service covered by Microsoft migration tools (DS Migrate and ADC), there are many more directory services that administrators would like to migrate to Active Directory services. Fortunately, there are other ways to migrate information into an LDAP-compliant directory service such as Active Directory services. Microsoft provides a few worth noting:

- DirSync
- The LDIFDE command-line utility
- ADSI scripting

## DirSync

DirSync is an industry-wide technology that enables developers to programmatically synchronize the information of two directory services. Additionally, Microsoft has created and submitted to the IETF an Internet Draft (it's still a draft at the time of this writing, though the capabilities described in it are built into Windows 2000 Server) that aims to provide a standardized means of synchronizing LDAP-compliant directory services, based on Microsoft's current DirSync efforts. Microsoft has created the draft to solicit feedback from the Internet community and plays an ongoing role in the directory synchronization effort described therein. DirSync is the technology behind MSDSS, mentioned earlier in the "Migrating from Novell NDS" section. MSDSS will be effective in migrating (or synchronizing) data from one directory service to Active Directory services (such as with Novell NDS) or synchronizing such data so that both directory services exist in the same network environment.

**More Info**   Because the life span of any Internet Draft is only six months (after which a new draft with a different name must be submitted), it's a bad idea to point those who want to review the draft to a specific file. (The initial DirSync draft expired in August 1999.) But there is hope: for more information about the Internet Draft proposed for DirSync, you can go to *http://search.ietf.org/search/brokers/ internet-drafts/query.html* and perform a search based on the keyword *DirSync*.

Application developers can take advantage of DirSync capabilities by getting information about DirSync on MSDN or MSDN Online, or from the *Active Directory Developer's Reference Library*, available from Microsoft Press. Microsoft is in the process of developing a product that will enable the synchronization of Active Directory services and NDS.

**More Info**   Need information from Microsoft on DirSync? Go to MSDN Online at *http://msdn.microsoft.com,* and do a search on *DirSync*.

## The LDIFDE Command-Line Utility

Microsoft provides a command-line utility that enables administrators to export information from a directory, modify that information, and import that information into Active Directory services. The LDIFDE utility is installed by default with Windows 2000 Server, and since its location (%WINDIR%\system32) is part of the environment path, you can execute LDIFDE commands (or batch files) from any directory on the computer.

LDIFDE creates and reads LDAP Data Interchange Format (LDIF) files. LDIF is a file format used for performing batch operations on LDAP-compatible directories. (LDIF is defined in an Internet Draft that is slated for the standards track.) LDIF files can contain both extracted data from a directory and instructions for updating information in an LDAP-compliant directory. Using LDIFDE, you can export information from a remote directory, move the LDIF-compliant file to your server, modify its contents (as long as the modifications maintain LDIF compliance), and import the file and its contents to your Active Directory services deployment.

As mentioned previously, LDIFDE is a command-line utility, but as command-line utilities go, it has a bunch of optional parameters that enable you to do all sorts of batch operations. Unfortunately, these parameters also make the utility confusing to use, especially when you're trying to figure out all its capabilities by a hit-and-miss or experimental approach. To help save you from such confusing or frustrating experiments, the Help screen associated with LDIFDE is provided here. (You can get the same information by typing LDIFDE ? at the command prompt.)

```
LDIF Directory Exchange

General Parameters
==================
-i              Turn on Import Mode (The default is Export)
-f filename     Input or Output filename
-s servername   The server to bind to (Default to DC of logged
                in Domain)
-c FromDN ToDN  Replace occurrences of FromDN to ToDN
-v              Turn on Verbose Mode
-j              Log File Location
-t              Port Number (default = 389)
-u              Use Unicode format
-?              Help


Export Specific
===============
-d RootDN       The root of the LDAP search (Default to Naming
                Context)
-r Filter       LDAP search filter (Default to "(objectClass=*)")
-p SearchScope  Search Scope (Base/OneLevel/Subtree)
-l list         List of attributes (comma separated) to look for
                in an LDAP search
```

*(continued)*

*(continued)*

```
-o list            List of attributes (comma separated) to omit from
                   input.
-g                 Disable Paged Search.
-m                 Enable the SAM logic on export.
-n                 Do not export binary values

Import
======
-k                 The import will go on ignoring 'Constraint
                   Violation'
                   and 'Object Already Exists' errors
-y                 The import will use lazy commit for better
                   performance

Credentials Establishment
=========================
Note that if no credentials is specified, LDIFDE will bind as
the currently logged on user, using SSPI.

-a UserDN [Password | *]            Simple authentication
-b UserName Domain [Password | *]   SSPI bind method

Example: Simple import of current domain
    ldifde -i -f INPUT.LDF

Example: Simple export of current domain
    ldifde -f OUTPUT.LDF

Example: Export of specific domain with credentials
    ldifde -m -f OUTPUT.LDF
            -b USERNAME DOMAINNAME *
            -s SERVERNAME
            -d "cn=users,DC=DOMAINNAME,DC=Microsoft,DC=Com"
            -r "(objectClass=user)"
```

While I'd love to take credit for creating and formatting all that useful explanatory information, I can't. You can have it with just a few keystrokes at your favorite Windows 2000 Server computer, by typing the following:

C:\>**ldifde**

For clarification, that's simply typing **ldifde** at any Windows 2000 Server command prompt, at which time Windows 2000 informs you that you've typed an invalid parameter and then goes on to explain all of its parameters as I provided a few paragraphs earlier. Can't find it? Did you get an error like the following when you entered the command?

```
C:\>ldifde
'ldifde' is not recognized as an internal or external command,
operable program or batch file.
```

That's probably because it's not available on computers running Windows 2000 Professional—you must be running Windows 2000 Server. Of course, if you want to be able to use it on your Windows 2000 computer (perhaps just to print out that useful parameter information), you can always simply copy the command (which is found in your Windows 2000 Server computer's %WINDIR%\system32 directory) to your local computer; if you put it into a local folder location that's in your environment's path variable, you can execute it from any local directory path when in your command prompt.

**Tip**   If you have problems with command-prompt usage and a given command-line utility, such as adding a local directory location to the path statement in your local environment and returning to the command prompt but still not getting it to work properly, try closing your command prompt and relaunching it. The command prompt loads environment variables upon startup and doesn't refresh them thereafter. If you made changes to any of your environment variables while your command-prompt window was open and then went back to the open command-prompt window expecting your changes to be reflected in that command window, forget it. Close it and relaunch the command prompt (or leave it open and just launch another instance), and your environmental variables will reflect the changes.

To change environmental variables, click the System applet in the Control Panel, click the Advanced property sheet, and then click Environment Variables (near the bottom of the property sheet).

As a simple LDIFDE example, the following command produces a file named testfile.ldif, which contains all Person objects in the Finance organizational unit.

```
ldifde -f testfile.ldif -s koala -d
    "ou=Finance,dc=iseminger,dc=com" -p subtree -r
    "(objectCategory=CN=Person,CN=Schema,CN=Configuration,
    DC=iseminger,DC=com)"
```

## ADSI Scripting

There is yet another way to get information into Active Directory, and that is by using the ADSI interfaces built into Windows 2000. ADSI enables you to programmatically manipulate information in Active Directory using VBScript or any COM-enabled language. ADSI itself is a COM interface for interacting with a directory service and is used by developers to write programs that read and manipulate information in Active Directory services. You can write scripts that use this interface and execute them at the command line in conjunction with the Windows Scripting Host, making ADSI a powerful tool for Windows 2000 administrators as well as for application programmers. In-depth ADSI definitions are beyond the scope of this book, but you can get ADSI information galore on MSDN, or you can have it in book form and at your fingertips if you have a copy of the Windows Programming Reference Series' *Active Directory Developer's Reference Library* (available from Microsoft Press). An entire book in that reference library is dedicated to explaining and referencing ADSI and its various scriptable interfaces.

The following is a quick example of how to manipulate data with VBScript. In this example, we're pretending that the finance organizational unit moves to another location. You need to update the address information for everyone in the organization, but the monotony of doing all that changing manually is enough to make you consider taking up ditch digging. So rather than edit each User object manually and individually, you create a file in Notepad with code that looks something like the following:

```
Sub ChangeAddr(ADObject)
Dim ADUser
For Each ADUser in ADObject
 Select Case ADUser.Class
  Case "user"
   oUser.Put "st","Washington"
   oUser.Put "streetAddress","234 Any Street"
   oUser.Put "postalCode","92111"
   oUser.Put "l","Mytown"
   oUser.SetInfo
  Case "organizationalUnit" , "container"
   ChangeAddr(ADUser)
 End select
Next
End Sub

Dim ADOrgUnit
Set ADOrgUnit = GetObject("LDAP://OU=finance,DC=iseminger,DC=com")
ChangeAddr(ADOrgUnit)
Set ADOrgUnit = Nothing
MsgBox "Done"
WScript.Quit
```

You then save the file with the name ChAddr.vbs. At the command prompt, you type the name of the file (ChAddr.vbs) to run the script, and your thoughts of buying a shovel and a pick go out the window. Of course, you need to be logged on as an Administrator with the necessary privileges to make these changes, but the idea is that you did all of those changes automatically, making your life as an administrator much easier.

## Conclusions

The idea behind Active Directory services' standards compliance and centralized, consolidated nature is that you, as an administrator, can be more effective when you don't have to manage multiple directories. While essentially every Windows 2000–based directory has been integrated with Active Directory services, there's still the issue of those other directory services out there. Fortunately, Microsoft has provided tools that allow migration from commonly used directory services—NDS, Exchange Server, and other LDAP-compliant directory services—to Active Directory, and they are in the process of creating another such tool—MSDSS.

Although MSDSS is not completed at the time of printing, I didn't want to leave you without access to information and recommendations about its usage when it does come available, so I'm providing information about MSDSS in a more immediate form (online content, that is) when MSDSS is finalized. I hope that providing information on MSDSS when it becomes available will help you get the information you need for directory synchronization or migration and thereby make your work life a little easier (or at least a little more informed).

And of course, Microsoft hasn't neglected its own similar directory service, Exchange Server, and has made it possible for users of Exchange Server 5.5 to make the transition into an integrated Exchange Server/Active Directory environment. By enabling information to be replicated one way or both ways, administrators gain flexibility in determining where data is best managed and security in knowing that the information is automatically propagated according to connection agreements they can configure to meet their organization's management and security requirements.

For everything else, Microsoft provides additional tools in DirSync, LDIFDE, and the extensive, complete, and powerful offerings found in ADSI. With careful planning and coordination, migrating from just about any directory to Active Directory services can be done in a controlled, partitioned manner that minimizes the impact on production environments.

# Chapter 13
# Making Postdeployment Organizational Changes

Your organization is going to change. Departments move, divisions get restructured, groups get realigned, new and improved products fall by the wayside, and the employees in those departments scatter with the wind of the next big thing. You, the administrator or IT planner, can be assured that such change is going to roll across your desk and fill up your to-do box. Fortunately, Microsoft Windows 2000 is quite flexible and has been designed to adapt to change on an ongoing basis.

This chapter addresses making postdeployment organizational changes based on the major Windows 2000 and Active Directory services structural components. Those structural components are as follows:

- Forests
- Domains
- Organizational units (OUs)
- Sites

**Note**  You can also apply much of the information in this chapter to the process of restructuring an existing Microsoft Windows NT environment. For more information about transitioning your existing Windows NT environment to Windows 2000, including recommendations for making the transition as smooth as possible, see Chapter 11, "Upgrading to Active Directory Services."

Each of the sections in this chapter is broken into two primary parts: "What You Can Change" and "What You Cannot Change." I've structured these in a way that will let you quickly identify aspects of your deployment that can or can't be modified so that you can easily reference this chapter if (or really, when) changes in your business or administrative activities require changes to your Windows 2000/Active Directory structure.

# Making Forest Changes

Forest changes affect your entire organization and, as such, should be considered with an eye to—well—avoiding them. Structural additions to the forest, such as adding a domain or domain tree to a forest, are expected and acceptable; changes to the parent of an existing domain tree (such as changing its name) have effects throughout the enterprise and should therefore be avoided as much as possible. Changes to the schema are not considered structural changes; they are more of an extension of the capabilities of Active Directory services since such changes often include the creation of new object classes or attributes.

The forest changes being addressed in this section are structural changes that modify such things as domain trees, forest roots, or other forest-structural elements of an Active Directory services deployment.

It's important to be familiar with two built-in groups whose members have significant control over the forest: the Schema Administrators group and the Enterprise Administrators group.

The *Schema Administrators group* is the only group whose members have permission to access Active Directory services' Schema container (also known as its namespace or its naming context—all of which are accurate terms). Don't take such permissions lightly; as explained in Chapter 10, "Working with the Active Directory Services Schema," schema changes are permanent and can have a significant impact on your entire organization.

Members of the *Enterprise Administrators group* have the final authority in a Windows 2000 network because they have administrative rights throughout the entire Windows 2000 deployment. They can take ownership of any object in the forest, regardless of what access controls have been placed on the object. They can create domains, create OUs, or delete such objects entirely. They have sweeping authority and as such can make sweeping changes to your forest whether they know it or not. Windows 2000 has been designed to enable extensive delegation of administrative authority, which enables you to design an administrative structure that limits the number of administrators who have extensive administrative permissions. Enterprise Administrators, however, are not limited in their administrative permissions, so guard membership to the Enterprise Administrators group carefully.

With the administrative warnings completed, it's time to consider just what kind of organizational changes you can make to an existing Windows 2000/Active Directory deployment. Note that the restrictions on modifications capable of being performed on existing forests, domains, OUs, and sites should be considered when you develop your preliminary forest plan. In other words, the information in this chapter should be considered alongside the information found in Chapter 7, "Planning an Active Directory Services Deployment," throughout the process of developing your Active Directory deployment plan. Doing so will help you gain perspective on which aspects of your planned Active Directory deployment structure will be ironclad once the structure's in place.

## What You Can Change

You can change the following after you create your Active Directory structure:

- **You can add a new domain to a forest.** Adding a new domain to an existing forest is no problem. After installing Windows 2000 Server, launch DCpromo.exe (the wizard that installs Active Directory services—also known as the Active Directory Installation wizard), choose to add a new domain in an existing forest, and specify your existing forest. There is a caveat, however; the new domain must be the child domain of an existing domain in the forest. More information on this and other domain-specific requirements is provided in the "Making Domain Changes" section later in this chapter. The process of using the Active Directory Installation wizard is described in detail (with lots of screen shots) in Chapter 9, "Managing Active Directory Services."

- **You can add a new domain tree to a forest.** Adding a domain tree to a forest is another option in the Active Directory Installation wizard. As mentioned throughout Chapter 7, "Planning an Active Directory Services Deployment," a forest can host multiple trees. When you deploy multiple trees in a forest, you must establish an explicit trust between the forest root and the top domain of any trees that you add, as displayed in Figure 13-1.

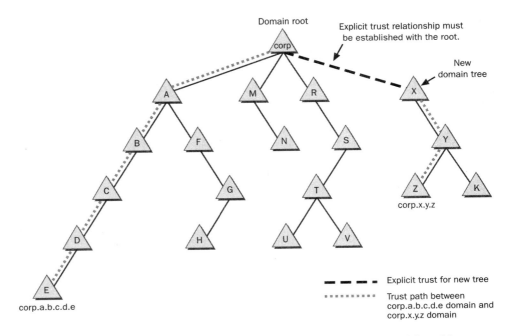

**Figure 13-1.** *The trust relationship established between the forest root and the additional tree's uppermost domain. Also illustrated is the way in which the forest root treats the trust relationship.*

When adding a tree to a forest, remember that the way in which Windows 2000 and Active Directory services manage trusts between domains in different trees can affect performance. Notice that the trust path in Figure 13-1 flows up through the additional tree, through the forest root, and then down through the other tree (or trees) in the forest. Such trust paths can introduce authentication delays if clients deep in the structure of one domain tree attempt to access resources deep in the structure of another domain tree. If such resource access is going to be a common occurrence between two particular domains, you can alleviate the performance hit by creating a cross-link trust. For more information on cross-link trusts, see the "Cross-Link Trusts" section in Chapter 3, "Windows 2000 Domains and Active Directory Services."

- **You can share resources between forests.** Such resource sharing requires that you set up an explicit, unidirectional trust relationship between the two domains participating in the resource sharing. Explicit trusts are *not* transitive and are unidirectional. That means if users in the *sales.corp.iseminger.com* domain needed to gain access to resources housed in *sampledomain.corp.microsoft.com*, administrators in both domains with appropriate permissions would have to set up a unidirectional trust in such a way that *sampledomain.corp.microsoft.com* trusted *sales.corp.iseminger.com*.

  Note that there's more administrative overhead associated with accessing resources outside the local forest than simply creating an explicit trust; resource access controls must be set, the explicit trust relationship must be managed, and so on.

**Note**  Users must explicitly search the trusted forest or domain to find external resources. Most user searches target the Entire Directory, which means that the forest's Global Catalog is searched. Users searching for objects that reside outside the forest will not find resources that are external to their forest in such searches because objects outside the local forest are not included in a forest's Global Catalog.

- **You can move objects between forests.** Moving objects between forests requires that the administrator moving the objects have appropriate permissions in both forests (whether as separate accounts or a single account), such as delete permissions in the source forest and create permissions in the target forest. Essentially, such moves are *migrations* of the objects from one Active Directory deployment to another. The most efficient way to migrate objects between two Active Directory deployments—and from a directory service to a different directory service—is to use the LDIFDE command prompt–based utility installed by default on all computers running Windows 2000 Server. Moving many objects between forests or directory services at once is often called a *bulk import*. See the "Migrating from Other Directory Services" section in Chapter 12, "Migrating to Active Directory Services," for more information about the LDIFDE utility.

## What You Cannot Change

You cannot change the following after you create your Active Directory structure:

- **You cannot merge forests in a single operation.** Merging forests cannot be done simply. You can clone security principals, migrate objects, and decommission domain controllers, downgrade them to member servers, and then add them to a new forest's domain and with those (complicated, administratively burdensome) steps, achieve the merging of forests, but there's no simple mechanism for doing so.

- **You cannot reinstall the root domain of a forest.** You must protect the forest root domain with all necessary and possible means, because losing it is a big deal and a bad thing. If you lose all of the domain controllers in a forest's root domain (through a fire, an earthquake, a theft, or whatever) and cannot restore even one domain controller (which implies that you didn't have even a minimal backup plan and brought the hardship on yourself), the Schema Administrators and Enterprise Administrators groups are lost forever, and there's no way to re-create them. You can't reinstall the root domain, so that means you'd have to (gulp) start all over with your Windows 2000/Active Directory structural deployment. The easiest way to prevent this is to ensure that you cannot lose all of your forest root domain's domain controllers in one catastrophic event (geographically disperse them) and ensure that you have a good backup plan *that is consistently executed,* with at least one full backup copy of the root domain's domain controller information sent to some very safe, accessible place that wouldn't be affected even if a catastrophic event did bring down your domain controllers. For more information about backup plans and recovery techniques, see Chapter 9, "Managing Active Directory Services."

- **You cannot move security principals between forests.** Within a forest, moving security principals such as users or groups between domains is fairly simple and is made possible by a couple of utilities that Microsoft has made available just for such situations. (See the next section, "Making Domain Changes," for more information on these utilities.) However, moving security principals between forests is not possible. Although Microsoft has made utilities available that can *clone* security principals (explained in the "Using ClonePrincipal" section later in this chapter), cloning security principals is not nearly as clean as moving them and will have a measurable, negative effect on the user's experience. (It isn't a smooth transition.) For more information about why this is the case, see the "Understanding SIDhistory" section later in this chapter.

## Making Domain Changes

Windows 2000 and Active Directory services offer a myriad of tools that enable administrators to easily handle change, including utilities that can help make domain changes as easy as possible on administrators. The Windows 2000 Resource Kit adds even more tools. While making changes to individual domains is relatively simple, changing a domain structure once it is in place is an involved and difficult undertaking. The following sections discuss the capabilities and constraints associated with making domain changes, as well as the constraints involved with undertaking domain tree–restructuring projects.

## What You Can Change

When changing domains in the Active Directory forest you can do the following:

- **You can add child domains to the Active Directory domain hierarchy.** As discussed previously in this chapter, you can add domains to the Active Directory hierarchy by installing a Windows 2000 Server computer, running the Active Directory Installation wizard on that computer, and choosing to create a new child domain in an existing forest.

- **You can remove an entire domain tree by demoting all of its domains' domain controllers.** To remove any collection of domains below the forest root (an entire domain tree or just a branch in the tree), you must simply remove each domain in the tree, starting with the lowest domain in the tree branch's hierarchy, and demote all the domains' domain controllers to member servers. (Member servers are Windows 2000 Server computers that are not domain controllers.) Note that to remove a domain, the domain cannot have any child domains. Therefore, the process of removing a branch of a domain tree simply involves deleting all domains in that tree, beginning with the lowest domain in the hierarchy and working your way up until the branch is removed.

- **You can have a NetBIOS domain name that is different from the domain's Domain Name Service (DNS) name.** I can't think of many reasons why you would want to do this, but it's possible. (I'm sure there are reasons out there, but planning for the future in your Windows 2000 deployment does not include hanging on to NetBIOS names.) An example of a NetBIOS name is the domain name assigned to domains in Windows NT. Even though you may never need to have different NetBIOS and DNS names for your domains, let's run through an example that illustrates when this might be necessary. Say you have a domain in your Windows NT deployment called BAD_NAME_CHOICE and for reasons specific to your deployment, you cannot or will not use Windows 2000 DNS for your DNS servers. If you were using Windows 2000 DNS, you could use the name in DNS because Windows 2000 DNS is capable of handling an underscore in a DNS name, but perhaps you're using BIND and your UNIX administrators must maintain control over the DNS servers. Underscore characters are illegal in DNS (Windows 2000 DNS handles them specifically to address the problem of underscores in existing Windows domains), so your naming convention for your Windows NT domains is incompatible with standardized DNS. This incompatibility affects your upgrade to Windows 2000 because, of course, domains in Windows 2000 are based on DNS rather than

NetBIOS. You might then have to leave the NetBIOS name of the domain as BAD_NAME_CHOICE, but use *better-choice.corp.[your DNS domain root].org* or something like that for the DNS name of the domain. (Dashes are legal in DNS.) In such an instance, Windows 2000 computers will identify the domain by its DNS name, while computers running earlier versions of Windows will identify the domain by its NetBIOS name. Anticipate user confusion if you do something like this.

I know, you didn't plan on having DNS as the primary locator service when you named your Windows NT domains using underscores, and I know that bad examples were provided, many of which used the underscore character, so you were imitating the examples and got caught in an upgrade pinch. That's not a pleasant situation to be in, but it happens (to all of us). I'd apologize for that if I were the person who thought of using underscores in examples, but I wasn't, so all I can do is commiserate. If it's any consolation, I've used underscores, too, such as in computer names—which with Windows 2000 become part of the extended DNS name of the network object, making them illegal and prime candidates for a new naming convention as well.

## What You Cannot Change

When changing domains in the Active Directory forest you cannot do the following:

- **You cannot change the name of the forest root domain.** This is fairly self-explanatory and is necessary because of the programmatic infrastructure of Windows 2000 and Active Directory services.

- **You cannot move domains between forests in a single operation.** A related topic was touched on earlier in the chapter when we discussed merging forests, and the logic that applied there applies here as well: you can clone or move the contents of a domain (such as its users, security groups, and resources), but you cannot move domains between forests in a one-step operation. For example, a simple tool that asks you, "Into which forest would you like to move this domain?" and then subsequently moves it in one automated step does *not* exist.

- **You cannot move a domain within a forest in a single operation.** For the same reasons you cannot move a domain between forests in one simple step (which include DNS hierarchy location, existence of child domains, security identifier [SID] and security token issues, and a multitude of other complicated domain-related dependencies), you cannot move a domain within a forest (such as moving it from one location in a domain tree to another) in one simple automated step. You can clone items in and move items from the domain, but you cannot move the entire domain itself. Microsoft provides a tool called MoveTree that can greatly help with the tasks associated with moving a domain within a given forest. (It cannot help you move a domain between two forests.) MoveTree is explained in detail later in this chapter.

- **You cannot rename a domain.** Although you cannot rename a domain, you can move its contents into a new domain with the name you want the existing domain to have (using the Windows 2000 Resource Kit utility MoveTree if the domain move is in the same forest) and achieve the same result. For those of you who are upgrading from an existing Windows NT deployment, the fact that you cannot rename a domain means that you should be sure about your domain naming convention before proceeding with either an upgrade or a restructure. This constraint provides yet another reason why it's good to base domain names in your Active Directory deployment plan on geographical location (such as countries or regions) rather than on your business structure, which is likely to change.

- **You cannot add a domain higher in the hierarchy than the root domain.** Regardless of the name of your root domain, you cannot add domains to your Active Directory structure that are higher in the DNS hierarchy than your root domain. If you have chosen to create a dedicated root domain called *corp.iseminger.com*, you cannot add a domain named *sales.iseminger.com* and have the domain participate in the forest.

- **You cannot add a parent for an existing domain.** The domain structure and the organizational structure of Active Directory services don't enable domain parents to be shoved into an existing structure; only child domains can be created.

- **You cannot split a domain into two domains in a single operation.** To split a domain, you must create a new domain and then move users and resources from the existing domain (per your desired split) into the new domain. Note that there is significant administrative overhead associated with performing such a manual split.

- **You cannot merge two Windows 2000 domains into one domain in a single operation.** To merge domains, you must remove all user accounts, groups, and resources from one of the domains and add them to the other domain and then demote all domain controllers in the empty domain and decommission it. You can use provided Microsoft utilities to help automate some of the process of doing such a manual merge.

## Understanding SIDhistory

Many of the features that enable administrators to move objects between domains in a forest are based on a Windows 2000 feature called SIDhistory (which is new to Windows). Put concisely, SIDhistory is an attribute of Active Directory security principals that enables security principals to be moved from a source container to another container while retaining SIDs from the source location—and to thereby retain permissions (resource access settings) based on those source SIDs.

As we know, SIDs are issued from a specific domain (rather than from a forest or any other organizational structure in Windows) and are unique for all time. (They are unique in every instance and are never identically reproduced, regardless of circumstance.) This uniqueness of SIDs not only ensures that a new user cannot be mistaken for a previous user, it also ensures that when a SID follows a user to another domain (which is enabled by SIDhistory), the SID is not at risk of conflicting with any other SID in the new domain. Think of it this way: Imagine your car is granted a license plate from one state (Washington State for the purpose of this example), and then you move to another state (California, for example) and get another license plate. If license plate numbers were unique for all time within a given state (so nobody else was ever issued the same Washington plate number that you had) and you stapled the Washington license plate onto your California license plate, a state trooper stopping you (you were speeding) could do a search based on your Washington license plate and unambiguously identify you (because your name and the car are uniquely identified with the Washington license plate number, which is unique for all time). By stapling the Washington State license plate with your more current California license plate, you've assured that any information associated with your Washington license plate number—such as unpaid parking tickets—could be unambiguously identified with you and considered in the final assessment of how big of a fine you should receive.

SIDhistory is similar to stapling that unique Washington State license plate to your California license plate; SIDhistory essentially staples your previous SID to the SID issued by the new domain to which a user is moved. When a user is moved from one domain to another within a given forest using an underlying SIDhistory-aware application programming interface (API) call, the user's security access token (which is the collection of all SIDs associated with the user, including his or her domain-based user SID, all group SIDs, and, in Windows 2000, the user's SIDhistory) includes SIDhistory in the new domain's security access token. When you attempt to access resources—perhaps in the domain from which you've recently been moved—the Windows 2000 computer hosting those resources reviews your SID and sees that your SIDhistory identifies you as the user in your current domain *and* as the user from your previous domain (with all associated security group memberships included), and it can grant access based on permissions contained in your current user account *and* on any permissions that remain from your user account in your previous domain.

The reason that SIDhistory is such a big deal (and it is a big deal) is that it enables administrators to move user accounts without needing to reassign resource permissions that would otherwise have been lost with the move—permissions that users should still have because they, as individuals, have not changed; only their home domain has changed. Since access restrictions can both deny and grant access, SIDhistory maintains security because any designations of "No Access" to a user's former group are also applied, due to the inclusive nature of SIDhistory. (It's simply another SID in a user's security access token, essentially treating a user's old SID like membership in a given security group.)

Microsoft Windows 2000 utilities that enable moves between domains in the same forest are built on SIDhistory-enabled API functions and therefore preserve SIDhistory capabilities. And since SIDhistory entries appear just like any other entries indicating security group membership, downlevel clients such as Windows NT 4.0 computers are also able to recognize SIDhistory.

With SIDhistory, the administrative overhead associated with moving security principals (such as users or groups) can be greatly reduced when SIDhistory-enabled utilities are used in the move process.

**Caution** You need to be aware of a problem that can occur as a result of the different ways that Windows NT 3.51 and Windows 2000 handle resource access. Windows NT 3.51 includes only SIDs from the local domain when it creates a user's security access token, which means universal groups (stored in the Global Catalog) and domain local groups from outside the Windows NT 3.51 domain are excluded from SIDs created on Windows NT 3.51 computers. This omission of groups to which the user actually belongs can result in the inability to deny resource access to users logging on to a Windows NT 3.51 computer and can be considered a potential security breach. (No Access permission settings based on universal group membership can be circumvented when a user logs on to a Windows NT 3.51 computer.) When moving security principals from Windows NT 3.51 deployments to Windows 2000, or if you are planning on leaving Windows NT 3.51 computers active in your Windows 2000 domain structure, you need to ensure these issues are taken into account.

## Using MoveTree

The Microsoft MoveTree utility is a command prompt–based, SIDhistory-enabled utility designed to make moving objects from one domain to another *in the same forest* easy on administrators. MoveTree is part of the Windows 2000 Resource Kit. When you go through the setup program, the Windows 2000 Support Tools Setup wizard walks you through the process of installing the tools on your system. Instead of using the wizard, you can view individual files in or extract individual files from the .cab file by right-clicking the .cab file in Windows Explorer and then clicking Explore.

**Note** You need to install the Resource Kit's Support Tools before you'll be able to find movetree.exe (and its required .dll file, movetree.dll), which you may have already learned by searching your Windows 2000 Resource Kit CD or the drive on which you installed Windows 2000 Server. The files you need (movetree.exe and movetree.dll) are packaged in a nice little 9-MB .cab file called support.cab.

MoveTree is capable of moving all sorts of objects, including (but by no means limited to) the following objects:

- OUs
- Security groups
- User accounts, with passwords preserved
- Computer accounts

### MoveTree Usage Constraints

MoveTree provides many advantages and capabilities, but it also has some important constraints, which are discussed in the next several paragraphs.

- **The source domain must be in mixed or native mode, and the target domain must be in native mode.** As we know, mixed mode requires that the Primary Domain Controller (PDC) in the existing Windows NT domain be upgraded to Windows 2000 Server and that Active Directory services be installed. Native mode, of course, requires that all domain controllers in the domain be upgraded to Windows 2000 Server and that the native-mode software switch be flipped.

- **Global groups must be empty prior to the move (and then repopulated when moved to the target domain).** This requirement involves a whole lot of administrative overhead, but if you don't follow it, MoveTree won't function properly. Global groups must be empty before you move them, due to SID-related issues associated with moving security principals from one domain to another. Although MoveTree is capable of retaining former SID settings through SIDhistory, it cannot move global groups that are not empty. This constraint also requires that any nested global groups in your native-mode domain be removed as well. (Nested groups are available only in native mode.) There is a better, less administratively burdensome approach to moving global groups with MoveTree than emptying all your global groups, and that is transitioning those groups to universal groups and then switching them back to global groups once the move has been completed. This approach is discussed a few paragraphs further on in this section.

- **Moved objects must be in closed sets.** Understanding closed sets can be tricky, so I'll provide a quick definition, an analogy, and then an explanation. A *closed set* is a self-contained collection of all objects associated with a given object. You can think of the requirement that all moved objects be in closed sets as a requirement that no stragglers or loose ends be left behind when MoveTree is used. In short, the set of moved objects must be complete.

Closed sets differ based on whether you're moving:

- A user or a global group
- A set of computers or domain local groups

Moving a user account or global group using closed sets can be compared to moving a family from one house to another. For example, pretend you and your family are moving from one house to another and you've hired a moving company to move you. For you to be completely moved, all the contents associated with your house must be moved. Pictures, lamps, attic storage boxes, and all other things that are associated with moving *you* must be included. Similarly, if a global group is moved, all its members must also be moved. (If a family switches houses, all possessions associated with the family move with it.) Likewise, if a user is moved, all global groups to which he or she belongs must also be moved. (If one member of the family were to move out, all belongings associated with him or her would need to move with that family member.) In either of these cases, if such requirements are not met, you do not have a *closed set*.

Moving a set of computers or domain local groups can be compared to moving a person who lives with roommates. For example, pretend that you live in an apartment that you share with two other roommates and your belongings in the central living area are fairly scattered and shared among all roommates. Now you have to move to another apartment; for the move to be complete (in a closed set), all your belongings must be collected from your room and from the shared living area (which includes a scattering of lamps and coasters, an area rug, and other random belongings). Also, you have to ensure that any personal information associated with you (such as your telephone number, utility bills, and mailing address) follows you to your new apartment. This example is similar to closed sets in domain local groups or computers. For each domain local group being moved (domain local group = the person moving), all computers containing resource access permissions that reference the domain local group (all computers referencing the group = all items associated with the person moving) must also be moved. For each computer being moved (computer being moved = person being moved), each domain local group referenced in its local resource access restrictions (all referenced local groups = all personal information associated with the person moving) must also be moved. In summary, closed sets equate to two one-to-many relationships, and all the "manys" equate to the items necessary to form the closed set.

### Avoiding Closed Sets

Because of the complexity often associated with determining a closed set, it isn't unusual for a closed set—even in its smallest complete incarnation—to include the contents of an entire domain. When this is not what you want, you should consider taking one of the approaches to moving objects described in the next several paragraphs. With these approaches, the closed set requirement of MoveTree is circumvented.

- **Transition all global groups to universal groups.** Transitioning groups to universal groups removes the requirement that they move with a domain. (Universal groups are, by definition, forestwide and not attached to a specific domain.) Because universal groups are not available in mixed-mode domains, however, this approach is possible only if your source domain is operating in native mode. Nevertheless, using this approach is much easier than having to deal with determining closed set membership or having to empty out global groups before using MoveTree. Once the user accounts are moved and settled, you can switch whichever global groups you transitioned (from your source domain) into universal groups back into global groups (in the target domain). Realize, though, that during the transition process, your universal group membership information will be propagated to the Global Catalog, and as long as those groups are universal groups, you will have to tolerate the additional replication overhead associated with having such membership information replicated across all enterprise Global Catalog servers. Despite that caveat, transitioning to universal groups is generally the easiest way to use MoveTree to get objects from one domain to the other within a given forest and involves the least amount of administrative overhead.

- **Create parallel groups in the target domain.** There may be reasons why you cannot transition the global groups in your source domain to universal groups. For example, your domains might be in mixed mode and have to stay in mixed mode (for whatever reason). Universal groups aren't available in mixed mode, so you need another solution. Creating parallel groups might be your solution.

  This option operates just as it sounds like it would. For each group in the source domain, create a corresponding group in the target domain. Identify all resources throughout the enterprise that reference the transitioning groups in their permission settings (their DACLs), and create entries in the settings for the newly created (parallel) groups that you create in the target domain. Yes, this is just as big, burdensome, administratively intensive, and hairy as it sounds.

- **Clone groups into the target domain.** Cloning is achieved with the Windows 2000 Resource Kit utility called ClonePrincipal, which is addressed in its own section below. This sounds easier than creating parallel groups (and it very well may be), but it has constraints of its own, which are detailed in the following section.

## Using ClonePrincipal

Microsoft provides a utility with Windows 2000 Server—called ClonePrincipal—that enables user accounts to be moved *between* forests. ClonePrincipal is provided in the Windows 2000 Resource Kit. The setup program initiates the Windows 2000 Support Tools Setup wizard, which walks you through the process of installing various tools on your system. Note that this is the same process that installs MoveTree and that you have to go through the Windows 2000 Support Tools Setup wizard only once to get all the available tools installed onto your system.

With ClonePrincipal, you can clone security principals that exist in a Windows NT (or Windows 2000) deployment and add them to a Windows 2000 native-mode domain in another forest. Cloning security principals is nondestructive to the source; when the cloning process is completed, the existing security principals located in the source domain are left intact, and replicas of those security principals are created in the target domain. ClonePrincipal is SIDhistory aware; during the process of cloning security principals in the source forest and adding them to the target forest, the source SIDs are copied into the cloned account's SIDhistory attribute, thereby retaining permissions to use existing resources that may have been associated with the source security principal's SID.

ClonePrincipal has the following restrictions:

- The source and target domains must not be in the same forest.
- The source SID cannot exist in the target forest, either as a primary SID or in the SIDhistory attribute. This restriction ensures that you cannot clone the same security principal and move it into a given forest more than once.
- You must have Domain Administrator permissions in the source domain and the target domain for ClonePrincipal to work.
- Auditing must be on in the target domain.

ClonePrincipal is actually a collection of files, all of which are included in the folder in which you directed the Windows 2000 Support Tools Setup wizard to place the files. (Often this is the C:\Program Files\Support Tools folder.) The files associated with ClonePrincipal are the following:

- **Clonepr.dll** Is a COM object with methods that enable ClonePrincipal operations
- **Clonegg.vbs** Clones all global group security principals in a given domain and moves them to a target domain in another forest
- **Cloneggu.vbs** Clones all global group and user account security principals in a domain and adds them to a target domain in another forest
- **Clonelg.vbs** Clones all local groups in a domain and moves them to a target domain in another forest
- **Clonepr.vbs** Clones a single security principal
- **Sidhist.vbs** Adds the SID of a source security principal to the SIDhistory of a destination security principal.

All the associated ClonePrincipal files that end in *.vbs* are sample scripts that you can modify as necessary to work for your deployment. The installation of the Windows 2000 Support Tools also includes the installation of a document (clonepr.doc) that goes into extensive detail about the ClonePrincipal utility.

## Making OU Changes

If you have to change something about the management or organizational structure in your Windows 2000/Active Directory deployment, make it your OUs. OUs were planned from the get-go to be easy to change, add, delete, and administer.

### What You Can Change

When changing your Active Directory OUs, you can do the following:

- **You can create complex OU structures quickly.** This can be good or bad, depending on whether doing so gets out of control (figuratively speaking, that is). OUs can be nested, enabling you to create the administrative structure that fits your organization without having to create a bunch of domains. All you need to create an OU are the appropriate administrative rights. Rights can be granted to create OU objects in a domain (granted by domain administrators) or to create OUs within OUs (nested OUs). Remember that simplicity is a good thing, and that you (or anyone in your organization who creates OUs) should have technical or administrative justifications for creating an OU.

- **You can delegate administration within any OU or OU structure.** With the capability to nest OUs, you also have the capability to have your administrative hierarchy reflected in the OU structure. For example, if you have three administrative teams—team1, team2, and team3—that have different levels of your administrative authority such that team1 is the top dog of the three administrative teams, team2 is next in line, and team3 is at the bottom of the management totem pole, you can nest OUs that correspond with each team. Say that team1 administers OU1, team2 administers OU2, and team3 administers OU3; you can nest OU3 within OU2, which is within OU1, the default result of which is that administrators in OU1 (that is, administrators in team1) have administrative control over OU1, OU2, and OU3. You can also configure OUs such that administrative permissions *do not* flow down through the OU structure, in which case only members of the true, domain-based top-dog administrative team (the domain administrators) have pervasive administrative rights through all nested OU structures. The point is OUs are flexible.

- **You can maintain control over whether OU administrators have the capability to create an OU structure within their OU.** You can specify whether OU administrators have full or partial control over their OU by specifying whether OU administrators are granted full control over an OU or only specific rights. With this administrative flexibility, you can control OU administrators' capability to extend their OU structure with additional nested OUs. Although this point was discussed in an earlier chapter, its administrative value is important enough for further clarification here.

  If you place an OU's administrator security group into the OU itself and grant full control over the OU to its administrators, you grant those administrators the authority to create additional nested OUs within their OU.

  If you place the OU's administrator security group into a parent OU (rather than into its own OU) and then grant those administrators specific access rights to the OU (such as rights to create User objects, Group objects, and resources), you limit the control they have over the structure of their OU. These two administrative options (granting full control vs. granting partial control) are illustrated in Figure 13-2.

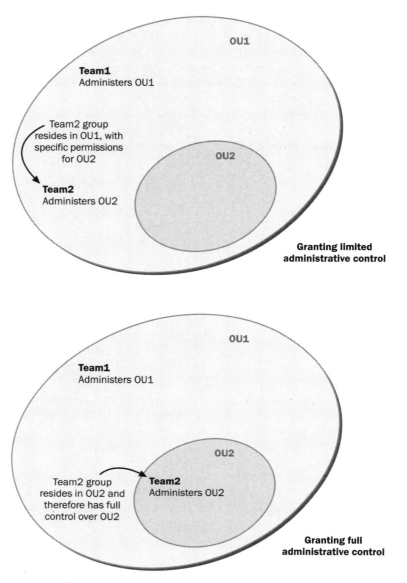

**Figure 13-2.** *Determining the control of OU administrators based on their OU administrative rights and their security group placement.*

Which administrative option you choose for your OUs depends on the IT staff structure you have in your organization, as well as the skill level of your OU administrators. If you are upgrading from Windows NT, keep in mind that many administrator groups that formerly managed their own domain will likely (and hopefully) have their domain become part of a larger domain, and as a result, the part of the organization over which they had administrative responsibility will become an OU. Part of managing such situations is clearly communicating that the change to an OU-based administrative structure (rather than a domain-based structure) does not minimize their importance or value as administrators, nor does it necessarily dilute their administrative control. (It might dilute their administrative control, and if it does, you should handle that tactfully.) The fact is that being responsible for "this new OU thing" is not quite as cool as being able to say that you're responsible for an entire domain, especially when it appears as though you've been stripped of your domain. Administrators are invaluable to the smooth running of any deployment, and skilled administrators are in high demand these days. How you handle the transition to an OU-based administrative structure can have a significant impact on how well the transition is received. Yes, that's the human side of a deployment, but it's reality, and if you handle the situation poorly (as in "Your domain's been demoted to an OU, and I'm stripping you of many of your administrative capabilities. Have a nice day."), you can jeopardize the overall success of your deployment. Enough said: the pulpit is hereby relinquished.

- **You can lose Group Policy settings by moving objects between OUs.** If you have Group Policy settings that are based on membership in an OU and you retire that OU or move objects (such as security principals or computers) from that OU to another, you could lose those Group Policy settings and adversely affect the productivity of associated users. Before making such modifications to your OU structure, you should review all Group Policy objects applied to the OU, as well as the Group Policy objects that will be inherited from any target OU into which you plan on moving objects. Note, too, that if you move objects between OUs that are in different domains or domain trees, you could lose access permissions that are based on domain membership.

## What You Cannot Do with OUs

When changing your Active Directory OUs, you cannot do the following:

- **You cannot assign access permissions based on OUs.** OUs are not security principals, and since they are not, objects within an OU cannot be granted or denied access to resources based on OU membership.

- **You cannot move objects between OUs unless you have proper permissions.** This might seem intuitive and simple, but it's worth mentioning: you must have proper permissions in both the source OU (delete object rights) and in the target OU (create object rights) to successfully move objects between OUs.

# Making Site Changes

Sites represent the physical network topology of your organization. Active Directory services has been designed to make infrequent changes to sites easy and manageable. Notice I said *infrequent changes*.

## What You Can Do with Sites

When changing your Active Directory sites, you can do the following:

- **You can introduce network congestion by making frequent site changes.** Active Directory services stores site information in the Configuration container, and the Configuration container resides on every domain controller in every domain in the forest. When changes are made to sites, the Configuration container must be replicated throughout the organization to keep all domain controllers updated with the latest information, and network traffic is thereby introduced. The best way to alleviate this problem is to perform site changes in batches, which means that you should gather site changes into a group and make all such modifications in one sitting. That way, the changes can be replicated throughout the organization in one transmission rather than in many transmissions.

- **You can limit the number of changes to sites by limiting the membership of the Enterprise Administrators group.** Only Enterprise Administrators can make changes to sites, and as mentioned throughout this book, Enterprise Administrators have other sweeping administrative permissions. To ensure that trivial site changes aren't made individually (but are instead collected and applied in batches), which would clog up the network, guard membership in the Enterprise Administrators group more tightly than you guard your favorite coffee mug.

- **You can optimize your overall Active Directory replication traffic by tuning site-link parameters.** Site-link parameters determine the route that replication traffic takes and when and how often replication is performed. You can optimize replication and its associated traffic to reflect your organization's WAN transmission priorities by properly setting your site-link parameters. Active Directory services requires that you provide values for the following site-link parameters any time you define a site link:
  - **Cost:** Used by Active Directory services to determine the most cost-effective route over which to send replication traffic.
  - **Replication schedule:** Enables administrators to specify when a given site link is available for replication traffic. Such availability could (and should) be based on the prioritized usage of the site link. For example, you could specify that the site link is unavailable between 8:00 A.M. and 11:45 A.M., which would then reserve the site link's bandwidth for mission-critical application usage rather than using it for Active Directory services.

---

**More Info**   Windows 2000 enables you to provide reserved bandwidth for users or applications, on a programmatic level, with a new technology called Quality of Service (QoS). For more information on QoS, check out MSDN or MSDN Online (*http://msdn.microsoft.com*). Note that to use MSDN Online, you must register, but rest assured, this is a free service.

---

- **Replication interval:** Specifies how often the system polls domain controllers on the opposite side of the site link for replication changes.
- **Transport:** Specifies the type of transport used for replication traffic.

Making postdeployment modifications to sites and site links is as easy as creating new sites (if appropriate) and modifying existing site-link parameters. For more information about the management of sites and site links, see Chapter 9, "Managing Active Directory Services."

---

## Conclusions

When your organization changes or reshapes, you're going to have to ensure that your Active Directory deployment can handle those changes gracefully. To do this, you might need to modify your forest, your domains, your OUs, or even your sites. Knowing what changes can be made to these Active Directory structural components is useful when such changes occur, but knowing about them *before* you complete your initial deployment or upgrade to Active Directory services is much, much better. That knowledge can help you create a well-designed, well-conceived initial Active Directory deployment plan that will enable you to head off requisite changes that might not be possible to make.

# Chapter 14
# Administratively Leveraging Active Directory Services

Throughout this book, the great capabilities that Active Directory services brings to a networked environment have been touted as the best thing since the invention of the mouse. But how do you actually get to use these capabilities to make administration easier? What has Active Directory done for me lately, you're probably asking—or more appropriately, what can Active Directory services do for me *right now*? This chapter answers those questions and gets you familiar with several important capabilities of Microsoft Windows 2000 (made possible by Active Directory services) that you can use to simplify network administration.

The sections in this chapter detail a handful of Windows 2000 capabilities and services that should be on your short list of features to implement in your network. The features explained in this chapter not only make your job as an IT professional more manageable, but they also empower users to get more use out of the network. Consequently, these features can significantly reduce the total cost of ownership (TCO) for your network.

Undoubtedly, more features and capabilities of this type, either from Microsoft or third-party vendors, will be made available to Windows 2000 as the technology gets put through its paces in deployments of all kinds. As it is, Windows 2000 already offers a number of time-saving, money-saving, TCO-reducing, and administrator productivity–enhancing features that you can immediately put to work for your organization. This chapter focuses on the following Windows 2000 features:

- Microsoft IntelliMirror
- Remote OS Installation
- Microsoft distributed file system (Dfs)

This certainly isn't a comprehensive list of useful technologies and features in Windows 2000; I'd need thousands of pages to go into detail about all the technologies that Windows 2000 makes available to administrators, users, and IT professionals. Instead, this is a list of three features that are extremely useful tools for IT professionals responsible for deploying and managing Windows 2000 networks in which Active Directory is deployed. Once you implement these three Active Directory–enabled Windows 2000 capabilities in your network, your job will become much easier, and that's always a good thing.

Surely one of the most important deployment considerations for you is: how do these features make my job easier? At the end of the explanation of each of these features is a section that compares administering and using Windows 2000 in your environment with that particular feature and without it. These sections either explain how the feature is used in a common task that administrators have to deal with daily in Windows environments, or they discuss how administering a Windows 2000 deployment would be handled without the explained technology. These sections firm up the explanations of how these features can make your life easier, and they should give you more real-life considerations for determining how to use these technologies to extend the usefulness of Active Directory services.

# Managing Change

*Change* happens. Business considerations change, hardware becomes obsolete, new employees join the fray and must be brought on line, and new must-have software becomes available. When changes occur, computers must be configured to accommodate these changes. Microsoft has included Active Directory–enabled features in Windows 2000 that help organizations manage change by simplifying configuration-related administration tasks.

Change—whether intentional or unintentional—doesn't come cheap. Even small changes that occur in an organization's network can have an impact on the availability and productivity of multiple members of the organization. This can result in a higher TCO of the network. (You've probably heard the term *TCO* and presumed only accountants, budget makers, and chief financial officers had to be concerned with TCO. That isn't the case at all; you, the IT professional, deal with issues every day that affect the TCO of your organization's computers and network.)

Consider, for example, how costly it can be when a user deletes a .dll file from his or her computer or when a user's hard disk crashes. You have to send a technician to the user's office to fix the problem, and the technician might not return for hours or days. That technician is getting paid to repair the computer (and is temporarily unavailable to work on other problems), but that isn't the end of the costs. The user, who depends on the now-defunct computer, can't get anything done while the computer is down, but he or she is still getting paid. What's the cost of owning that computer now? Tack on the cost of paying the temporarily unavailable technician, the temporarily unproductive user, and the additional IT staff members who must be hired because problems of this type are so time-consuming. (If three computers crash in an organization each day, at least three technicians must be available to handle the problems in a reasonable amount of time, presuming it takes a full day to restore or fix a computer.) In addition, factor in the costs associated with regenerating user settings, restoring lost data, reconfiguring the computer, and restoring or reinstalling applications once the computer is functioning again. The cost of a single computer failure in an enterprise environment is significant, and generally, the cost of the replacement part (a bad hard disk, for example) is just the beginning.

The bottom line is that computers are expensive—much more expensive than their original purchase price. The collection of costs associated with owning computers is the TCO, a concept whose relevance in your daily work life is hopefully a bit clearer now. In an effort to reduce the cost associated with owning computers, Windows 2000 has a handful of features geared specifically to enable IT professionals (administrators, managers, and decision makers for technology purchases) to reduce the cost of ownership by efficiently handling change. These features are collectively known as the Change and Configuration Management initiative, and they rely on the capabilities available to Windows 2000 when Active Directory services is deployed.

Simply put, when you implement the features of Windows 2000 Change and Configuration Management with your Active Directory deployment, the task of administering your Windows 2000 network becomes more manageable. (These features are included in Windows 2000, but you do have to implement them.) Your job becomes easier, your effectiveness and efficiency are increased, and users are less affected by software and hardware failures and other changes that occur on the network. Because everyone is more productive, your TCO is reduced. You may have heard this initiative to reduce TCO referred to by another name—ZAW, or Zero Administration for Windows.

Two of the Change and Configuration Management features available in a Windows 2000 deployment that also implement Active Directory services are:

- IntelliMirror
- Remote OS Installation

Organizations that want to extend the functionality offered by these Change and Configuration Management capabilities (for example, organizations with enterprise systems that want further control over their users' hardware and software environments) can buy Microsoft System Management Server (SMS) 2.0. This chapter doesn't discuss SMS because it is sold separately from Windows 2000.

---

**More Info**   For more information about SMS 2.0, check out the Microsoft SMS Web site at *http://www.microsoft.com/smsmgmt/default.asp*.

---

## What Change and Configuration Management Enables

So what's the big deal about Change and Configuration Management? What can IntelliMirror and Remote OS Installation do that will make the members of your IT department more productive and make their jobs easier? With Change and Configuration Management and Active Directory services, administrators can centrally create and enforce computing environment policies for groups of users and computers. With the policies in place, administrators can then rely on the system (Windows 2000 and Active Directory) to enforce these computing environment policies throughout the enterprise.

Another important benefit that the Change and Configuration Management features provide—which is a result of the policy-based, centrally administered computing environment—concerns users. IntelliMirror and Remote OS Installation make a user's computing experiences much more consistent and make computers and applications more readily available to users (increasing productivity and thereby reducing TCO).

> **Note**  IntelliMirror not only relies on the availability of Active Directory services, it also relies on Group Policy definitions. To take advantage of the most powerful features of IntelliMirror, you must use Active Directory and Group Policy in your Windows 2000 deployment. In fact, most organizations with Windows 2000 networks should use Active Directory and Group Policy (as well as IntelliMirror and Remote OS Installation). For more information on Group Policy, check out Chapter 9, "Managing Active Directory Services."

In the bulleted list that follows this paragraph, the benefits of deploying IntelliMirror and Remote OS Installation are described in more detail. If the items in this list are attractive to you, you should seriously consider incorporating IntelliMirror and Remote OS Installation capabilities into your Active Directory deployment. (If they are not attractive to you, check your pulse.) With Change and Configuration Management deployed, an administrator can do the following:

- **Define computing-environment settings centrally:** Computing environments for groups of computers, as well as for groups of users, can be centrally defined. Once defined, these settings will be enforced by the system (Windows 2000 and Active Directory services).

- **Replace faulty or damaged computers much more easily:** Administrators can quickly replace a computer when IntelliMirror and Remote OS Installation work in concert. Once the new computer is in place, the operating system can be installed with Remote OS Installation and IntelliMirror can automatically regenerate the computer's and user's environment, restoring data, applications, preferences, and administrative policies. Note that all of this (with the exception of putting the new computer in place) is possible without a visit to the computer.

- **Enable users to roam to any Windows 2000 computers on the network:** With IntelliMirror, administrators can enable users to roam to any Windows 2000 Professional computer on the network. The user can have the same (or a very similar) computing environment (including access to their data, applications, and preference settings) on any Windows 2000 Professional computer in the Active Directory deployment as they would have on their local computer.

- **Enable users to have the same computing experience on line and off line:** With IntelliMirror, files that users store on their local computer can be mirrored to a location on the network. This feature enables users to quickly find all their files (because a user's files are stored in the same place whether the user is working on line or off line) and to access their network files even when working off line. With intelligent caching, files are cached locally and automatically synchronized between the server (the mirror) and the local version.

- **Centrally manage software installation, repairs, updates, and removal:** With these capabilities, made possible by IntelliMirror, administrators can reduce their visits to users' workstations. For example, when users damage applications by "cleaning up" their local computer's files (read "deleting all those unnecessary .dll and .ini files"), you don't have to send out a technician. Instead, IntelliMirror (with the help of Windows Installer) automatically reinstalls the application or missing files, keeping the user productive.

- **Automate the installation of the Windows 2000 operating system:** With Remote OS Installation, administrators can automate the installation of Windows 2000 on remote computers and can secure such installations by properly configuring Group Policy or by limiting such installations to appropriate computers or users. Administrators can centrally configure a standard desktop image, with whatever customized settings they prefer, and that image will appear when they install operating systems using Remote OS Installation. If an administrator chooses not to do this, the desktop image will be like the one that is created when Windows 2000 is installed from a CD.

Clearly, the Change and Configuration Management features of Windows 2000, which take advantage of the centralized characteristics of Active Directory services, make administration of a distributed network easier. They are perfect examples of the types of features that are possible when a centralized directory service (such as Active Directory services) is part of a network environment.

The following two sections provide more details on the Active Directory–enabled capabilities of IntelliMirror and Remote OS Installation, discuss the technologies that enable these capabilities, and explain how to implement IntelliMirror and Remote OS Installation.

## Using IntelliMirror

IntelliMirror is a feature new to Windows that aims to increase the availability of Windows-based computers while reducing the overall cost of administering the computers and users. IntelliMirror is a primary component of Change and Configuration Management, a group of Windows 2000 technologies that implements Microsoft's ZAW initiative.

IntelliMirror greatly simplifies the management of Windows-based computers. Before IntelliMirror, desktop management usually meant employing a staff of technicians. A technician needed to be available to visit a given computer, sit in front of the computer for a while and assess problems (anywhere from software glitches to missing files to broken hard drives), and then make the necessary configuration changes to hopefully get the waiting user back up and running. With the advent of IntelliMirror, much of this burden is shifted to the system (Windows 2000 and Active Directory). IntelliMirror also minimizes many problems associated with the loss of a computer by enabling administrators to mirror data stored on users' computers on the network.

In addition to its ability to reduce the frequency of IT staff visits to desktop locations, IntelliMirror enables users to roam the network and while doing so, to have their data, applications, and settings appear wherever they end up.

IntelliMirror is composed of three features, all of which are integrated into the Windows 2000 operating system:

- **User Data Management:** Mirrors a user's data (generally, a collection of specific folders) to a predefined network share, which is then synchronized with the user's local copy. To the user, the data always appears local but can be accessed regardless of whether the user is at his or her primary computer, at another computer on the network, or off line (such as at home with a company laptop).

- **Software Installation and Maintenance:** Enables a Windows 2000 computer to ensure that a certain administratively defined set of applications is either present on (assigned to) or available to (published to) a certain set of computers. Additionally, applications can be assigned to or published for groups of users. This feature also ensures that Windows Installer–enabled applications that are damaged or missing files get repaired on the fly.

- **User Settings Management:** Mirrors a user's preferred desktop settings (like wallpaper, color schemes, and so on) to a location on the network. Anytime the user logs on to a Windows 2000 computer in the Active Directory deployment, these settings are applied.

One of the big advantages to these approaches to desktop management is that users don't have to know what's going on behind the scenes. Administrators can use the necessary tools to configure IntelliMirror to work in their Windows 2000/Active Directory environment (these tools and the configuration process are discussed later in this chapter), and users can simply work productively without worrying about copying files to the network, synchronizing files stored both locally and on the network, or any of that confusing stuff. In short, IntelliMirror works transparently, greatly increasing the likelihood that it will work effectively in your organization.

When you implement IntelliMirror *and* Remote OS Installation in your Windows 2000 deployment, you enable administrators to centrally control what is almost certainly the largest administrative burden to IT staffs: desktop management. To better visualize how these features can benefit your organization, consider the illustration found in Figure 14-1.

As you can see from the illustration, the idea behind IntelliMirror is essentially that all of a user's computing experiences in a Windows 2000 environment should be almost identical, regardless of whether the user logs on to the same computer every day or a different computer every day, and regardless of whether the user's computer is connected to the network.

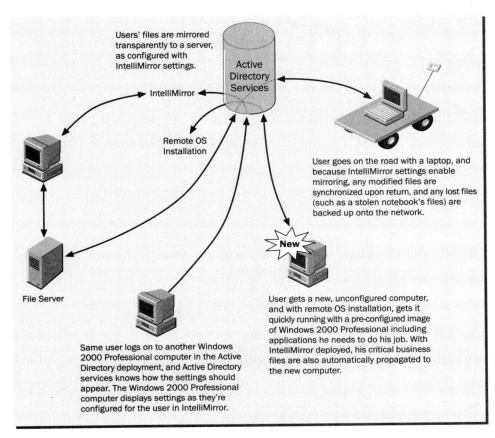

**Figure 14-1.** *How IntelliMirror and Remote OS Installation combine to create a complete Change and Configuration Management solution for Windows 2000/Active Directory deployments.*

The tools used to implement IntelliMirror are somewhat hidden within various management and administrative interfaces used for general Windows 2000 administration. There is no IntelliMirror snap-in, nor is there one simple lever, as it were, that you can point to and say, "Flip that switch and IntelliMirror is activated." The IntelliMirror implementation process is a little more involved and a little less straightforward than this, but IntelliMirror is not terribly difficult to implement. The next section explains how IntelliMirror depends on various Windows 2000 technologies and hopefully sheds light on why IntelliMirror implementation tools are scattered across a couple of management tools. Once you understand where these technologies and tools are located and how they interact, you will see that IntelliMirror is fairly simple to implement.

## Technologies That Enable IntelliMirror

IntelliMirror is made possible by a collection of interdependent technologies. While these technologies' interdependencies are sometimes difficult to clearly see, you need to understand them to understand how IntelliMirror works. Understanding these interdependencies will also help clarify why the administrative interfaces that you use to implement IntelliMirror (Active Directory snap-ins, for the most part) are not specifically "IntelliMirror tools." The following bulleted paragraphs explain the major technologies on which IntelliMirror is either based or dependent and detail the role these technologies play in making IntelliMirror possible:

- **Active Directory:** Active Directory centralizes management, and desktop management (or Change and Configuration Management—whichever you choose to call it) is no exception. IntelliMirror is managed through Group Membership and Group Policy, both of which are objects maintained in the Active Directory information store.

- **Group Policy:** IntelliMirror settings and usage are based on Group Policy, which is configured and stored in Active Directory. To centralize the tasks associated with IntelliMirror, Windows 2000 bases IntelliMirror settings on computer groups and user groups, both of which are subject to Group Policy. In other words, IntelliMirror is centrally managed based on group membership, group membership is the unit of management by which policies are applied (through Group Policy), Group Policy is centrally managed and is maintained in the Active Directory information store, and the Active Directory information store is configured through its various management interfaces, such as the Active Directory Users And Computers snap-in.

- **Roaming user profiles:** IntelliMirror uses roaming profiles to implement its User Settings Management capabilities. Using a roaming user profile enables a given user's profile settings (the contents of the ntuser.dat file)—such as color schemes, wallpaper, Start menu customizations, and other information—to be centrally stored at an administratively specified network location. Each time that user logs on to a Windows 2000 computer participating in the Active Directory environment, the user profile is pulled from the network location and its settings applied. Customizations to the user's settings made during a given logon session are saved to the profile when the user logs off, making those customizations available the next time the user logs on—regardless of whether the next logon is performed at the same computer or another computer. The alternative to a roaming user profile is a local profile. When local profiles are used, a user's settings are available only when that user logs on to the computer on which the settings are saved.

- **Folder Redirection:** IntelliMirror uses the Folder Redirection technology built into Windows 2000 to enable users to keep seemingly local files and folders on a network drive. This feature is one of the primary enablers of the User Data Management feature of IntelliMirror.

- **Offline Folders:** IntelliMirror uses Offline Folders capabilities, which complement and are dependent on Folder Redirection technology, to automatically synchronize local copies of files and folders with their network-based mirror copies, thereby enabling users to transparently work with files on line and off line. If version conflicts occur, such as would be the case if the cached (offline) version and network-resident version of a file were modified when the user was off line (for example, if two people worked on the file at home overnight), the user is prompted to resolve the conflict. With Offline Folders, users can have a single set of files (from the user perspective) that offers the benefits of both local and network files. Because files are stored on the network (and are therefore being backed up), they are much more secure from loss than if the files were stored only locally. Additionally, unlike files that are stored only locally, redirected and synchronized files are available if the user moves to another computer. And because files are still stored locally, users can work on them whether their local computer is connected to the network or not.

The following sections explain the three features that compose IntelliMirror and discuss how IntelliMirror uses the technologies just outlined.

## User Data Management

With IntelliMirror's User Data Management feature, Microsoft's goal is to have users say, "Wow, my documents and personal files follow me wherever I go, on or off the network. Isn't this neat? I'm way more productive this way."

As mentioned previously, User Data Management enables administrators to make the data users see and work with on a day-to-day basis, such as documents and other user-created files, more secure from loss and more readily available. When implementing this feature, administrators first redirect the data that users would usually keep on their local computers (often, with Windows 2000 computers, this is the My Documents folder) to a location on the network. Then administrators set this location to be available for offline use. With this configuration, whenever a user saves a document in a local folder that the administrator has configured for network redirection (and offline use), the document is actually saved to the network location and then synchronized back to the local computer. When users consistently store their documents within the directory structure configured for redirection to the network (such as the My Documents folder and its subfolders), a number of advantages are achieved.

- Users can work the same way, regardless of whether they have access to the network. Temporary network outages do not disrupt workflow, nor does taking home a computer (such as a laptop for which User Data Management is configured) and working on documents there.
- Synchronization occurs in the background and is transparent to the user. Users don't have to configure anything or concern themselves with remembering to synchronize their data with the network version—it happens automatically, and the user is involved only if conflicts between the local version and the network version arise.

- Important company data that the user might be working on is better protected. By redirecting data to a network location (and synchronizing the network version of the data with the local version), administrators can use IntelliMirror to manage mission-critical operations such as backup and recovery, without having to involve users and without relying on users to do their own backups.

- Hardware failures occurring on user computers have less impact than they otherwise would. With User Data Management in place, a hard-disk failure or computer failure doesn't result in as large a loss of productivity (or data); the new hard-disk or computer can be simply deployed, the local directories can be synchronized with the directories at the user's network-redirected data location, and the user is back in business with little or no lost data and with much less lost productivity.

Sounds good, doesn't it? User data is centrally managed and maintained and is always available, enabling users to work more productively and enabling administrators to more effectively manage mission-critical data. Information about how to put User Data Management to work in your organization is explained in the "Implementing IntelliMirror" section found later in this chapter.

## Software Installation and Maintenance

With the IntelliMirror Software Installation and Maintenance feature, Microsoft's main goal is to have users say, "Wow, the applications I use are always available on this computer and on any Windows 2000 Professional computer I log on to. Isn't this neat? I'm way more productive this way."

Microsoft's second goal with the IntelliMirror Software Installation and Maintenance feature is to have administrators say, "Wow, the users I support don't require hands-on desktop visits nearly as often as they used to. IntelliMirror fixes broken applications and installs required applications automatically. I'm going to get another latte and a day-old scone, and read my stock quotes."

Software Installation and Maintenance enables administrators to push applications onto computers selectively and provides all the benefits associated with self-healing applications. With the Software Installation and Maintenance features of IntelliMirror, organizations can deploy software in a just-in-time (JIT) manner. This means that applications can be installed based on a specified group of either users or computers and can be deployed automatically upon first attempted use, or they can be installed proactively.

Software Installation and Maintenance is not only about applications. With it, administrators can apply service packs, upgrade drivers, deploy new utilities, and so forth.

When planning the implementation of Software Installation and Maintenance in your organization, you should keep the following things in mind about this feature:

- **It is dependent on Group Policy.** The IntelliMirror Software Installation and Maintenance feature is configured through settings made to a given group's Group Policy. While some Group Policy features are available in Microsoft Windows NT 4.0, they are implemented in a different way than in Windows 2000 and won't work with IntelliMirror. (In Windows NT, they are essentially static registry entries that effectively "tattoo" the registry with settings. Windows 2000 Group Policy makes registry settings, but unlike tattooed registry settings, Windows 2000 Group Policy settings can be removed as a matter of course.)

- **It is dependent on Active Directory.** Since the IntelliMirror Software Installation and Maintenance feature is dependent on Group Policy and Group Policy is dependent on Active Directory (because Group Policy Objects [GPOs] are stored in Active Directory), the IntelliMirror Software Installation and Maintenance feature is dependent on Active Directory.

- **It is most effective with Windows Installer–enabled applications.** Windows Installer technology enables maintenance and repair of installed applications on the fly. Windows Installer–enabled applications detect when files are missing and, rather than simply fail, can go to a distribution point, get the required files, and then launch the application. Windows Installer also enables the installation of applications whenever users attempt to launch files associated with uninstalled applications (sometimes called *document invocation*). While the details about what Windows Installer technology does and how it works are beyond the scope of this book, you should at least know that Windows Installer is an advanced set of requirements to which Windows 2000– certified applications must adhere, and that enable automated software installation and maintenance.

- **It is functional with applications that are not Windows Installer– enabled.** Not all applications that users need are going to be immediately Windows 2000 certified (and thus Windows Installer capable). In fact, some of them will probably never be certified. Nevertheless, you can make such applications work with IntelliMirror by manually providing certain settings in a ZAW application package (.zap) file.

### Assigning Applications vs. Publishing Applications

The IntelliMirror Software Installation and Management feature can make software available to users in two ways: it can assign software, or it can publish it. Assignment or publication can apply to two groups in Group Policy: users and computers. (For those familiar with Group Policy, this is old news.) There are differences between assigning software to a group of computers versus assigning software to a group of users. Included in this section is a chart that clarifies these differences. But before we look at that, let's first explain the difference between assigning and publishing software.

Administrators *assign* software when users need it to perform their job. Software that is assigned appears automatically on the desktops of certain computers or of certain users' computers. If a user subsequently removes the software (through the Add/Remove Software Control Panel applet or otherwise), the software will still be available the next time the user logs on and will be reinstalled if the user attempts to launch a document that is associated with the removed software. Assigned software "sticks," regardless of what the user does.

Administrators *publish* software when that software might be useful for certain users (or on certain computers) but isn't necessary for users to perform their jobs. Software that is published appears in the list of software that is available in the Add/Remove Software Control Panel applet. Users can individually install published software; published software is not installed by default and does not stick in the way that assigned software does.

To put it into simple terms: when software is published, it is available to certain users or on certain computers and must be installed from an Add/Remove Programs applet on whatever Windows 2000 Professional computer it is to be added to. When software is assigned, it appears in the Start menu of certain computers (in the case of computer group assignments) or appears in the Start menu of any computer to which certain users log on (in the case of user group assignments) as though it is already installed (whether it's already installed or not).

Software behaves differently depending on whether it is assigned or published to user groups or to computer groups. Figure 14-2 illustrates the differences between applications that have been published and those that have been assigned, and it also shows the difference between applications assigned to groups of users and those assigned to groups of computers.

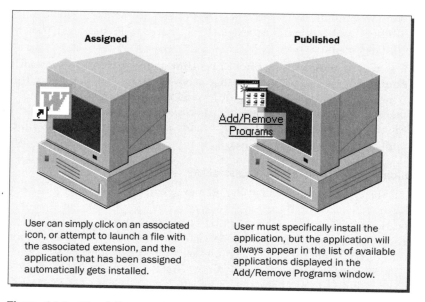

**Figure 14-2.** *The differences between applications that have been published and those that have been assigned.*

An explanation of how to put Software Installation and Maintenance into service in your organization is explained in the "Implementing IntelliMirror" section later in this chapter.

## User Settings Management

With the IntelliMirror User Settings Management feature, Microsoft's goal is to have users think as they're productively plugging away at whatever Windows 2000 workstation they visit, "Am I logged on to my primary computer, or am I logged on to some random Windows 2000 computer in a corner of the company I rarely visit? Gee, I can't really tell because my computing experience is the same on every workstation."

User Settings Management enables users to roam around the network, log on to any Windows 2000 Professional computer (assuming they have permission to do so), and have their familiar settings follow them, so to speak. Not surprisingly, the primary enablers of this "follow me" settings management technology are Group Policy and Active Directory. All the information that the User Settings Management feature of IntelliMirror uses is associated with a particular user and is stored in Active Directory. There are three types of settings information associated with a given user.

- **User and administrative information (*vital information*):** User information is the set of computing-environment characteristics users are accustomed to having available throughout their computing day, such as Web browser favorites, cookies, quick links, desktop backgrounds, and so on. Administrative information is the set of administrator-controlled settings that users are accustomed to having applied to their environment, such as Start menu settings (such as hiding the Run command in the Start menu), user-viewable items in Control Panel, and so forth.

- **Temporary files and settings (*temporary information*):** Temporary files and settings include Web browser history (such as the Microsoft Internet Explorer cache), the Documents list from the Start menu, and so forth.

- **Information specific to the local computer (*local information*):** Local-computer information consists of settings information that is specific to the computer on which a given user works, such as which folders or files are marked for offline use.

Only vital information follows users as they roam across the network. Most of the vital settings information associated with a given user is kept in the user's profile. (As you might have guessed, setting up roaming profiles for users is a primary step in implementing User Settings Management.) Most of the rest of a user's vital settings information comes from settings assigned to GPOs that are applied to groups to which the user belongs. I'll get more detailed than this about configuring the settings information that User Settings Management uses (and about other aspects of implementing the User Settings Management feature of IntelliMirror) in the "Implementing IntelliMirror" section found later in this chapter.

### How Much Do I Need This Technology?

One thing to keep in mind throughout this discussion is the following: IntelliMirror, or any other Windows 2000 feature that you'd consider deploying, should somehow enhance your computing experience, make your job easier, or increase your productivity—otherwise, you shouldn't use it. If you work for a small organization—with seven employees, for example—and it's going to take you two weeks and a new server to get IntelliMirror working in your organization, the costs of implementing IntelliMirror will probably outweigh the feature's benefits. How long would it take you to reinstall an operating system for one of the seven users? Not too long, probably, compared to how long it would take you to ensure IntelliMirror was working, to apply Group Policy, and to complete the other necessary tasks associated with using IntelliMirror. Of course, with seven users you might not be deploying Active Directory services, either.

It's easy to get wrapped up in technology simply because it's there, but you should assess whether it's going to make your life easier. Often, these cool empowering and enabling technologies do just that, but every situation is different. Yours might be an exception to the rule; to know if that's the case, evaluate the benefits and the deployment costs well enough to make an informed decision.

## Implementing IntelliMirror

To get IntelliMirror operational in your organization, you must meet IntelliMirror's requirements. IntelliMirror requires the following:

- Windows 2000
- An Active Directory services environment
- Group Policy (to get full functionality)

Additionally, you can use IntelliMirror only with Windows 2000 Professional workstations. If you're using Windows 98, Windows 95, or Windows NT 4.0 or earlier on your desktops and want to implement the features available with IntelliMirror, you have the following two options:

- Upgrade the desktops you want to manage to Windows 2000 Professional.
- Deploy SMS 2.0.

Now that the conditions and requirements have all been aired, let's discuss the steps that you need to take to use IntelliMirror features in your Active Directory–enabled Windows 2000 environment.

## How to Implement User Data Management

To implement User Data Management (the feature that enables you to make data that users are accustomed to working with on a daily basis, such as files and documents, more secure from data loss and more readily available), you must complete the following steps (which are described in detail in the sections that follow):

- Create a network share to which users' folders will be redirected.
- Enable Folder Redirection.

### Creating a Network Share

Creating a network share is a common administrative task that you are probably already familiar with, but it won't hurt to review the few simple steps involved in creating a share. There are a bunch of ways to create a share in Windows 2000, and the method I am about to describe is one of them. If you're more comfortable with a different approach, by all means use it. The approach we'll review (creating a share by using the command prompt) is quick and easy and lets the administrator stay where he or she can often be found—in front of the blinking little line from which Windows 2000 can be configured, inspected, administered, and otherwise interrogated.

The first step in the process is to invoke the command prompt, which you can do quickly by typing and executing **cmd** in the Run dialog box. Next, create the share by typing the following command-line directive at the command prompt:

```
net share [sharename]=[path to the root of the share]
```

If the name of the share that resided on your server (which we'll call BigServer) were UserDocs and the path to the location you wanted to be the root of the share were d:\Users\OfflineFolders, the command-line directive you would type is:

```
net share UserDocs = d:\Users\OfflineFolders
```

I'll continue to refer to this example throughout the rest of this section. You, of course, should substitute whatever share name you create wherever I refer to the UserDocs share.

### Enabling Folder Redirection

You enable Folder Redirection through the Active Directory Users And Computers snap-in. To access the snap-in, click the Start button, point to Programs, point to Administrative Tools, and then click Active Directory Users And Computers. The steps you'll need to take to enable Folder Redirection are the following:

1. In the Active Directory Users And Computers snap-in, select the domain or organizational unit (OU) or site in which the users for whom you want to enable Folder Redirection reside, as shown in Figure 14-3.

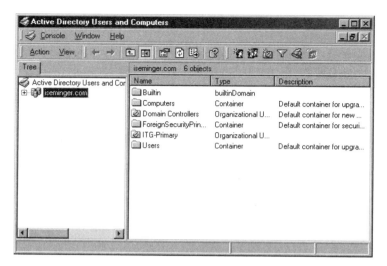

**Figure 14-3.** *The domain selected in the Active Directory Users And Computers snap-in.*

2.  Right-click the domain OU or site for which you want to enable Folder Redirection, and then click Properties, as shown in Figure 14-4.

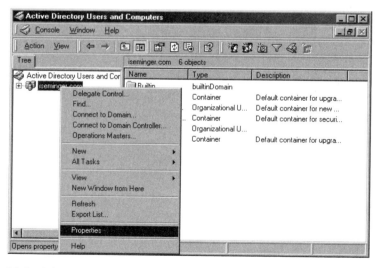

**Figure 14-4.** *Selecting Properties from the shortcut menu.*

3.  On the property sheet, shown in Figure 14-5, click New to create a new GPO, name it appropriately (Folder Redirection, for example), and then press ENTER.

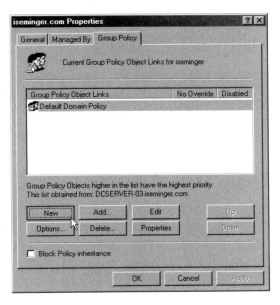

**Figure 14-5.** *The Properties property sheet.*

4.  Select the GPO you've just created, and then click Edit to configure the GPO. The Group Policy snap-in appears, as shown in Figure 14-6.

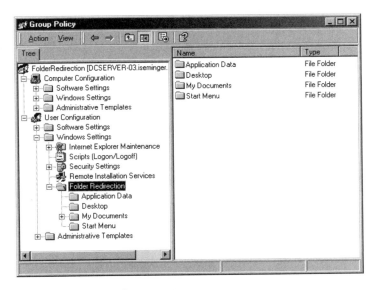

**Figure 14-6.** *The Group Policy snap-in.*

5.  From the new snap-in, expand the User Configuration folder, expand Windows Settings, Folder Redirection, right-click My Documents (to redirect the My Documents folders), and click Properties. A property sheet appears, as shown in Figure 14-7.

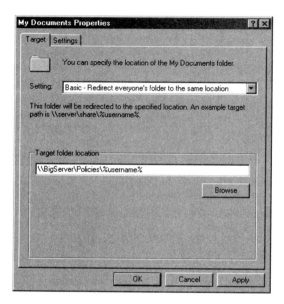

**Figure 14-7.** *The property pages associated with redirecting the My Documents folder in the Group Policy snap-in.*

6.  In the Target property page, select the setting you want to use from the drop-down box located to the right of the Setting caption (such as Basic – Redirect Everyone's Folder To The Same Location).

7.  In the Target Folder Location frame, type the path to the share you created earlier (such as **\\BigServer\UserDocs**). You can use system-based variables to ensure each user gets his or her own directory, such as the %username% system variable shown in Figure 14-7.

8.  In the Settings property page, configure the settings for the folder redirection as appropriate. The optional settings are shown in Figure 14-8.

That's it—you've enabled Folder Redirection for the group you selected in step 2. You can enable Folder Redirection for any other groups by performing these steps for each group. You should enable Folder Redirection as high up in the object hierarchy as possible to reduce the number of times these steps must be completed.

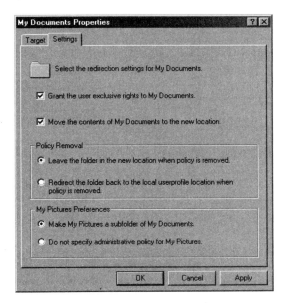

**Figure 14-8.** *The Settings property page for My Documents properties.*

What about synchronization of these redirected folders? Fortunately, that's all done by the operating system; administrators do not have to explicitly configure Offline Folders technology, and users have access to redirected files and folders once the administrator has configured Folder Redirection. Having Offline Folders technology built into Windows 2000 is like having fuel injection built into your car: it's a feature that improves performance, and there's nothing that the user (or technician) has to do to reap its benefits because the manufacturer has built it in as a fundamental capability.

## How to Implement Software Installation and Maintenance

You enable Software Installation and Maintenance (the feature that enables you to automate software installation and repair) by creating distribution points for the software that you want to make available to users, and you configure this feature by creating a GPO with appropriate settings. These steps are described in detail in the next two sections.

### Creating a Software Distribution Point

A software distribution point is where the IntelliMirror Software Installation and Maintenance feature goes to get the software that must be installed on Windows 2000 Professional computers that are targeted to receive the software. To create a software distribution point, you need to do the following:

1. Create a network share from which the software will be installed. The "How to Implement User Data Management" section earlier in this chapter explains how to create a network share.

2. Copy the software (from the application's installation CD, for example) to subfolders of the network share. If you wanted Microsoft Office 2000 to be part of your organization's managed software, for instance, you would create a subfolder called Office2000 and place the contents of the Office 2000 CD into that subfolder.

### Creating a GPO that Deploys the Software

As you read in Chapter 9, "Managing Active Directory Services," you can create multiple GPOs and simply apply as many objects to a given user or computer group as appropriate. For Software Installation and Management, you should create as many GPOs as necessary for groups (such as a domain, an OU, or an entire site) to have appropriate software deployments. In other words, if you wanted to assign Office 2000 to a group of users and to assign Office 2000 and Quake Arena to a group of computers, you could create one GPO for Office 2000 software and another GPO for Quake Arena, and then apply the Office 2000 GPO to both groups and the Quake Arena GPO to the computer group.

The steps involved in creating a GPO that enables you to assign or publish software are the following:

1. Launch the Active Directory Users And Computers snap-in, and select the object for which you want to create a GPO. For example, if I wanted to create a GPO for an OU, I would select that OU in the Active Directory Users And Computers snap-in. Figure 14-9 shows the Active Directory Users And Computers snap-in, with the OU (ITG-Primary) selected that we created in Chapter 9, "Managing Active Directory Services."

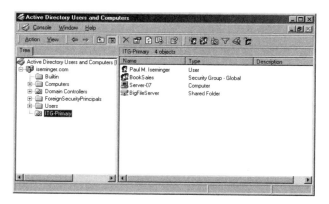

**Figure 14-9.** *OU (ITG-Primary) selection in the Active Directory Users And Computers snap-in.*

2.  Create a new GPO. This is done by right-clicking the selected object with which you want the policy to be associated, clicking Properties, selecting the Group Policy property page, and then clicking New. Figure 14-10 shows the Group Policy property page. As you can see, the New button is the top left button in the group of six buttons found toward the bottom of the property page.

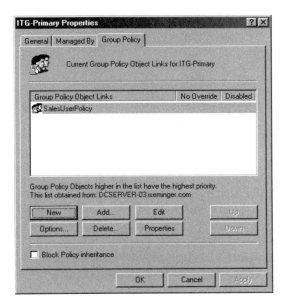

**Figure 14-10.** *The Group Policy property page.*

3.  Provide an appropriate name for the new GPO. If you have a reasonably large organization, you should consider establishing a GPO naming convention plan, similar to file server naming conventions or printer naming conventions, so that you can easily identify the origin, container, or owner of each GPO created. Figure 14-11 illustrates how you specify the name for a new GPO.

4.  Notice the appearance of an Up button and a Down button in Figure 14-11; multiple GPOs assigned to any container have an order of precedence associated with their appearance in this window. To increase the precedence of a given GPO, select it and click the Up button until it fits into the hierarchy as you want it to. For more information about the impact of applying multiple GPOs to a given container (such as a group or a site or an OU), consult Chapter 9, "Managing Active Directory Services."

5.  Select the newly created GPO, and then click the Edit button. You'll see the window shown in Figure 14-12.

**Figure 14-11.** *Specifying a name for a new GPO.*

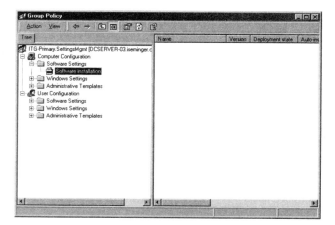

**Figure 14-12.** *The Group Policy window.*

6.  Under Computer Configuration (or User Configuration if you're configuring the policy for users), expand Software Settings, and then select Software Installation.

7.  Right-click Software Installation, and then click Properties, as illustrated in Figure 14-13.

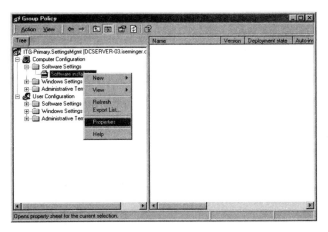

**Figure 14-13.** *Selecting Properties from the shortcut menu.*

8.   Set the default package location to the network share you configured earlier.
(This will save you many clicks during subsequent software management configurations.) If you don't know the location or path to the network share, you
can click the Browse button on the Software Installation property page. Figure
14-14 shows how easy it is when you know the network share location ahead
of time. (You simply type in the location.)

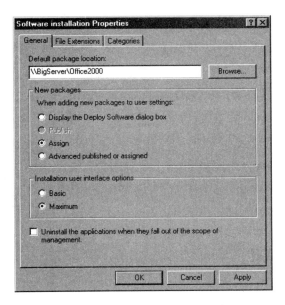

**Figure 14-14.** *The Software Installation property sheet.*

9.  From this window, you can choose to either assign or publish software residing in this location, using or making other settings modifications based on the other two property pages associated with the software package.

You have all sorts of options at this point regarding your software distribution; the associated property pages enable you to set your options, and from those settings you can formulate a Software Installation and Maintenance strategy that fits your needs.

### How to Implement User Settings Management

To implement User Settings Management (the feature that enables a user's familiar desktop settings to be applied on any Windows 2000 workstation on the network), you have to deploy roaming user profiles. The steps involved in deploying roaming user profiles for an organization are similar to the steps associated with deploying other features of IntelliMirror and are as follows:

1.  Create a network share.
2.  Use the Active Directory Users And Computers snap-in to select the users (or groups) to whom you want roaming user profiles to apply.
3.  Configure the user properties (or group properties) to store users' profiles on the network share created previously.

## Life Without IntelliMirror

It's fairly easy to imagine life without IntelliMirror—it's the same life led by IT administrators prior to Windows 2000, where computers required that the user install any software that was needed or a technician would either prepare the computer with the software or be sent to the computer to perform the installation. And if the software was broken (because of a deleted .dll file, a missing file, or some other problem), the technician would have to revisit the computer, troubleshoot the problem, and then fix it. As discussed previously, there are costs associated with such visits. IntelliMirror can reduce those visits, make software available, and install software, thereby counteracting users' unwitting attempts at breaking it. In life prior to Windows 2000 and IntelliMirror, there was no safeguard against the all-too-common problematic situations present in a Windows environment. Life without IntelliMirror results in more computer visits and associated headaches and less availability of appropriate applications for users, not to mention the inability to centrally manage which applications a given container (such as a group or site) should always have available.

## Using Remote OS Installation

Remote OS Installation enables IT departments and other groups responsible for the ongoing operation of workstations to greatly simplify the process of deploying or repairing workstations. As the name implies, Remote OS Installation enables Windows 2000 Professional (the operating system, or OS) to be automatically installed on remote computers without requiring a technician to visit each computer. Technician visits are often a significant and complicated part of desktop administration. Microsoft added the Remote OS Installation feature to Windows 2000 in response to customers' requests for a better desktop deployment solution.

> **Caution**   A warning is presented on the workstation on which the operating system installation is being performed, but an additional word of caution is worth including here. Using Remote OS Installation to install an operating system on a desktop computer removes all information on that computer's hard disk, so plan on losing whatever information exists on the computer's hard disk when you use Remote OS Installation.

Remote OS Installation creates a preboot execution environment (PXE) that enables the client to get basic network connectivity. Once basic connectivity is established, a series of scripted operations can lead the client to a point at which the installation or repair of the operating system can occur across the network. The value of this capability should be immediately apparent to anyone who has had the distinct displeasure of attempting to install an operating system when no operating system (nor installation CD, nor boot disk) is available. Perhaps the following scenario sounds familiar: You're trying to get *any* (pronounced with a hint of desperation) compatible client up and running without an installation CD and without a boot floppy disk that has the appropriate network interface card (NIC) driver. To add to the frustration, all the software you need is right on the network and the client has a network card installed, but you still can't get to it because the client can't boot with network connectivity. That's where Remote OS Installation shines, and the value of such a centralized operating system installation faculty in Windows 2000 is immediately apparent. Those of you who have not had to endure such an ordeal should take my word for it—this Windows 2000 feature is a time-saver, a frustration-saver, and a gray-hair-saver.

Once Remote OS Installation is implemented in your organization's Windows 2000/ Active Directory environment, you can configure it to perform the following installations:

- A CD-like installation of Windows 2000 Professional
- A customized installation of Windows 2000 Professional

This capability for automatic software installation empowers you to do the following:

- Deploy new computers more easily with less administrative overhead.
- Repair damaged computers remotely with less administrative overhead. (When this capability is used with the capabilities provided by IntelliMirror, administrators can, after a damaged computer is replaced, regenerate the computer's environment with very little administrative intervention.)

These capabilities enable organizations to lower the cost of deploying and maintaining computers. As you remember from earlier in this chapter, this is one of the main goals of Microsoft's Change and Configuration Management initiative (which is designed to help fulfill Microsoft's ZAW initiative), of which Remote OS Installation is a part.

Figure 14-15 reminds you where Remote OS Installation fits in the Windows 2000 Change and Configuration Management initiative.

| Feature | | Benefits | Technologies |
|---|---|---|---|
| **Change and Configuration Management** — **IntelliMirror** | **User Data Management** | **My data and documents follow me!** Users can have access to the data they need to do their jobs, whether on line or off line, when they move from one computer to another on the network. Administrators manage this feature centrally by policy to minimize support costs. | • Active Directory<br>• Group Policy<br>• Offline folders<br>• Synchronization Manager<br>• Enhancements to the Windows Shell<br>• Folder Redirection<br>• Disk quotas |
| | **Software Installation and Maintenance** | **My software follows me!** Users have the software they need to perform their jobs. Software and optional features install "just in time." Once installed, software is self-repairing. Administrators manage application and operating system upgrades as well as application deployment centrally by policy. This minimizes support costs. | • Active Directory<br>• Group Policy<br>• Windows Installer<br>• Add/Remove Programs in the Control Panel<br>• Enhancements to the Windows Shell |
| | **User Settings Management** | **My preferences follow me!** Users see their preferred desktop arrangements from any computer. A user's personal preferences and settings for desktops or software are available wherever the user logs on. Administrators manage this feature centrally by policy to minimize support costs. | • Active Directory<br>• Group Policy<br>• Offline folders<br>• Roaming user profiles<br>• Enhancements to the Windows Shell |
| | **Remote OS Installation** | Administrators can enable remote installation of Windows 2000-based operating systems and desktop images on new or replacement computers without on-site technical support. | • Active Directory<br>• Group Policy<br>• Dynamic Host Configuration Protocol (DHCP)<br>• Remote Installation Services |
| **IntelliMirror + Remote OS Installation** ⟶ **Machine Replacement** | | | |

**Figure 14-15.** *The Windows 2000 Change and Configuration Management map.*

As you can see from Figure 14-15, IntelliMirror and Remote OS Installation enable administrators to perform many tasks from a central location—tasks that once required multiple and often protracted visits to users' workstations. Minimizing such visits significantly increases IT staff members' productivity, not to mention their availability to deal with the inevitable slew of other administrative tasks.

## Technologies That Enable Remote OS Installation

The Remote OS Installation feature of Windows 2000 is dependent on a handful of technologies; some are new to Windows, others are simply technologies required for networking that enable the automated discovery and negotiation (explained later) involved in the process of installing an operating system remotely. The following list enumerates and describes the technologies that must be available in the Windows 2000 network for which you want to enable Remote OS Installation.

**Remote Installation Services (RIS):**  RIS is a service running on a Windows 2000 Server computer that listens for requests from client computers for Remote OS Installation services, effectively functioning as a boot server. For Remote OS Installation to function in a Windows 2000 environment, at least one server must run RIS. The Windows 2000 Server/RIS computer also houses the operating system images that get installed on client computers. RIS enables more than one Windows 2000 Professional image to be available to computers, and RIS can house modified installation images that can be made available to certain clients. With multiple-operating-system image availability, administrators can customize a basic operating system installation to include base applications and settings that are appropriate for their organization's environment.

More specifics about RIS, OS images, and the features and restrictions of each are provided later in this section. You might have noticed one of the restrictions already: only Windows 2000 Professional can be installed with Remote OS Installation. (There is one exception—you'll find out more about that in the "Creating OS Images" section later in this chapter.)

**Microsoft Domain Name Service (DNS) server:**  DNS is the locator service that enables clients to find RIS servers on a network. Windows 2000 computers hosting RIS register the RIS service (and associate their IP address with that service) with Microsoft DNS Server computers. This RIS registration and the standard DNS registration process that domain controllers undergo to enable clients to find Active Directory resources are what enable clients to find RIS servers on a network. Clients requiring services of Remote OS Installation query DNS for a RIS server and use the results to establish contact with the RIS server.

**DHCP server:**  Clients that require the services of Remote OS Installation must first locate a RIS server, and to locate a RIS server, the client must first dynamically obtain an IP address. Windows 2000 uses DHCP to enable this connectivity.

**Active Directory services:**  The dependency of Remote OS Installation on Active Directory services is no surprise—if Active Directory services wasn't a primary enabler of Remote OS Installation, there wouldn't be much reason to discuss Remote OS Installation in this book. RIS uses Active Directory to get information about network configurations and about permissions. For example, RIS uses Active Directory to locate computer accounts in a given domain (because permission to perform a remote operating system installation on a given computer can be regulated through permissions set in Active Directory) for the following reasons:

- To determine if Group Policy settings affect whether the user or computer should be allowed to remotely install the operating system
- To determine the appropriate RIS server to use (based on network configuration such as site information)

- To set a naming policy for new computers
- To specify the location (domain or OU) in which the new computer should reside

Because of these dependencies, the Windows 2000 server on which RIS is enabled must have access to Active Directory services. A RIS server can be serviced by (that is, the service can be running on) either a Windows 2000 domain controller or a stand-alone Windows 2000 Server computer. RIS servers must also be authorized to serve as RIS servers in a Windows 2000 environment, and such authorization is enabled through settings in Active Directory.

**PXE-compliant clients:** For Remote OS Installation to work properly, the client computer on which the remote OS installation is to be performed must be PXE compliant. PXE-compliant computers are computers capable of obtaining and executing network-based boot instructions instead of booting from potentially nonexistent local computer–based boot instructions. Computers can comply with PXE by:

- Designating themselves as PXE compliant (certain Dell Latitude laptops, for example).
- Having NICs that interoperate with a boot floppy disk–based initiation of Remote OS Installation. (A listing of compatible NICs is provided later in this section.)
- Having a PXE-compliant motherboard BIOS.
- Meeting the requirements of the NetPC or Managed PC standard.

    Any computer that complies with the NetPC or Managed PC standard (also known as the PC98 standard) is PXE compliant.

## Implementing Remote OS Installation

Before you implement Remote OS Installation, you should understand the remote operating system installation process. In particular, you should understand the interactions that take place between a client and a RIS server during this process. An understanding of this process and these interactions will help you better understand Remote OS Installation in general, as well as the features and requirements of RIS servers and their clients.

Let's start with a summary of the process: a client boots, gets instructed to initiate a remote operating system installation, gets an IP address and locates a RIS server, authenticates, and then installs the operating system from a selection of operating system images. That's it—but of course, there are more details to be explained.

The following list describes the steps involved in the remote operating system installation process. Note that some of these steps have been simplified to avoid certain issues that are either beyond the scope of this book (such as the DHCP protocol) or not important to understanding the process (such as how Trivial File Transfer Protocol [TFTP] differs from FTP).

1.  During the boot sequence, the client computer is directed to initiate a remote operating system installation. The option to initiate a remote operating system installation is generally available in the early part of the boot process.

2.  The client instructed to initiate an operating system installation broadcasts a DHCP request—specifically, a DHCP DISCOVER message—containing PXE client extension tags that identify the client as a PXE client.

3.  The DHCP request is answered by a DHCP server, which responds with appropriate DHCP settings, such as an IP address and the address of the default DNS server. If the DHCP server (or the proxy DHCP server) is capable of responding by using the extended PXE-enabling protocol, it also returns a list of appropriate boot servers (RIS servers).

4.  The client contacts the RIS server and receives the name of an executable file that resides on the RIS server.

5.  The client downloads the executable file from the RIS server using TFTP (a very simple and light version of FTP).

6.  The client runs the downloaded executable file, which then leads the client through the process of remotely installing Windows 2000 Professional, and provides an option that enables the user to choose which Windows 2000 image to install, if multiple images are available.

The process that a client goes through in finding its RIS server has other issues associated with it that you should understand, such as which server the client determines should serve as the installation source for its operating system installation. One thing you should consider is the following: since any remote installation of Windows 2000 requires a significant number of files to traverse the network, it's highly recommended that any remote operating system installation take place between a client and server that have LAN-speed connectivity between them. Fortunately (and as mentioned previously), Active Directory attempts to locate a RIS server that is best suited to serve the client's remote operating system installation needs. Active Directory will try to find a RIS server within the client's site, which ensures (assuming proper planning and deployment of Windows 2000 sites) that the RIS server and the client will be connected at LAN speeds.

Another issue associated with deploying RIS servers is load balancing. To determine whether you should deploy one RIS server in every site or multiple RIS servers, you'll need to analyze your network usage, as well as your Remote OS Installation usage.

### Configuring Clients to Work with Remote OS Installation

Users who perform remote operating system installations on their computers are guided through the installation process by the Client Installation wizard, which is a set of selections presented to users when they press F12 during the boot process of a PXE-capable computer. Administrators must ensure certain settings are properly configured on PXE-capable computers for this feature to work properly.

For a PXE-capable computer to take advantage of Remote OS Installation capabilities, the computer must be configured (in its BIOS settings) so that the first boot device selected is the NIC. When configured in this manner, a computer enables the user to choose whether the computer should be booted from the network (which thereby enables Remote OS Installation). Normally, the user chooses this option by pressing F12 within a certain time period, the duration of which is displayed on the computer monitor and after which the computer boots from the next device in the list, generally the C: drive. Clients need to have sufficient hard disk space on their target drive—usually the C: drive—to handle the installation process. The amount of installation space required depends on the amount needed by the optional software or settings that are included with the installation.

During the installation of the operating system on the client computer, the user (who is sitting in front of the computer that is about to receive the operating system installation) is presented with a set of setup options. Administrators specify which options are available by using Windows 2000 Group Policy settings. The administratively set options available are as follows:

- **Automatic setup:** This is the default setup option enabled for all Client Installation wizard users. When this setup option is set, the installation process begins immediately (rather than consulting the user for input). In this setup situation, the user is simply prompted for logon credentials and confronted by a caution message about the impending operating system installation. If no further options are enabled, the installation proceeds.

- **Custom setup:** This setup option is similar to automatic setup but enables administrators or other helpdesk personnel to prepare computers on behalf of other users in the organization with appropriate customization options. This is useful for enabling the preparation of workstations for subsequent delivery to the desktop.

- **Restart a previous setup attempt:** This option is useful when the installation process is interrupted. An installation can be interrupted, for example, when a client loses connectivity with the RIS server.

- **Maintenance and troubleshooting:** This option enables OEMs or independent software vendors to provide maintenance and troubleshooting utilities and capabilities. Vendors such as AMI and Phoenix Technologies provide such utilities.

## Client Requirements

As mentioned previously, for Remote OS Installation to function, the client computer on which an installation is to be performed must be PXE compliant. For clients to be PXE compliant, they must meet one of the following requirements:

- Meet NetPC or PC98 requirements

- Have an installed NIC and a motherboard BIOS that is PXE compliant
- Have a NIC that is compatible with the remote installation boot floppy disk and be booted from the PXE boot floppy disk (also referred to as the remote installation boot floppy disk)

### NetPC and PC98 Requirements

To meet the requirements of the NetPC or PC98 standard, a computer must have PXE functionality included in its feature set. (Realize, however, that the NetPC and PC98 standards provide more than PXE functionality. Consult the NetPC and PC98 standards for all the other requirements they must meet—our focus is on PXE compliance.) NetPC and PC98 computers must be equipped with version 1.0b or later of their respective standard to function properly with Remote OS Installation.

### Compatible Network Cards

If your computers don't meet the NetPC requirements, the PC98 requirements, or PXE requirements, there's still hope: if a client computer has a NIC that is compatible with the remote installation boot floppy disk and if the computer boots from the remote installation boot floppy disk, that computer can still make use of Remote OS Installation. Although there are a fair number of NICs on the following list of compatible NICs, it's important to know that this list cannot be expanded. You cannot add network adapters to the list or drum up support for adding other NICs; the NICs on this list are the only cards supported. The following list is the most current list of available compatible NICs:

**Table 14-1. NICs Compatible with the Remote Installation Boot Floppy Disk**

| Manufacturer | Model |
| --- | --- |
| 3Com | 3c900 (Combo and TP0)<br>3c900B (Combo, FL, TPC, and TP0)<br>3c905 (T4 and TX)<br>3c905B (Combo, TX, and FX) |
| AMD | AMD PCNet and Fast PCNet |
| Compaq | Netflex 100 (NetIntelligent II)<br>Netflex 110 (NetIntelligent III) |
| DEC | DE 450<br>DE 500 |
| Hewlett-Packard | HP Deskdirect 10/100 TX |
| Intel | Intel Pro 10+<br>Intel Pro 100+<br>Intel Pro 100B (including the E100 series) |
| SMC | SMC 8432<br>SMC 9332<br>SMC 9432 |

**Note**   Because of Plug and Play requirements, only PCI cards are supported by RIS. Since PCMCIA cards are excluded, laptop or notebook computers on which you want to perform a remote operating system installation must be attached to a docking station with a PCI-based NIC from operating system previous list installed in the docking station.

### PXE-Capable Motherboard BIOS

Some motherboards come with a BIOS that is PXE capable. On such systems, the BIOS handles the software necessary to make the computer PXE capable. A motherboard's documentation or manufacturer's Web site will have specifics about whether the motherboard supports such capabilities. Also, most motherboards these days are flash-upgradeable, which means that more recent versions of their BIOS are available through their manufacturer's Web site. While flashing a BIOS is not a trivial task (and requires a visit to the computer), it might make otherwise non-PXE-capable computers PXE capable.

**Real World**

Flashing a BIOS on a motherboard isn't something that should be done on a whim. You should have a specific reason for doing so, and you must ensure that the flash process is completed or you can render the computer completely unusable. It will require some serious, involved troubleshooting (usually by someone outside your IT department) to get the motherboard functioning again. Make sure you have the proper version of the upgraded BIOS and that you test it on a non-production-environment computer before you go flashing a user's BIOS. While flashing a BIOS might save you some costs associated with upgrading NICs or entire computers, if care isn't taken during the flash process, you can wreak havoc.

### Creating the RIS Boot Floppy Disk

During the RIS installation on a Windows 2000 Server computer, the utility that is used to create a RIS boot floppy disk is also installed. The location of the utility, which is simply an executable file called rbfg.exe, is the following:

```
\\[server name]\[RIS directory]\admin\i386
```

So, if the Windows 2000 server on which RIS was installed was named RISServer24 and the directory in which the services were installed was RISFolder, the path would be the following:

```
\\RISServer24\RISFolder\admin\i386
```

To create the boot floppy disk, simply run the utility. You can do so by typing the location of the utility into the Run dialog box (accessed from the Start menu) or at the command prompt. Using the previous server name example, from the command prompt (or the Run dialog box, for that matter), you would need to execute the following command:

```
\\RISServer24\RISFolder\admin\i386\rbfg.exe
```

This would bring up a wizard that would walk you through the simple steps (stick a floppy disk in the drive, click OK, and so on) involved in creating the remote installation boot floppy disk.

### Implementing Servers

The steps involved in preparing a RIS server—that is, a Windows 2000 Server computer on which RIS runs—are as follows:

1.  Run the RIS Setup wizard by typing **RISetup.exe** at the command prompt on a Windows 2000 Server computer. Alternatively, you can type **RISetup.exe** in the Run dialog box (accessed from the Start menu). (This has the same effect as typing **RISetup.exe** at the command prompt.) You're presented with the Welcome screen shown in Figure 14-16.

**Figure 14-16.** *The welcome screen of the Remote Installation Services Setup wizard.*

2.  When you click Next, you are prompted to type the location of the remote installation folder, as shown in Figure 14-17.

3.  Complete all the steps in the setup process. (Most of the steps are self-explanatory, as many wizard screens are, and therefore aren't explained individually here.) Throughout the process, you should keep a few things in mind. First, the drive on which you install RIS is the drive on which you will place your operating system images (such as the Windows 2000 CD image or your customized Windows 2000 Professional image), and to provide the necessary security on the drive, you must format that drive with the NTFS 5.0 file format. Second, you'll be asked whether the RIS server should respond to clients that request remote installation service. (If you don't enable this option, this RIS server won't respond to clients that need service.) This seems like a silly question—if you didn't want it to respond, why would you be installing the service?—but it's actually not because you could be setting up a backup RIS server. Third, you'll be asked whether the RIS server should respond to

unknown client computers. An unknown client is a client that does not have a preexisting computer account in Active Directory. By enabling this option (which means that the server won't respond to unknown clients), you can ensure that only clients with proper accounts will be allowed to remotely install Windows 2000 Professional from this RIS server (and, because of the automation of the installation/deployment process associated with Remote OS Installation, begin functioning in *your* Windows 2000/Active Directory environment). I highly suggest enabling this option; it provides your network with better security (even though, as you'll see later, a remote operating system installation cannot occur if the user requesting it does not have an existing user account).

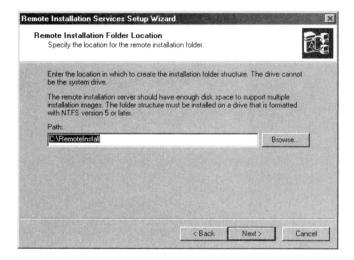

**Figure 14-17.** *The Remote Installation Folder Location screen.*

4. Authorize the RIS server to run on your network. You must do this to put your RIS server into service. Although the authorization information is housed in Active Directory, you actually must authorize the server using the DHCP Manager snap-in. This isn't a big deal; remember, you must have DHCP running in your Windows 2000/Active Directory environment to deploy Remote OS Installation. The authorization process is straightforward. In the DHCP Manager snap-in, right-click DHCP (upper-left corner), and then click Manage Authorized Servers, as shown in Figure 14-18.

5. Click Authorize in the dialog box that appears, as shown in Figure 14-19.

6. Type the name of the RIS server or its IP address, as shown in Figure 14-20.

Once the system verifies the address of the server, your RIS server is authorized to perform its duties in your Windows 2000 environment.

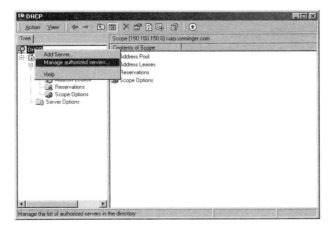

**Figure 14-18.** *The DHCP snap-in.*

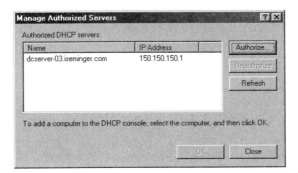

**Figure 14-19.** *The Manage Authorized Servers dialog box.*

**Figure 14-20.** *The Authorize DHCP Server dialog box.*

**Note**   You need to be logged on as a Domain Administrator to be able to authorize a RIS server in the DHCP Manager snap-in.

When determining where to store your operating system images on your Windows 2000 Server computer, you should keep in mind the following:

- As mentioned previously, you must store operating system images on a drive formatted with NTFS 5.0.

- You cannot place an operating system image on the same volume on which Windows 2000 Server is installed. This means that you will need at least two logical partitions on the Windows 2000 Server computer on which RIS is installed.

- You'll need between 800 megabytes (MB) and 1 gigabyte (GB) of free hard disk space for each image you intend to make available through RIS.

- If you deploy multiple RIS servers, it is the administrator's responsibility to ensure that they house identical images. Neither Windows 2000 nor RIS makes any effort to check operating system images or replicate images between or among RIS servers. You can, however, use File Replication Services (FRS), which is built into Windows 2000, to manually configure such replication.

### Creating Operating System Images

Imagine that you could take a snapshot of a given configuration so that certain applications were installed, certain registry settings were in place, and all other such computing environment settings were configured and then cloned onto another computer. This snapshot, often called an *image,* could make rolling out multiple computers much easier; rather than installing the operating system and then having to go to each client and install given applications and make certain settings, you could simply roll all that information and all those settings into one simple installation. This capability is built right into Remote OS Installation.

Your organization might have a collection of primary software and settings to which every computer and every user must have access. You might call this a *base image,* from which users and groups further modify their workstations. Wouldn't it be convenient if you could include all those settings and applications when you install an operating system remotely? Answer: Yes. Fortunately, Remote OS Installation lets you do just that. You can create an image of a given Windows 2000 Professional installation and push that image onto any Remote OS Installation–compatible client.

There are three ways you can create an operating system image:

- **Use the standard Remote Installation Setup wizard.** This method enables administrators to set up a remote operating system installation that will be just like an installation from the Windows 2000 Professional CD. It does not enable administrators to include base applications or customized settings with the distribution of the operating system. This approach is initiated by running the file called RISetup.exe. (This is the same file used to install RIS on a Windows 2000 server.) To get more information about using the Remote Installation Setup wizard, follow the steps outlined in the previous section, "Implementing Servers."

- **Use the Remote Installation Preparation wizard.** The Remote Installation Preparation wizard provides administrators with more flexibility in their deployment of Windows 2000 Professional installations. This approach, initiated by running the RIPrep.exe file on a Windows 2000 Professional computer, enables administrators to include applications and computer settings in the operating system image.

- **Use the System Preparation tool.** This method of creating an operating system image, implemented by running the executable file called SysPrep.exe, enables administrators to configure a given Windows 2000 Professional computer with the software and settings that they want other Windows 2000 Professional computers to have and then uses a third-party disk-imaging software (not included in Windows 2000) to take a snapshot of the image. One advantage of this approach is that it enables the remote installation of Windows 2000 Server. The other advantage of using the System Preparation tool is that, because it interacts with the third-party imaging software, it can circumvent the need for an Active Directory infrastructure.

---

**Note**  With any of these approaches, all image or installation data must be contained on one logical drive. Also, as mentioned previously, all data on the hard disk of the computer on which the operating system is being installed will be deleted during the remote operating system installation process.

The approach you use depends on which set of capabilities is best suited for your deployment and what the limitations of your deployment are. Before finalizing your decision on any of these approaches, you should test all approaches you are considering by using a spare or test computer as the computer on which the remote operating system installation is performed. Your test computer should have a configuration and capabilities similar to the configuration and capabilities of the computers on which you'll be remotely installing the operating system in the production environment.

## Living Without Remote OS Installation

Like IntelliMirror, Remote OS Installation is new with Windows 2000, so determining what it is like to live without the ease of use it brings to your Active Directory services environment is as simple as considering how you must achieve these results in a Windows NT environment. In Windows NT, installation of an operating system can be somewhat automated by providing an answer file (a file that provides installation settings that the installation process uses to determine certain settings provided in that file), but that solution is far inferior to the Remote OS Installation feature. Installing an operating system used to entail a technician visiting the computer, installing the operating system, and then hopefully being able to install all the applications that the user had before the installation of the new operating system. With Remote OS Installation (especially when deployed in concert with IntelliMirror), much of the work associated with those technicians' tasks can be automated, centralized, and easily managed.

# Using Distributed File System

Distributed file system (Dfs) does for file servers what Active Directory services does for networks: it centralizes, consolidates, hierarchically organizes, and simplifies. With Dfs, the scattering of physical file servers that exist throughout an organization—with their unique, vague, stupidly systematic, or sometimes unbelievably obtuse naming conventions (if such patterns can be called naming conventions)—can be brought together under one logical, hierarchically structured namespace, enabling users to more easily find the files and data they need. To summarize what Dfs does: it takes multiple file servers that are physically separated and collects them into one logical location, making those separated file servers appear to the user as though they are one big, well-organized, easy-to-navigate file server.

I'm a big fan of Dfs, mainly because I've endured trying to quickly find a file that I use occasionally, but not often enough to commit its location to my over-used personal memory, and that resides on a server whose name has nothing to do with the organizational structure to which the file's contents belong. With Dfs, finding such files becomes infinitely easier because poorly created naming conventions based on tree types, bird names, snack brands, coffee smells, world cities, skin ailments, or other lists of unassociated short terms are no longer used.

Perhaps one of the easiest ways to explain what Dfs can do for your organization is to provide a before-and-after example. Say your organization has the collection of file servers illustrated in Figure 14-17. The servers are scattered throughout the domain *corp.iseminger.com*, and all of them are accessed by various users and groups. In fact, individual files and folders on each server and its network shares are accessed by and restricted to diverse collections of groups. When the new Windows 2000 deployment is complete, some of these groups will be based in other domains within the *iseminger.com* forest.

As you can see from the illustration, there appears to be no sensible naming convention associated with the various server names and share names. For example, the data located at \\itchy\bedbugs has to do with marketing material, but further down the path in that same server share—in the folder \\itchy\bedbugs\projects\oatmeal—resides a bunch of files that have to do with a new horror novel being released next year and that can be accessed only by a group of copy editors and graphic designers. In addition, the rest of the marketing data is located at \\zebrafinch\decaf\marketstudies.

When you implement Dfs in this organization, however, data can be organized more logically and therefore accessed much more easily. Figure 14-22 illustrates how the organization's servers appear after Dfs is deployed.

As you can see, Dfs enables a bunch of scattered file servers to be consolidated into one logical, hierarchical, centrally managed, and centrally accessed tree. What's better yet is that users who are accustomed to using the original (but disorganized) naming structure to locate servers and files can still do so. There's no disruption introduced when Dfs is deployed; users can access data using either the Dfs tree or the original physical share names and paths.

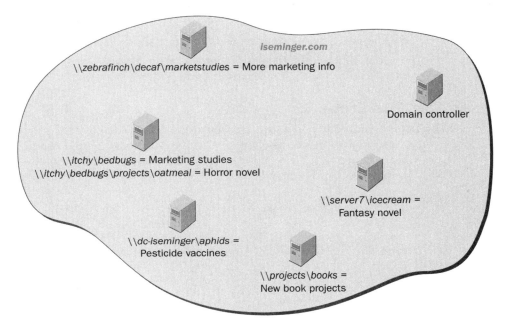

**Figure 14-21.**  *The collection of file servers scattered across* iseminger.com.

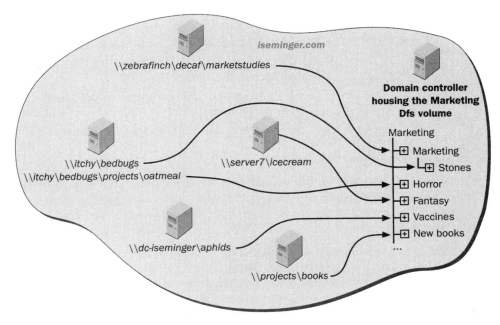

**Figure 14-22.**  *The collection of file servers as they appear in a Dfs tree.*

In short, Dfs offers the following advantages:

- To users, the network appears as one big, easily navigated file system.
- To administrators, the file system infrastructure is more easily managed, more scalable, more fault tolerant, and ultimately more available.

## Technologies That Enable Dfs

When Dfs is deployed in a Windows 2000 environment, Dfs makes extensive use of Active Directory services to enhance its offerings. Dfs is available with Windows NT 4.0 as well, but obviously Windows NT 4.0 deployments cannot take advantage of the Dfs offerings made possible through the interaction between Dfs and Active Directory services.

Dfs makes use of Active Directory services in the following ways:

- Dfs stores its tree topology and server information in the Active Directory information store, enabling the native multimaster replication system of Active Directory to provide the Dfs structure with fault tolerance.
- Dfs uses Active Directory services for keeping all computers participating in the collective logical view of the Dfs tree in synchronization, enabling users to see a synchronized view of the Dfs structure. Compare this Active Directory–enabled approach to individual servers maintaining information about the Dfs tree structure; modifications in one location of the tree wouldn't necessarily be propagated to other participating members of the Dfs tree, resulting in a different view of the tree based on which server responded to a client's request to view the Dfs structure.
- Dfs uses site configuration information stored in Active Directory to enable clients to intelligently select the appropriate replica (if replicas are available). Replicas are explained later in this section.
- Dfs uses Active Directory to manage administrative information associated with the Dfs tree's maintenance, structural information, and configuration.
- Dfs uses the FRS feature of Windows 2000 to keep replicas synchronized.

## Dfs Technical Details

To help clarify the way Dfs provides the service it does, you need to understand some of the technical details associated with the way Dfs performs its operations, which the following terms and their associated explanations provide. You should be familiar with these terms and capabilities when deploying Dfs in your Windows 2000 environment.

**Partition Knowledge Table (PKT):** The *PKT* is the table that manages the mapping of logical locations in the Dfs hierarchy (also often referred to as the Dfs tree) to the physical servers that actually house the associated data. If the Dfs root is housed on a Windows 2000 domain controller—and thus becomes integrated with Active Directory—the PKT is maintained as part of the Active Directory information repository. When client computers access a Dfs volume (or any part of a Dfs volume), they do so through a query process that transparently points them from the logical Dfs name to the physical server name and path that houses the target folder or document. This information, which is actually just an entry in the PKT, is kept in a locally cached table on the client. The client table keeps entries for a certain amount of time (5 minutes is the default timeout) before flushing them, and if the resource (folder or file) is needed again after the timeout expires, a new query to the Dfs server must be initiated. For performance reasons, clients always consult their local cache when attempting to resolve a Dfs resource. (Local lookups are much faster than referrals.)

**Note**   If a client computer attempts to access a resource before its information is flushed from the local cache, the entry's timeout is reset. In a scenario in which another query is made before the timeout expires, the timeout period would be reset and the entry in the client's cache would live for another 5 minutes, unless it was accessed again (and got another 5-minute lease on life). If the 5 minutes expire, the entry is flushed from the cache.

**Dfs link:** To make Dfs useful, you must be able to associate separate physical file-server shares (or file-server directory locations) with any given Dfs volume. These associated file-server shares, which exist below the Dfs root, are called *Dfs links*. In earlier versions of Dfs, Dfs links were also called junctions.

**Replica:** A replica is an identical copy of a given share point—a junction—of a Dfs hierarchy. For example, if you have an installation point for your software, and that installation point is overloaded, you might want to put an exact replica on another server and divvy up the workload so that each server can be more responsive. That second version of the installation point is considered a *replica* of the first (original) version. Each replica of a given source (share point) has a different physical location. File replication is based on replication policies associated with each link and can be automatically synchronized (and the replicas subsequently treated as multiple masters of the same information) when Dfs is deployed on a Windows 2000 domain controller—as long as you configure FRS to automate data replication between replicas. (FRS is *not* enabled between replicas by default.) Dfs automatically manages the traffic associated with replicated junctions with appropriate consideration given to the network topology. If multiple replicas exist in an Active Directory site, Dfs provides basic load balancing among replicas. (Clients randomly choose from among the replicas on the list.) If replicas exist in multiple sites, the connection referral (the pointer to the physical share location for the data the client is requesting) passed to the client connects that client to the closest replica (based on information about network topology stored in Active Directory). In earlier versions of Dfs, replicas were called alternate volumes.

## Implementing Dfs

You can implement Dfs in a couple of ways: as a stand-alone Dfs volume, which is housed on a stand-alone Windows 2000 Server; or as an Active Directory–based Dfs volume, which is housed on a Windows 2000 domain controller. Dfs has its own snap-in, called the

Distributed File Service snap-in. (You'll see this snap-in later in this section.) As with many Windows 2000 features, when Dfs leverages Active Directory services to carry out its feature set, it becomes a more powerful feature.

A Dfs deployment that is based on Windows 2000 domain controllers—and thus takes advantage of Active Directory services (and is the best kind of Dfs deployment)—starts by creating a Dfs volume at the domain level (versus creating a stand-alone Dfs volume or creating one based in an OU). A Dfs volume in the *iseminger.com* domain might be called \\iseminger\marketing, and its Dfs root might be housed on the Windows 2000 domain controller called IseServe23 in the *iseminger.com* domain. The other two Dfs roots in the domain might be called \\iseminger\sales and \\iseminger\production, but each of those would have to be housed on a different Windows 2000 domain controller.

A Dfs root equates to the root of the logical Dfs share. Dfs roots are hosted on Windows 2000 domain controllers. The Dfs root is simply the very top of the Dfs hierarchy. Figure 14-23 illustrates the relationship between a Dfs root and other shares that are part of the Dfs volume.

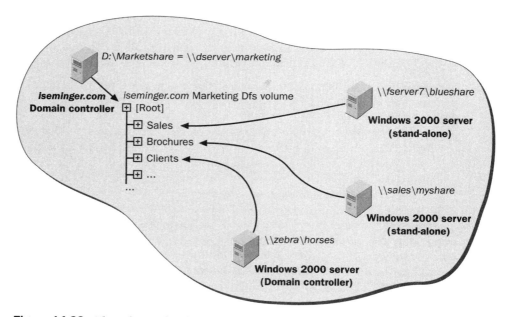

**Figure 14-23.** *The relationship between the Dfs root and other shares that make up the Dfs volume.*

**Note**  Dfs roots can also be hosted on Windows NT 4.0 Server computers but are limited to one Dfs root per Windows NT 4.0 Server computer. You'll get more functionality and capabilities out of your Dfs deployment, however, if you choose to place your Dfs root on a Windows 2000 Server computer or (better yet) on a Window 2000 domain controller.

**More Info**   Since I've explained that Dfs roots are housed on Windows 2000 Server computers, it might be helpful to understand how Dfs functions, in terms of its programmatic operational environment, on a Windows 2000 server. Dfs functions as a background process (making it unobtrusive to more important processes and introducing no impact on performance) that simply maintains a table of logical-to-physical locations for Dfs and physical file-share resources. Because Dfs is a background process, you can be assured that when you deploy Dfs on your domain controller, you won't be endangering that server's ability to service other Active Directory–related work. A background process, by definition, has a lower precedence than other processes (such as a foreground process) and is preempted whenever another, more important process needs to do work.

While it is possible for a stand-alone Windows 2000 server to host a Dfs root, realize that the root will not be able to provide any Active Directory–enabled benefits—and most of the scalability-related and availability-related benefits associated with a Dfs root are made possible by Active Directory.

Setting up a Dfs root is easy. Once you have the plan for how you want your Dfs deployment structured—which should specify the Windows 2000 domain controller on which you want to place the root, the physical shares you want to include in the Dfs root, and how you want them to appear to users viewing the Dfs volume—just follow these steps:

1.   Click the Start button, point to Administrative Tools, and then click Distributed File System. The Distributed File System snap-in appears, as shown in Figure 14-24.

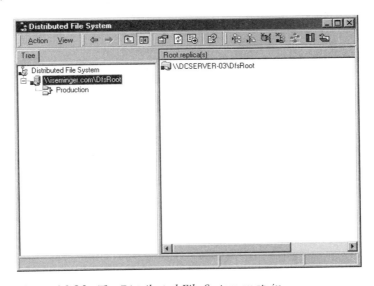

**Figure 14-24.**  *The Distributed File System snap-in.*

2. Right-click Distributed File System in the left pane of the Distributed File System snap-in, and click New Dfs Root in the shortcut menu that appears.

3. The Create New Dfs Root wizard starts; its welcome screen is shown in Figure 14-25. During the wizard, you will enter the planning information that you've already written down. (You *did* formulate a plan and write all your planning information down as recommended earlier, didn't you?) The following instructions illustrate the process of creating a new Active Directory–enabled Dfs root based in the *iseminger.com* domain. You, of course, would substitute the generic "DfsRoot" name of this Dfs root with something that more accurately reflected the Dfs root you created, such as "Marketing" or "Manufacturing".

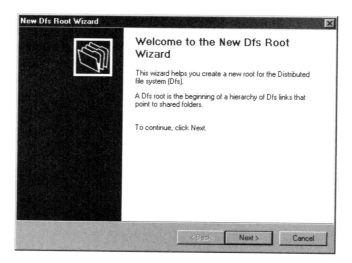

**Figure 14-25.** *The Welcome screen of the New Dfs Root wizard.*

4. Click Next to display the Select The Dfs Root Type screen, as shown in Figure 14-26. You can create a domain Dfs root or a stand-alone Dfs root. For this example, choose to create a domain Dfs root.

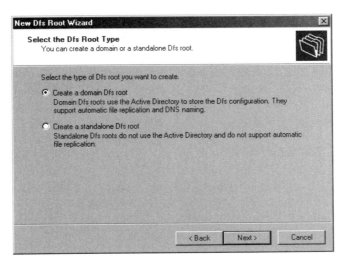

**Figure 14-26.**  *The Select The Dfs Root Type screen of the New Dfs Root wizard.*

5.   Click Next to display the Select The Host Domain For The Dfs Root screen, as shown in Figure 14-27. Here you choose the domain name.

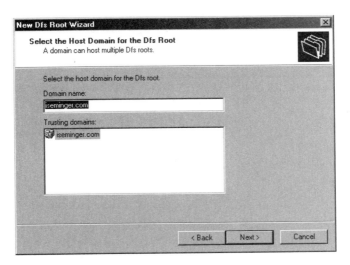

**Figure 14-27.**  *The Select The Host Domain For The Dfs Root screen.*

6. Click Next to display the Specify The Host Server For The Dfs Root screen, as shown in Figure 14-28. Here you specify the host server name.

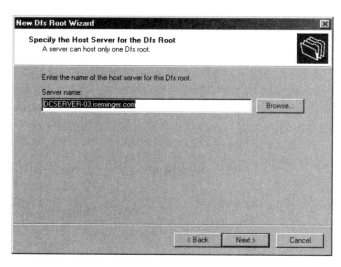

**Figure 14-28.** *The Specify The Host Server For The Dfs Root screen.*

7. Click Next to display the Specify The Dfs Root Share screen, as shown in Figure 14-29. Here you specify the share name.

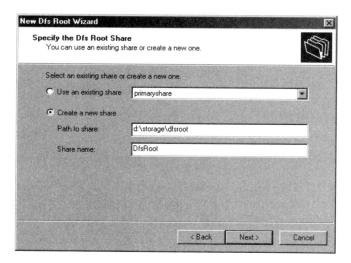

**Figure 14-29.** *The Specify The Dfs Root Share screen.*

8. Click Next to display the Name The Dfs Root screen, as shown in Figure 14-30. Here you specify the Dfs root name.

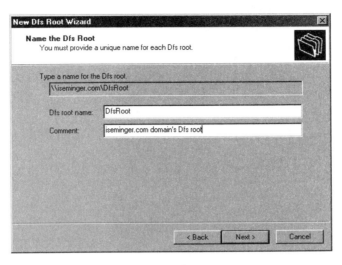

**Figure 14-30.** *The Name The Dfs Root screen.*

9.   Click Next to display the summary screen of the wizard, as shown in Figure 14-31.

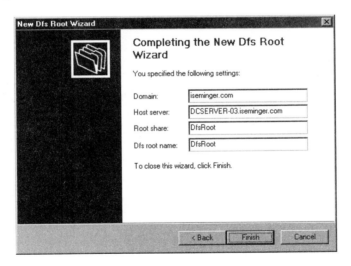

**Figure 14-31.** *The summary screen.*

Once the wizard is completed, your new Dfs root will be available for you to add shares to the Dfs volume and thereby create a unified Dfs tree that logically represents the scattering of servers you may have in the domain—which is, as you remember, the goal of using Dfs.

Next, you should add Dfs links to flesh out the Dfs tree. These links can include Windows 2000 network-share paths (such as \\zebrafinch\decaf), deeper paths in a Windows 2000 computer (such as \\itchy\bedbugs\projects\oatmeal) instead of a standard share path, or paths to network shares in a computer that is not running Windows 2000 (such as the network share \\Seattle\saltines on a Windows 95 computer). To add Dfs links, follow these steps:

1.  In the Distributed File System snap-in, right-click a Dfs root (such as the Dfs root you just created), and click New Dfs Link, as shown in Figure 14-32.

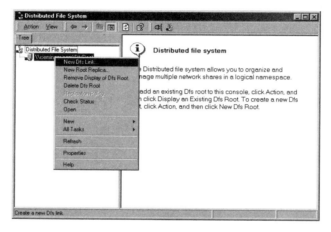

**Figure 14-32.** *The first step in adding a Dfs link.*

2.  The Create A New Dfs Link dialog box appears, as shown in Figure 14-33. Here you provide information about the new Dfs link you're adding to the Dfs root.

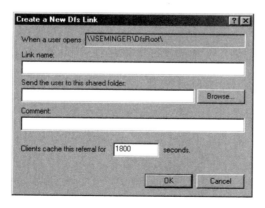

**Figure 14-33.** *The Create A New Dfs Link dialog box.*

3. Click OK. Now you should specify replicas for the Dfs root or its links. As mentioned previously, creating replicas enables administrators to easily back up data shares and also to avoid data loss during back-up operations because data remains available even if one replica fails. Creating replicas also makes load sharing possible because busy servers can use replicas to divide the load among multiple file servers. Dfs-aware clients automatically select the nearest replica, based on Active Directory services' site configuration information. You specify a replica for a given Dfs link by right-clicking the Dfs Link in the left pane of the Distributed File System snap-in and then selecting New Replica, as shown in Figure 14-34.

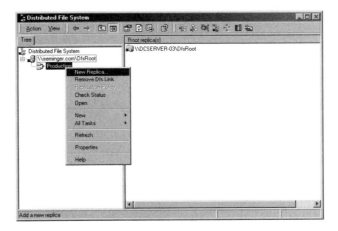

**Figure 14-34.** *The Distributed File System snap-in.*

4. You then manage Dfs replication from the Distributed File System snap-in. The snap-in is the standard management interface for a Dfs volume. Since Dfs volumes are considered a domain-based "service," management of the Dfs volume is reserved for administrators with appropriate permissions (which are configurable, of course). Only administrators with proper administrative privilege can perform administrative tasks such as moving or removing replicas, adding hard disk space, or even decommissioning replicas and replacing entire servers. The great feature of Dfs, however, is that administrators can do all this without users ever knowing about the maintenance, since Dfs enables administrators to provide such administrative services without making users endure a disruption in service.

**Caution** Don't use the backup utility included in Windows 2000 to back up a Dfs volume. You need to find a Dfs-aware backup solution if you're planning on performing backups that use the Dfs hierarchy as the source of the files. There are certain architectural requirements that must be met for a backup utility to be able to back up and (especially) restore a Dfs hierarchy, and that additional functionality is not built into the backup software provided with Windows 2000. No, I don't know why the Windows 2000 backup utility can't do this. Yes, you'd think it would.

### Dfs Limitations

There are a handful of limitations associated with Dfs that you should consider when preparing your Dfs deployment plan.

- The maximum number of characters per file path is 260.
- The maximum number of replicas in a replica set is 32.
- The maximum number of Dfs roots per server is 1. (You can have unlimited Dfs roots in a given domain, however.)
- The maximum number of Dfs links or shared folders per Dfs root is 1,000.

### Dfs Security

The deployment of Dfs has no effect on network security. Dfs simply manages the logical appearance and the hierarchical structure of a collection of physical servers and shares, but it makes no presumptions about or changes to their security. Security and access control lists (ACLs) continue to be maintained on the physical locations associated with the various logical representations of each file server. This is the best, most logical approach to security, and it makes a lot of sense when you consider that each physical server can remain locally maintained even if it's globally published.

## Conclusions

Active Directory services makes Windows more extensible, scalable, available, and capable than ever before. Active Directory creates an infrastructure on which all sorts of services can be built—including services that can make the management of the user experience more efficient and effective. Active Directory services' capabilities have enabled a trio of extremely powerful tools to be developed—IntelliMirror, Remote OS Installation, and Dfs.

IntelliMirror can make managing the user experience a snap; no longer do IT professionals have to deal with their organization's potentially thousands of computers individually—computers that must be working in order for users to stay productive. Instead, users' information and settings can be managed and protected centrally and effectively, increasing everyone's productivity.

Remote OS Installation significantly reduces the costs associated with the numerous and time-consuming visits to users' workstations that are necessary for administrators to install operating systems, reinstall software, or apply patches and upgrades. With Remote OS Installation, all such work can be largely automated, centralized, remotely executed, and most important, managed, maintained, and controlled.

When used together, IntelliMirror and Remote OS Installation provide a comprehensive disaster recovery safety net. No longer is a user banished to two days of lost productivity when his or her computer's hard disk fails. You can drop in a new or repaired computer, remotely install the operating system, and replicate the user's *centrally managed* data and settings; within an hour or two, the computer is up and running again.

And to top off these user-experience enhancements, Dfs and its Active Directory–enabled enhancements enable users to easily find documents and files that are scattered across a network. With Dfs and Active Directory, a network becomes a single entity—a navigable tool that all users, not just technically savvy ones, can take advantage of. The burden of providing the framework to which user services can be added is finally being placed where it belongs: on the shoulders of the operating system, which is managed and orchestrated by the administrator, and simplified for all.

# Part III
# Appendixes

# Appendix A
# Windows 2000 DIT Classes

ACS-Policy
ACS-Resource-Limits
ACS-Subnet
Add-In
Addr-Type
Address-Book-Container
Address-Template
Application-Entity
Application-Process
Application-Settings
Application-Site-Settings
Attribute-Schema
Builtin-Domain
Category-Registration
Certification-Authority
Class-Registration
Class-Schema
Class-Store
Com-Connection-Point
Computer
Configuration
Connection-Point
Contact
Container
Control-Access-Right
Country
CRL-Distribution-Point
Cross-Ref
Cross-Ref-Container
Device
Dfs-Configuration
DHCP-Class
Display-Specifier
Display-Template

DMD
Dns-Node
Dns-Zone
Domain
Domain-DNS
Domain-Policy
DS-VI-Settings
DSA
File-Link-Tracking
File-Link-Tracking-Entry
Foreign-Security-Principal
FT-Dfs
Group
Group-Of-Names
Group-Policy-Container
Index-Server-Catalog
Infrastructure-Update
Intellimirror-Group
Intellimirror-SCP
Inter-Site-Transport
Inter-Site-Transport-Container
Ipsec-Base
Ipsec-Filter
Ipsec-ISAKMP-Policy
Ipsec-Negotiation-Policy
Ipsec-NFA
Ipsec-Policy
Leaf
Licensing-Site-Settings
Link-Track-Object-Move-Table
Link-Track-OMT-Entry
Link-Track-Vol-Entry
Link-Track-Volume-Table
Locality

Lost-And-Found
Mail-Recipient
Meeting
MHS-Public-Store
MS-Mail-Connector
ms-Exch-Configuration-Container
MSMQ-Configuration
MSMQ-Enterprise-Settings
MSMQ-Queue
MSMQ-Settings
MSMQ-Site-Link
MS-SQL-OLAPCube
MS-SQL-OLAPDatabase
MS-SQL-OLAPServer
MS-SQL-SQLDatabase
MS-SQL-SQLPublication
MS-SQL-SQLRepository
MS-SQL-SQLServer
NTDS-Connection
NTDS-DSA
NTDS-Service
NTDS-Site-Settings
NTFRS-Member
NTFRS-Replica-Set
NTFRS-Settings
NTFRS-Subscriber
NTFRS-Subscriptions
Organization
Organizational-Person
Organizational-Unit
Package-Registration
Person
Physical-Location
PKI-Certificate-Template
PKI-Enrollment-Service
Print-Queue
Query-Policy
Remote-Mail-Recipient
Remote-Storage-Service-Point
Residential-Person
RID-Manager
RID-Set
Rpc-Container
rpc-Entry

rpc-Group
rpc-Profile
rpc-Profile-Element
rpc-Server
rpc-Server-Element
RRAS-Administrator-Connection-
    Point
RRAS-Administrator-Dictionary
Sam-Domain
Sam-Domain-Base
Sam-Server
Secret
Security-Object
Security-Principal
Server
Servers-Container
Service-Administration-Point
Service-Class
Service-Connection-Point
Service-Instance
Site
Site-Link
Site-Link-Bridge
Storage
Subnet
Subnet-Container
SubSchema
Top
Trusted-Domain
Type-Library
User
Volume

# Appendix B
# Base DIT Class Hierarchy

ACS-Policy
ACS-Resource-Limits
ACS-Subnet
Address-Book-Container
Application-Entity
    DSA
Application-Process
Application-Settings
    NTDS-DSA
    NTFRS-Settings
Application-Site-Settings
    Licensing-Site-Settings
    NTDS-Site-Settings
Attribute-Schema
Builtin-Domain
Certification-Authority
Class-Schema
Class-Store
Configuration
Container
    Group-Policy-Container
    ms-Exch-Configuration-Container
    Rpc-Container
Control-Access-Right
Country
CRL-Distribution-Point
Cross-Ref
Cross-Ref-Container
Device
Dfs-Configuration
DHCP-Class

Display-Specifier
Display-Template
    Address-Template
DMD
Dns-Node
Dns-Zone
Domain
    Domain-DNS
DS-UI-Settings
File-Link-Tracking
    Link-Track-Object-Move-Table
    Link-Track-Volume-Table
File-Link-Tracking-Entry
Foreign-Security-Principal
FT-Dfs
Group
Group-Of-Names
Infrastructure-Update
Intellimirror-Group
Inter-Site-Transport
Inter-Site-Transport-Container
Ipsec-Base
    Ipsec-Filter
    Ipsec-ISAKMP-Policy
    Ipsec-Negotiation-Policy
    Ipsec-NFA
    Ipsec-Policy
Leaf
    Category-Registration
    Class-Registration
    Connection-Point
        Com-Connection-Point
        Index-Server-Catalog
        Print-Queue
        rpc-Entry
            rpc-Group
            rpc-Profile
            rpc-Profile-Element
            rpc-Server
            rpc-Server-Element

Service-Connection-Point
    MS-SQL-OLAPServer
    MS-SQL-SQLServer
    Service-Administration-Point
        Intellimirror-SCP
        Remote-Storage-Service-Point
        RRAS-Administration-Connection-Point
Service-Instance
Storage
Volume
Domain-Policy
Link-Track-OMT-Entry
Link-Track-Vol-Entry
NTDS-Connection
Secret
Service-Class
Trusted-Domain
Locality
    Physical-Location
Lost-And-Found
Mail-Recipient
Meeting
MS-SQL-OLAPCube
MS-SQL-OLAPDatabase
MS-SQL-SQLDatabase
MS-SQL-SQLPublication
MS-SQL-SQLRepository
MSMQ-Configuration
MSMQ-Enterprise-Settings
MSMQ-Migrated-User
MSMQ-Queue
MSMQ-Settings
MSMQ-Site-Link
NTDS-Service
NTFRS-Member
NTFRS-Replica-Set
NTFRS-Subscriber
NTFRS-Subscriptions
Organization
Organizational-Role

Organizational-Unit
Package-Registration
Person
    Organizational-Person
        Contact
        User
            Computer
    Residential-Person
PKI-Certificate-Template
PKI-Enrollment-Service
Query-Policy
Remote-Mail-Recipient
RID-Manager
RID-Set
RRAS-Administration-Dictionary
Sam-Domain
Sam-Domain-Base
Security-Object
    Sam-Server
Security-Principal
Server
Servers-Container
Site
Site-Link
Site-Link-Bridge
Sites-Container
Subnet
Subnet-Container
SubSchema
Type-Library

# Appendix C
# Windows 2000 Base DIT
# *attributeSchema* Objects

Account-Name-History
ACS-Aggregate-Token-Rate-Per-User
ACS-Allocable-RSVP-Bandwidth
ACS-Cache-Timeout
ACS-Direction
ACS-DSBM-DeadTime
ACS-DSBM-Priority
ACS-DSBM-Refresh
ACS-Enable-ACS-Service
ACS-Enable-RSVP-Accounting
ACS-Enable-RSVP-Message-Logging
ACS-Event-Log-Level
ACS-Identity-Name
ACS-Max-Aggregate-Peak-Rate-Per-User
ACS-Max-Duration-Per-Flow
ACS-Max-No-Of-Account-Files
ACS-Max-No-Of-Log-Files
ACS-Max-Peak-Bandwidth
ACS-Max-Peak-Bandwidth-Per-Flow
ACS-Max-Size-Of-RSVP-Account-File
ACS-Max-Size-Of-RSVP-Log-File
ACS-Max-Token-Bucket-Per-Flow
ACS-Max-Token-Rate-Per-Flow
ACS-Maximum-SDU-Size
ACS-Minimum-Delay-Variation
ACS-Minimum-Latency
ACS-Minimum-Policed-Size
ACS-Non-Reserved-Max-SDU-Size
ACS-Non-Reserved-Min-Policed-Size
ACS-Non-Reserved-Peak-Rate
ACS-Non-Reserved-Token-Size
ACS-Non-Reserved-Tx-Limit

ACS-Non-Reserved-Tx-Size
ACS-Permission-Bits
ACS-Policy-Name
ACS-Priority
ACS-RSVP-Account-Files-Location
ACS-RSVP-Log-Files-Location
ACS-Server-List
ACS-Service-Type
ACS-Time-Of-Day
ACS-Total-No-Of-Flows
Additional-Information
Additional-Trusted-Service-Names
Address
Address-Book-Roots
Address-Entry-Display-Table
Address-Entry-Display-Table-MSDOS
Address-Home
Address-Syntax
Address-Type
Admin-Context-Menu
Admin-Count
Admin-Description
Admin-Display-Name
Admin-Property-Pages
Allowed-Attributes
Allowed-Attributes-Effective
Allowed-Child-Classes
Allowed-Child-Classes-Effective
Alt-Security-Identities
ANR
Application-Name
Applies-To

App-Schema-Version
Asset-Number
Assistant
Assoc-NT-Account
Attribute-Display-Names
Attribute-ID
Attribute-Security-GUID
Attribute-Syntax
Attribute-Types
Auditing-Policy
Authentication-Options
Authority-Revocation-List
Auxiliary-Class
Available-Authorization-Packages
Available-Distributions
Bad-Password-Time
Bad-Pwd-Count
Birth-Location
Bridgehead-Server-List-BL
Bridgehead-Transport-List
Builtin-Creation-Time
Builtin-Modified-Count
Business-Category
Bytes-Per-Minute
CA-Certificate
CA-Certificate-DN
CA-Connect
Canonical-Name
Can-Upgrade-Script
Catalogs
Categories
Category-Id
CA-Usages
CA-WEB-URL
Certificate-Authority-Object
Certificate-Revocation-List
Certificate-Templates
Code-Page
COM-ClassID
COM-CLSID
COM-InterfaceID
Comment
Common-Name
COM-Other-Prog-Id

Company
COM-ProgID
COM-Treat-As-Class-Id
COM-Typelib-Id
COM-Unique-LIBID
Content-Indexing-Allowed
Context-Menu
Control-Access-Rights
Cost
Country-Code
Country-Name
Create-Dialog
Create-Time-Stamp
Create-Wizard-Ext
Creation-Time
Creation-Wizard
Creator
CRL-Object
CRL-Partitioned-Revocation-List
Current-Location
Current-Parent-CA
Current-Value
Curr-Machine-Id
DBCS-Pwd
Default-Class-Store
Default-Group
Default-Hiding-Value
Default-Local-Policy-Object
Default-Object-Category
Default-Priority
Default-Security-Descriptor
Delta-Revocation-List
Department
Description
Desktop-Profile
Destination-Indicator
dhcp-Classes
dhcp-Flags
dhcp-Identification
dhcp-Mask
dhcp-MaxKey
dhcp-Obj-Description
dhcp-Obj-Name
dhcp-Options

dhcp-Properties
dhcp-Ranges
dhcp-Reservations
dhcp-Servers
dhcp-Sites
dhcp-State
dhcp-Subnets
dhcp-Type
dhcp-Unique-Key
dhcp-Update-Time
Display-Name
Display-Name-Printable
DIT-Content-Rules
Division
DMD-Location
DMD-Name
DN-Reference-Update
Dns-Allow-Dynamic
Dns-Allow-XFR
DNS-Host-Name
Dns-Notify-Secondaries
DNS-Property
Dns-Record
Dns-Root
Dns-Secure-Secondaries
Domain-Certificate-Authorities
Domain-Component
Domain-Cross-Ref
Domain-ID
Domain-Identifier
Domain-Policy-Object
Domain-Policy-Reference
Domain-Replica
Domain-Wide-Policy
Driver-Name
Driver-Version
DSA-Signature
DS-Core-Propagation-Data
DS-Heuristics
DS-UI-Admin-Maximum
DS-UI-Admin-Notification
DS-UI-Shell-Maximum
Dynamic-LDAP-Server
EFSPolicy

E-mail-Addresses
Employee-ID
Employee-Number
Employee-Type
Enabled
Enabled-Connection
Enrollment-Providers
Extended-Attribute-Info
Extended-Chars-Allowed
Extended-Class-Info
Extension-Name
Facsimile-Telephone-Number
File-Ext-Priority
Flags
Flat-Name
Force-Logoff
Foreign-Identifier
Friendly-Names
From-Entry
From-Server
Frs-Computer-Reference
Frs-Computer-Reference-BL
FRS-Control-Data-Creation
FRS-Control-Inbound-Backlog
FRS-Control-Outbound-Backlog
FRS-Directory-Filter
FRS-DS-Poll
FRS-Extensions
FRS-Fault-Condition
FRS-File-Filter
FRS-Flags
FRS-Level-Limit
FRS-Member-Reference
FRS-Member-Reference-BL
FRS-Partner-Auth-Level
FRS-Primary-Member
FRS-Replica-Set-GUID
FRS-Replica-Set-Type
FRS-Root-Path
FRS-Root-Security
FRS-Service-Command
FRS-Service-Command-Status
FRS-Staging-Path
FRS-Time-Last-Command

FRS-Time-Last-Config-Change
FRS-Update-Timeout
FRS-Version
FRS-Version-GUID
FRS-Working-Path
FSMO-Role-Owner
Garbage-Coll-Period
Generated-Connection
Generation-Qualifier
Given-Name
Global-Address-List
Governs-ID
GPC-File-Sys-Path
GPC-Functionality-Version
GP-Link
GP-Options
GPC-Machine-Extension-Names
GPC-User-Extension-Names
Group-Attributes
Group-Membership-SAM
Group-Priority
Groups-to-Ignore
Group-Type
Has-Master-NCs
Has-Partial-Replica-NCs
Help-Data16
Help-Data32
Help-File-Name
Home-Directory
Home-Drive
Icon-Path
IndexedScopes
Initial-Auth-Incoming
Initial-Auth-Outgoing
Initials
Install-Ui-Level
Instance-Type
International-ISDN-Number
Inter-Site-Topology-Failover
Inter-Site-Topology-Generator
Inter-Site-Topology-Renew
Invocation-Id
Ipsec-Data
Ipsec-Data-Type

Ipsec-Filter-Reference
Ipsec-ID
Ipsec-ISAKMP-Reference
Ipsec-Name
IPSEC-Negotiation-Policy-Action
Ipsec-Negotiation-Policy-Reference
IPSEC-Negotiation-Policy-Type
Ipsec-NFA-Reference
Ipsec-Owners-Reference
Ipsec-Policy-Reference
Is-Critical-System-Object
Is-Defunct
Is-Deleted
Is-Ephemeral
Is-Member-Of-DL
Is-Member-Of-Partial-Attribute-Set
Is-Privilege-Holder
Is-Single-Valued
Keywords
Knowledge-Information
Last-Backup-Restoration-Time
Last-Content-Indexed
Last-Known-Parent
Last-Logoff
Last-Logon
Last-Set-Time
Last-Update-Sequence
LDAP-Admin-Limits
LDAP-Display-Name
LDAP-IPDeny-List
Legacy-Exchange-DN
Link-ID
Link-Track-Secret
Lm-Pwd-History
Locale-ID
Locality-Name
Localization-Display-Id
Localized-Description
Location
Lockout-Duration
Lock-Out-Observation-Window
Lockout-Threshold
Lockout-Time
Logo

Logon-Count
Logon-Hours
Logon-Workstation
LSA-Creation-Time
LSA-Modified-Count
Machine-Architecture
Machine-Password-Change-Interval
Machine-Role
Machine-Wide-Policy
Managed-By
Managed-Objects
Manager
MAPI-ID
Marshalled-Interface
Mastered-By
Max-Pwd-Age
Max-Renew-Age
Max-Storage
Max-Ticket-Age
May-Contain
meetingAdvertiseScope
meetingApplication
meetingBandwidth
meetingBlob
meetingContactInfo
meetingDescription
meetingEndTime
meetingID
meetingIP
meetingIsEncrypted
meetingKeyword
meetingLanguage
meetingLocation
meetingMaxParticipants
meetingName
meetingOriginator
meetingOwner
meetingProtocol
meetingRating
meetingRecurrence
meetingScope
meetingStartTime
meetingType
meetingURL

Member
MHS-OR-Address
Min-Pwd-Age
Min-Pwd-Length
Min-Ticket-Age
Modified-Count
Modified-Count-At-Last-Prom
Modify-Time-Stamp
Moniker
Moniker-Display-Name
Mscope-Id
MS-DS-Consistency-child-Content
MS-DS-Consistency-Guid
MS-DS-Creator-SID
MS-DS-Machine-Account-Quota
MS-DS-Replicates-NC-Reason
Msi-File-List
Msi-Script
Msi-Script-Name
Msi-Script-Path
Msi-Script-Size
MSMQ-Authenticate
MSMQ-Base-Priority
MSMQ-Computer-Type
MSMQ-Cost
MSMQ-CSP-Name
MSMQ-Dependent-Client-Service
MSMQ-Dependent-Client-Services
MSMQ-Digests
MSMQ-Digests-Mig
MSMQ-Ds-Service
MSMQ-Ds-Services
MSMQ-Encrypt-Key
MSMQ-Foreign
MSMQ-In-Routing-Servers
MSMQ-Interval1
MSMQ-Interval2
MSMQ-Journal
MSMQ-Journal-Quota
MSMQ-Label
MSMQ-Long-Lived
MSMQ-Migrated
MSMQ-Name-Style
MSMQ-Nt4-Flags

MSMQ-Nt4-Stub
MSMQ-OS-Type
MSMQ-Out-Routing-Servers
MSMQ-Owner-ID
MSMQ-Prev-Site-Gates
MSMQ-Privacy-Level
MSMQ-QM-ID
MSMQ-Queue-Journal-Quota
MSMQ-Queue-Name-Ext
MSMQ-Queue-Quota
MSMQ-Queue-Type
MSMQ-Quota
MSMQ-Routing-Service
MSMQ-Routing-Services
MSMQ-Services
MSMQ-Service-Type
MSMQ-Sign-Certificates
MSMQ-Sign-Certificates-Mig
MSMQ-Sign-Key
MSMQ-Site-1
MSMQ-Site-2 ·
MSMQ-Site-Foreign
MSMQ-Site-Gates
MSMQ-Site-Gates-Mig
MSMQ-Site-ID
MSMQ-Site-Name
MSMQ-Sites
MSMQ-Transactional
MSMQ-User-Sid
MSMQ-Version
msNPAllowDialin
msNPCalledStationID
msNPCallingStationID
msNPSavedCallingStationID
msRADIUSCallbackNumber
msRADIUSFramedIPAddress
msRADIUSFramedRoute
msRASSavedCallbackNumber
msRASSavedFramedIPAddress
msRASSavedFramedRoute
ms-RRAS-Attribute
ms-RRAS-Vendor-Attribute-Entry
MS-SQL-Alias
MS-SQL-AllowAnonymousSubscription

MS-SQL-AllowImmediateUpdatingSubscription
MS-SQL-AllowKnownPullSubscription
MS-SQL-AllowQueuedUpdatingSubscription
MS-SQL-AllowSnapshtFilesFTPDownloading
MS-SQL-AppleTalk
MS-SQL-Applications
MS-SQL-Build
MS-SQL-CharacterSet
MS-SQL-Clustered
MS-SQL-ConnectionURL
MS-SQL-Contact
MS-SQL-CreationDate
MS-SQL-Database
MS-SQL-Description
MS-SQL-GPSHeight
MS-SQL-GPSLatitude
MS-SQL-GPSLongitude
MS-SQL-InformationDirectory
MS-SQL-InformationURL
MS-SQL-Keywords
MS-SQL-Language
MS-SQL-LastBackupDate
MS-SQL-LastDiagnosticDate
MS-SQL-LastUpdatedDate
MS-SQL-Location
MS-SQL-Memory
MS-SQL-MultiProtocol
MS-SQL-Name
MS-SQL-NamedPipe
MS-SQL-PublicationURL
MS-SQL-Publisher
MS-SQL-RegisteredOwner
MS-SQL-ServiceAccount
MS-SQL-Size
MS-SQL-SortOrder
MS-SQL-SPX
MS-SQL-Status
MS-SQL-TCPIP
MS-SQL-ThirdParty
MS-SQL-Type
MS-SQL-UnicodeSortOrder
MS-SQL-Version
MS-SQL-Vines
MTA-Local-Desig

Must-Contain
Name-Service-Flags
NC-Name
NETBIOS-Name
netboot-Allow-New-Clients
netboot-Answer-Only-Valid-Clients
netboot-Answer-Requests
netboot-Current-Client-Count
Netboot-GUID
Netboot-Initialization
netboot-IntelliMirror-OSes
netboot-Limit-Clients
netboot-Locally-Installed-OSes
Netboot-Machine-File-Path
netboot-Max-Clients
Netboot-Mirror-Data-File
netboot-New-Machine-Naming-Policy
netboot-New-Machine-OU
netboot-SCP-BL
netboot-Server
Netboot-SIF-File
netboot-Tools
Network-Address
Next-Level-Store
Members
NT-Mixed-Domain
Nt-Pwd-History
NT-Security-Descriptor
Obj-Dist-Name
Object-Category
Object-Class
Object-Class-Category
Object-Classes
Object-Count
Object-Guid
Object-Sid
Object-Version
OEM-Information
OM-Object-Class
OM-Syntax
OMT-Guid
OMT-Indx-Guid
Operating-System
Operating-System-Hotfix

Operating-System-Service-Pack
Operating-System-Version
Operator-Count
Option-Description
Options
Options-Location
Organizational-Unit-Name
Organization-Name
Original-Display-Table
Original-Display-Table-MSDOS
Other-Login-Workstations
Other-Mailbox
Other-Name
Other-Well-Known-Objects
Outbound-Host
Owner
Package-Flags
Package-Name
Package-Type
Parent-CA
Parent-CA-Certificate-Chain
Parent-GUID
Partial-Attribute-Deletion-List
Partial-Attribute-Set
Pek-Key-Change-Interval
Pek-List
Pending-CA-Certificates
Pending-Parent-CA
Per-Msg-Dialog-Display-Table
Per-Recip-Dialog-Display-Table
Personal-Title
Phone-Fax-Other
Phone-Home-Other
Phone-Home-Primary
Phone-Ip-Other
Phone-Ip-Primary
Phone-ISDN-Primary
Phone-Mobile-Other
Phone-Mobile-Primary
Phone-Office-Other
Phone-Pager-Other
Phone-Pager-Primary
Physical-Delivery-Office-Name
Physical-Location-Object

Picture
PKI-Critical-Extentions
PKI-Default-CSPs
PKI-Default-Key-Spec
PKI-Enrollment-Access
PKI-Expiration-Period
PKI-Extended-Key-Usage
PKI-Key-Usage
PKI-Max-Issuing-Depth
PKI-Overlap-Period
PKT
PKT-Guid
Policy-Replication-Flags
Port-Name
Possible-Inferiors
Poss-Superiors
Postal-Address
Postal-Code
Post-Office-Box
Preferred-Delivery-Method
Preferred-OU
Prefix-Map
Presentation-Address
Previous-CA-Certificates
Previous-Parent-CA
Primary-Group-ID
Primary-Group-Token
Print-Attributes
Print-Bin-Names
Print-Collate
Print-Color
Print-Duplex-Supported
Print-End-Time
Printer-Name
Print-Form-Name
Print-Keep-Printed-Jobs
Print-Language
Print-MAC-Address
Print-Max-Copies
Print-Max-Resolution-Supported
Print-Max-X-Extent
Print-Max-Y-Extent
Print-Media-Ready
Print-Media-Supported

Print-Memory
Print-Min-X-Extent
Print-Min-Y-Extent
Print-Network-Address
Print-Notify
Print-Number-Up
Print-Orientations-Supported
Print-Owner
Print-Pages-Per-Minute
Print-Rate
Print-Rate-Unit
Print-Separator-File
Print-Share-Name
Print-Spooling
Print-Stapling-Supported
Print-Start-Time
Print-Status
Priority
Prior-Set-Time
Prior-Value
Private-Key
Privilege-Attributes
Privilege-Display-Name
Privilege-Holder
Privilege-Value
Product-Code
Profile-Path
Proxied-Object-Name
Proxy-Addresses
Proxy-Generation-Enabled
Proxy-Lifetime
Public-Key-Policy
Purported-Search
Pwd-History-Length
Pwd-Last-Set
Pwd-Properties
Quality-Of-Service
Query-Filter
QueryPoint
Query-Policy-BL
Query-Policy-Object
Range-Lower
Range-Upper
RDN

RDN-Att-ID
Registered-Address
Remote-Server-Name
Remote-Source
Remote-Source-Type
Remote-Storage-GUID
Replica-Source
Repl-Property-Meta-Data
Repl-Topology-Stay-Of-Execution
Repl-UpToDate-Vector
Reports
Reps-From
Reps-To
Req-Seq
Required-Categories
Retired-Repl-DSA-Signatures
Revision
Rid
RID-Allocation-Pool
RID-Available-Pool
RID-Manager-Reference
RID-Next-RID
RID-Previous-Allocation-Pool
RID-Set-References
RID-Used-Pool
Rights-Guid
Role-Occupant
Root-Trust
rpc-Ns-Annotation
rpc-Ns-Bindings
rpc-Ns-Codeset
rpc-Ns-Entry-Flags
rpc-Ns-Group
rpc-Ns-Interface-ID
rpc-Ns-Object-ID
rpc-Ns-Priority
rpc-Ns-Profile-Entry
rpc-Ns-Transfer-Syntax
SAM-Account-Name
SAM-Account-Type
Schedule
Schema-Flags-Ex
Schema-ID-GUID
Schema-Info

Schema-Update
Schema-Version
Scope-Flags
Script-Path
SD-Rights-EffectiveSearch-Flags
Search-Guide
Security-Identifier
See-Also
Send-TNEF
Seq-Notification
Serial-Number
Server-Name
Server-Reference
Server-Reference-BL
Server-Role
Server-State
Service-Binding-Information
Service-Class-ID
Service-Class-Info
Service-Class-Name
Service-DNS-Name
Service-DNS-Name-Type
Service-Instance-Version
Service-Principal-Name
Setup-Command
Shell-Context-Menu
Shell-Property-Pages
Short-Server-Name
Show-In-Address-Book
Show-In-Advanced-View-Only
SID-History
Signature-Algorithms
Site-GUID
Site-Link-List
Site-List
Site-Object
Site-Object-BL
Site-Server
SMTP-Mail-Address
SPN-Mappings
State-Or-Province-Name
Street-Address
Sub-Class-Of
Sub-Refs

SubSchemaSubEntry
Superior-DNS-Root
Super-Scope-Description
Super-Scopes
Supplemental-Credentials
Supported-Application-Context
Surname
Sync-Attributes
Sync-Membership
Sync-With-Object
Sync-With-SID
System-Auxiliary-Class
System-Flags
System-May-Contain
System-Must-Contain
System-Only
System-Poss-Superiors
Telephone-Number
Teletex-Terminal-Identifier
Telex-Number
Telex-Primary
Terminal-Server
Template-Roots
Text-Country
Text-Encoded-OR-Address
Time-Refresh
Time-Vol-Change
Title
Token-Groups
Token-Groups-no-GC-Acceptable
Tombstone-Lifetime
Transport-Address-Attribute
Transport-DLL-Name
Transport-Type
Treat-As-Leaf
Tree-Name
Trust-Attributes
Trust-Auth-Incoming
Trust-Auth-Outgoing
Trust-Direction
Trust-Parent
Trust-Partner
Trust-Posix-Offset
Trust-Type

UAS-Compat
UNC-Name
Unicode-Pwd
Upgrade-Product-Code
UPN-Suffixes
User-Account-Control
User-Cert
User-Comment
User-Parameters
User-Password
User-Principal-Name
User-Shared-Folder
User-Shared-Folder-Other
User-SMIME-Certificate
User-Workstations
USN-Changed
USN-Created
USN-DSA-Last-Obj-Removed
USN-Intersite
USN-Last-Obj-Rem
USN-Source
Valid-Accesses
Vendor
Version-Number
Version-Number-Hi
Version-Number-Lo
Vol-Table-GUID
Vol-Table-Idx-GUID
Volume-Count
Wbem-Path
Well-Known-Objects
When-Changed
When-Created
Winsock-Addresses
WWW-Home-Page
WWW-Page-Other
X121-Address

# Index

*Page numbers in italics indicate illustrations.*

forests, *continued*
  moving
    domains, 361
    objects, 358
    user accounts, 367–68
  multiple, 126
  number of, 125–27
  planning, 119, 124–27
  resource sharing, 358
  root, upgrading from NT, 325
  root domain installation, 359
  Schema Administrators group, 356
  security principals, 359
  transitive trust relationships, 230
  upgrade planning, 321
forestwide FSMO roles, 265
forwarders, 89–91, *90*
FQDN (fully qualified domain name), 84, *85*
FRS (File Replication Services)
  Dfs (distributed file system), 414
  upgrading from Windows NT, 331–32
FSMO (flexible single–master operation), 68–70
  role holders, 68–69
  submenu, ntdsutil, 280–81
FSMO roles
  categories, 265
  domain based, 265–66
  locating, 265–66
  managing, 265–70
  seizing, 270
  transferring, 269–70
Full Control, 142
fully qualified domain name. *See* FQDN (fully qualified domain name)
full zone transfers, 96–97, *97*
function of Active Directory, 5
function keys, command line, 276

# G

genealogy constraints, 294
GeneralizedTime, 291, 312
Global Catalog, 52, 58–64
  ADSI, 63
  housing, 62
  namespace, 59
  naming contexts, 61

Global Catalog, *continued*
  objects, 59–60
  operation, 62–64
  replicate attributes to, 240–41
  schema, 61–62
  searches, 63–64
  servers
    domain controllers, 147–48
    SRV RRs, 107–8
    type designation, 105
  universal groups, 122
global groups, 121
governsID, 298–99
GPOs (Group Policy objects), 261–65
  boundaries, 127
  create new, 395
  Folder Redirection, 390–91
  software deployment, 394–98
Group Policies, 261–65. *See also* GPOs (Group Policy objects)
  domain trees, 129–30
  IntelliMirror, 378, 382
  OUs, 143, 371
  property page, 263, 395, *395*
  Software Installation and Maintenance feature, 385
Group Policy snap-in, Folder Redirection, 391–92, *391*
groups. *See also* Group Policies
  adding, 213–14
  built-in, 123–24
  delegating control to, 241–46
  domain local, 121–23
  e-mail distribution lists, 120
  Enterprise Administrators, 124, 130, 356
  export objects, 282–83
  global, 121, 123
  GPOs, 261–65, 390–98
  local, 121, 123
  maximum number of members, 121
  MoveTree utility, 365–67
  moving to OUs, 336
  naming, 213
  native mode, 329
  nesting, 121
  non–security, 120
  planning, 120–24

**David Iseminger**  David is an independent consultant at Microsoft and has worked on Windows NT (since Windows NT 3.5) and Windows 2000 as a networking and router performance analyst, telecommunications specialist, and performance tool developer. He is the Series Editor (author) of the *Windows Programming Reference Series*, available from Microsoft Press, and generally writes a few books a year (computer books and novels). David works with Microsoft's Developer Documentation Group as a programming writer, creating and maintaining many of the Platform SDK's established and emerging networking technologies. Find out more about this book, the Windows Programming Reference Series (WPRS), and other projects David is involved in at *http://www.iseminger.com*.

The manuscript for this book was prepared and galleyed using Microsoft Word 2000. Pages were composed by Microsoft Press using Adobe PageMaker 6.52 for Windows, with text in Garamond and display type in Franklin Gothic. Composed pages were delivered to the printer as electronic prepress files.

Cover Designer:              Girvin Strategic Branding & Design
Cover Illustration:          Tom Draper Design
Interior Graphic Designer:   James D. Kramer
Interior Graphic Artist:     Joel Panchot
Principal Compositor:        Dan Latimer
Manuscript Editor:           Elizabeth Cate
Indexer:                     Bill Meyers

*For information about Microsoft Press®*
*products, visit our Web site at*
**mspress.microsoft.com**

**Microsoft**·*Press*